The Reconstruction
of Southern Education

The Reconstruction
of Southern Education

The Schools and the 1964 Civil Rights Act

Gary Orfield
*Woodrow Wilson Department of
Government and Foreign Affairs
University of Virginia*

WILEY-INTERSCIENCE
A DIVISION OF JOHN WILEY & SONS
New York · London · Sydney · Toronto

Library of Congress Catalog Card Number: 72-77832
SBN 471 65690 9
Printed in the United States of America

To my Antonia

Preface

Standing before the Lincoln Memorial on August 28, 1963, a black preacher from Georgia told 200,000 marchers of his vision. "I have a dream," Martin Luther King said. "It is a dream deeply rooted in the American dream." Across the South, he told the country, the day would come when the walls of racial separation would be pulled down. "One day, right there in Alabama," he said, "little black boys and black girls will be able to join hands with little white boys and white girls as sisters and brothers."

His dream was improbable. His movement challenged the deepest social customs and governmental traditions of a vast and politically powerful region. His dream was a call for revolution in the truest sense of the word. For a time the movement seemed irresistible. Five years later, however, he was dead and the public was undisturbed as policemen tore down Resurrection City, his last dream. As Dr. King died for his revolution in 1968, Alabama's leading segregationist was emerging as a major force in American politics, largely on the basis of his pledge to reverse the tide of racial change begun in 1963. Neither black nor white Americans could still feel the hope and unity of that distant summer day.

When the Supreme Court ruled in 1954 that school segregation denied black students their Constitutional rights, a great test of American government became inevitable. The struggle between national rights and local power, between an abstract commitment to equality and the concrete fact of caste separation, reached a decisive stage in 1964 when Congress authorized use of the power of the executive branch to make the 1954 decision a reality in the schools of the South. In the years that followed the powerful national commitment to fundamental social change expressed in the 1964 Civil Rights Act, the impulse was seriously delayed and dissipated by the decentralized structures of power in American federalism.

The subject of this book is the political and administrative struggle over the future of southern education set in motion by passage of the 1964 Civil Rights Act. My basic conclusion is that the institutions of American federalism and the popular beliefs associated with them make long-term national intervention in local race relations possible only under the most extraordinary conditions. The best that can be expected within the normal pattern of political relationships is a temporary use of Federal power against the local status quo. Temporary intervention, however, is no small accomplishment, particularly when it exposes the fallacy of the extreme racial stereotypes used to justify local segregation. Even a brief exercise of national authority can relieve local leaders of the political burdens of implementing a deeply resented change and can create a new status quo which some local leaders will defend.

The obstacles inherent in American federalism hamper the implementation of virtually all reform legislation but they become peculiarly formidable in the case of a bitterly divisive issue. Both the Constitutional structure and the congressional system are so constructed that a passive national majority cannot enforce a change intensely opposed by any politically important minority holding regional power. In Congress the seniority system makes it highly unlikely that all key decision points within the decentralized committee structure will respond to majority feeling on a divisive issue. Both the vast seniority accumulated by southern Democrats and the Senate filibuster system magnify the power of the South to frustrate a majority desire to protect the constitutional rights of southern blacks.

Normally the congressional system guarantees that Federal administrative power will not be used to disrupt race relations. Passage of the 1964 Act was possible only because the entire remainder of the country was temporarily strongly determined to override tradition and willing to pay the cost of an indefinite deadlock in the entire legislative process to forestall the regional veto.

The public assumed that the success of the 1964 civil rights coalition in finally pushing the historic measure through Congress actually settled the question of legal discrimination in the South. It was, of course, only the first act in a new phase of the national struggle. The real policy questions were merely transferred from the floor of Congress to the bureaucracy, the courts, and the meeting rooms of appropriations subcommittees which must provide funds if new programs are to be implemented.

The bureaucracies upon which the new civil rights responsibilities were imposed were living organizations, operating within a web of commitments to programs and constituencies tied to the status quo. Administrators knew that the continuation and growth of their programs demand good relationships with these constituencies and with senior members of

Congress who largely control their agency's legislation and money. Because Federal bureaucracies are so intimately connected with and responsive to Congress, there are continuing opportunities for opponents of administrative actions to threaten basic existing agency functions.

Federal education officials found themselves in a uniquely sensitive position because of the widespread belief that anything approaching "Federal control" of the schools was wrong. Although the idea of equal educational opportunity was widely accepted, the commitment to local control of education remained a cardinal principle of American political ideology. In communities practicing discrimination a strong Federal commitment on behalf of equality necessarily restricts local control and increases the political vulnerability of Federal school authorities.

The enforcement effort confronted not only political storms, but also grave administrative difficulties. The simple fact was that the great bulk of the administrative machinery of American education is located at the state and local levels. Short of using military force or engaging in battles in the courts, Federal administrators faced with massive noncompliance have only two real choices—end the local program by cutting off funds or settle for whatever local officials will concede and quietly ignore further demands of the law. The fund cutoff weapon, however, is a dangerous two-edged sword which not only punishes local recalcitrance but also ends a needed program and subjects the agency to political attacks. In the absence of an overwhelming demand for extraordinary measures, general practice is to accept whatever can be obtained through negotiation.

The inertia built into the federal system means that change tends to be incremental. The resulting gradualism in school desegregation not only allowed time for the crystallization of local resistance but also greatly lengthened the period of political vulnerability of the enforcement effort. The policy implications of American federalism explain the bitter comment of a black attorney in Virginia. They seem to think, he said of the desegregation effort, that it is making it easier for a dog whose tail must be cut off to cut an inch at a time. The problem is that our basic traditions of government make it almost impossible to take more than an inch. By stretching out the process of change the problem of the reformers in keeping public attention focused on the issue is greatly increased even while the opportunities for attack by defenders of the status quo are multiplied.

The intention of this study is to assess the capacity of American political and administrative institutions to solve the American dilemma. In my analysis of a policy issue of great intrinsic importance I have tried to move beyond the traditional preoccupation with the inner workings of governmental institutions within a basically stable status quo toward an understanding of the relationship between these institutions and fundamental social change. Surely a political science that assumes a constant social environment for governmental action is of little utility at a time when rapid social change is a basic fact of national experience and when there is a serious question about the adequacy of our governmental machinery for the task of resolving bitter and highly volatile social divisions. This study is concerned with the output of the political system, with the substance of policy, and the adequacy of that policy for the realization of the social transformation envisaged by the Civil Rights Act.

This book has many "details" for the simple reason that policy commitments and administrative strategies often are far more the product of an accumulation of limited decisions about details than of a conscious choice between fundamental alternatives. The book also incorporates two case studies intended to serve several purposes. The chapter that analyzes the abortive effort to desegregate Chicago's public schools is intended to fulfill the dual objectives of explaining the decisive incident in the evolution of the policy conclusion that the Civil Rights Act was largely irrelevant to the problems of northern schools and of examining the political environment within which a northern desegregation effort would have to operate. The study of enforcement in Virginia is an effort to examine the substantive problems and consequences of national policy making within the context of existing state and local educational politics. The intent of the Virginia chapter is to move beyond the Washington perspective to suggest more adequately the interplay of local, state, and national power in determining what the Civil Rights Act actually means in practice.

This study depends very heavily on the generous cooperation and helpful explanations provided by many dozens of men and women on all sides and levels in this historic battle over school discrimination. The frankness of former Assistant Commissioner of Education, David Seeley, and his decision to grant me full access to internal Office of Education documents were vital to my formulation of the essential questions of the study. A Danforth Fellowship and a Brookings Institution Research Fellowship financed by the Johnson Foundation provided needed resources. The continuing encouragement of Professor Grant McConnell was very helpful. I have profited greatly from the comments and corrections of those who have read all or part of the manuscript—David Greenstone, Paul Peterson, Meyer Weinberg, Francis Keppel, David Filvaroff, G. W. Foster, Jr., Antonia Orfield, David Seeley, Hayes Mizell, David Barus, and my student assistant, Dianne Mathiowetz.

Admittedly, this book lacks the completely value-free character of much contemporary social science literature. Although I have attempted to explain the positions taken by all participants in this social revolution as fairly and honestly as possible, I cannot claim personal neutrality. I believe that it is neither necessary nor possible for all scholars to assume a pose of scientific detachment on every issue. Although the work of defining concepts and systematically testing hypotheses is essential, so too is the work of intellectual exploration motivated by personal commitment. If a science of politics is possible, it will surely not develop by an ordered set of rational steps; like the other sciences it will proceed often through insights growing from intense personal curiosity and involvement in basic social questions.

I am convinced that the use of governmental power to break up the remnants of the American caste system is the most pressing public issue of this generation. If the effort begun in 1964 should fail, we shall kill something central to the American dream. My deepest hope, and the hope of many southern educators, is that in the end we shall overcome. My fear is that we may fail, largely because of the inadequacies of our governmental system.

GARY ORFIELD

Charlottesville, Virginia
November 1968

Contents

The Reconstruction
of Southern Education

1

Background to Reconstruction

There has been a quiet social revolution in the schools of the South since 1964. As public attention has been diverted from the rural South to the urban North, southern racial barriers that seemed impenetrable in the 1950's have been breached in many hundreds of communities. Ironically, however, interest in the old cause of southern school integration has fallen just as the lengthy struggle is finally yielding basic change.

It is hard to imagine a more vivid symbol of the bitter intensity of the American racial dilemma than the picture of black students walking into a Little Rock high school while bayoneted U.S. paratroopers held back jeering segregationists. To understand the magnitude of the social transformation in the South since 1964, that portrait of hate must be compared to a new image of tense but peaceful change. Even in the stagnant red clay counties in rural backwaters, where racial attitudes had not changed much for a century, dozens or even hundreds of black children have recently crossed rigid caste lines to enter white schools. Counties with well-attended Ku Klux Klan cross-burnings have seen the novel and amazing spectacle of Negro teachers instructing white classes. It has been a social transmutation more profound and more rapid than any other in peacetime American history.

This is a revolution whose manifesto is a court decision and whose heroes are bureaucrats, judges, and civil rights lawyers. It is a critical battle in the continuing war between local elites and Federal action to protect nationally guaranteed rights. It is a decisive episode in the continuing struggle between those who wish the public schools to be truly committed to equal opportunity and those who desire the schools to perpetuate the local culture and social order. Finally, it is a revolution that tests the ability of American institutions of government to heal the inherited wounds of centuries of separation and black subordination and thus to make of the nation a single people.

The Supreme Court solemnly proclaimed a basic principle of Constitu-

1

tional law in 1954, but it did not actually integrate the schools. The philosophic right could only become an operating reality when resources were found to overcome the powerful weapons for defense of the local status quo inherent in American federalism. The decision had no impact in the local community until Negro parents and civil rights attorneys took their school board into a Federal court and won a court order. Black students could obtain what was theirs by right only by overcoming organized state and local harassment and delay. Black communities had few resources to challenge the massed economic and political power of white leadership.

The struggle over school desegregation acutely reflected a fundamental tension in the American political system. An order from the insulated precincts of a court directing a profound restructuring of the central public institution in the local community inevitably produced a contest between local strength and national authority within the political system. Each in the lengthening procession of Septembers since 1954 has been a test of the ability of the Federal government to protect the rights of its people. The maps showing the glacial spread of desegregation during the first decade of struggle showed a substantial national victory in the border states, where there were many local sympathizers. In the South, however, the battle against local resistance had only begun, and the outcome remained very much in doubt. Ninety-nine out of 100 black children remained in segregated schools.

The courts and the civil rights organizations had set a crusade in motion, but they lacked the force necessary to achieve a lasting victory. Supporters of change found that the forces of continuity were far better organized and had far better access to many crucial centers of decision. In the struggle to bring the authority of the executive branch to the support of desegregation, civil rights leaders learned the ways in which decentralization of power within Congress and the pervasive local sensitivities of many congressmen twist and deflect popular demands opposed by local elites. The extent and diversity of successful local resistance made clear the broad range within which state and local officials can redefine national rights. It became clear that a new departure in American federalism, commiting the national Administration to the battle for local change, was essential.

Until 1964 thousands of southern communities openly defied the Constitution, and there was little Federal officials could do about it. A little-noticed provision in the 1964 Civil Rights Act, however, fundamentally altered the equation of power, opening the way for a far-reaching reconstruction of race relations in southern schools. By forbidding the use of Federal aid in segregated school systems and by authorizing the Attorney

General to bring lawsuits on behalf of Negro children, the new law put the weight of the Federal bureaucracy on the side of change.

Southern politicians had long feared the consequences of a strong Federal role in education for the future of southern society. When a national definition of equal opportunity and racial justice was imposed in place of regional norms as a condition to local participation in the huge 1965 school aid program, these old fears proved correct. The existing social order could not be preserved when Federal officials had both strong financial leverage and a clear congressional mandate to use the power of that money to challenge the tradition of unrestricted localism in education and to force recognition of the rights of black students.

The first year of the transformation wiped out most of the large pockets of total resistance. In almost every southern school district, September 1965 found at least a few Negro students defying ancient walls of separation. By the next fall most school systems were making some tentative gestures toward the formerly unthinkable goal of faculty integration, a long step in communities convinced that all blacks were intellectually inferior to the least able white. Local officials who had hoped to indefinitely postpone even token integration now found the entire system of separate schools threatened. As the educational system was attacked, so too was the pattern of rigid stereotypes and exclusiveness the schools helped perpetuate.

It has been a strange sort of revolution. There has been only isolated violence, and few people outside the South knew that anything significant was happening. There have been no manifestoes, but only dry bureaucratic documents. Instead of charismatic figures, the leaders have been a small group of civil servants from the Office of Education and the Department of Health, Education, and Welfare. Low-ranking Washington officials, working in the drab green offices of a shabby World War II temporary building and in the anonymous corridors of the regional General Services Administration headquarters, have labored to restructure racial practices in hundreds of southern towns.

This vast change has not been accepted passively and is still far from complete. The Civil Rights Act altered the law, but not the political system. Southern congressmen have continued to call on every tactic to undermine the enforcement process. Many state and local officials continue to draw on their large reserves of administrative discretion to frustrate Federal directives.

Working against rapid enforcement were both the continuing decentralization of political power in the United States and the historic American ideology of local control of the schools. The attempt to use Federal power to drastically rearrange local school systems was a striking break in a powerful national tradition of localism. Since 1964 a social revolution has been well begun. The ultimate outcome, however, is still in doubt.

LOCALISM, RACE, AND THE SCHOOLS

No two issues have been so troublesome for American federalism as the protection of Negro rights and the support of local schools. If the issue of Negro rights has been the American dilemma, the promise of education for all has been the American answer to social problems. In a nation with a strong historic and philosophic commitment to local self-government, local and state authority over education and race relations has normally been taken for granted. Education is the most important function of local government, but it is at the local level that discrimination is strongest. Thus the problems of the Negro in the white-dominated local community have been reinforced by discrimination in the locally controlled institution that holds the key to social mobility.

Throughout the past century reform efforts to use Federal power to increase educational opportunity or to alter racial patterns at the local level generally have collapsed in the face of determined opposition. Again and again, in fact, the issues of Federal aid to education and Federal protection of civil rights have become entangled. Most proposals for Federal education programs have been fought both by those defending the tradition of local control of the schools and by southerners afraid of Federal leverage over a local institution basic to the maintenance of racial separation. The South has had the most critical need for Federal help, but southern politicians have often led the battle against aid plans.

Even as late as the 1950's, the question of race blocked passage of a Federal aid program. As Congress divided between those who insisted that money go only to integrated schools and to those violently opposed, it seemed that the two great issues of education and civil rights had grown so intertwined that no significant national action was possible in either field.

The first two years of the Johnson Administration brought a sudden and massive break with tradition. Passage of historic civil rights legislation was quickly followed by creation of an unprecedented program of Federal aid to elementary and secondary schools. The 1964 Civil Rights Act forbade Federal subsidies to support segregated programs. The 1965 Elementary and Secondary Education Act provided large new Federal grants under a formula favoring poor southern school districts. The interaction of these two laws confirmed the worst fears of southern leaders and prompted revolutionary change in southern schools. Federal pressure, in turn, provoked a massive political and congressional counterattack on both the education program and the Civil Rights Act. The tradition of localism still had very powerful champions.

Traditional American Federalism

The meaning and even the rhetoric of the battle that was to break over the schools were deeply rooted in American history and political speculation. The preference for local rather than national control of major public institutions has been a dominant theme of American political philosophy. Most Americans have always shared the belief expressed by Jefferson:

> It is not by the consolidation, or concentration of powers, but by their distribution, that good government is effected. Were not this country already divided into states, that division must be made, that each might do for itself what concerns itself directly, and what it can do much better than a distant authority. . . .[1]

In American politics attacks on overcentralization in Washington are exceeded in frequency only by praise for the virtues of the grass roots. American political ideas were forged in a time when the national government was a distant presence and when what public action was necessary for a simple society was concentrated in the community or in the state. These beliefs have an independent life of their own and continue to shape political choices long after the disappearance of the conditions that originally produced them.

The commitment to local control is reinforced by the structure of the American party system. Operating within a highly decentralized party system, politicians know that nomination and re-election depend far more on local standing and the handling of local demands than on the support of the national party leadership. Power within the system flows upward from those with local political influence. "Except during periods of crisis," one observer noted, "not even the President . . . requesting action from a congressman or senator can command the sort of accommodating response that, as a matter of course, follows requests from an individual, an interest group, or a mayor of a city in the legislator's district." [2]

The nature of the political system demands that congressmen be primarily concerned with home district problems. Since Congress not only establishes the broad authority for Federal programs but continually examines and interferes in the implementation of those programs, most

[1] Walter Hartwell Bennett, *American Theories of Federalism* (University, Ala.: University of Alabama Press, 1964), p. 90.
[2] Morton Grodzins, "Centralization and Decentralization in the American Federal System," *A Nation of States,* Robert A. Goldwin, ed. (Chicago: Rand McNally, 1961), p. 7.

programs are designed to serve but not disrupt local interests. Only an overwhelming and continuing national majority can successfully use the machinery of the Federal government to force change in a basic local value.

The complex of Federal-state-local relationships that was to grow up amid these popular attitudes and political realities was one that emphasized the primacy of state and local authority. Because state governments retain independent bases of both constitutional and political power, successful Federal enterprises must normally rely on state and local cooperation. Cooperation is so essential that, except in extraordinary circumstances, divisive issues must be muted.

In theory, the Civil War settled the issue of the supremacy of federal authority. War needs justified great expansion of the Federal establishment, and victory ended doubts about the supremacy of the national government. After the war Reconstruction leaders, like contemporary civil rights spokesmen, recognized that the normal pattern of Federal-state relations bought cooperation by betraying the Negro. Local discretion meant local repression. It was clear that the new rights of the freedmen would be meaningless unless the power of local white leaders was broken. The ensuing effort to limit local abuses brought a fundamental change in constitutional structure. Constitutional amendments to abolish slavery, protect Negro voting rights, and guarantee equal protection of the laws were forged to pit the power of the nation against local discrimination.

The surge of reform generated bitter southern resistance. Change had been made possible by temporary southern exclusion from Congress, but the reform program soon encountered growing public apathy and renewed southern political power. In the electoral crisis following the contested presidential election of 1876, the Republican party abandoned the vestiges of Reconstruction in exchange for southern agreement to steal the election from the Democratic candidate. The Supreme Court completed the retreat by narrowly defining the laws and constitutional amendments adopted during Reconstruction. Thus the solemn language of national commitments was rendered meaningless until the courts began to reexamine these guarantees in the next century.

The Reconstruction measures were an anomaly in the federal system. They could be sustained only as long as they were strongly supported by a large national majority. When concern for the freedman fell, southern cries of Federal tyranny gained a growing audience. As the South regained the balance of political power, it was a simple matter to dismantle the enforcement apparatus. The old patterns of local white domination were soon restored. Local use of governmental power to enforce rigid racial separation was not to be seriously challenged until 1954.

Localism and Federal Aid Programs

It is impossible to understand the nature of American domestic programs without knowing the ideological and political context within which they emerged. From the beginning, a Congress sensitive to localism has created programs characterized not by Federal control, but by a bargaining situation, with the states and localities operating at a substantial advantage. The Federal-state relationship has been one of diplomatic cooperation, with national officials trying to advise or persuade rather than direct local and state administrators.

A typical pattern of Federal grant programs began to develop even before the adoption of the Constitution. Congress under the Articles of Confederation started a tradition of grants to the states for specific purposes, with little or no Federal supervision. Federal officials found that they had to rely on the good will of local administrators. Attempts to force local change produced political attacks that endangered the programs. From the beginning, state leaders and state congressional delegations "were continuously present and involved, always prepared to question an administrator's action, enlarge or decrease an appropriation, and contact the appropriate bureau on behalf of a public or private constituent." [3] Without the strength to successfully dominate, Federal agencies had no choice but to come to terms with the local centers of power.

States and local communities have often been able to misuse Federal grants with impunity. Widespread failure to use proceeds from grants of public lands for colleges, for example, led Congress to provide authority for withholding Federal funds in future programs. Federal administrators could deny public money to states violating the law, but the states were authorized to appeal this denial to Congress.[4] The withholding authority, the ancestor of the provision denying federal funds to segregated programs in the 1964 Civil Rights Act, was seldom used.

Federal bureaucrats soon learned that the withholding of funds is a dangerous two-edged sword. The recalcitrant state agency is punished, but the Federal program is also wounded through loss of vital local support, political attacks, and general disruption of cooperative relationships needed for the successful operation of other programs. Officials who believe their programs are useful are naturally reluctant to deny services

[3] Daniel J. Elazar, *The American Partnership, Intergovernmental Co-operation in the Nineteenth-Century United States* (Chicago: University of Chicago Press, 1962), pp. 299–300, 303. Council of State Governments, *Federal Grants-In-Aid* (Chicago: Council of State Governments, 1949), p. 1.

[4] V. O. Key, Jr., *The Administration of Federal Grants to the States* (Chicago: Public Administration Service, 1937), pp. 156–58.

to people in need who have nothing to do with the state violation of Federal regulations.

The first attempts to cut off Federal cash failed badly. The initial controversy was ignited by educational discrimination. Acting under the "separate but equal" provision of the Land Grant College Act, the Secretary of the Interior denied an annual payment to South Carolina in the 1890's until state officials allowed more money for the Negro land grant college. The state appealed to Congress, however, and the funds were restored. This ended any attempt to question state decisions about "equality." In other programs, similar experiences made officials cautious. Two Agriculture Department efforts to close totally inadequate experiment stations met the same fate in Congress.[5] Even successful efforts to deny funds can well cost more than they gain. Ohio politicians were indignant for decades after the Social Security Administration acted in 1935 to cut off $2 million in payments because the Ohio governor refused to create a nonpolitical administrative staff for the program.

Federal aid officials, who are often drawn from positions in state agencies, prefer to operate through quiet cooperation with state officials.[6] Such a relationship can only work when Federal authorities make no demands that would generate local political turmoil. This system has given aid programs a politically powerful constituency and has minimized any threats to the professional, political, or social status quo from Federal programs. The price has often been Federal willingness to let local officials deal with controversial problems, and a principal victim has been the Negro. From the 1890's until 1964, the proliferating grant programs accepted and subsidized the southern caste system. Southern programs were thoroughly separate and often shockingly unequal.

Title VI of the Civil Rights Act was intended to reverse the long history of Federal tolerance of local discrimination in nationally financed programs. The sanction was to be the fund-withholding power, a power that had always been seen as a drastic remedy rarely to be used. Rather than use this power, a leading student concluded that most Federal agencies would often "close their eyes to frequent departures from the conditions of the federal grants." [7] The agency most strongly influenced by the new responsibility was the Office of Education, one of the most cautious and traditional Federal agencies.

[5] *Ibid.*, pp. 161–62.
[6] U.S., Congress, Senate, Committee on Government Operations, Subcommittee on Intergovernmental Relations, *The Federal System as Seen by Federal Aid Officials*, 89th Cong., 1st Sess., 1965, p. 98.
[7] Key, p. 167.

Federal Submissiveness in Education

Nowhere has the tradition of local power been more pronounced than in education. Throughout its history the Office of Education has been caught between the powerful American impulse for educational progress and a deeply rooted belief in locally controlled schools. Historically the conviction that education was a central local function was so strong that decades of agitation were required even before the Office of Education could be established as a powerless office for collecting educational statistics and publishing miscellaneous reports. The survival and success of the agency has depended upon its ability to accommodate state and local school officials.

Until very recently, the Office of Education did little more than collect data on school systems. Even this enterprise was disorganized and ineffective because the Office could only passively accept the often inadequate data provided by state authorities. The Office's role in the national educational system was trivial, and much of its limited staff time was frittered away providing advisory services for school districts near Washington. Its program of educational research was unimpressive, and findings were not effectively communicated to the education profession.[8] The Federal education agency was a feeble operation, obviously lacking the resources to significantly change local school systems.

Race and Federal Aid to Education

Since the Civil War serious discussions of Federal help for the schools have aroused southern fears of racial change. At first southern spokesmen were worried about the prospect of a better educated, less contented black community; later they became alarmed at the danger of direct interference with school segregation itself. During the Reconstruction era and after the 1954 Supreme Court decision, these fears were magnified by northern ideas on Negro education expressed during debates on the aid proposals.

Active consideration of Federal aid programs generally came during periods of growth of the national government's power. Most of these periods, particularly the Civil War, Reconstruction, the New Deal, World War II, and the 1960's, were also characterized by heightened interest in Negro rights. When the national mood encourages expansion of Federal activities, it is natural that demands be made for strengthening and equal-

[8] Charles H. Judd, *Research in the United States Office of Education.* "Staff Study Number 19" (Washington: The Advisory Committee on Education, 1939), pp. 15–18, 24–43.

izing the public school system and for remedying the most serious blot on American democratic ideas.

Only in the midst of the great centralization of powers brought by the Civil War did the first major education program become law. The states' rights objections of the absent southerners were over-ridden as the Land Grant College Act was passed. In 1867, shortly after the war, the Office of Education was created.

The Reconstruction period produced the first great educational program directly administered by the national government. Much of the work of the Freedman's Bureau, established to ease the dislocation caused by the end of slavery, involved the organization of Negro colleges and training institutes. Within five years of the war, a quarter-million blacks were in school, largely as a result of the Federal initiative.[9]

The debate on the creation of the Office of Education reflected the northern belief that better schools were the key to remolding southern society. Education, said a Minnesota congressman, would inspire the southern white to "love the great nation that lifts him up," while enabling the freedman to use his new power "to his own advantage and the glory of his country." Without schools to provide civil training, the powerful Senator Charles Sumner argued, suffrage would be a "barren scepter" to the Negro. Better schools must be provided, said a member of the House, because "the attempt to . . . build a great, wise nation upon an ignorant, bigoted, and brutalized population has cost half a million lives. . . ." [10]

At the end of the Civil War, southern education was in desperate condition. Even before the war, the average state in the South had spent only $50,000 a year for public education. Facing the devastation of the war, many southerners recognized the need for Federal funds and, at first, joined with northerners in urging assistance for the schools. By the late 1870's, Congress was flooded with petitions asking for Federal grants, and 90 per cent of them came from the South.[11] Under the spur of this interest, aid bills were seriously considered several times between 1870 and 1890.

Even when the need was greatest, however, there was some southern suspicion. Discussing President Ulysses S. Grant's aid plan in 1872, one southern congressman was concerned that "this measure would ultimately

9 John Hope Franklin, *Reconstruction: After the Civil War* (Chicago: University of Chicago Press, 1961), pp. 36–38.
10 *Congressional Globe*, 39th Cong., 1st Sess., 1866, p. 2965; *ibid.*, 39th Cong., 2d Sess., 1867, p. 1843.
11 *Ibid.*, 39th Cong., 1st Sess., 1866, p. 2965; Gorden Canfield Lee, *The Struggle for Federal Aid, First Phase.* "Teachers College, Columbia University Contributions to Education," No. 957 (New York: Teachers College Bureau of Publications, 1949), p. 61.

mean mixed schools for the South. . . ." House acceptance of an amendment permitting states to segregate reassured only two southern congressmen.[12] Northern members heightened suspicions when they emphasized the political importance of schooling for southern blacks and casti-
gated white Democratic leaders who would be threatened by effectively
used Negro political power.[13]

As the South began to recover economically from the war, southern
support for Federal aid faded. During the 1880's opinion crystallized
increasingly on sectional lines. Time after time New Hampshire's Senator
Blair pressed for enactment of his program to distribute federal funds to
the states according to the number of illiterates in the state's population.
The Blair bill repeatedly passed the Senate, but foundered in a House that
was under Democratic control during much of this period. The bill required that each state provide free primary schools for all children "without distinction of race or color, either in the raising or distributing of
school revenues or in the school facilities provided." [14] By 1890 the
Democratic party was firmly committed to opposition. "Freedom of education," declared the 1892 party platform, ". . . must not be interfered
with under any pretext whatever." [15]

Even as the South was turning against a Federal role in education, so
too was the education profession. The most influential schoolmen, the
state and city superintendents, moved from their postwar support of
Federal aid to opposition by 1890. Protecting the status quo of state and
local power became a central objective. "The unfettered working of the
State systems," said the Connecticut superintendent, ". . . has now become our settled policy, which no lobby in Washington can change if it
would. . . ." [16] Local control and local support, said President Charles
Eliot of Harvard, was the "genuine American method," in contrast to the
subsidy which "saps the foundations of public liberty." [17] State educators
now assumed a powerful position in the fight against aid bills. Thus the
localism deeply ingrained in the American political system and in national
political ideology combined with southern resistance to defeat Federal aid
proposals.

The only significant education bill to emerge from Congress between
the Civil War and the presidency of Woodrow Wilson was the second
Morrill Act, which increased grants to state colleges. This law conflicted
neither with the interests of the state education establishments nor with
the southern desire for segregation; it allowed colleges to discriminate if
separate Negro institutions were maintained. Thus Congress wrote the

[12] *Ibid.,* p. 82.   [13] *Ibid.,* p. 75.   [14] *Ibid.,* p. 90.   [15] *Ibid.,* pp. 95, 144.
[16] *Ibid.,* p. 67.   [17] *Ibid.*

separate but equal doctrine into education legislation six years before the Supreme Court read it into the Constitution.[18]

The only important federal breakthrough before the 1950's was in vocational education. A national campaign by a Progressive era coalition of labor, education groups, and business won congressional approval of the vocational program in 1917.[19] One of the factors that made southern support possible in the wartime battle for passage was the adoption of a southern attitude on race relations by the Wilson Administration. A Cabinet that systematically segregated Federal agencies, dismissed those who objected, and fired or demoted many black employees in the South was hardly likely to use the new program to tamper with school segregation. "Now it seemed," wrote a leading student of Wilson's presidency, "that for the first time since the Civil War the Federal government had placed its approval on the southern caste system." [20]

The attitude of the time had been expressed forcefully in the 1914 debate on the Smith-Lever Act, which provided funds for agricultural training through state colleges. This program did not even promise separate but equal treatment, and an attempt to insert such a guarantee failed badly in the Senate. Hoke Smith, a leading southern spokesman, argued that Negroes only needed a few months of schooling and were not ready for the complicated courses offered in the white schools. Mississippi's Senator Vardaman told the Senate that blacks were already voting too much and that it was never "intended by the creator that the two races should live together upon equal terms." [21] The Senate refused to adopt the separate but equal provision in spite of the fact that one member revealed that more than six times as much money had been invested in white agricultural land grant schools as in their southern black counterparts.[22]

In theory the new Vocational Education Act of 1917 gave the government broad authority over state programs, but the realities of American federalism were soon reflected in actual administrative practice. Discrimination was rampant and supervision so lax that some towns used training funds to offer free workers for new businesses.[23] Within two decades, Federal regulation was virtually nonexistent. The states simply

[18] Dawson Hales, *Federal Control of Public Education, A Critical Appraisal.* "Studies in Education" (New York: Columbia University Press, 1954), p. 56.
[19] Lawrence A. Cremin, *The Transformation of the School* (New York: Vintage Books, 1964), pp. 50–55.
[20] Arthur S. Link, *Woodrow Wilson and the Progressive Era* (New York: Harper and Row, 1963), pp. 64–65.
[21] Rayford W. Logan, *The Betrayal of the Negro, From Rutherford B. Hayes to Woodrow Wilson* (New York: Collier Books, 1965), p. 369.
[22] *Ibid.,* p. 368.   [23] Key, p. 98.

sent in their administrative regulations once every five years. No reports were required either on the effectiveness of existing programs or on plans for the future. Supervision was so loose that some professionals were seriously worried that their whole field would be discredited by the extremely weak programs in some states.[24]

The southern vocational education efforts faithfully reflected local racial attitudes. Research during the New Deal found that black vocational teachers were paid less than half as much as whites, although Federal funds paid the total salaries of both groups. Similarly, white programs received more than twice as much per pupil. The Negroes that did get into the programs were concentrated in the agriculture program, with only one in six receiving trade or industrial arts preparation.[25] Change was possible, a Negro scholar concluded, only through Federal pressure, preferably in the form of denying funds unless all students were treated equally.[26]

Discrimination in Federal school aid fortified the historic pattern of unequal education in the post-Civil War South. Believing that "the Negro could not and should not be educated at all," most southern communities simply did not provide any Negro schools for some time after the Civil War.[27] As late as the eve of World War I, not a single black high school was operating in the entire rural South. In 1920 fewer than one-sixth of the Negro students were in grade five or higher.[28] In 1930 the South could afford to spend only half the national per pupil average, even for white students. Support for black students, however, was only one-eighth the national norm, a mere $12.57 per student each year. In the Deep South the discrepancy was greater.[29]

Federal school aid was a godsend for educators in the poor southern states, but only once before 1964 did Federal administrators seriously attempt to exercise leverage against unequal education. During the New Deal a series of school programs were spawned on an emergency basis, operating outside the normal pattern of Federal-state relationships. Pressure on state officials from the Works Progress Administration succeeded in raising Negro teachers' pay to 80 per cent of the white level. Both the WPA and the National Youth Administration directed state authorities to

[24] *Ibid.*, pp. 73–74.
[25] Doxey A. Wilkerson, *Special Problems of Negro Education.* "Staff Study Number 12" (Washington: The Advisory Commitee on Education, 1939), pp. 92–96.
[26] *Ibid.*, pp. 109–10.
[27] Raymond B. Fosdick, *Adventure in Giving: The Story of the General Education Board* (New York: Harper and Row, 1962), pp. 81, 83.
[28] *Ibid.*, p. 100.
[29] Charles W. Dabney, *Universal Education in the South* (Chapel Hill: University of North Carolina Press, 1936), II, 495.

enroll black students at least in proportion to their population in the state. The WPA exceeded this figure.[30] The experiment made clear the potential power of Federal bureaucracies in improving educational opportunities for Negroes.

The New Deal education plans died during World War II, but the war and its aftermath gave birth to the important new "impacted areas" program. Eventually this effort was to give the Office of Education some leverage over local racial practices in certain school districts. Temporary Federal aid was provided during the 1940's for school systems seriously strained or "impacted" by World War II and Korean War military buildups. The extremely popular program paid both current expenses and building costs with no strings attached. In 1950 it was put on a permanent basis.[31]

The high concentration of military bases in the South made the new program particularly important there. Recognizing this fact, southerners had originally succeeded in writing into the bill a requirement that even schools wholly financed and operated by Federal agencies must abide by all state education laws, including those demanding racial separation. President Harry S. Truman vetoed the bill, explaining that it would require resegregating Federal schools already successfully integrated in the seventeen southern and border states. The President's action was defensive, designed only to prevent use of the program as a weapon against existing integration.[32]

Congress acted in 1956 to increase the attractiveness of the program in the South by adopting a national minimum contribution, thus providing a large windfall for poor southern districts.[33] Not until after the Little Rock crisis, however, was the relationship between the Federal subsidies and the 1954 Supreme Court decision seriously examined. When Virginia's "massive resistance" program closed schools serving thousands of military-base children, President Dwight D. Eisenhower requested authority to reopen and operate the schools on an integrated basis. After a long debate Congress granted the Administration a very limited power to run the schools that had been built with national funds to educate children of Federal servicemen.[34] With this minor exception, Federal programs continued to help finance school systems operating in defiance of the Constitution.

In administering Federal grants within the context of the American

---

[30] Wilkerson, p. 141.
[31] I. M. Labovitz, *Aid for Federally Affected Public Schools.* "The Economics and Politics of Public Education," No. 9 (Syracuse, New York: Syracuse University Press, 1962), pp. 19–37.
[32] *Ibid.,* p. 51.   [33] *Ibid.,* p. 56.   [34] *Ibid.,* pp. 78–79.

political system and serving a public deeply committed to local control of the schools, the Office of Education had to adjust to its environment. Like other Federal grant agencies, the Office adopted an attitude of permissiveness and deference toward state and local authority. The price of success included a willingness to leave racial issues in the South to the local white leadership. Consequently, Federal money passively financed school programs that not only enforced rigid separation but also systematically discriminated against black students and teachers in the allocation of funds. Until a vast change in national attitudes occurred, spreading the conviction that protection of Negro rights justified a major exception to the tradition of localism, Federal bureaucrats were powerless. This transformation was begun by the 1954 Supreme Court decision and came to fruition in the 1964 Civil Rights Act.

THE FIGHT TO ENFORCE THE SUPREME COURT DECISION

When the Supreme Court ruled that segregated schools violated the constitutional rights of black students, a massive shadow fell over Federal-state relations in education. A majority of the population readily accepted at least the principle of some desegregation of southern schools.[35] The decision helped neutralize the philosophic argument for localism by an appeal to the more fundamental American ideals of egalitarianism and educational opportunity. In spite of the decision, however, political power remained localized, a fact that was carefully weighed by the Court itself in deciding upon a cautious and gradual approach to implementing the decision.

The Supreme Court had to confront the fact that it possessed no enforcement machinery and that it lacked effective support from either an executive branch led by a president who couldn't make up his mind about civil rights or a legislative branch hobbled by a built-in southern veto on racial questions. Even the internal structure of the Federal judiciary itself was heavily influenced by the traditions and politics of American federalism. The Court's 1955 order which spelled out the means for implementing the preceding year's decision, reflected the belief that only a gradual process under the day-to-day control of southern judges serving on the lower Federal courts was enforceable. The Court declared:

> Full implementation of these constitutional principles may require solution of varied local school problems. School authorities have the primary responsibility

[35] See Gallup Poll figures from 1954 to 1959, cited in John M. Fenton, *In Your Opinion* (Boston: Little Brown and Co., 1960), pp. 146–147.

for elucidating, assessing, and solving these problems; courts will have to consider whether the action of school authorities constitutes good faith implementation. . . . Because of their proximity to local conditions and the possible need for further hearings, the courts which originally heard these cases can best perform this judicial appraisal.[36]

The decision to rely on plans approved by Federal district courts put the burden of initiating the hated changes on the shoulders of the district judges. Once black litigants brought a school board into court, the responsibility for working out the crisis of federalism was handed to men born and trained in the South, active in the community and political life of their states, and appointed to the bench with the endorsement of the state's leading politicians. This crucial responsibility was given to men sworn to uphold the Constitution, but men who were also very much part of a region where 80 per cent of their fellow whites opposed the Supreme Court decision.[37]

The strong local influence on appointments to the district courts suggested that enforcement would be slow. The 1955 decision on implementation, commented one Mississippi attorney, was a "very definite victory for the South."

We couldn't ask for anything better than to have our local, native Mississippi federal district judges consider suits. . . . Our local judges know the local situation and it may be 100 years before it's feasible.[38]

In fact the desegregation process under the Federal district judges proved to be a moderate, localized, sporadic, and delay-prone struggle to obtain token integration.

The situation confronting the judges was unprecedented. Men accustomed to trying individuals for concrete violations were now asked to put an entire white community on trial for violation of a broad but unspecific constitutional interpretation. For several years the judges worked with little specific guidance from the Supreme Court. They had to find agreement on a plan for radical change from black and white community leaders who did not even discuss the subject with each other. The puzzle of finding a way to breach the ancient wall of legal segregation was often left to a Federal judge who had neither standards nor experience to guide him.[39]

[36] *Brown v. Board of Education,* 347 U.S. 483 (1955), reprinted in Hubert H. Humphrey, ed., *School Desegregation: Documents and Commentaries* (New York: Thomas Y. Crowell Co., 1964), p. 30.
[37] Fenton, p. 152.
[38] Reed Sarratt, *The Ordeal of Desegregation* (New York: Harper and Row, 1966), p. 200.
[39] Interview with Professor G. W. Foster, Jr., June 6, 1967. Professor Foster traveled widely through the South in the late 1950's, interviewing federal judges and white and Negro community leaders.

When the law seemed unclear, the tendency of the district judges was to resolve doubt in favor of local claims. Judges had to live in their home communities. Even lifetime tenure cannot insulate men from what one appeals court judge described as "the unconscious urge for the approbation of their fellow man, and fellow man most often means those of like interests and backgrounds, business and professional experiences and even prejudice." [40] A leading observer commented: "These judges will do what they must; they can hardly be expected on their own initiative to move against the local power structure. If their instructions from above are ambiguous, the ambiguity will be resolved to conform to the judge's own convictions and the mores of his district." [41]

In the period immediately following the 1955 decision, the federal system produced significant progress. In the border states and, initially, in some areas of the Middle South, local leaders were willing to accept some token integration on a gradual basis. In several states, in fact, desegregation began on a voluntary basis, without any court orders. In the six border states outside the old Confederacy, progress continued and very substantial desegregation was achieved in the decade after 1954. Progressive local leaders, a more moderate tradition of race relations, and the fact that the proportion of Negroes in the student population was only about half what it was in the South, all helped to produce compliance. Where local leadership was cooperative, federalism was successful.

In the South, however, the Federal courts soon confronted a leadership united in resistance. Once again conservative southern politicians stirred up the race issue to consolidate their positions and forestall the political changes that seemed to be brewing in a rapidly modernizing South. Leaders personally opposed to integration both on social and on philosophic "states' rights" grounds found their inclination strengthened by the obvious political profits involved. In 1956 the decision of southern political leadership was expressed in the "Southern Manifesto," signed by 101 members of Congress. The manifesto denounced the 1954 decision as "contrary to the constitution" and made it good politics across the South to endorse fanciful resolutions interposing the sovereignty of the state against the Federal courts.[42] The southern statesmen had given their blessing to a systematic campaign to use every resource of state and local government to defy the law of the land.

After 1956 moderate southern school officials willing to peacefully desegregate faced increasing harassment from state officials. By 1957 at least

[40] Sarratt, p. 201.

[41] J. W. Peltason, *Fifty-eight Lonely Men* (New York: Harcourt, Brace and World, Inc., 1961), pp. 12–13.

[42] Anthony Lewis and the *New York Times, Portrait of a Decade* (New York: Bantam Books, 1965), p. 39.

136 new laws and state constitutional amendments designed to delay or prevent integration were on the lawbooks. The most common device was the pupil assignment law, giving local school boards power to establish criteria for assigning students. By manipulating the various requirements, local officials could generally preserve segregation. State laws made the process more expensive and lengthy for black applicants by creating elaborate administrative procedures.[43] Thus, each Negro student had to clear a set of high hurdles before he could appeal the predictable ultimate rejection to the Federal courts.

Federal judges confronted southern resistance without much support from either the Administration or the Supreme Court. From 1955 until its decision on the Little Rock case in September 1958, the Court remained silent, leaving local crises to the lower courts. President Eisenhower's continuing refusal to endorse the Supreme Court decision was notorious. Although Eisenhower finally intervened dramatically in Little Rock, he permitted local disturbances to thwart court orders in a number of cases.[44] The Justice Department limited itself to a handful of "friend of the court" briefs. For several years, a judge ordering integration had to act without any clear guidance from the Supreme Court and without any assurance that his order would be enforced by the executive branch. He had to place himself to the left of the President and defy the very political organization that had sponsored his appointment. Facing enormous local opposition, many district judges were inclined to accept at face value state laws plainly designed to prevent enforcement of the Supreme Court decision.

With the Administration taking a neutral and passive position, the judicial struggle was left, by default, to the black community. With limited resources and under constant harassment by state legislatures, the NAACP was able to launch only a scattered attack, focusing at first on the major cities and the Middle South. Ten years after the 1954 decision most southern school districts had never been confronted with a challenge to their unconstitutional separate school systems.

Even when attorneys from the NAACP Legal Defense Fund brought a school board into court, many district judges tended to approve "almost anything" the board was willing to submit as an integration plan. Most judges were very grateful for any kind of local suggestion taking the burden of decision from them. Until the 1960's, most Federal judges were ready to approve plans allowing more than a decade for token integration of all grades.[45]

---

[43] Patrick E. McCauley, "Be It Enacted," *With All Deliberate Speed*, Don Shoemaker, ed. (New York: Harper and Brothers, 1957), pp. 130, 136–39.
[44] Peltason, pp. 51–52.   [45] *Ibid.*, p. 99.

In the years following the Supreme Court decision, the impression spread widely throughout the South that the most a community would have to do was to admit a few selected Negroes into its white schools. This impression was strengthened greatly by the often quoted 1955 opinion of the Fourth Circuit Court of Appeals in the Claredon County, South Carolina case. "The Constitution," Judge Parker wrote for the court, ". . . does not require integration. It merely forbids discrimination." Unless black students chose to enter white schools, the school board could send them to segregated schools.[46] This interpretation, which was generally accepted until the mid-1960's, limited the constitutional right to equal education to those Negro students willing to pay the price for defiance of basic community values.

The principal success of the Federal courts in the 1950's came in the gradual dismantling of state laws intended to prevent even token desegregation. The Supreme Court finally provided some leadership in its firm and urgent decision on the Little Rock case in 1958. Federal judges subsequently became increasingly impatient with the endless evasive tactics of the state governments and overturned the vaunted legal barricades of "massive resistance." The united front of total resistance was broken, and small areas of token integration began to appear south of the Virginia border in the late 1950's.

As the 1960's began Federal judges were gradually tightening the requirements and increasing the speed of the desegregation process. President John F. Kennedy openly supported the Supreme Court decision and ordered expanded Justice Department activity in support of Negro litigants. Although the Supreme Court had not spelled out the meaning of "deliberate speed," some courageous Federal judges now began to accelerate change in the southern states. In 1961, for instance, Federal District Judge Bailey Brown rejected the standard "grade-a-year" plan submitted by one Tennessee school board. "I don't think the idea should get around," he said, "that every school district can simply wait until they are sued and then come in with the most conservative plan that has ever been approved and expect to have it approved." [47] Decisions were handed down requiring districts that had long delayed desegregation to begin more rapidly. In 1962 the Sixth Circuit Court of Appeals challenged the grade-a-year plan, a position given support by a 1963 Supreme Court ruling questioning the adequacy of desegregation plans that would have sufficed in the mid-1950's. In the border states, several decisions ordered immediate desegregation of all grades.[48] In one 1964 case, the Supreme

[46] Sarratt, p. 208.   [47] *Ibid.*, p. 216.
[48] *Ibid.*, pp. 216–18; U.S. Commission on Civil Rights, *Survey of School Desegregation, 1966*, pp. 7–8.

Court expressed the conviction that "there has been entirely too much deliberation and not enough speed" in the desegregation process.[49]

During the period immediately before the Civil Rights Act, the Federal courts were not only working to step up the rate of change but also to expand the substantive and procedural requirements. Some decisions began to explore the relationship of faculty integration to successful student desegregation, the need for positive local action to abolish legally separate schools, and a variety of mechanisms to improve the means by which black students and their parents could express their preference for an integrated school.

After ten years of struggle, the Federal courts were beginning to produce more adequate definitions of the rights of Negro students. Judicial compulsion combined with occasional voluntary action and sporadic assistance from the executive branch to begin desegregation in every state by 1964. In the states of the former Confederacy, however, the persistance of an extremely low level of actual integration suggested that school desegregation simply could not be fully implemented through the normal machinery of the federal system. Only Texas and Tennessee, the two southern states with the lowest percentage of black enrollment, had more than 2 per cent of their Negro students in integrated schools in 1964. In seven states, a decade of effort had brought fewer than a hundredth of the Negro pupils into white schools.[50] The system of Federal-state judicial relationships evolved to handle normal disputes between state and national law could not cope with state governments and local officials determined to misuse the court system for delay and obstruction. In the Deep South, the system sometimes approached total collapse.

While most Federal judges subordinated personal preference and enforced the Constitution when directives from superior courts were clear, some Deep South jurists used the Federal bench to openly oppose the Supreme Court decision. In Mississippi and Louisiana, some judges repeatedly showed their contempt for the clear decisions of higher courts. A suit to desegregate schools in Mississippi's two largest cities was dismissed by a judge who asserted that genetic differences between the races made school integration unfeasible. A Georgia judge asserted that he could not order desegregation because the intellectual inferiority of all Negroes meant they could never be accepted in white schools.[51] A severe strain on the Federal court system was obvious in a Louisiana case in which the Fifth Circuit Court of Appeals was forced to take control of

[49] *Griffin v. County School Board*, 337 U.S. 218, 229 (1964).
[50] Lewis, pp. 256–57.
[51] Leon Friedman, "The Federal Courts of the South: Judge Bryan Simpson and His Reluctant Brethren," *Southern Justice*, Leon Friedman, ed. (New York: Pantheon Books, 1965), p. 192.

the internal business of a district court because its judge refused to obey repeated orders of the appellate court.[52]

Even judges fully prepared to enforce the Constitution were hamstrung by the traditions of federalism in the judiciary. Out of respect for the laws and constitutions of the states, Federal courts had developed procedures for handling challenges to the constitutionality of state laws with great care. "It is," wrote one student of the courts, "one of the operating assumptions of our federal system that no state law is clearly unconstitutional." [53] Thus Federal courts require that a litigant suing in a state court appeal through the entire state judicial system before coming to the Federal courts. This procedure lessens Federal-state conflicts by giving state judges an opportunity to either invalidate a law on their own grounds or to construe the statute so narrowly that it is constitutional. Although this practice is useful in normal situations, it permitted unconscionable state delay in school desegregation.

The assumption that no state would intentionally and flagrantly defy the Constitution proved wrong in hundreds of instances during the battle over the 1954 decision. When the issue at stake was a revolutionary local racial change, other assumptions basic to the operation of the Federal courts were undermined. Although the burden for initiating lawsuits remained with private parties, the assumption that any litigant could obtain a lawyer and safely test his legal claim was no longer true in a situation in which the entire local white leadership was in opposition and fear of retaliation was pervasive both among those claiming their rights and black attorneys. A system designed to adjust controversies between individuals and businesses was seriously inadequate to administer the enforcement of a bitterly contested national policy in a region where all the resources of governmental power were in the hands of opponents.

As the head of the Justice Department's Civil Rights Division during the early 1960's, Burke Marshall was at the center of the effort to make the institutions of the federal system work to protect Negro rights. Writing in 1964, Marshall concluded that the massive disrespect for established legal principles was "testing . . . the durability of the federal structure." [54]

> It is as if no taxpayer sent in a return until he personally was sued by the Federal government. . . . The crisis is more deplorable, of course, because it is not private persons . . . who are failing to comply with laws, but the states themselves. . . .[55]

[52] Shirley Fingerhood, "The Fifth Circuit Court of Appeals," *Southern Justice*, p. 219.
[53] Peltason, p. 109.
[54] Burke Marshall, *Federalism and Civil Rights* (New York: Columbia University Press, 1964), p. 7.
[55] *Ibid.*, p. 8.

Southern states treated desegregation suits not as a way to determine the law but as illegitimate attacks on the social order.

> In the view of the state, it is legitimate and right not to move until forced to do so, and then barely to budge. The assertion of Federal rights . . . can be realized only through the processes of the Federal courts, case by case, in an endless chain of litigation.[56]

A constitutional right has very little real value if it can be obtained only when a member of a vulnerable minority is willing to fight a protracted battle with the legal authorities of his community and state. The federal system had failed, Marshall concluded, and Negro rights could be protected only by bringing the full weight of national power to bear on behalf of those whose rights were denied.[57] Continued decentralization of power meant continued domination by local white elites and continued deprivation of Negro rights. Failure of the court system in much of the South brought to the fore proposals to either increase Justice Department intervention in desegregation suits or to use the financial power of the federal bureaucracies to end defiance of the Constitution.

The Proposal for Justice Department Intervention

In the years immediately following the 1954 Supreme Court decision, the reform proposal most seriously considered called for a move toward equalizing the courtroom conflict by allowing the Attorney General to sue local school boards on behalf of black children. This idea was based on the assumption that the courts could cope with the problem if only the staff and prestige of the Justice Department were available to those claiming their rights. The nature of the case-by-case process, however, would remain the same, and the crucial decisions would continue to be made by Federal judges.

The proposal to extend the authority of the Justice Department was first seriously debated in 1956, when it was put forward as the most far-reaching segment of the civil rights bill assembled by Attorney General Herbert Brownell. The possibility of a GOP breakthrough among urban black voters created a strong incentive for enactment of the bill, and the South fought bitterly. During the decisive Senate struggle on the bill in 1957, the leader of the southern forces, Senator Richard Russell of Georgia, denounced the bill as "cunningly designed to vest in the Attorney General unprecedented power to bring the whole might of the Federal government, including the armed forces if necessary, to force a com-

---

[56] *Ibid.*, p. 6.   [57] *Ibid.*, pp. 7, 83.

mingling of white and Negro children in the state-supported schools of the South. . . ." [58]

President Eisenhower's obvious doubts about the value of this important change combined with the traditional southern threat of filibuster in the Senate to veto this central element of the civil rights bill. Because a two-thirds vote was required to end debate in the Senate, any 34 senators who felt strongly enough about an issue could simply talk it to death. There were 34 senators from states operating segregated schools in 1954, and filibuster had long been the fate of even such proposals as anti-lynching bills. The Attorney General was not to receive authority to intervene until 1964. Even then this power was strictly limited.

After the emasculation of the 1957 bill and the failure of Congress to confront the school issue in the 1960 act, the Justice Department began to make more vigorous use of what little authority it did possess. The department, which had generally participated in school cases only in a few instances when the judge had asked for assistance, now launched some new initiatives. It asked the court involved for permission to become a party to the suit against the Prince Edward County, Virginia, school system. One of the counties involved in the initial 1954 decision, Prince Edward County had closed its schools completely rather than begin integration. In this case, the department argued, it must be a participant in the litigation rather than a passive "friend of the court." Such involvement was essential to "prevent the circumvention and nullification of the prior orders of this court and to safeguard . . . the integrity of the judicial processes of the United States." [59] Under congressional pressure, the Administration also attempted to initiate suits against several segregated school districts receiving Federal impacted areas money. The district courts, however, refused to permit the direct intervention of the Attorney General without specific congressional authorization.[60]

The impasse left the job to the agonizingly slow processes of the Federal district courts and to the limited staff of the NAACP Legal Defense Fund. As the Civil Rights Act was debated in 1964, fewer than a fifth of the school districts of the South had begun desegregation, and many hoped to permanently escape the threat. Ten years of litigation had failed to win recognition of the constitutional rights of more than 99 per cent of the black students in most southern states. This was an issue so fundamental to the future of a regional social structure that the normal assumptions of American federalism simply broke down. Without a massive use

---

[58] Cited in James L. Sundquist, "For Minorities, Equal Rights," (unpublished manuscript, 1966), p. vi–15.
[59] Sarratt, p. 69.   [60] *Ibid.*, pp. 70–71.

of national power, civil rights leaders predicted that another century would be required for complete school desegregation.

Until the Birmingham demonstrations erupted into the national consciousness in the spring of 1963, the Kennedy Administration began no significant action to meet this constitutional crisis. Judging that his narrow congressional majority meant that any real effort to change the racial status quo would only kill other needed programs, Kennedy ignored his campaign promises and offered no civil rights bill until February 1963, when he sent to Congress a collection of minor changes far more modest than the 1956 Eisenhower program. The President asked for no new authority to fight school segregation.[61] Only after a sudden and striking change in popular attitudes did the Administration ready the bill that ultimately became the 1964 Civil Rights Act.

Harlem's Congressman and the Struggle to Bypass the Courts

Deeply frustrated by the "deliberate speed" of the southern courts in enforcing the 1954 *Brown* decision, civil rights advocates began very early to think about the creation of administrative sanctions. The idea was to use the financial leverage of the executive branch to force immediate local action without endless delays. The hope was to change the enforcement problem from one in which the individual Negro had to sue for his rights to one in which all school districts would be required automatically to meet general standards of desegregation or lose Federal subsidies. The leading proponent of this new approach in the 1950's was Congressman Adam Clayton Powell.

Ever since the Civil War, there had been recurrent discussion of the possibility of using Federal aid programs to force an improvement in the conditions of Negro education. Fear that this would in fact be done was a major reason for southern opposition to most aid bills. The idea, however, was absolutely contrary to the traditions of localism in Federal grant programs and had never had any impact on the administration of federal education programs.

The 1954 decision provided a persuasive new argument for administrative regulations. Should the Office of Education continue its practice of subsidizing local racial separation, public money collected from all citizens would be used to aid defiance of the Constitution. This new argument was quickly put forward. Whereas in the 1940's the NAACP had asked only that Federal aid be provided equally for black and white schools, the organization demanded that the 1955 aid-to-education bill be amended to withhold money from states not complying with the Su-

[61] *Ibid.*, p. 73.

preme Court decision. This suggestion was enough to postpone action in the southern-dominated congressional committees for the rest of the session.[62]

The following year, the NAACP position was taken up by Adam Clayton Powell, the leading black spokesman in Congress. The mercurial Harlem Congressman had a long-standing concern with school segregation. In the mid-1940's he urged action to end segregated and unequal schools in the District of Columbia, and he proudly claimed to be the "first Negro since Reconstruction to have any legislation made into law" after the 1946 adoption of his amendment forbidding states to refuse food to Negro children in the new school lunch program.[63] Powell quickly became the leading congressional spokesman for the NAACP proposal.

During 1956 hearings on the school construction bill, Powell warned that unless the Administration voluntarily agreed to deny aid to states defying the Supreme Court decision he would attempt to write such an amendment into the bill. The Administration took the position that only a Supreme Court order directing such withholding would justify this action.[64]

Once again it seemed as if the questions of Federal aid to the schools and Federal responsibilities for civil rights were so entangled that nothing could be done on either front. With southern seniority on the committees controlling education legislation in each house, with a shrewd southern leader as chairman of the House Rules Committee, with a large group of senators prepared to filibuster, and with northern conservatives firmly committed to local control of the schools, it was clear that the Administration could not pass a school bill that threatened integration. Both the localistic orientation of Congress and the dispersion of power within Congress to a number of veto positions, generally allocated on the basis of seniority, make any significant challenge to a vital regional interest extraordinarily difficult. Without a national demand strong enough to persuade a majority to override normal congressional procedures, significant change on the race issue was impossible.

Until a vast change occurred, congressional barriers were so impassable that the Powell amendment was initially opposed by the liberal forces that helped make the principle it embodied into law eight years later. Leading liberal organizations and even other black congressmen de-

[62] James L. Sundquist, "For the Young, Schools" (unpublished manuscript, 1966), p. v–10.
[63] Neil Hickey and Ed Edwin, *Adam Clayton Powell* (New York: Fleet Publishing Corp., 1965), pp. 95, 106.
[64] Robert Bendiner, *Obstacle Course on Capital Hill* (New York: McGraw-Hill, 1964), p. 125.

nounced this amendment that was certain to kill the chances of passing an education bill. A National Education Association spokesman said that the amendment "would not hasten the integration of a single school system." [65] Powell persisted, however, arguing that the Negro people "are willing to wait a few more years rather than see a bill passed which will appropriate Federal funds to build a dual system of Jim Crow schools in defiance of the law." [66] While splitting with white liberals, Powell accurately reflected the sentiment of NAACP leaders who saw no other alternative to endless litigation.

Powell's proposals presented a dilemma for liberals: they had to either vote to enforce the Supreme Court decision and thus kill the school bill or risk being branded as supporters of segregated education. Conservative Republicans found themselves in the delightful position of making a meaningless gesture of support for civil rights and killing a Federal aid bill at the same time. Knowing that the amendment would consolidate southern opposition and surely doom the bill in the Senate, many southerners sat out the vote, permitting easy passage of the nondiscrimination proviso. The amendment transformed the school bill into a civil rights bill and split the Democratic party cleanly on sectional lines, producing virtually unanimous southern opposition. A Georgia congressman who originally supported Federal aid denounced the amended version as an attempt "to bribe my state and the South with school construction money to accept the mixing of the races. . . ." This, he announced, would "break down the social barriers which at present prevent the temptation to intermarriage of the two races. . . ." [67]

The issue continued to generate controversy. Powell claimed that his desertion of the Democratic ticket in the 1956 presidential election was caused by Adlai Stevenson's refusal to support the withholding of Federal funds from segregated schools.[68] The following year the Powell amendment again helped doom an education bill.

Only the national shock generated by the launching of the Soviet sputnik was sufficient to float the one major new education program of the Eisenhower Administration over the shoals of the civil rights issue. The National Defense Education Act, designed to meet serious deficiencies in the educational system, particularly in sciences and modern languages, was carefully drawn to provide aid largely to individuals rather than

[65] *Ibid.*, pp. 125–26.
[66] *Congressional Record*, 85th Cong., 1st Sess., 1956, p. 1191, quoted in Sundquist, "For the Young, Schools," p. v–12.
[67] J. W. Anderson, *Eisenhower, Brownell, and the Congress* "The Inter-University Case Program" (University, Ala.: University of Alabama Press, 1964), p. 76.
[68] Hickey and Edwin, p. 122.

schools. Its fellowship and teacher training programs provided aid directly to the person involved. Powell settled for a provision forbidding consideration of race in granting aid to students, but not preventing enrollment of students or creation of special programs in segregated institutions.[69]

Passage of the NDEA was an exception rather than a harbinger of change. The same stubborn basic issue of Federal rights was again raised by the Harlem congressman in 1960, when a strongly Democratic Congress was eager to pass a school construction bill before the coming election. Once again the House adopted the Powell amendment. For the first time, the amended bill passed the House. At this juncture, Virginia's Representative Howard Smith used his power as Chairman of the House Rules Committee to take the extraordinary step of blocking an effort to work out a compromise with the Senate, which had earlier passed the bill without the amendment.[70] Once again a single member had forced Congress to recognize the connection between the Federal role in education and equal opportunity for black students. Once again Powell's action activated the opposition of the powerful southern minority, and that minority was able to use positions of power in Congress to veto action on either front.

In the 1950's, Powell's actions seemed like needless and damaging obstructionism. He was continually insisting that Congress do something that seemed plainly impossible or else there could be no action to meet the critical problems of the schools. In retrospect, however, Powell's achievement is far more important. A massive federal aid program geared to the maintenance of separate schools in the South did not appear. When the Elementary and Secondary Education Act was finally passed in 1965, the new program was not encumbered by years of accommodation with the status quo in the South; together with the Civil Rights Act, it proved to be a powerful engine of racial change.

A Beginning in the Bureaucracy

When President Kennedy took office, the arena of struggle over discrimination in Federally financed education programs shifted for a time to the bureaucracy. Between 1960 and 1963, there was no major congressional action on the question, but it was seriously debated within the Department of Health, Education, and Welfare.

The issue was removed from congressional discussions of education legislation by a change of heart of Congressman Adam Clayton Powell. Just as the Kennedy Administration began, the seniority system made

[69] Sundquist, "For the Young, Schools," pp. 21–27.
[70] Bendiner, pp. 167, 169–70.

the chairman of the Education and Labor Committee. Elected from as stable a one-party district as any southern Democrat could wish for, Powell was now handed, by virtue of the decentralization of power in Congress, decisive control over new education legislation and powerful influence over the operations of HEW and the Labor Department. Thus the Kennedy Administration was vastly relieved when the new chairman withheld his antisegregation amendment from the high-priority education bill. Accepting Kennedy's pledge to use executive powers against discrimination, Powell removed the race issue from the education debate for two years, only to see the bill killed by religious controversy. By 1963 Powell had become disenchanted and began once again to insist on antidiscrimination provisions in new legislation.[71]

The nondiscrimination issue raised serious policy dilemmas within the Federal bureaucracy. Serious discussion began in late 1959 when President Eisenhower asked Cabinet members from HEW, Labor, and Justice to study racial discrimination in grant programs and to prepare a paper on the topic for the Cabinet.[72] For more than a year, the study languished in the depths of HEW, the conglomerate department operating more programs than any other agency.

When a preliminary report to the Secretary of HEW concluded that the department already had power to cut off money from segregated institutions, the HEW legal staff counterattacked. HEW General Counsel Parke Banta expressed the views of many of the grant program administrators when he argued that the Secretary had no authority to enforce the Constitution, but that he must follow the particular words of each law directing him to make grants, even if grants aided defiance of the Constitution. He concluded that "mere segregation" in an otherwise fairly run program was not so contrary to program objectives that fund withholding would be justified.[73]

The issue remained unresolved as the Kennedy Administration began. Outgoing HEW Secretary Flemming decided that discretionary authority probably did exist, at least in certain programs, but that the basic policy decision should not be left to individual program administrators. Action, he wrote, "should be taken on an across-the-board basis by order of the President."[74]

Pressure came from outside the Administration as well. The U.S. Civil

[71] *Ibid.*, p. 198.
[72] Memorandum from HEW Secretary Flemming to the Secretary of the Cabinet, January 19, 1961.
[73] Memorandum from Parke Banta, HEW General Counsel, to Secretary Flemming, September 16, 1960.
[74] Flemming to Secretary of the Cabinet, January 19, 1961.

Rights Commission, an advisory body of eminent citizens set ı
to study discrimination, called for denial of Federal grants to
colleges both late in the Eisenhower years and early in the __
Administration.[75] Kennedy received similar recommendations from the
Leadership Conference on Civil Rights, the Washington-based confederation of national civil rights groups, and the moderate Southern Regional
Council. The Leadership Conference memo, handed to the President by
Roy Wilkins, pointed out that a fourth to a tenth of the budgets of
southern states consisted of Federal money, much of which was used to
strengthen the segregated institutions operated by state authorities.[76]

Kennedy promised to consider the idea, but his Administration took
only modest steps in the suggested direction. At first, in fact, HEW
Secretary Abraham Ribicoff tried to quiet southern fears about the 1961
education bill by stating that HEW had no authority to withhold grants
because of segregation.[77] Neutralization of the race issue won the votes
of 17 previously opposed southern congressmen. The gain was not
enough to offset the losses caused by Catholic opposition to the bill providing no aid for parochial schools, and Federal aid did not become a
reality for another four years.[78]

The limited progress that was made by 1963 within HEW can largely
be credited to Representative Powell's use of his committee chairmanship
to check up on the performance of Kennedy's promise for change by
executive action. Powell named a subcommittee on integration in Federal
aid programs. Executives of agencies running school programs were
called to testify, and Powell called them back to report on progress.
Needless to say, an official did not enjoy appearing before an angry
chairman of the committee controlling his legislative proposals and budget authorization with nothing to report.

From the perspective of the South, the Powell influence over HEW
represented localism gone wrong. The seniority system that had so long
magnified the strength and influence of the rural southern whites now put
the administrators of the nation's existing education programs at the
mercy of a militant New York City black.

Under pressure, Secretary Ribicoff took the first step, quietly inserting
a nondiscrimination clause in contracts with colleges running National
Defense Education Act programs.[79] HEW, however, was reluctant to
require desegregation in school systems receiving impacted areas aid. In

---

[75] Sarratt, p. 63.
[76] Arthur M. Schlesinger, Jr., *A Thousand Days* (Boston: Houghton Mifflin Co., 1965), p. 951.
[77] Letter from Secretary Ribicoff to Senator Prouty, May 17, 1961.
[78] Sundquist, "For the Young, Schools," p. v–41.   [79] Sarratt, p. 64.

1962 Ribicoff testified against a bill calling for fund withholding, stating the Administration's preference for the old Eisenhower proposal authorizing the Attorney General to intervene in desegregation suits.[80] Enforcing the constitutional requirements in impacted area schools, he said, was "a congressional problem, not an administrative one." [81]

Plainly unhappy with this position, Powell asked Ribicoff to return in a month. This pressure was decisive within HEW in resolving the continuing dispute between officials concerned about civil rights and program administrators worried about maintaining their relationships. Ribicoff returned to announce that HEW funds could no longer be used to pay local school districts that forced children living on southern military bases to attend segregated schools.[82] The victory was only partial, however. Military children living off-base were not affected because HEW attorneys decided that the Federal interest in these students was less direct. The words of the law, the lawyers told Ribicoff, gave HEW no authority to stop subsidies in this situation.[83] This limited ruling was the only major administrative action within HEW until the enactment of the 1964 Civil Rights Act.

Reactions to the Ribicoff ruling that segregated schools were "unsuitable" for base children suggest the dilemma that confronted HEW and the Administration. A handful of active civil rights supporters denounced the department's failure to deal with the total problem. New York's Senator Kenneth Keating called the limited decision a "surrender to the forces which have been defying the law of the land," while Senator Jacob Javits repeatedly argued that the President could easily solve the whole problem with an executive order.[84] South Carolina's Senator Strom Thurmond, however, bitterly characterized the Ribicoff action as "the rankest type of economic blackmail," warning that southerners would never be deceived again by assurances that there could be Federal aid without Federal control.[85]

As the civil rights movement gained momentum, it was increasingly difficult to answer embarrassing questions about discrimination. Yet the Administration saw serious obstacles both within the Federal establishment and in the states that were preventing further change. The traditions of American federalism and the popular commitment to locally run schools meant that any education program administrator who acted

[80] Letter from Secretary Ribicoff to Powell, April 24, 1962.   [81] Sarratt, p. 65.
[82] Ibid.; I. M. Labovitz, Aid for Federally Affected Public Schools. "The Economics and politics of Public Education." No. 9 (Syracuse, N.Y.: Syracuse University Press, 1962), p. 94.
[83] Ibid., p. 93.   [84] Ibid., p. 94.   [85] Quoted in Labovitz, p. 184.

forcefully was inviting destructive cries of "Federal control." Normal supervision, for example, was so lax that a national survey of educators showed a virtually unanimous belief that the impacted areas program involved neither direct nor indirect Federal control.[86] This was the way the public and Congress wanted things to be and the way things had always been done in the Office of Education. The cautious attitude of program officials was reflected in the finding of the HEW legal staff that the aid laws permitted very little administrative discretion on the civil rights issue. The administrative relationships expressed fundamental political and social realities. The Negro movement had not yet become sufficiently broad and deep to overcome the ingrained traditions of federalism.

As time passed liberals in Congress became increasingly restive. Powell's Education and Labor Committee contained a strong group of liberals, and pressure built for passage of a bill to end the flow of money into segregated systems. HEW spokesmen testified that the measure was "essentially negative and punative in character," but the committee found that Federal money was highly concentrated in states with segregated schools and that some action was necessary. Alabama, for instance, remained absolutely segregated although one-sixth of its total capital outlays for schools came from Federal aid. The Powell committee reported out a bill limiting future payments to districts making some progress toward integration, but it was blocked in the Rules Committee. In the Senate, liberal forces were almost successful in an effort to write a non-discrimination proviso into an appropriations bill.[87]

In spite of the liberal attack, the Kennedy Administration refused to extend the HEW ruling to cover off-base military students. Instead, the Justice Department went to the courts. A handful of lawsuits were filed against what was described as "unconstitutional school segregation in an area where such segregation directly affects the armed forces." [88] In the years to come the tactic of avoiding controversial policy decisions by leaving them to the courts was to become an exceedingly familiar one.

Again and again the idea of widespread withholding of Federal aid was put forward, and again and again it was dismissed. Because it was a basic alteration in Federal-state relations, it appealed to civil rights advocates; for the same reason it was opposed both by locally oriented politicians and by program administrators. Black spokesmen insisted that localism guaranteed continued segregation while white opponents argued that expansion of Federal power would disrupt cooperative federalism and produce a dangerous centralization of authority.

---

[86] Labovitz, p. 179.   [87] *Ibid.*, pp. 93, 99–100, 94.   [88] *Ibid.*, p. 95.

The two attitudes were perfectly clear in the controversy over the Civil Rights Commission's report on Mississippi in early 1963. The commission was profoundly shocked by the outcome of localism in the Magnolia State:

> Citizens of the United States have been shot, set upon by vicious dogs, beaten, and otherwise terrorized because they sought to vote. Since October, students have been fired upon, ministers have been assaulted . . . children, at the brink of starvation, have been deprived of assistance by the callous and discriminatory acts of Mississippi officials administering Federal funds.[89]

In its brief emergency report to President Kennedy, the commission noted that Mississippi received Federal grants amounting to twice the tax revenue produced in the state. Thus the people of other states were heavily subsidizing Mississippi's "subversion of the Constitution." [90]

President Kennedy, a moderate with a background in localistic politics and an appreciation of congressional attitudes, was disturbed by the commission's call to cut off funds for such projects as the new jet airport in Jackson designed with segregated facilities. Kennedy said that he possessed no such authority and felt that the report was not "constructive." "Such power," he told a commission official, "might be dangerous." [91] He told a news conference that "it would probably be unwise to give the President . . . that kind of power because it would start in one State and for one reason or another it might be moved to a State which was not measuring up as the President would like to see it measure up in one way or another." [92] He conceded that new programs should be administered in a nondiscriminatory manner, but wrote to the Civil Rights Commission that cutting off funds to existing programs would often be a self-defeating gesture, particularly damaging to many Negroes benefiting from Federal aid programs.[93] It was evident that the President accurately mirrored congressional sentiment when the House, in April 1963, summarily defeated antidiscrimination amendments on two education bills after five minutes of debate on one and ten on the other.[94] Yet two months later President Kennedy was to send to a receptive Congress a historic civil rights bill that included a provision for fund withholding.

[89] Quoted in Schlesinger, p. 952.   [90] Sarratt, p. 66; Schlesinger, p. 952.
[91] *Ibid.*, pp. 951, 953.
[92] John Fitzgerald Kennedy, *The Public Papers of the President, 1963* (Washington: Government Printing Office, 1964), p. 333.
[93] *Ibid.*, pp. 333–35.
[94] U.S., Congress, House, Committee on the Judiciary, Subcommittee No. 5, *Hearings, Civil Rights,* 88th Cong., 1st Sess., 1963, p. 960.

THE CALL TO REVOLUTION: BIRMINGHAM
AND THE CIVIL RIGHTS BILL

The Birmingham Crisis and Public Opinion

Year after year those engaged in the civil rights movement demanded national action and insisted that Negro rights would be denied until American federalism was altered to use national power to balance local intolerance. While generally sympathetic, the public in the North did not grasp the urgency of the need. In the spring of 1963, when the President was dismissing out-of-hand the proposals of the Civil Rights Commission, only one person in 25 saw civil rights as the primary national problem.[95] Without broad and intense public support on this highly sensitive issue, Congress was not prepared to make a radical break with the tradition of localism.

Suddenly, in May, 1963, a great symbolic confrontation took place in the streets of Birmingham, Alabama. The dimensions of the need for immediate Federal action became clear to a shocked and angered public.

Newspaper pictures and television film from the streets of Birmingham made possible an alteration in American federalism that had eluded civil rights leaders for many years. The viciousness of Eugene ("Bull") Connor's police force created a powerful symbol of lawless localism. Constitutional abstractions might have limited appeal, but anyone watching TV could understand what it felt like to have a dog, capable of tearing a man apart, lunge at him during a peaceful march. One photo of a woman held down by five policemen, one with a knee across her throat, was worth a million pious words about local responsibility. Brusque arrests of kneeling marchers and brutal use of powerful fire hoses to knock down demonstrators made the crisis clear in homes across the country.[96]

There was a classic moral clarity and simplicity about the confrontation between the crude and die-hard segregationist police chief and the eloquent religious determination of the marchers and their leader, Martin Luther King, Jr. The confrontation sent surging energy through the civil rights movement across the country and generated the national anger that made basic change possible.

The shift in the tide of public opinion quickly influenced Congress. One of the first responses to the Birmingham crisis was the introduction of a large number of bills demanding the end of Federal complicity in the

[95] *Washington Post,* July 14, 15, and 21, 1963.
[96] Michael Dorman, *We Shall Overcome* (New York: Delacorte Press, 1964), pp. 143–87.

operation of segregated schools. In the House, 53 congressmen rapidly introduced bills, a typical example being Representative Gill's proposal that future education grants go only to totally desegregated school systems or those submitting an acceptable desegregation plan to the Commissioner of Education.[97] Even before the Administration's civil rights bill was assembled, Representative Powell had scheduled hearings on these proposals.

Within the Administration, the Birmingham confrontation made obvious the minor and inadequate nature of the civil rights program submitted several months earlier. Now civil rights specialists were called in to pull together an adequate Federal response to the wave of concern sweeping the nation. Men who had been quietly fighting within the bureaucracy for years to make marginal changes now found that the most far-reaching of the measures on the "laundry list" of possible legislation prepared by the President's advisers at the beginning of the year were insufficient. Suddenly the President sensed that the country was ready to accept a wide expansion of Federal power into such vital areas as protection of equal access to public accommodations and examination of employment discrimination.

In a magnificent, quickly drafted speech delivered the evening of June 12, Kennedy put the question to the nation. The talk built on the concern stirred by Birmingham and by the tense confrontation earlier in the day between Governor George Wallace and Federal authorities over the entrance of black students to the University of Alabama. "The heart of the question," Kennedy said, "is whether all Americans are to be afforded equal rights and equal opportunities, whether we are going to treat our fellow Americans as we want to be treated."

If an American, because his skin is dark, cannot eat lunch in a restaurant open to the public, if he cannot send his children to the best public school available, if he cannot vote for the public officials who represent him, if, in short, he cannot enjoy the full and free life which all of us want, then who among us would be content to have the color of his skin changed and stand in his place? Who among us would then be content with the counsels of patience and delay? . . . . .

The events in Birmingham and elsewhere have so increased the desires for equality that no city or state or legislative body can prudently choose to ignore them. The fires of frustration and discord are burning in every city, North and South, where legal remedies are not at hand. . . . .

Next week, I shall ask the Congress of the United States to act, to make a commitment it has not fully made in this century to the proposition that race has no place in American life or law.[98] . . . .

[97] H. R. 9938, 88th Cong., 1st Sess., June 11, 1963.
[98] Reprinted in Dorman, pp. 324–25.

In his address to the nation, the President called for enormous strength-ening of Federal authority to protect the rights of black Americans, but he did not mention the fund-withholding principle. The school desegre-gation tool he requested was the old device of extending the Attorney General's power to initiate lawsuits. When the White House bill went to Congress a week later, however, it did include a weak fund-deferral pro-vision.

In putting together his civil rights bill, Kennedy asked for more than he expected or wanted to get. "A hell of a lot of things," said Lee White, his aide for civil rights, "were thrown in to demonstrate the comprehen-siveness of the proposal." [99] The decision to incorporate fund with-holding into the bill, Theodore Sorensen recalled, was stimulated by the suggestions of members of the Congress.[100] In a message to Congress, the President suggested that the new authority would end the perennial "Powell amendment" controversy. "Instead of permitting this issue to be-come a political device," he said, "often exploited by those opposed to social or economic progress it would be better . . . to pass a single com-prehensive provision making it clear that the Federal Government is not required, under any statute, to furnish any kind of financial assistance . . . to any program or activity in which racial discrimination occurs." [101]

Civil rights leaders were still disappointed. The President's bill asked that program officials be *permitted* but not *required* to cut off funds in case of discrimination. The decision was at the discretion of the adminis-trator.[102] This, civil rights spokesmen argued, represented no change in the status quo.

The Administration continued to view expansion of the Attorney Gen-eral's authority as the key to school desegregation. The loosely drawn early version of Title VI was seen as an unimportant and expendable part of the entire package. The Administration had no intention of using this power to set up federal desegregation standards for all school districts. Such a measure, the assistant attorney general testified, would be "com-pletely unworkable" and would require massive military intervention.[103]

Kennedy sent his bill to Congress assuming that Birmingham was the crest of national concern and that his requests would be pared down at the tight spots in the congressional ordeal. The initial public reaction, in fact, was that the President was moving too fast. Very shortly, however, greatly heightened public concern and broad approval for the central provisions on public accommodations, job opportunities, and voting rights

[99] Interview with Lee C. White, June 21, 1967.
[100] Theodore C. Sorensen, *Kennedy* (New York: Harper and Row, 1965), p. 497.
[101] Kennedy, *Public Papers, 1963*, p. 492.   [102] Sorensen, p. 497.
[103] *Washington Post*, June 14, 1963.

were evident. Polls taken two months before Birmingham and one month after the President's speech showed a 1200 per cent increase in the number of Americans believing civil rights to be the most urgent issue before the nation. By midsummer there was an overwhelming national sentiment that "Negroes deserve a better break than they have been getting," and even in the South there was a majority in favor of federal action on jobs, voting rights, and public accommodations.[104] As the congressional battle began, the tide of concern continued to rise. The breadth and strength of the national movement was underlined in Washington by the descent on Capitol Hill of religious leaders from communities scattered across the country and by the extraordinary success of the March on Washington. When the bill went before Congress, many members were eager to demonstrate their commitment to civil rights and to produce an act even stronger than the President's bill. The survival and the vital strengthening of Title VI were indirect results of this concern. Intense public awareness of the need for extended national powers removed the central barrier to change in American federalism.

Strengthening Title VI

The discretionary language of the Administration's draft of Title VI was rapidly criticized. The day the bill was sent to Congress from the White House, some senators called for mandatory withholding at a conference of Republican senators.[105] New York's Senator Javits, long an advocate of administrative action against segregation, told the Senate that the title was superfluous because the President already had the power.[106] This criticism was countered by Senator Sam Ervin of North Carolina in the hearings of the southern-dominated Judiciary Committee. "No dictator," he said, "could ask for more power than Title VI confers on the President." [107] At the Senate hearings, Attorney General Robert Kennedy minimized the importance of Title VI, explaining that the permissive approach was far superior to the automatic cutoff of funds required in bills submitted by a number of members of Congress.

The protracted southern resistance to the civil rights bill generated months of debate and produced an incredibly long record of discussion on its major issues. One of the most remarkable features of this debate was the relatively slight attention given to Title VI, which became the most controversial section of the act within a year. The tremendous bulk of the debate focused on the public accommodations provision, singled out

---

[104] *Ibid.*, July 14, 15, 21, and 22, 1963.   [105] *Ibid.*, June 20, 1963.
[106] *Ibid.*, July 3, 1963.
[107] U.S., Congress, Senate, Committee on the Judiciary, *Hearings, Civil Rights—The President's Program, 1963*, 88th Cong., 1st Sess., 1963, p. 59.

by both southerners and conservative Republicans as the most intolerable and constitutionally dubious portion of the bill. Ironically, this section was quickly and easily enforced across most of the South, whereas the little-noticed Title VI gave the government a tool to change the central public institutions of the southern caste system. The failure to recognize and focus attention on the central importance of Title VI represented a major tactical error in the fight against the bill.

During the first months of congressional consideration, liberals succeeded in transforming Title VI from an almost meaningless permissive statement into a positive requirement. In the House, the Education and Labor Committee exerted pressure by reporting out bills for mandatory withholding in several HEW programs.[108] In the Senate, GOP Senator Keating of New York and Democratic Senator Ribicoff of Connecticut were the leading critics of the Administration draft. They called for a compromise that would make some kind of enforcement action mandatory, but would also provide administrative flexibility by permitting the option of either fund cutoff or a lawsuit against the discriminating institution.[109] Failure to exercise existing discretionary authority, leading GOP liberals argued, made change essential. This concern was shared by Roy Wilkins, speaking for the dozens of organizations in the Leadership Conference on Civil Rights. "We feel," he said dryly, "that unless it is made mandatory, all sorts of discretion will be exercised and until it is demonstrated . . . that discretion . . . does not mean discrimination then we would want mandatory phraseology in there." If the government was really willing to act voluntarily, he remarked, it would have been done years ago.[110]

The first decisive test for the civil rights bill came in the House Judiciary Committee. Because the Senate Judiciary Committee was chaired by Senator James O. Eastland of Mississippi, serious committee work on the bill was confined to the House group. When the Justice Department sent the House committee a revised Title VI closely following the Keating-Ribicoff suggestions, several of the House Judiciary subcommittee Republicans were concerned, but the liberal Democrats still dismissed the proposal as inadequate and insignificant. Most subcommittee members shared a normal congressional distrust of bureaucrats, and even House Judiciary Chairman Emanuel Celler warned of "this tremendous power . . . in the control of someone who would turn the spigot on or off with whim or caprice." [111]

The House Judiciary Committee is a committee of lawyers, and they

108 House Judiciary Subcommittee, 1963, p. 2161.
109 *Washington Post*, August 18, 1963.
110 House Judiciary Subcommittee, 1963, p. 2161.   111 *Ibid.*, pp. 1531–32.

were bothered by the possibility of arbitrary executive action that might endanger the rights of local authorities. Before Title VI emerged from the committee, it had been amended to allow the courts back into the process by permitting judicial review of fund-cutoff actions. Thus the long-desired "administrative remedy" for discrimination was made subject to some of the same possible delays that had held back school desegregation.

Liberals were skeptical about Title VI. Even if Federal agencies enforced it, there was not enough money going to most southern school districts to provide much leverage. Civil rights supporters generally favored the approach incorporated in the 1960 Democratic platform: a simple requirement, unconnected to aid programs, that every school district be required to file an acceptable desegregation plan with the government. A Civil Rights Commission spokesman argued that Title VI gave the President nothing he did not already have and that a far more direct approach would be needed to begin desegregation across the South.[112] All of the assumptions about Title VI would, of course, have been radically revised had there been any way of knowing that less than a year after the Civil Rights Act became law a large school program would make Federal aid a powerful factor in school financing in almost all southern districts.

Attitudes in the House reflected the belief that the South was a special case and that federalism was to be disturbed only in areas where defiance of the Constitution was clear. Thus when HEW Secretary Anthony Celebrezze testified that Title VI was written broadly enough to permit Federal action against de facto segregation in the neighborhood schools of the North, the issue quickly aroused some of the committee's members.[113] When the bill emerged from committee, the original language authorizing action against racial imbalance was eliminated.[114] On the floor of the House, this attitude was again apparent when members worried about possible Federal requirements for bussing black children to white schools in the North wrote into another section of the bill an explicit prohibition on efforts to enforce racial balance. The language of Title VI itself was unclear on this issue.

Another House amendment further reflected both the caution and the lawyerly approach of many members. The protection of judicial review was not deemed sufficient. The House also insisted on the provision of administrative hearings, involving an elaborate quasi-judicial process, before any money could be terminated. This process was intended to fur-

---

[112] *Ibid.,* pp. 1102–3.   [113] *Ibid.,* pp. 1514–15, 1519, 1522.
[114] U.S. Congress, House, Committee on the Judiciary, *Civil Rights Act of 1963,* 88th Cong., 1st Sess., 1963, House Report No. 914, pp. 44, 85.

ther limit the possibility of arbitrary decision and to encourage the creation of uniform enforcement standards.[115] In fact, however, the amendments tended to frustrate the development of genuinely independent administrative standards and to closely tie the exercise of the fund-cutoff authority to standards developed in the case law of the courts. An administrator facing the prospect of formal administrative hearings and possible appeal to the courts had to strongly consider the probable reaction of the courts. Naturally, he would be most certain that his actions would be sustained in the courts if his agency's standards were derived from criteria developed in the courts. Although the courts had failed to cope effectively with southern resistance, Congress was unwilling to exclude the courts from a continuing role in supervising the exercise of administrative power.

Two days before the murder of President Kennedy, the civil rights bill, with Title VI, was reported to the House floor. Within the Administration, the title was not seen as a "make or break item," but as something "kind of tucked away among some giants." [116] Had Kennedy lived, it was one of the segments of the bill that might possibly have been traded to the South for an end to the Senate filibuster.

The assassination brought in a new President for whom both personal inclination and political reality demanded an uncompromising stand in favor of enactment of the complete measure that had become identified in the public mind with Kennedy's "martyrdom." In his first days in office, President Lyndon B. Johnson pledged to civil rights leaders that he would accept no weakening. Johnson guaranteed passage of the entire bill when he made perfectly clear the Administration's willingness to tolerate a complete cessation of all legislative activity in the Senate for months.[117] It was a rare historic moment when the President, congressional leadership, and the public all recognized that protection of the rights of black Americans was the fundamental issue. Normal barriers fell, and a revolution in American federalism was accomplished.

During the endless Senate debate, Title VI was little discussed and received virtually no public attention in the media. Even the background materials prepared by the Justice Department for the bill's supporters belittled the significance of the provision. The effect of Title VI, the department claimed, was merely to eliminate the separate but equal pro-

---

[115] U.S. Department of Justice, Untitled analysis of the 1964 civil rights bill (two looseleaf notebooks of mimeographed material used by bipartisan floor leaders during Senate debate), pp. 7, 9.

[116] Interview with Lee C. White.

[117] Rowland Evans and Robert Novak, *Lyndon B. Johnson: The Exercise of Power* (New York: New American Library, 1966), pp. 376–380.

viso in some aid programs and to provide procedural safeguards for the exercise of a withholding power most agencies already possessed.[118] The title was expected to have little impact on school desegregation because of the minor importance of Federal money in most districts and because of language specifying that enforcement actions be consistent with the objectives of the aid program. Thus "cutoff of funds would . . . generally be inconsistent with the objectives of the school lunch program, which are to provide urgently needed food for growing bodies. . . ." As long as both white and black children were fed, the Justice Department attorneys suggested, money would continue to flow even to totally segregated systems. Rather than end a needed program, the analysis said, it would be more appropriate for the agency to wait for normal desegregation suits brought either by the parents or by the Attorney General.[119] When actual enforcement began the Justice Department was to retain a strong preference for the case-by-case approach over general independent administrative standards.

The Justice Department saw the Office of Education as playing a minor role, one in proportion to its puny role in most local school systems. The Commissioner of Education "would be warranted in relying on any existing plans of desegregation which appeared adequate and effective, and on litigation by private parties or by the Attorney General . . . as the primary means of securing compliance. . . ."[120] The Administration regarded Title VI merely as a recognition of the Commissioner's authority to require some gradual plan of integration as a condition for continued Federal aid. It was predicted that even when school districts were totally adamant the Commissioner would normally rely on civil rights attorneys or the Justice Department to take the local school board to court. Fund withholding was simply not a very credible threat when the average district would lose only a few thousand dollars, easily absorbed at the local level.

Senate Majority Whip Hubert Humphrey, the Administration's floor manager for the civil rights bill, accepted the Justice Department's interpretation and relied on it during the brief debates on the title. As the recognized spokesman for the Administration, Humphrey spoke with authority, and his words were later to be carefully weighed by agency officials, the courts, and southern politicians engaged in the dispute over what had been the real "intent of Congress" in writing the nondiscrimination requirement into law.

While it is logically impossible to assert that the majority of congressmen actually support anything other than the language approved by formal votes, much of the maneuvering involved in congressional debate is

---

[118] Justice Department notebook, pp. 1–3, 36.   [119] *Ibid.*, pp. 30–31, 50.
[120] *Ibid.*, pp. 29–30.

directed at influencing the "legislative history" of a statute. Because statutory language is often broad and compromises frequently produce intentionally vague language, Federal courts have increasingly tended to weigh committee reports and floor debates in interpreting laws. Thus "members of Congress . . . often take pains to get statements into the *Congressional Record* which will support their view of the intent of the legislative language being adopted." [121] After the civil rights bill became law, many of the political and legal arguments about Federal enforcement standards revolved about the question of the extent to which the sweeping words of Title VI were limited by rather cautious interpretations made at some points during the Senate discussions.

In opening the short discussion of the title, Senator Humphrey saw the provision as virtually noncontroversial.

> If anyone can be against that, he can be against Mother's Day. How can one justify discrimination in the use of Federal funds? . . . President after President has announced that national policy is to end discrimination in Federal programs.[122]

Title VI, he emphasized, did not require instant desegregation, especially when a "Federal court may have found such a plan impracticable." [123] The title was a "moderate" and "cautious" mechanism, not one demanding "drastic action which local officials and local public opinion regard as harsh and punitive." [124] Although the poor record of the courts had been a basic reason for the withholding proposal, the Minnesota senator predicted that court-order desegregation plans would be accepted under Title VI in order to prevent "an unseemly conflict between Federal agencies and Federal courts." [125]

As Administration spokesman, Senator Humphrey frequently adopted the exact words of the Justice Department analysis, clearly endorsing the idea of gradualism in implementation. Although the key term "discrimination" was not defined in Title VI, the Administration assumed that the title forbade only that discrimination found unconstitutional by the courts. Fund withholding was pictured as a last resort, to be invoked only when the local school officials would accept no reasonable plan. Even then, the remedy might well be a traditional lawsuit.[126] Humphrey's argument suggested that the title was not the instrument of revolution feared in the Powell amendments, but merely a moderate grant of power to be used against only highly recalcitrant local officials.

---

[121] Walter F. Murphy and C. Herman Pritchett, eds., *Courts, Judges, and Politics* (New York: Random House, 1961), p. 403.
[122] *Congressional Record* (Permanent edition), 88th Cong., 2d Sess., March 30, 1964, p. 6543.
[123] *Ibid.,* p. 6546.   [124] *Ibid.,* pp. 6544, 6547.   [125] *Ibid.,* p. 6546.
[126] *Ibid.,* p. 6545.

While Humphrey could speak with authority about the intentions of the Justice Department draftsmen and the Administration's enforcement plans, his was by no means the unanimous view of the meaning of Title VI. In fact a more forceful vision was put forward by Senator John O. Pastore, to whom Humphrey had assigned the more detailed defense of the title. In the beautifully organized struggle against the southern filibuster, particular members were delegated to defend specific segments of the legislative package, and the Rhode Island senator offered a strong supporting argument. The Supreme Court decision, he said, meant that school segregation was "absolutely wrong" and Title VI would end the use of the "common wealth of the people of the United States to promote . . . that kind of system." Separate school systems would be eliminated "once and for all." [127] In contrast to Humphrey's gradualism, Pastore argued that a court-ordered plan taking five or six years would not be adequate. "I can see," he said, "how it might require two months, six months or a year, but the process cannot take an eternity." [128]

The South mounted only a sporadic, scattered, and ineffectual attack on Title VI. What discussion there was indicates that concerned southern members disagreed with the Majority Whip's assessment of the meaning of the title. The proposal was called "unprecedented," "dictatorial," and "the most dangerous grant of power . . . ever proposed in the long history of this Government. . . ." But these were only occasional remarks, lost amid a torrent of abuse directed against the public accommodations section of the bill.[129]

The endless floor debates were overshadowed by private negotiations between the Administration and Minority Leader Everett M. Dirksen of Illinois. With the votes to decide the fate of the southern filibuster, Dirksen was in the position to demand some concessions. He negotiated a new draft of the bill, the "Dirksen-Mansfield substitute," which incorporated two significant alterations in Title VI. The senator obtained an agreement to limit Federal ability to regulate northern racial practices by forbidding fund cutoff for discriminatory employment practices, except when the job itself was a primary concern of the Federal program. Dirksen also added still more procedural safeguards to those already adopted by the House and made explicit the understanding that funds would be denied in a case of local discrimination only to the particular locality violating the law rather than a state's entire program.[130]

[127] *Ibid.*, April 7, 1964, p. 7057.
[128] *Ibid.* (Daily Edition, No. 110), pp. 13, 937–38.
[129] *Ibid.* (Permanent Edition), April 18, 1964, p. 8191.
[130] A state's aid could, of course, be denied if the state agency itself was discriminating. See discussion in *Ibid.*, June 5, 1964.

The Dirksen version, however, still did not satisfy Senator Robert Byrd of West Virginia, one of Capitol Hill's most determined segregationists. He was worried about the compulsory bussing issue that had agitated the House. Under pressure of Byrd's questioning and his threat to try to amend the title, Senator Humphrey made clear his belief that the title had no application to de facto segregation and that the prohibition against school bussing that the House had written into another part of the bill applied to Title VI as well. Since Title VI required presidential approval for regulations on fund withholding, Humphrey sought to reassure Byrd by promising that President Johnson would reject any "racial balance" requirement. Senator Javits, who had been involved in drafting the title, agreed with Humphrey, saying that any school district ordered to bus could easily get a court order to release Federal funds.[131]

Humphrey did leave an opening for future regulation of northern school systems should the courts find that unconstitutional segregation existed. By developing an interpretation of Title VI depending on current judicial decisions, he implied that judicial action to expand constitutional protections would also affect the meaning of Title VI. A specific prohibition of de facto segregation, he said, had been eliminated from the bill because of the recent refusal of the Supreme Court to review the Gary, Indiana, case in which the NAACP had unsuccessfully argued that de facto segregation was unconstitutional. Summarizing current court doctrine, he said that this case showed that "while the Constitution prohibits segregation, it does not require integration." Title VI "does not attempt to integrate the schools, but it does attempt to eliminate segregation in the school systems." [132] Less than four years later, the Supreme Court was to make clear that the Constitution does require complete abolition of separate schools in the South, and the lower Federal courts were beginning to more closely examine northern segregation.

At the time Title VI was under consideration in Congress there was little in the debate to indicate that the provision would quickly revolutionize southern education. Congress did not favor a general restructuring of the federal system, but reasonably strong and carefully limited Federal intervention when the Constitution was blatantly defied. Certainly there was no majority in Congress ready to act on the controversial northern neighborhood school issue before it had been defined by the courts.

The frequently stressed relationship between Title VI and the desegregation standards evolved by the Federal courts was to be both a source of serious program weaknesses and, later, a source of much-needed flexibility. The close linkage precluded immediate use of the new power to

131 *Ibid.*, June 4, 1964, reprinted *ibid.*, September 28, 1966, pp. 22336, 22337.
132 *Ibid.*, p. 22337.

completely eliminate the segregated schools of the South or to begin dismantling northern de facto segregation. It set strict limitations on the ability of program administrators to create independent administrative standards. Acceptance of the Humphrey argument about the meaning of Title VI, however, did have one highly important advantage. Title VI was not constructed as a static requirement, but was defined in relationship to judicial interpretations of the Constitution. Thus it left open the possibility that evolution of constitutional law would expand the requirements. As the Federal courts in the South very rapidly tightened their standards in the years after 1964, this linkage required reflection of the stronger requirements in the Title VI enforcement process.

In the Senate, the only significant attack on Title VI was led by Senator Albert Gore of Tennessee. A supporter of earlier civil rights bills, Gore found Title VI too radical a change for his moderate temperament. He saw it as the most disruptive change in the entire bill. Gore's fears were much like those that had troubled President Kennedy before Birmingham. He saw the title as a large and undefined power expanding the authority of the executive branch and making possible future use of Federal aid money for political purposes.[133] The basic premise, he feared, was that "this social revolution must be accomplished overnight." [134] What was later to emerge as a dramatic break with the tradition of federalism was quietly and easily passed by a Senate concentrating on what seemed to be far more basic changes. The Tennessee senator's motion to strike Title VI from the bill was crushingly defeated, 69–25, receiving the votes of only two senators outside the southern and border states.[135]

The heart of the title was intact after the lengthy congressional ordeal. "No person in the United States," proclaimed the first section, "shall, on the ground of race, color, or national origin, be excluded from participation in, be denied the benefits of, or be subjected to discrimination under any program or activity receiving Federal financial assistance."

Amendments written into the law had put some limits on the seemingly vast scope of the power conferred by the first sentence. Complicated procedural protections made arbitrary actions extremely unlikely and built delays into the enforcement process. The usefulness of the power outside the South was also called into question, particularly in regard to compulsory school bussing to alleviate de facto segregation. The Senate debate also produced a series of commitments by the Administration through Senator Humphrey. The Majority Whip had said that court orders then existing would be adequate compliance, and he had closely

133 *Ibid.*, April 25, 1964, pp. 9083, 9096.   134 *Ibid.*, June 9, 1964, p. 13126.
135 *Ibid.*, June 10, 1964, p. 13418.

tied the enforcement process to judicial standards. With two relatively minor exceptions, however, there had been no further limitations actually written into the text of Title VI. A powerful Senate majority had turned back an attempt to kill the provision. Title VI created the possiblity of a revolution in Federal-state relations, a basic change that would have been unthinkable a year earlier.

In the months after the Civil Rights Act became law, two external developments began to transform what had seemed a rather innocuous proviso into a charter for a social revolution in southern education. As the Office of Education was formulating its desegregation requirements, the Federal courts were rapidly moving toward a more extensive definition of the rights guaranteed black students by the Constitution. Judicial standards rapidly evolved from the minimum of gradual token integration in 1964 to a demand for more rapid progress by the time Federal enforcement began and, by 1968, to a requirement for root-and-branch elimination of the entire system of separate schools. Even as the courts were expanding the meaning of Title VI, Congress was giving the Office of Education the means to force local compliance. Passage of the 1965 Elementary and Secondary Education Act magnified Federal financial leverage over local school systems. These two developments turned a device for gradual transition into an engine of revolution.

The Meaning of Title VI

The public school system is the most important public institution in American life, and the crisis in race relations is the central social problem. When these two issues touch, as in the 1954 Supreme Court decision, the outcome is of enormous importance for American society. The 1954 decision set in motion a fundamental change in constitutional law, challenged the basic premises of southern life, and called into being a powerful social movement strongly influencing both the psychological orientations and the political beliefs of millions of Negroes and whites.

Although the Supreme Court began the process of tearing down rigid caste barriers in the schools, the procession of change soon became bogged down in the realities of American federalism, a system that tends to transform all basic political issues into questions of local versus national power. The Court was confronting a powerful tradition of Federal-state-local cooperation in which the price of local help is Federal willingness to respect the local status quo. This pattern of local dominance has historically been particularly striking in questions relating to the schools and to race. In ten years of struggle, the Federal judiciary had won some local toleration for token integration, but almost 99 per cent of black students in the 11 southern states remained in segregated schools.

For a decade the civil rights movement found itself fighting, through the Federal courts, to destroy a system heavily supported by Federal aid grants. Throughout the history of the grant programs, the local concentration of power in American politics and education had precluded any attempt to alter local patterns of race relations. Until there was a revolution in public attitudes and in political leadership, only marginal changes were possible. The insistence of Adam Clayton Powell forced Congress to confront this unpleasant issue in the 1950's, but then the only result was the destruction of education legislation. Only the circumstance of Powell's elevation to a position of great power within Congress stimulated the first timid use of administrative power to protect the constitutional rights of black children. President Kennedy summarized a very general feeling in early 1963 when he dismissed the idea of massive fund withholding as radical and dangerous. Before basic change could occur, the American public had to recognize the incompatibility of Negro rights with local control in the South.

The Birmingham confrontation, the national movement that it generated, and the leadership of two Presidents produced the public commitment to broad expansion of Federal power needed to break with tradition and engage Federal authority in the battle to protect Negro rights from local abuse. For the first time in the twentieth century, Congress was determined to put the question of equal rights at the top of the national agenda. As one part of a sweeping civil rights measure, Congress approved Title VI, a compromise requirement demanding that executive agencies act against segregation, withholding funds if necessary. This apparently minor provision, when expanded by subsequent court decisions and given force by massive Federal aid programs, was to prove as important in the actual dismantling of caste institutions as the Supreme Court decision had been in sapping their legitimacy. Within a year after President Johnson signed the Civil Rights Act, unknown bureaucrats were drawing on the authority granted by Title VI to administer a major social revolution in thousands of southern school districts.

2

The Evolution of Administrative Policy:

from the Law to the Guidelines

The afternoon of July 2, the day the Civil Rights Act was signed, a small group of concerned officials was called to a meeting in the office of the Commissioner of Education. Thus began the confrontation between the leadership of a Federal bureaucracy strongly tied to the status quo in American education and a law expressing the demands of a great social movement for basic local change. No one yet knew the implications of Title VI. This meeting saw the first groping attempts to estimate the changes that would be necessary in the Office of Education's day-to-day relationships with thousands of state and local education officials.

Although no one knew just how the broad injunction of the new law would be translated into the rules and procedures of the education bureaucracy, those meeting with Commissioner Francis Keppel saw that most of the agency's many grant programs would be affected and that some kind of promise of nondiscrimination would be required from those receiving grants. Beyond this, however, there was confusion. Central problems such as the definition of "discrimination" in Title VI and the relationship between judicial standards and the administrative requirements could not be resolved. Perhaps, one of the participants suggested, the White House staff would settle the policy issues.

The civil rights movement and the passage of the Civil Rights Act required that Federal agencies use the leverage provided by Federal money to force recognition of Negro rights in locally operated programs. Where the localities were adamant, Federal officials were required to completely sever the program relationship. After generations of passive Federal tolerance of local segregation, the law required a sudden and radical change in the entire relationship. Within the Office of Education, however, the formal responsibility for civil rights enforcement confronted the continuing realities of staff attitudes, local resistance, and

47

exposure of the Office to locally generated political pressures. Although the impulse behind the Civil Rights Act was a powerful one and although Commissioner Keppel was fully committed to enforcement, passage of the act was only the beginning of a lengthy internal struggle for a vigorous enforcement policy.

The broad principle of nondiscrimination in Federal programs seemed clear enough to civil rights advocates, but the imposition of a sweeping but nonspecific demand on scores of programs with different purposes, mechanics, traditions and even different constituencies proved to be a job of enormous complexity. Only after months of struggle between officials oriented toward the continuance of existing program relationships and those oriented toward the law and the courts or the civil rights movement did the basic form of the Federal regulations emerge. Only after further months of attempting to administer these general regulations did the Office of Education produce the detailed standards that became known as the school desegregation guidelines. In these months Office of Education officials were dealing with political questions of the first magnitude, and the decisions they made altered American federalism and profoundly affected the future of race relations in thousands of American communities.

FIRST STEPS

The Office of Education and the Tradition of Local Control

The task of civil rights enforcement was superimposed on an agency that had developed for almost a century in an environment in which the tradition of local control of the schools was accepted as a cardinal principle of political ideology. The modern history of the Office has been sharply influenced by this central fact.

The great expansion of Federal functions brought by the New Deal altered the role of the national government in many areas of American life but did nothing to diminish the preference for local control of education. Two National Advisory Committees on Education appointed by President Roosevelt concluded that the Office should confine itself primarily to research work. While formally processing some grant applications, the committee concluded, the agency should have absolutely no role in administering schools, even those directly under the jurisdiction of the Federal government.[1] From 1917 to 1950 no major permanent education programs were added, and the Office of Education grew slowly.

[1] Public Administration Service, "A Report on an Administrative Survey of the U.S. Office of Education of the Federal Security Agency," 1951, p. 7. (Mimeographed.)

As the 1950's began the Office remained an insignificant operation by Washington standards, with a total staff of less than 400, including secretaries. The staff operated more like a school of education faculty than an administrative agency, turning out studies of interest to a specialist or a professional group. Even the research effort showed little originality: the studies were commonly "compilations, opinions, or other kinds of secondary research" and tended to "reflect the orthodox viewpoint of those in the education profession." [2]

The Office reflected the status quo in American education and suffered from a serious case of professional inbreeding. All major positions were filled by committees of educators who generally relied on the recommendation of the division head, thus protecting the agency from anyone who might question existing arrangements. The strong tendency was to recruit elderly specialists, taking little notice of the "administrative, supervisory, and other characteristics which . . . distinguish a position in a Federal agency from one in a school or university system." [3]

The Office of Education had always had to cope with an environment extremely hostile to the expansion of its powers. To survive, it had to create a role for itself that did not threaten local power centers; it exercised only the loosest kind of formal control over grant programs. The staff members the Office recruited fervently shared the belief in locally controlled schools. "The Office," an administrative report for the Hoover Commission noted in 1950, "has always been a champion of the rights of the states to develop their educational programs, and has insisted whenever possible that programs operate by placing initiative and responsibility on state school systems. . . ." [4] This commitment pervaded official statements, producing frequent promises to "work primarily through State and local educational agencies," using methods "free of any taint of 'Federal control.' " [5] The staff, concluded a 1961 analysis, was still "dedicated to servicing local, State and institutional policies rather than a national policy." [6] The Office of Education accommodated itself to its political environment by renouncing ambitions for leadership in education and by faithfully serving local interests.

In spite of the passive tradition of the Office of Education, the specter of Federal control rose again whenever any program of general aid to

[2] *Ibid.*, p. 17.　　[3] *Ibid.*, pp. 53–54.

[4] Hollis P. Allen, *The Federal Government and Education* (New York: McGraw-Hill, 1950), p. 190.

[5] Public Administration Service, p. 4, quoting a 1950 statement of the Commissioner of Education.

[6] U.S., Office of Education, Committee on the Mission and Organization of the Office of Education, *A Federal Education Agency for the Future* (Washington: Government Printing Office, 1961), p. 6.

education was seriously discussed. Postwar debate continually returned to the themes of Federal bureaucratic inflexibility and the destructive impact of national programs on the development of local leadership. Arguing from a widely accepted dogma, so strongly believed that generations of contrary experience could be discounted, Federal aid opponents warned of a power-hungry national bureaucracy, generating endless red tape and extending its influence into the most vital local concern. Federal direction of the schools, some asserted, could even lead to dictatorship.[7]

Even strong supporters of Federal aid made clear that although they valued the Federal tax resources they would tolerate no significant Federal policy initiatives. A 1964 statement of the influential Educational Policies Commission summarized the conventional wisdom of the profession:

> Under commonly accepted interpretations of the Constitution, education, as such, is not a Federal function. Education is among those matters reserved to the states. . . . The tradition of diffused control exists not only for Constitutional reasons, but also for practical reasons. Decisions on education ought to rest on information best available to the respective states and localities. Therefore the Federal government ought not to interfere . . . ; decisions on curriculum and staffing—in effect, the decisions that govern actual educational procedures—should continue to be made locally under general state control.[8]

School administrators in the early 1960's, one researcher reported, continued to see the nation's education system as 50 separate compartments, each containing a number of school districts operating under the leadership of a state department of education. The separate compartments were vaguely connected to the Office of Education, an insignificant element in the total system. Educators feared any change that would breach the compartmental walls and subordinate the states to a national agency. The officials surveyed uniformly agreed that the Office of Education should have nothing to do with local schools and should deal only with the state departments. Federal officials, it was felt, should provide advice only on request.[9] Local beliefs established the limits of permissible Federal behavior:

> The officials of the Office of Education are emphatic in saying that they do not desire to dictate school curriculum or education . . . policy to state and local school bodies. This is almost a reflex response to any question which even vaguely infringes upon state or local autonomy. In specific the Office of Education respon-

[7] Hales, pp. 6–10.
[8] Educational Policies Commission, *Educational Responsibilities of the Federal Government* (Washington: National Education Association, 1964), p. 5.
[9] Sidney C. Sufrin, *Administering the National Defense Education Act.* "The Economics and Politics of Public Education," No. 8 (Syracuse, N.Y.: Syracuse University Press, 1963), pp. 54–55. Hereafter cited as NDEA.

dents insist that they come into states only on the request of the states, and even then usually make it a point never to deal with local officials unless state officials are present.[10]

Federal caution aided the growth of the Office of Education's programs. The sputnik crisis forced the nation to give attention to serious educational deficiencies, and the administration of the National Defense Education Act proved that Federal programs could meet such needs with virtually no control of local school systems. With President Kennedy strongly committed to Federal aid and with state and local school systems confronting severe financial crisis rooted in inadequate local tax resources, grant programs began to multiply at an increasing rate. The hearings on the first Kennedy aid-to-education bill indicated both what had changed and what had remained constant in national attitudes. Testimony showed that "the essential argument that schools could be improved by Federal funds was almost universally agreed upon." [11] Administrators were deeply concerned with public intolerance for further increases in the very rapidly rising local property tax rates and with school indebtedness expanding at a rate many times more rapid than that of the Federal government. With interstate tax competition for industry preventing the development of new tax resources and with very severe differences in taxable income per child, some kind of Federal assistance was necessary to cope with the problems of booming enrollments.

The obvious need for Federal money, however, did nothing to weaken opposition to Federal control. All witnesses at the 1961 hearing shared the belief that Federal control of education was undesirable. An observer commented, that no one "sensitive to the American tradition and familiar with the American temper seriously argues that the curricula, textbooks, school buildings, faculty requirements, and all the other factors which make up a school should be controlled by the Federal government." [12]

The Office of Education, in the early 1960's was five times as large as the 1950 staff, and its budget had climbed from $40 million to $600 million in 12 years, but it still had not become a major factor in the national system of education. The responsibility for some 30 new pieces of legislation failed to change "the basic, operating structure of USOE or its traditional norm of bureaucratic staffing and behavior." [13] The Office

---

[10] Sufrin, NDEA, pp. 62–63.

[11] Sidney C. Sufrin, *Issues in Federal Aid to Education.* "The Economics and Politics of Public Education," No. 4 (Syracuse, N.Y.: Syracuse University Press, 1962), p. 56.

[12] *Ibid.,* p. 57.

[13] Stephen K. Bailey, "The Office of Education: The Politics of Rapid Growth," a paper presented at the 1966 annual meeting of the American Political Science Association, pp. 5–6. (Mimeographed.)

remained a loose grouping of largely autonomous programs administering only a sixth of total Federal expenditures in education. The vacuum of internal leadership created by a rapid turnover in the Commissioner's office had led professionals in each program to create alliances with congressmen and professional leaders making the programs service agencies for the institutions and associations representing the status quo in American education.

The problems of the Office were continually reinforced by its method of recruiting personnel. To administer its growing programs, it selected elderly specialists, not young men with broad backgrounds and administrative ability. Competitive tests were circumvented by creating specialized positions only after officials had selected the man they wished to employ. Staff members generally had spent most of their careers in local and state school systems, coming to the Federal agency at an average age of 50.[14]

It is difficult to imagine any agency less prepared in terms of temperament, tradition, and philosophy to forcefully set in motion a major social revolution. Yet within two years of the time the Office of Education was given this responsibility by the Civil Rights Act; thus the agency that had always eschewed any hint of Federal control had moved strongly to protect the constitutional rights of black children in southern schools. The Office set down the school desegregation guidelines and enforced, with some vigor, detailed regulations governing the assignment of students, placement of faculty, student transportation, districting, and a variety of other factors of great importance to school administrators in the segregated school districts of the 17 southern and border states. These requirements, unimaginable a few years earlier, were a measure of the change in American federalism produced by the civil rights movement.

Enforcement Action before the Civil Rights Act

The Office of Education bureaucracy had been little affected by demands for using Federal aid funds to force desegregation during the 1950's and early 1960's. Critics pointed out that, whereas the Defense Department had taken major steps to end segregation in schools operated by the military on southern bases even before the 1954 Supreme Court decision, HEW, in which the Office of Education is located, delayed until 1962 before taking any action to end segregated programs it financed for the same group of children.[15]

[14] *Ibid.*, p. 17.
[15] U.S., Congress, House, Committee on Education and Labor, Subcommittee on Integration in Federally Assisted Public Education Programs, *Integration in Public Education Programs*, 87th Cong., 2d Sess., 1962, p. 89.

The basic problems of discrimination in Office programs were outlined in a series of policy papers prepared during 1960. The Commissioner of Education and high HEW officials saw four major issues. In the first place the Land Grant College Act, the oldest aid program, was still being administered in accordance with the separate but equal provision written into the act almost 70 years earlier. Second, there was the persisting problem of segregation in vocational education. The problem of discrimination had also clearly emerged in the National Defense Education Act. Finally, there was the question of the "suitability" of segregated schools for children on southern military bases.[16] The problems were outlined in 1960, but only halting steps toward solutions were taken before passage of the 1964 act.

Within HEW Secretary Ribicoff assigned much of the responsibility for developing civil rights policy proposals to Assistant Secretary James Quigley, a genial Catholic ex-congressman from Pennsylvania. He was intensely sympathetic to the civil rights movement and had requested the assignment after learning that the department was weak in this field. Representing HEW both on Vice-President Johnson's equal employment committee and a White House sub-Cabinet group on civil rights, Quigley was an early and lonely voice for the civil rights movement within the councils of the department. Until 1962 Quigley's advocacy made no significant headway against the resistance of the department's operating agencies.

This situation was changed only by the extraordinary situation that a militant Negro happened to control the congressional committee with jurisdiction over HEW. The power that an actively concerned committee chairman can use to change the terms of debate within an executive agency was clearly illustrated by Ribicoff's "suitability ruling." In early 1962 Secretary Ribicoff went before the Powell committee with a promise that all new education programs of the Kennedy Administration would be administered in a nondiscriminatory manner, but the Harlem congressman was far from satisfied with what amounted to a theoretical commitment for programs that might be enacted at some future date. The Secretary, Quigley recalls, "took a rather bad beating" from the committee and was directed to return.[17] Ribicoff agreed to support limited action against school segregation on military bases, the boldest move of the Kennedy Administration against segregation in Federally financed education programs.

The fact that Ribicoff issued a ruling that protected only the rights of

[16] David Seeley and Lucille G. Anderson, "Chronological Statement on Civil Rights in the Office of Education," October 1965.
[17] Interview with James Quigley, January 23, 1967.

children living on military bases, leaving children of off-base military personnel in Federally supported segregated schools, reflected a division of opinion within the department. Just as the HEW General Counsel of the Eisenhower era had argued that the Secretary had no authority to enforce the Constitution but must carry out the particular requirements of the various laws, Ribicoff's top legal advisor approved imposition of a desegregation requirement when he felt that the words of the law gave the Secretary broad discretion, but interpreted another section of the law in such a manner that the Secretary had no alternative to distributing Federal funds without any conditions. This ruling was hotly challenged by Senator Javits, who argued that HEW was the only major agency in the Federal government that failed to recognize "the authority and even the obligation under the Fifth Amendment to withhold funds from segregated Federal programs and activities." [18] The very cautious ruling of the HEW legal staff, however, accurately reflected the views of the men administering the department's basic programs.

Limited as it was, Secretary Ribicoff's decision to discontinue support for segregated schools on military bases posed a major enforcement problem. The manner in which this responsibility was handled strongly influenced decisions made during the first months of Title VI enforcement. The assignment was given to Assistant Secretary Quigley, who threw his considerable skills of persuasion and negotiation into the effort.

Quigley traveled through the South with the director of the impacted areas program; he made a "hard pitch" for compliance, arguing, "twisting arms," and sometimes threatening to cut off funds. Although the school districts stood to lose only the cost of educating children they would no longer be responsible for since base children would enter base schools, Quigley's effort proved successful outside the Deep South. Later, after enactment of Title VI, Quigley was to engage in a lengthy and futile attempt to extend the method of personal negotiation that had worked in dealings with a handful of districts to the process of administering a more demanding federal requirement affecting thousands of school districts.

During the first two years of Kennedy's presidency the Administration argued that no further legislation was needed for civil rights and that major advances could be made within the executive branch. By mid-1963, the Office of Education had taken some action against discrimination in grant programs for library facilities, manpower training programs, educational television services, and adult education programs in addition to the limited impacted areas requirement.[19] Even when the Administration did

[18] *Congressional Record*, 88th Cong., 2d Sess., May 7, 1964, pp. 7102–3.
[19] U.S., House, Committee on the Judiciary, Subcommittee No. 5, *Hearings, Civil Rights*, 88th Cong., 1st Sess., 1963, pp. 1540–41.

submit its first civil rights bill, Kennedy proposed nothing more than technical assistance to communities attempting to desegregate, a minor remedy for the terribly unequal educational opportunities he eloquently described.[20] The prevailing attitude in the Administration before Birmingham was stated by Assistant Attorney General Burke Marshall:

> I am not sure what the effect would be of a bill . . . which would state that every school district has to start desegregation immediately. Obviously they would not. We have a great problem in maintaining respect for the law. This law would not be obeyed. . . .
>
> It would perhaps be constitutionally permissible to destroy the federal system for all practical purposes in some states until school segregation has been ended. Obviously however, this is no minor matter. . . . Closed schools on a large scale are also a serious possibility which should be thought about seriously and responsibly before embarking the nation on this course.[21]

In the Office of Education Commissioner Francis Keppel was strongly and publicly committed to the objectives of the civil rights movement. His attitude was expressed in a speech entitled "The Emerging Partnership of Education and Civil Rights," given after the passage of the Civil Rights Act.

> For the past decade this Nation has been struggling through a period of crisis, testing whether our democracy can establish in fact what it has long and nobly proclaimed in words. The Civil Rights movement is the embodiment of this effort, and the Civil Rights Act of 1964 is its highest expression. . . .
>
> . . . It stands as a great watershed dividing the past from the present in our national life. . . .
>
> Many difficulties clearly lie ahead. Important social changes never occur without disagreement and controversy. But the major thing is that we are agreed on the inevitability of change. To paraphrase the words of a leading Southern school official: we are no longer debating the merits of desegregation; we must now try to find means of achieving it.[22]

Although the Commissioner's personal stance was clear, civil rights was a secondary concern, subordinated until 1965 to the achievement of the two basic goals President Kennedy had given him: to make the Federal government a significant force in American education through passage of a general aid-to-education bill and to reorganize the Office of Education to mold its scattered and ineffective segments into an instrument capable of stimulating educational change. Believing that the Office of Education

[20] John F. Kennedy, *Public Papers of the Presidents of the United States* (Washington: Government Printing Office, 1964), pp. 222–26.
[21] Letter from Assistant Attorney General Marshall to Leslie Dunbar, February 26, 1963.
[22] Francis Keppel, "The Emerging Partnership of Education and Civil Rights," *Journal of Negro Education*, Vol. XXIV (Summer 1965), 204.

could not exert major leverage for racial change, at least until Federal aid programs were much larger, Keppel delegated civil rights matters to a young assistant, David Seeley. Seeley, who had a Yale law degree, experience with the HEW legal staff, and had studied under Keppel at the Harvard Graduate School of Education, was later to emerge as a decisive figure in Title VI enforcement. Keppel's sympathies eventually made possible vigorous enforcement of the Civil Rights Act. In the short run, however, he made little impact on the strong preference for local control deeply embedded throughout the programs of the Office of Education.

Most Office of Education officials saw the civil rights movement as a threat. Just when sputnik and the advent of the New Frontier had finally produced rapid growth in Office programs, the demands of the civil rights movement threatened vitally important state and local support. "Here," recalls one high official, "were a bunch of fellows struggling to get into the sun." They would say, " 'We are professionals. Keep us out of this social reform movement.' " The crisis in Birmingham, however, set in motion a chain of events making this most traditional of agencies responsible for instituting a revolution in race relations in local school systems.

The sense of rage produced across the nation by brutality in Birmingham rapidly generated proposals both in Congress and at the White House for ending Federal subsidies to school systems defying the Constitution, but the issue failed to stir enthusiasm within the Office of Education. Commenting on proposals before the Powell committee, Keppel's civil rights advisor questioned the appropriateness of the remedy, echoing President Kennedy's earlier concern that the result might be denial of needed programs without achieving integration.[23] At the Powell committee hearings Assistant Secretary Quigley opposed legislation requiring cutoff of funds and argued that the national interest might demand continued support to segregated programs under certain circumstances. Quigley urged enactment of legislation that would permit but not require withholding.[24]

President Kennedy's decision to include even a weak withholding provision took HEW by surprise. When he read the Administration bill, Quigley says, "I couldn't believe my eyes." [25] When HEW Secretary Celebrezze appeared to testify on the Administration proposal he argued very strongly for administrative discretion, asserting that it would be administratively impossible to suddenly impose nondiscrimination re-

[23] David Seeley, typed note, undated.
[24] UPI news clip, June 26, 1963. Quigley, of course, could not support a proposal more far-reaching than the President's bill.
[25] Quigley interview.

quirements on all of the thousands of projects financed by 130 different HEW programs. He pointed out that it had taken him almost a year to make the necessary decisions on desegregation requirements for a handful of programs. "I think," he said, "that the administrator must have some degree of flexibility so his programs just don't go down the drain." [26]

The enforcement program then visualized by HEW leadership was centered in the department's regional offices, largely staffed by local people. These officials, said Celebrezze, "know the complexity of the problem and the people involved." [27] Suggesting that perhaps 50 additional staff members would be needed, Celebrezze leaned strongly toward a negotiating approach. "The way I suggest we administer this . . . is to have us judge, as we sit down with the school officials, whether they are really making a diligent effort, what their problems are and how we can work out their problems." [28]

In their testimony on the President's proposal, both Quigley and Keppel made optimistic estimates about the response of southern schoolmen. Quigley pointed out that the number of southern districts involved in the extremely popular impacted areas program was "legion" and predicted that attitudes would cover the spectrum from "defiant resistance to an anxious desire to do something." [29] With Federal encouragement, Commissioner Keppel predicted, there were areas in every state, including Alabama and Mississippi, where "integration could occur tomorrow in the public school system without incident or any disturbance." [30]

Attitudes Within the Office of Education

In June 1963, as the President's bill went to Congress, administrators of the Office's major programs were asked to analyze the impact of the proposed requirement. Throughout the Office, administrators tooling up expanded programs saw civil rights enforcement as a major obstacle. The responses clearly illustrated the failure of Commissioner Keppel to shake the Office's deeply ingrained attachment to the status quo.

Predictably, the primary concern was that programs would be weakened by disruption of carefully developed relationships with state and local educators. Thus the director of the impacted areas program gloomily predicted that many southern districts would simply withdraw from his program. Most school districts in Alabama, Mississippi, South Carolina, Louisiana, and some sections of Georgia, he felt, would rather lose the money than begin integration. In the other states, he guessed, many school officials would be willing to begin integration, because they "know

---

[26] House Judiciary Subcommittee, *Hearings, Civil Rights*, pp. 1521, 1553.
[27] *Ibid.*, p. 1553.   [28] *Ibid.*, p. 1548.   [29] *Ibid.*, pp. 1549–50.
[30] *Ibid.*, p. 1551.

they will soon have to integrate whether or not they receive federal funds." He saw fund withholding as a negative step that "would seriously affect the quality of the education program for Negro and white students alike in some of the applicant school districts. . . ." [31]

Similar disruption was feared in college programs. Sixteen states, one administrator reported, still maintained separate but equal land-grant institutions that would presumably be affected. The official was also worried that termination of National Defense Education Act student loan programs at segregated colleges would mean that "considerable numbers of needy students might be expected to drop out of college." [32]

In most Federal programs, actual administrative control over local projects rested with state departments of education, with the Office of Education simply forwarding funds and receiving reports. Washington staff members were troubled by the prospect of transforming the existing Federal-state cooperation, with state domination of operating decisions, by assuming responsibility for a controversial Federal-local regulatory function that would bypass state officials. Development of effective cooperative relations with the states had always been the first essential for operating a successful Federal program. Now administrators who functioned largely as professionals in developing and using this kind of relationship were distressed by the threat of the most explosive kind of disruption. Both in the NDEA and vocational education programs, high officials pointed out the obvious rupture of administrative relationships that would be required. [33]

Those responsible for the Office's oldest activity—the collection of education statistics and the dissemination of information on promising educational programs—shared this concern. An Educational Research and Development Bureau staff member wrote that these programs "would be adversely affected by Federal requirements external to the programs involved. We rely on voluntary cooperation from educational agencies. This cooperation would be seriously injured by any investigative or policing functions lodged in the Office of Education." [34] Another bureau functionary clearly expressed the conservatism of the Office, questioning the constitutionality of the fund-cutoff proposal. The idea, he wrote, "carries us a long distance from a 'Government by law' to a 'Government by men.'" He saw the constitutional question as "larger than the current

[31] Memorandum from Rall I. Grigsby to John R. Ludington, June 25, 1963; Memorandum from Rall I. Grigsby to Arthur Harris, July 3, 1963.
[32] Memorandum from Kenneth W. Wildenberger to Arthur Harris, June 25, 1963.
[33] Memorandum from Ralph J. Becker to Arthur Harris, June 25, 1963.
[34] "Effect of 'Non-Discrimination' Requirement on Programs in ERD," author not indicated, July 3, 1963.

issue of 'civil rights' even though it is, of course, less pressing politically." [35]

The reaction in the Office was echoed by the HEW legal staff. General Counsel Willcox was particularly disturbed by the bill's failure to define the central term "discrimination." This flaw, he suggested, might force the department into extremely sensitive areas of regulation. Willcox proposed a cautious, flexible, and gradual approach. The aid funds, he wrote, had been granted "for a bewildering array of programs supported by the department pursuant to the authorizations of many statutes enacted over a span of generations" and "abrupt action would be both unwise and unfair."

> Many activities of State and local government and many private institutions have become heavily dependent on financial aid. . . . Perhaps we . . . have been remiss in letting them so long continue to receive aid while discriminating. . . . But the fact is that we have done so, and in all fairness they should not be subjected to disruption of their finances if they cannot mend their ways overnight. We should not right one wrong by doing another.
>
> . . . There must be a reasonable middle ground between this course and further protracted delay. The appropriate course, I think, will necessarily vary from program to program. . . .[36]

A careful lawyer oriented toward protection of the web of legal and practical relationships that had evolved through years of experience in administering the various grant programs, General Counsel Willcox shared the fear of disruptive change and the sudden breach in long-term agreements that would be involved in immediate imposition of an extremely important new requirement for every Federal program.

At the outset it was clear that both the leaders of the major education grant programs and the HEW legal staff were hostile to the fund-withholding idea. Relationships with state officials were seen as a precious asset of the various programs, not to be jeopardized for any extraneous purpose. The administrators, a number of them southerners, felt that not only would the Office be weakened, but educational opportunities would decline for both white and black students. Given the limited importance of Federal funds in education, it was assumed that many school districts, particularly in the Deep South, would simply withdraw from Federal programs. To limit the difficulties, the HEW legal office favored modification of the legislation to limit the department's responsibilities, indicating a predisposition to interpret the legislation narrowly.

After an initial flurry of concern, however, interest in the issue within the department died down for almost a year. There was a widespread

[35] Memorandum from Herbert S. Conrad to Ralph Flynt, June 25, 1963.
[36] Memorandum from General Counsel Willcox to agency heads, June 25, 1963.

belief that Title VI would never become law. "We never expected Title VI to remain in the bill," Quigley remembers. "We thought that this was a loss leader." [37] Although an Office of Education task force on the issue was theoretically in operation, lack of pressure created an atmosphere of inaction in the bureaucracy. Only in the final weeks before passage of the Civil Rights Act did it become evident that the southerners' strategy of concentrating their fire on the public accommodations section would permit enactment of Title VI. This miscalculation meant that the Office of Education had no significant role in drafting the legislation that was to give the agency its most difficult administrative responsibility. Apart from some inconclusive discussion about the possible use of HEW auditors as compliance investigators, almost no planning had been done in the Office of Education until the Civil Rights Act was very near final passage.[38]

About a week before the President signed the act, the wheels began to turn within the Office. David Seeley, the Commissioner's assistant, began to search for information to use in negotiations with school districts during the coming summer months. In a well-intentioned but unfortunate gesture, the Office had ceased to collect comparative data on white and Negro schools after the 1954 Supreme Court decision; now the Office had no information on the existing racial situation in southern school districts. Nor was there anyone in the Office of Education with a clear idea of the standards to be used in evaluating the desegregation plans school districts would submit to remain eligible for Federal funds. Seeley's initial hope was that the staff of the Civil Rights Commission could provide both information and compliance standards. If the commission failed to suggest standards, Seeley proposed reliance on either the HEW General Counsel or the Justice Department.[39] All three of these sources were to play a role in settling some of the basic policy questions, but in the long run, the job of developing detailed enforcement standards was to rest with the Office of Education itself.

Uncertainty about policy was compounded by uncertainty about administrative structure. Although the Commissioner of Education had final authority and responsibility for education grants, he was subordinate, particularly in political matters, to the secretary of HEW. Both Assistant Secretary Quigley and Commissioner Keppel were committed to civil rights enforcement, and it was unclear whether administrative machinery would be located at the departmental level in HEW or at the Office level.

[37] Quigley interview.
[38] Memorandum from David Seeley to Lisle Carter, March 19, 1964; memorandum from Carter to Seeley, April 10, 1964.
[39] Seeley Chronology. This took place on June 24, 1964.

Several contradictory assumptions about enforcement methods could be supported by different sections of a memo circulated by Secretary Celebrezze shortly before the signing of the act. He stated that each of HEW's constituent agencies would have full responsibility for enforcement of the antidiscrimination requirement, a statement that might suggest the creation of agency-level compliance operations. He also, however, designated Quigley as department-wide coordinator, a task that might well demand the development of an enforcement staff in Quigley's office. Finally, Celebrezze strongly emphasized "voluntary compliance," directing each program to attempt to employ personnel with experience in interracial relations work.[40] This final suggestion implied that enforcement would become part of the responsibility of the staff on each grant program and was consonant with the Administration-wide position that enforcement responsibility would "pervade" the operating programs and would not require any significant additional staff. Months were to pass before the administrative requirements for Title VI enforcement were understood and before the lines of responsibility were clarified.

When Commissioner Keppel called together a group of important staff members the day the Civil Rights Act became law, the program administrators seemed to lean toward a minimum compliance provision that would require school systems receiving aid to file a written assurance of nondiscrimination. This pledge would be accepted, with the Office reserving the right to demand proof should any suspicion of noncompliance arise.[41]

Title VI provided that the basic administrative rules for enforcement must be incorporated in a formal regulation signed by the President. The process of drafting this legal document began in the HEW legal office shortly before passage of the Civil Rights Act. In their early discussions, program administrators hoped that this regulation would resolve the basic policy issues. The Office of Education decided to continue business as usual pending action on the regulation, with the understanding that, upon approval, new agreements would immediately be subjected to the nondiscrimination requirement.

Alerting the South

Before any serious compliance effort could be mounted it was essential that southern educators be made aware of the new law. While discussions on the regulation were getting underway, Quigley and several Office of Education officials discussed Title VI with groups of school administrators assembled in several southern cities. At the outset the Federal officials

[40] Memorandum from Secretary Celebrezze to HEW agency heads, June 25, 1964.
[41] Notes of July 2, 1964, meeting; author not indicated.

found that southern educators "generally weren't aware that they were required to do anything." [42] Keppel rapidly took action to include notices about Title VI with various communications from the Office of Education, and the HEW team organized a first series of meetings within weeks of the law's enactment. Because they were most heavily affected, the superintendents from districts depending on impacted areas aid were called together first for closed sessions in three southern cities.[43]

Both in the initial meetings and in five additional sessions in late July with more broadly representative groups of educators, the worried superintendents raised a variety of specific questions. Since many basic issues were unresolved within the Administration, the Federal representatives could often only promise rapid issuance of the presidential regulation. Approval of the regulation was expected in time to take effect for the school year beginning in September.[44] Even in these early sessions, however, some analysis of the requirements was made, and interpretations were announced that later served to limit the freedom of action of the Office of Education.

During these sessions Quigley and Seeley, Keppel's choice as Office liaison to Quigley's operation, took positions on three important issues that seemed clear then but later were to become highly controversial. Because of Senator Dirksen's success in incorporating into Title VI a limitation on Federal authority to regulate employment practices, both Federal spokesmen were initially convinced that the Office of Education had no authority to deal with the explosive question of faculty desegregation. Seeley remained convinced on this issue for some time, but by a late July session in Memphis, Quigley was hedging on the issue, saying that he didn't know the answer and that the question would be "one of our toughest, most difficult, most knotty problems to solve." [45] The educators were told, however, that there would be no faculty integration requirement, at least for the first year.

The Office of Education commitment on this issue betrayed a lack of understanding of both the legislative history of Title VI and the evolution of the faculty desegregation question in constitutional litigation.

[42] Interview with David Seeley, June 17, 1967.
[43] Seeley Chronology.   [44] Seeley interview, June 17, 1967.
[45] Assistant Secretary Quigley, tape recording of a meeting with school officials in Memphis in late July 1964. The language in Title VI, proposed by a Republican Senator during the negotiations between Senator Dirksen and the Justice Department, had then been justified as a necessary step to eliminate overlap between Title VI and Title VII, concerned with job discrimination. Justice Department concern that this language not preclude faculty desegregation requirements had led to a statement by Senator Humphrey specifically mentioning the possibility of such requirements under Title VI during the floor debate.

During the Senate debate, Humphrey specifically stated that faculty integration could be required, citing a court decision to support his argument. Some important court decisions had treated faculty integration not as a question of employment discrimination but as a necessary element in a successful student desegregation program. Months later, when leading officials realized that a mistake had been made, the Office found itself in a position in which it could demand nothing without being accused of breaking its pledges on an issue of the first importance in many communities. The commitment also confronted the Office with a serious political problem when it did change the requirements to insist on faculty desegregation in 1966.

On two other issues that later became controversial, the Federal spokesmen relied on Senator Humphrey's narrow construction of the title during Senate debate rather than upon the words of the law itself. Southern schoolmen were told that, "We've pretty well decided that a school district that is desegregating under a court order . . . will be considered to be in compliance." [46] This meant that the Office could require no further progress from major urban school systems operating under court-ordered plans allowing another decade for token integration of all grades. Perhaps even more important was the question of "freedom of choice" desegregation plans.

Relying on Humphrey's comments and current court decisions, Quigley and Seeley assured school officials that districts providing theoretical freedom for Negro students to choose to enroll in white schools would be eligible for funds. The following exchange at a meeting in Biloxi, Mississippi, indicates the kind of commitments that were made:

MISSISSIPPI SCHOOL OFFICIAL: "You're going to say we're guilty of discrimination even though not a single Nigger in a district will want to go to school with a white."

DAVID SEELEY: "So far as I know the court decision did not require . . . integration, it merely required desegregation. In other words it doesn't require you to force Negro students to go to school with white students. . . . It just requires that the actions of the school district in assigning students not be based on race. . . . If you have . . . a free choice system . . . and you end up with most of the Negro students going to one school and the white kids going to another, or all of them for that matter, this could, conceivably be found to be non-discrimination, so long as it was clear that this was not by policy of the board but by choice of the students." [47]

Although the meetings did bring some public commitments on issues that were later to prove embarrassing, they also served to make the South

[46] David Seeley, tape recording of a meeting with school officials in Biloxi, Mississippi, July 25, 1961.
[47] *Ibid.*

aware of the Federal determination to force change, at least as far and as fast as the higher Federal courts had decided the Constitution demanded. The courts, Seeley told the Memphis session, "have become increasingly impatient," and "delays after this time are very hard to justify on the basis of good faith." [48] The central effort was to make the school officials come to terms with the fact that important changes had to be made, but that they were not going to have to do anything impossible. The essential success of this effort was evident in the comment of the Mississippi superintendent at the end of the Biloxi meeting. After telling a Gospel parable and making a bitter comment about civil rights laws, Superintendent Tubb spoke to the local school officials:

> We're going to be calling on all of you, whether you are a county superintendent, a district superintendent, or consolidated superintendent, in the next few months. And we're expecting each of you to carry a pretty heavy burden. And believe me all of you are going to carry a pretty heavy burden. I'm not pessimistic. But let's remember that I think that we have the strength to handle the problem.[49]

The President himself played a role in spreading awareness of the new law. In mid-July, Jack Valenti of the White House staff informed Keppel that President Johnson wished to meet with several hundred educators to discuss the impact of the Civil Rights Act on education. The session was then rapidly organized and held less than a month after the signing of the act.[50]

Enforcement: The First Months

The public commitment of the Administration to vigorous enforcement of Title VI was not soon reflected in the allocation of administrative resources. This failure was not due to an absence of determination to do the job, it was due to a lack of understanding of the nature and magnitude of the necessary effort. Requests from both Keppel and Quigley for funds to administer Title VI ran afoul of a government-wide underestimation of the administrative requirements. The Budget Bureau assumed that Title VI could be handled by existing staff just as any other change in the legal requirements for Federal grants. Responsibility for civil rights enforcement was to "pervade" the operating programs. If additional staff were granted to the Office of Education, Budget officials argued, every agency operating grant programs would come in with demands for additional personnel.

While the idea of "pervasive" enforcement sounded plausible, it soon became evident that the people running the Federal aid programs were

[48] Seeley, Memphis tape.   [49] Biloxi tape.
[50] Memorandum from Commissioner Keppel to Jack Valenti, July 17, 1964.

radically unsuited, in terms of their values and in terms of their relationships with state and local officials, to be administrators of a law bringing to bear Federal power to force basic changes in the local social order. From the very outset, Commissioner Keppel realized that there would have to be some focus for the Office of Education effort. He engaged in a futile effort to find a prominent educator willing to coordinate what was then dimly perceived as a compliance investigation unit. With neither staff, budget, nor provision for high rank and high salary, the job had little to recommend it.

During the first summer there was not a single person in the Office of Education devoting full time to what was soon to become the Office's most visible public responsibility. As it became obvious that the HEW Title VI regulation would not be completed in time for the coming school year, concern about enforcement machinery subsided. Keppel's assistant, David Seeley, spent most of his summer working on War on Poverty programs.

With no administrative apparatus in existence in the Office, early enforcement problems were forwarded to Assistant Secretary Quigley. Very shortly after the Civil Rights Act was signed, Quigley was confronted with a difficult decision. Across the South, the Federal government was financing construction of schools in segregated school systems receiving impacted areas aid. Passage of the act found 76 projects partially paid for. Title VI left unsettled the question of whether the Office should withhold the remaining payments until the schools desegregated. Worried local school officials, who had made large commitments on the basis of assured reimbursement, quickly began to pressure the Office for release of funds.[51]

Quigley was determined to use the leverage provided by one of the Office's most important programs to negotiate desegregation plans. At his request, Keppel held up the payments. Quigley himself negotiated by telephone with some of the local schoolmen. Some districts remained adamant however, demanding unconditional release of the Federal money needed to meet the pressing demands of local contractors. The issue came to a head in August in Houston County, Georgia, where the school officials refused to accept any plan requiring more than a notoriously weak court order in a neighboring county.

When the local congressman demanded release of the funds, program officials stalled, blaming congressional delay in acting on appropriations for the current fiscal year. After the bill passed, an adamant and angry

[51] Memorandum from B. Alden Lillywhite to Assistant Secretary Quigley, July 16, 1964.

local superintendent again asked his congressman to intercede. The congressman called, demanding to know who was responsible. At this point, B. Alden Lillywhite, the program official caught between local demands and Quigley's orders, turned to Keppel. Concerned about the possible impact on congressional relations, he questioned Quigley's judgment and informed the Commissioner that the HEW General Counsel had "serious reservations" about the legality of withholding the final construction payments.[52] Already the split between administrators and lawyers oriented toward existing program relationships and those primarily concerned with an activist enforcement policy was becoming evident.

Quigley, an excellent negotiator, exasperated program officials with his continued refusal to tell local educators what the minimum requirements for obtaining Federal funds were. His approach was to build up pressure on the districts to get as much desegregation as possible in each situation, rather than to establish an officially sanctioned minimum.[53] His unpredictable approach to administration was clearly illustrated in the final resolution of the Houston County crisis. After discussing the crisis by phone with an angry congressman, he ordered release of the funds. Realizing that his authority was not clear, Quigley was determined to push as hard as he could but to retreat before the threat of a dangerous confrontation. Even after this reversal, however, he favored further delay in other southern school districts. Quigley did not see the problem in terms of overall standards, but saw each school district as a separate arena of struggle for the best possible desegregation plan.

From the beginning, there had been a legal argument against Quigley's maneuver. Title VI provided that funds be withheld in conformance with presidentially approved regulations. Since the regulation was still in preparation HEW possessed no clear legal authority. Quigley was less concerned with legal technicalities than with using the power of Federal money to break local defiance of the Constitution. His approach put program officials in a very difficult position. Both program administrators and HEW legal technicians questioned Quigley's authority and were concerned with resulting damage to necessary program relationships. After the Houston County retreat, Quigley met with General Counsel Willcox and high Office of Education administrators. The group decided to avoid further confrontations by releasing not only the payments still due on projects approved before Title VI became law, but also payments on projects in segregated districts approved between the time the act was

---

[52] Memorandum from B. Alden Lillywhite to Commissioner Keppel, September 22, 1964; note by David Seeley, August 21, 1964.
[53] Quigley was following the approach used by the courts since the 1954 decision in tailoring a distinct plan to meet the special circumstances in each school district.

passed and the issuance of the department's Title VI regulation.[54] There was no further pressure on Federally subsidized schools to desegregate in the fall of 1964. This early dispute was the harbinger of future differences.

Drafting the Regulation

Less visible than the early administrative gropings, but of far greater importance, were the months of discussion within the Administration as the lawyers and policy makers worked to translate the sweeping injunction of Title VI into a series of concrete and carefully defined administrative requirements to be approved by the President as the charter for civil rights compliance programs throughout the executive branch. Throughout the summer and well into the fall the drafting process continued.

The fact that presidential approval of the regulation was necessary meant that the HEW decisions concerned not merely the department but the entire Administration. The White House called on the Justice Department's Office of Legal Counsel, which had been prominently involved in drafting the act, to coordinate an effort to draft uniform regulations applicable to all Federal agencies administering grant programs. Two days after President Johnson signed the bill, the Justice Department circulated a guide to all agencies asking submission of draft regulations to the Office of Legal Counsel within two weeks. The Justice memorandum asked that agency drafts either provide for the use of fund withholding as a penalty or for the insertion of a nondiscrimination clause in contracts, making possible lawsuits against violators.[55]

HEW, the department most affected by the new requirement, had made only a minor effort to draft regulations before the act became law. No one in the department had been sufficiently involved in the drafting process to know what the language of Title VI meant. When the White House decided before passage of the act that the HEW regulation, because of the scope and variety of HEW programs, would serve as a model for the entire government, a deputy General Counsel was put to work drafting legal language.[56]

Looking at the record of the congressional debate, Reginald Conley of the General Counsel's office found little to guide him. The debate was "so damn voluminous—everybody said everything until he was blue in the

---

[54] Memorandum from Lillywhite to Keppel, September 22, 1964; memorandum from Arthur Harris to Keppel, September 30, 1964.
[55] Assistant Attorney General Norbert A. Schlei, "Guide for Issuance of Regulations under Title VI of the Civil Rights Act of 1964," July 3, 1964.
[56] Interview with Reginald Conley, March 22, 1967; memorandum from General Counsel Willcox to Assistant Secretary Quigley, May 26, 1964.

face." [57] Left without clear guideposts, Conley attempted to interpret the face value of the words. In the earliest draft, grant recipients were asked only to submit a very general promise of nondiscrimination. This was simply an extension into the field of civil rights of the general procedure of general reliance on the good faith of local officials. This approach, together with a recognition of the department's authority to impose specific demands if necessary, seemed reasonable enough to those working in the context of existing program relationships. Even this minimum requirement, it was suggested, could be dispensed for a year and a half by the Secretary and indefinitely by the President should it interfere with the achievement of the basic objectives of the grant program.[58]

What seemed reasonable to program-oriented officials seemed highly ineffective to those more aware of the record of southern resistance since 1954. The large loophole created by possible dispensation from the desegregation requirement was tightened substantially in the next draft.[59] Early discussions within the department, the General Counsel reported, revealed differences of opinion on such basic questions as the impact of Title VI on the issue of faculty desegregation and the propriety of incorporating the judicial doctrine of gradualism into the HEW regulation.[60]

The Federal agency most closely connected with the civil rights movement, the U.S. Civil Rights Commission, made an initial assessment of Title VI very different from that produced in HEW. Commission staff members proposed that no new grant programs be initiated in a given area until the nondiscrimination demand was fully complied with, and that existing programs be continued only if local officials submitted a concrete plan for "prompt" elimination of discrimination by a specific date. Moreover, the enforcement procedure should not rely on complaints but should require regular reports from all localities concerned.[61] The commission favored a sudden reversal in the pattern of Federal-state relations and close scrutiny of local performance.

Eager to produce regulations rapidly, Lee White of the President's staff called together a meeting of concerned officials the same day the act was signed. Quigley emphasized to White the need for very rapid action on the school regulations to permit enforcement action before Labor Day. White assured him that the President was "very much interested in tim-

[57] Conley interview.

[58] "Preliminary Working Draft" of Title VI regulation, May 19, 1964.

[59] Reginald Conley, notes of civil rights meeting in the Treaty Room of the Executive Office Building, July 2, 1964.

[60] General Counsel Willcox, "Outline of D/HEW Regulations under Title VI of H.R. 7152," May 22, 1964, draft prepared for submission to the White House.

[61] Justice Department, "Preliminary Guide to Departments on Title VI Regulations," June 18, 1964.

ing" and that the regulations would indeed be ready by September. President Johnson underlined the importance of immediate implementation at a Cabinet meeting the same day.[62]

In spite of the Administration's commitment, the weeks that had been allotted for preparation of the regulations were to stretch into months. The task of overcoming the massive inertia of the great agencies, of fundamentally restructuring relationships built up by agencies with diverse missions expressed in hundreds of different programs, and of reconciling sharply distinct orientations toward the civil rights movement consumed month after month.

Within HEW the split between those oriented toward the movement for Negro rights and those primarily concerned with program relationships was clearly reflected in the debate over the faculty integration issue. All of the department's operating agencies opposed any attempt to desegregate professional staffs. Office of Education officials felt particularly strongly, arguing that any attempt to cover teachers would promptly raise claims that HEW was violating the title's language proscribing regulation of employment practices. The result would be "such charges of arbitrary action as to impair seriously our chance of getting voluntary compliance with respect to students." [63] Quigley's deputy, Lisle Carter, Jr., the department's ranking Negro official, read Title VI differently; he argued that only employment that was "extraneous to the Federal purpose" of a given program could not be regulated.[64] Justice Department staff members who had been close to the drafting process came down somewhere in between, arguing that employees such as faculty members and health professionals, whose work was directly related to the accomplishment of the purpose of the grant, could be covered.[65]

What was really involved in this dispute was a basic difference in the perspectives from which the issue was considered. Office of Education staff members separated the issues of student and faculty integration not only because of the words of Title VI, but also on the grounds that a very clear and politically important distinction was made between the two issues in the communities with which the Office had to deal. While many southern localities were prepared to tolerate a few Negro students in the white schools, the general popular assumption was that there were no Negro teachers competent to teach in white schools and that white teachers would absolutely refuse assignment in Negro schools.

While program officials viewed the issue in terms of what seemed

[62] Conley meeting notes, July 2, 1964.
[63] Willcox, "Some Principal Issues under Title VI of the Civil Rights Act," July 14, 1964.
[64] Memorandum from Lisle Carter to Willcox, July 9, 1964.
[65] Willcox, "Principal Issues . . . ," July 14, 1964.

possible in the existing situation, Quigley's office and the Justice officials considered the question in terms of the requirements of the Constitution, the intent of Congress, and, simply, in terms of the steps necessary to eliminate the system of racially separated schools. Increasingly, Federal courts were holding that integration of faculties was a necessary element in desegregation plans. Black students were obviously far more likely to choose to enter an integrated school if there were Negro teachers on the faculty. Similarly, placement of white teachers in Negro schools was an essential step in the process of breaking down the community identification of certain schools as wholly Negro and therefore necessarily inferior. From this perspective, action against faculty segregation was clearly in order.

When the regulation was finally issued, the question of teacher segregation was left unresolved. The document forbade racially motivated denial of opportunity to take part in a Federally supported program, "including the opportunity to participate as an employee." The right to participate as an employee, however, was defined to cover only programs designed primarily to provide jobs, work experience, aid for the handicapped, or subsidized employment for graduate students.[66] Not until early 1966 was the final resolution of the issue clear.

Faculty integration was only one of a series of issues that emerged in the drafting process. Within HEW, Quigley organized a task force on Title VI under Lisle Carter, Jr. Policy questions were examined by four work groups, each including a member from each of HEW's operating agencies.

The reports of the work groups generally reflected a cautious approach to the enforcement responsibility. The work group on construction grants, for example, recommended continuing aid to any district involved in desegregation litigation which promised to comply with the eventual court order. With its invitation for years of delay, this procedure promised very little progress, particularly in the Deep South where many Federal district courts could be expected to delay and to grant only slight relief to Negro litigants. Similarly, the compliance work group proposed the requiring of only a general assurance from recipients. Under this plan the responsible local official need only list the grants made to his organization, state that the Civil Rights Act had been obeyed, and summarize the steps that had been taken.[67]

After this initial pledge was filed, the basic enforcement responsibility was to rest with local Negro citizens and with the HEW regional offices. The work group incorrectly predicted that the beginning of enforcement

[66] *Federal Register,* Title 45, Subtitle A, Part 80.3.
[67] "Compliance Report," draft by Mr. Nash, August 6, 1964.

activity would set off a "barrage of complaints" that would play a central role in triggering investigations. The regional offices, using regular program personnel, were to evaluate state reports and make on-the-spot investigations of complaints. In Washington the effort would be coordinated by a compliance report unit in the Secretary's office, which would assemble and review information about a given institution or school system and direct further action when necessary.[68] This plan put heavy reliance for civil rights enforcement on regional staff members, whose basic professional interest lay in developing and maintaining good working relationships with state and local officials.

The discussion of the basic assumptions of the enforcement process generated a dispute between HEW and the Civil Rights Commission staff. The commission, putting enforcement of the Constitution first, supported compulsory investigation of the local racial situation before any Federal grant could be made. HEW, however, argued for initial acceptance of a written promise, even when there was suspicion of noncompliance, claiming that the commission's approach would bring all of the department's programs grinding to a halt for an indefinite period. This, one HEW official recalls, was a fight between the "far-outers" and the "practical types." Lee White, of the President's staff, decided in favor of practicality, thus limiting the immediate impact of the Act.[69]

On another point of debate between the department and the commission staff, the limited view of Title VI powers lost. Discussing the issue of eligibility for Federal funds, the HEW General Counsel proposed that the flow of Federal money continue to institutions that operated Federally supported programs on an integrated basis but otherwise remained totally segregated. The commission argued for treating total educational institutions or school districts on a systemic basis. Because a total institution was under centralized administrative control and was commonly perceived as a unit in the community, the commission held that any grant would tend to strengthen the entire institution, thus giving Federal agencies the responsibility for regulating the racial practices of the total organization. Justice attorneys supported the commission's argument, and it was endorsed at the White House level.[70] The regulation provided that a college receiving a grant from any program must guarantee wholly non-discriminatory treatment of all students.[71]

While several issues shaping the contours of enforcement policy stimulated policy battles, one of the most important was very easily settled. Most of the large city school systems of the South were already desegre-

[68] Memorandum from Louis H. Rives, Jr., to Lisle Carter, August 7, 1964.
[69] Conley interview.   [70] *Ibid.*
[71] *Federal Register*, Title 45, Subtitle A, Part 80.4 (d).

gating under court orders resulting from NAACP lawsuits by the time the Civil Rights Act became law. The issue was whether the Office of Education should simply accept existing, and often inadequate, court-order plans as compliance with Title VI, or whether the Office should attempt to second-guess the local Federal judges and impose new requirements on these same districts. Both in the Justice Department and in HEW, the commitments made by Senator Humphrey during the Senate debate were seen as leaving the Administration no alternative to continuing aid to districts obeying court orders.[72] The contrary remarks of Senator Pastore, floor manager for Title VI, were not seriously considered. Even a militant Negro lawyer then in HEW recalls that the question seemed closed and that the small number of school districts under court order tended to mask the importance of the decision.[73]

The willingness to accept court orders was reinforced by fears of a confusing and damaging conflict between the Federal courts and the Federal executive. A decision to reject court orders would put executive agencies in the difficult position of pitting their judgment of the appropriate remedy for unconstitutional segregation against that of the local Federal judge who had explored all the details of the case. Should a local school board in such a situation use the judicial review provision in Title VI to test the legality of the agency's demands, the case might well be heard in the same Federal district court. Even without court challenges, Federal officials would confront local feelings that a requirement rejected by a Federal judge and then imposed by an administrator was of questionable legality.

Although it was later challenged by civil rights groups, Administration policy makers felt that the legislative history of Title VI permitted no further requirements of districts operating under court order. Although fewer than one-tenth of the southern school districts were affected, this decision meant that Title VI was a dead letter in most of those large cities that might well be most responsive to rapid change. Acceptance of court-order desegregation plans also set limits on what could be required of other school districts. If a substantial group of the most important districts of the South were to continue receiving Federal aid while stretching the process of token integration over the period of a decade, more backward districts not under court order could not reasonably be forced to immediately abolish the system of racial separation in the schools.

[72] Conley interview. The Justice Department had accepted this limitation because of the belief that it would be possible to strengthen existing court orders and develop new legal principles through litigation authorized by Titles IV and IX of the Civil Rights Act.
[73] Interview with Mordecai Johnson, March 1, 1967.

Given the court-order situation, equity required that HEW accept voluntary desegregation plans from other school districts incorporating at least some element of the gradual approach ordained by the courts. Thus, although grant recipients in programs outside the field of education were plainly required to end segregation at once, the regulation was to offer school districts three options. Each district could submit either an assurance that its schools were totally desegregated, an agreement to abide by a court-ordered desegregation plan, or a voluntary desegregation plan. Thus the decision to accept court orders as adequate compliance determined the whole structure of enforcement policy. Policy makers, however, saw this much less as a new decision than as a reaffirmation of a commitment clearly made by the Administration during the Senate debate.

As seen from the White House, the months of discussion of Title VI regulations resulted in HEW's operating agencies and the General Counsel calling for the narrowest construction of the new authority. Justice Department attorneys and Assistant Secretary Quigley advocated more vigorous enforcement, although Justice was very sensitive to commitments made by Administration spokesmen during the congressional debate. Predictably, the Civil Rights Commission staff put forward the broadest interpretation of the title. Time after time, three major strands of argument had appeared—that of the program administrator sensitive to the needs of his state and local constituents, that of the lawyer oriented toward the courts and concerned with faithful reflection of the intent of Congress, and that of the activist primarily concerned with finding a way to protect the rights of black Americans.

White House aide Lee White played the role of mediator, but he assigned basic drafting responsibility to Assistant Attorney General Norbert Schlei. The Justice Department, responsible for much of the language in the Civil Rights Act and the only Federal agency with experience in enforcing civil rights laws in the South, was generally deferred to in the important matter of interpreting the legislative intent. When important policy issues remained unresolved, both White and the President himself were called on for decisions. The President's concern, White recalls, was that the regulation be "as fair and invincible to attack as possible." [74] The Administration desired a policy that was enforceable and immune to the very serious political damage to the enforcement program that would arise from a defeat in the courts. Because the Justice Department apparently had the best information available for assessing both the response in the South and the reaction of the courts, the White

[74] Interview with Lee White, June 21, 1967.

House generally supported Justice proposals when disputes occurred. The administration was also eager to observe the commitments made during congressional debate, and the close involvement of Justice attorneys in the legislative struggle permitted the department to offer authoritative interpretations of the legislative history. The knowledge and experience brought by the Attorney General's staff to the policy conferences generally overbalanced HEW's desire to protect program relationships from any possible damage.

Two ideas were dominant at the White House reviews: there was both a desire to use this powerful Federal sanction carefully and within the law and also a desire to make a forceful and determined response to the national demand for racial progress. "My attitude," White recalls, "was that this was an exceedingly potent weapon but that it ought to be used with tremendous care because it was so damn dangerous." [75] The President and his staff accepted neither the cautious approach of the HEW lawyers and program administrators nor the radical changes proposed by the Civil Rights Commission. Generally, they endorsed the judgment of the Justice Department, supporting what they believed to be full and vigorous enforcement of the law.

The struggle within the Administration over the shape of the regulation cost a year in the process of desegregating southern schools. The delay was required by protracted policy arguments, often couched in legalisms, over the basic issues of professional integration and the treating of educational institutions as systemic wholes.

The mixture of law and politics characteristic of the rule-making process was evident in the faculty integration issue. The HEW draft regulation first submitted for Administration approval held that such coverage was prohibited by the act.[76] Relying on court decisions and legislative history, the Justice Department promptly took the position that teaching staff should be covered. Shifting the argument from legal abstractions to political reality, Commissioner Keppel reported the feeling of southern educators that such a requirement "would very definitely generate the impression that we are twisting this law to be as harsh as possible. It would undermine our efforts to indicate that we are merely implementing the law of the land. . . ." School districts prepared to begin student desegregation, he wrote, might change to total resistance, since faculty integration was "a much more difficult problem in most cases." [77] In a mid-August memo to Lee White the HEW General Coun-

[75] *Ibid.*
[76] Memorandum from Secretary Celebrezze to Kermit Gordon, July 16, 1964.
[77] General Counsel Willcox, "Regulation under Civil Rights Act," July 20, 1964; memorandum from Keppel to Willcox, July 24, 1964.

sel maintained that a general faculty integration requirement would "invite a charge that we had broken faith with Congress." [78] Eventually the regulation was drawn to permit but not to demand faculty integration requirements.

With the President ready to sign the regulation, HEW continued to dispute the question of awarding graduate fellowships to segregated institutions. Although the Justice Department, the Atomic Energy Commission, the National Science Foundation, National Aeronautics and Space Administration, and the Defense Department all favored treatment of institutions as wholes, HEW continued to urge separate treatment of each program. After prolonged delay the Justice position prevailed.

The policy decisions incorporated in the final document bore directly on the central missions of several agencies. The central goal of HEW is the effective distribution of billions of dollars of Federal money provided to the states, the local governments, and various private institutions for the accomplishment of national purposes. The success of these programs demands the maintenance of effective working relationships permitting Federal leadership through persuasion. The necessity of maintaining these relationships tends to make HEW a representative of local interests within the Administration, a tendency that was strongly reflected in early Title VI policy discussions. The Justice Department's central role as legal advisor to the Administration, and its large commitment to the defense of civil rights guaranteed by the Constitution and Federal laws, represented very different interests in the policy struggle. The Justice interest was in a careful and "lawyerly" interpretation of Title VI that could be readily defended in the courts, and in the creation of an enforcement tool that would supplement the litigation undertaken by the department's Civil Rights Division. The final decisions on the policy issues substantially aided the Justice Department in the accomplishment of its civil rights mission while weakening HEW's ability to effectively handle its basic program responsibilities.

The time given to Administration-wide policy discussion produced important gains. Had HEW been permitted to draft its own regulations, much of the revolutionary force of the law would undoubtedly have been lost through narrow interpretations by the department's legal staff and operating agency heads. The involvement of the President and the leading role of the Justice Department resulted in a regulation closely conforming to the interpretation presented by Administration spokesmen on the floor of Congress. On December 3 1964 President Johnson signed the regulation. A month later it was to take effect.

[78] Memorandum from Willcox to Lee White, August 17, 1964.

Creation of the Office of Education Compliance Machinery

During the months of policy discussions, the Office of Education was involved only sporadically. Commissioner Keppel and his assistant, David Seeley, spoke to groups of southern educators and were marginally involved in the drafting process. What enforcement activity there was centered in the office of Assistant Secretary Quigley.

Keppel's attempt to recruit a prominent educator to coordinate Office of Education civil rights responsibilities resulted in failure. Michigan's state superintendent was expected to take the job, but he changed his mind shortly before the Title VI regulation took effect. Keppel's wish to set up an enforcement unit was frustrated further by the Budget Bureau's assumption that no new personnel were required for this function and by the impossibility of gaining approval for the "supergrade" position necessary to give the top position high status and salary.

Only a fortunate circumstance made the budget problem surmountable. Another section of the Civil Rights Act had provided funds to aid communities undergoing desegregation and to finance a national survey on the educational significance of segregated schools. Thus, although there was no Title VI budget, the Office did have funds for the creation of a small unit concerned with school desegregation when the appropriation became available in the fall of 1964.

As serious planning began, no one in the Office was aware of the intensity of the resistance to be encountered and of the administrative demands the compliance responsibility would generate. This was part of a government-wide underestimation of the task. Thus, although the relatively unimportant Community Relations Service was readily granted a number of supergrade positions giving its executives the prestige associated with the top three levels of the civil service, the director of the effort to revolutionize race relations in southern schools was not to hold such a rank for months. In the words of one participant, there was simply a "general lack of appreciation of the monstrousness of the task before us." [79]

With the regulation finally approved, a handful of people in the Office set to work preparing for the expected influx of voluntary desegregation plans from southern school districts. The regulation did not define what must be included in such a plan, and the ad hoc group of staff members taking shape around David Seeley recognized that some instructions would have to be sent to local educators together with the legalistic regulation.

[79] Seeley interview, June 17, 1967.

The instructions were mailed, along with the regulations, to thousands of school districts in a frantic last-minute rush on New Year's Eve, 1964. School officials received a broad outline of the points to be covered in a minimally acceptable plan. Any plan would have to provide a nonracial method for assigning students entering the earliest grade as well as specify the time schedule the district would follow in opening the other grades to some method of integration. Racial gerrymandering of school boundary lines was not to be allowed. Public notice of the plan would be required, and school systems establishing a plan based on the choices of the students would have to pledge that Negro decisions to enter white schools would be honored.[80] Beyond these very general requirements, local school boards were without guidance in drawing up their plans.

Perhaps more important than the broad outline of the desgregation plan was the indication in this early document that the Office was prepared to begin holding up funds immediately. The instructions directed state agencies to authorize no new programs and to renew no continuing programs after January 3 until the Commissioner of Education certified the local district's compliance with Title VI.[81]

The decision to immediately freeze all Federal aid money for new programs and renewals meant that thousands of school districts began to feel the full force of the cutoff power in the spring of 1965 as they were planning school budgets for the coming fall. Had the Office chosen to rely on lengthy termination proceedings in each individual case rather than to defer all funds until plans were submitted, far more time would have been lost before local officials confronted the necessity of change. Commissioner Keppel's willingness to hold back funds until May, together with the promise of vast new sums of Federal aid under the Elementary and Secondary Education Act, made Title VI a matter of urgent concern across the South.

The regulation took effect three days into 1965, and the Office of Education had a major new program to administer. Having failed again in his attempt to recruit a prominent schoolman, Keppel turned to his youthful assistant, David Seeley, and asked him to take leadership on a temporary basis. Seeley, who had been Keppel's civil rights aide but had been giving most of his time to the poverty program, now took command of the nascent enforcement staff.

Keppel's last-minute choice turned out to be peculiarly apt. To some extent, Seeley combined all three of the major perspectives in terms of

[80] Office of Education, "Instruction to School Districts Regarding Compliance with Title VI of the Civil Rights Act of 1964: Nondiscrimination in Federally Assisted Programs."
[81] *Ibid.*

which civil rights policy was discussed, a fact that made it possible for him to communicate effectively with a remarkably wide range of people. In the first place, Seeley was a lawyer with experience in the HEW legal office. Training at the Harvard Graduate School of Education and a variety of program responsibilities as Keppel's troubleshooter gave him a good understanding of the problems of the administrators of the Office's grant programs. Finally, experience in handling civil rights issues for Keppel and a rapidly increasing sensitivity to the problems of school segregation gave him a growing sympathy for the demands of the activists. Thus Seeley could not be attacked, as many other Federal officials were, either for ignorance of the law or for lack of experience in educational programs. Nor could he easily be attacked by civil rights groups.

When he took charge, Seeley had puny resources for the administration of a social revolution. Funds for administering grants to desegregating communities had been used to assemble a staff of six and to employ one important consultant, Professor G. W. Foster, Jr. The necessity of coping with the flood of mail, phone calls, and the endless delegations that soon came pouring into Washington forced Seeley to borrow staff from the desegregation grant program and from various parts of the Office of Education.

During the first weeks, the dominant theme was confusion. The staff was installed in a borrowed conference room near Seeley's office. No one knew what the lines of responsibility were or whether final decisions would be made by Commissioner Keppel or Assistant Secretary Quigley. No one was able to give authoritative guidance to school officials asking questions left unanswered by the regulation and the instructions. There was confusion of authority even within the tiny staff in the conference room. Theoretically the new Equal Educational Opportunities Program was divided into two branches, one concerned with desegregation grants and the other dedicated to Title VI enforcement. The administrative assistant of a prominent senator had been recruited to head the enforcement section, but it rapidly became apparent that neither his background nor his temperament suited him for the explosive and sensitive responsibility. During this period, one participant recalls, "there was no order." [82]

Little attention was given to the problem of organizing the work of the small staff. A secretary was sent in to organize the rapidly accumulating correspondence and chose to file it by states, a circumstance that may have influenced the later organization of the program along geographical lines. External pressures on the informal operation were rapidly accumulating. "By the middle of January," a consultant remembers, "superintendents were just crowding the halls . . . up by Keppel's office. . . .

[82] Interview with G. W. Foster, Jr., June 6, 1967.

There just had to be somebody to get these people moving and out of sight." [83]

The crisis was met by the creation of an extraordinary group of consultants led by Professor G. W. Foster, Jr., of the University of Wisconsin Law School. Foster, who had become deeply interested in the role of the Federal judiciary in the confrontation between national rights and local power in the late 1950's, combined recognized expertise in school desegregation law with an activist temperament. He saw Title VI as a "golden opportunity" for taking the intolerable pressure of the school cases off the Federal judges by introducing a powerful new force for school integration. Foster eagerly volunteered his help and rapidly became Seeley's leading advisor.

The basic decisions to accept either court orders or voluntary desegregation plans as adequate compliance with Title VI presupposed some relationship between judicially developed standards and the minimums to be imposed by the Office of Education. Thus Foster's knowledge of the complex body of legal doctrine developed in desegregation decisions was obviously relevant to the solution of the problems constantly presented to the inexperienced enforcement staff by southern educators.

Amid the "absolute shambles" of the first weeks, Foster gained Seeley's support for assembling a group of part-time consultants, law professors who had previously worked together on Civil Rights Commission studies. During the critical formative period of the first months, this group became the core of the Title VI program. The pressure for decisions forced the Office to rely on those who could accurately interpret the standards evolved in the courts. From the knowledge and judgment of this group of professors emerged the standards that were to be codified and imposed on the South. The result, of course, was to tie Office of Education enforcement criteria very closely to the decisions of southern Federal courts.

The early conception of the enforcement responsibility was one of monitoring and negotiating a flow of local plans, in which local officials would invent programs designed to take into account the particular problems and opportunities of each community. At the outset, the staff optimistically hoped for honest plans that promised substantial local progress, failing to realize that it was impossible politically for many local leaders to propose anything that might later turn out to be more than the minimum demanded of another community. Seeley was simply "unprepared for the massiveness of the unwillingness to come up with decent plans or any plans." [84] The frustrating attempt to deal with the wholly inadequate plans submitted during the first months were to produce the recognition that far more explicit Federal leadership was necessary.

---

[83] *Ibid.*   [84] Seeley interview, June 17, 1967.

The consultants began by carefully reviewing the first plans submitted. The proposal of each school district was Xeroxed and given to each of the professors who flew into Washington for part of every week. Each man would write a memo on the plan, discussing the legal and policy issues involved. Group discussions of the plans revealed that all of the early proposals were seriously below current standards of Federal courts of appeals in the South. The plans continually presented new policy issues, and the discussions among the consultants began to produce common approaches to translating the case law into general administrative standards. These discussions were the first step in the development of the school desegregation guidelines, the document that became the charter for the transformation of race relations in southern education.

The five consultants, crowded into a single room down the hall from the Commissioner's office, had little time for legal speculation. The flow of urgent requests from local officials who felt a terrible need to know what they would have to do was channeled to the law professors.

> If a school superintendent and a school board lawyer came in from Fiddlesticks, Mississippi and they demanded to see somebody who knows something about it, they weren't going to take some clerk. They were going to insist that they see Mr. Keppel.[85]

Keppel's office referred the visitors to Seeley's secretary, who would send them on to see the consultants, who were, therefore, often completely bogged down in discussions. Whenever the phone would ring, one of the consultants would answer and try to explain the issue troubling the local school official. The professors were also expected to go into the South to meet with school authorities and explain the law to them.

The consultants quickly assumed a central role not because of any power inherent in their positions but because they were the only people in the Office able to answer pressing questions. In this case, knowledge was power. The practical necessity for decisions, together with the fact that the only existing standards were embodied in a complex body of case law mastered by only a small number of experts, gave the law professors an opportunity to transform their scholarly knowledge into national policy in a realm of the greatest sensitivity. The consultants knew the court decisions, there was a widely shared assumption that Title VI was designed to enforce the Constitution as interpreted by the courts, and no one else in the Office had any idea about a source of desegregation standards to rely on in answering the continuing barrage of questions. The urgent administrative need for standards forced the Office to operate on the assumption that "discrimination" in Title VI meant what the courts

[85] Foster interview, June 6, 1967.

had decided was unconstitutional, and then to rely on the consultants to extrapolate from court decisions to the specific issue under discussion.

A month of chaos was sufficient to convince both Seeley and Foster that ad hoc advice to individual superintendents was not adequate. Further policy guidance was clearly necessary. Foster reported to Seeley that there were simply not enough experts available to help thousands of districts draft adequate individual plans. Asserting that it was "abundantly clear that a great many districts simply want to be told what they must do," Foster urged that principles be extracted from court decisions to "spell out some of the minimum alternative choices." [86] At the same time, Seeley concluded that southern state political leaders were trying to deal with the uncertainty of Federal requirements by "sounding us out as to what would be acceptable compliance." [87]

Seeley argued that both the local political needs and the administrative necessity of coping with thousands of districts with a very small staff required formulation of explicit minimums. Failure to make clear Federal requirements would only result in the submission of thousands of plans that had received community endorsement but would require extensive negotiation to bring up to the level of current judicial standards. Since the Title VI staff was hopelessly inadequate for the massive negotiations, this situation would present the Office with the unhappy dilemma of either accepting meaningless promises of compliance or ending needed programs in large areas of the South. The answer, Seeley wrote to Quigley, was to call together various concerned Federal agencies to draw up "guidelines for the acceptability of the desegregation plans." After such standards were informally cleared with the White House and civil rights groups, he suggested, there would be a firm basis for negotiation with state political and educational leaders toward statewide compliance agreements.[88]

Quigley, however, strongly opposed this idea, arguing that it would be politically unwise and might be a barrier to achievement of maximum desegregation. Inflexible written standards, he asserted, could only be set at the lowest common denominator so that compliance was possible in the Deep South. The Assistant Secretary favored simply permitting pressure to mount on school districts until it was so intense that the community would submit a plan that in fact represented the maximum change that could be tolerated locally. Quigley strongly believed that a school board was far more likely to effectively implement a plan developed locally than one imposed from Washington.

[86] Memorandum from Foster to Seeley, January 25, 1965.
[87] Memorandum from Seeley to Assistant Secretary Quigley, January 25, 1965.
[88] *Ibid.*

The problem of different basic conceptions of the enforcement process was magnified by an uncertain division of authority between Quigley and Keppel. Although Keppel had statutory responsibility for grant programs and civil rights authority under the HEW regulation, Quigley had been clearly designated from the outset as department-wide coordinator for Title VI enforcement. While the bulk of day-to-day business was handled in the Office of Education, Quigley's office frequently became involved both in specific cases and in policy decisions. While Seeley was temporarily borrowing staff members from other Office programs, Quigley was using funds allocated for staffing his responsibilities in the field of pollution to support a growing civil rights staff. Quigley estimates that three-fourths of his time was consumed by civil rights matters during this period.

From the beginning most of the political questions went to Quigley. While most school officials came to the Office of Education, Quigley handled cases in which a congressman or a senator's office had arranged an appointment for the school official. Thus Quigley carried out individual negotiations. He also took an active role in urging the department's regional offices to become heavily involved in the enforcement process. Thus several distinct centers of authority were simultaneously involved.

The most important early negotiations took place between Quigley and the political leadership of South Carolina. Had these discussions succeeded, the entire future of the enforcement program might well have been transformed. Governor Russell, a moderate, desired a statewide arrangement under which all districts would submit the same plan. HEW enforcement officials were uniformly eager to obtain the help of the state political establishment, which would be of immense value in making the program work. Through representatives, the governor proposed a statewide plan based on the recent court-order plan imposed on the Darlington County school system by a Federal district court in South Carolina.[89]

Before responding, Quigley sent the plan to the legal consultants, who were unanimously horrified. Although the freedom of choice plan demanded a good deal by South Carolina standards by calling for a theoretical opening of all 12 grades to Negro students immediately, it lacked the specific protections necessary to make freedom of choice a plausible route to integration in the Deep South. Experience had shown that in communities fundamentally opposed to any integration, specific guarantees in black and white about the notice to be provided to Negro parents and the method for exercise of the choice were essential. Obviously, if the plan was not made known to the Negro community or if a transfer

[89] Seeley interview, June 17, 1967.

applicant had to confront an official gauntlet designed for intimidation, "freedom of choice" was reduced to a euphemism for segregation. The law professors responded with an addition to the plan, summarizing protections that had been supported by the Federal court of appeals having jurisdiction over South Carolina.

Governor Russell was informed that the plan was basically sound, but that it would be necessary to make explicit certain things that were implicitly or informally understood between the district judge and the Darlington school authorities. After several weeks of delay, the Governor decided to negotiate the proposal and sent his son and the state attorney general to Washington. After a long and tough session with Quigley, a tentative agreement was reached; it included a proviso that HEW would relax somewhat the requirements on notice set forth by the law professors.

Had the agreement been concluded, enforcement of the more stringent standards soon to be established in the guidelines would have been impossible. In South Carolina, however, educational leaders advised the Governor to reject the compromise.[90] Ironically, Governor Russell's decision to refuse the plan thus was crucial to the success of the civil rights program.

A second political crisis was generated by a movement led by another southern moderate governor, Carl Sanders of Georgia. As it became obvious that the Office of Education would not approve desegregation plans that would accomplish nothing, school districts in several states tried to take advantage of what they hoped was a loophole in the Federal regulation. The regulation had provided three possible methods of compliance with Title VI—the voluntary desegregation plan, the court order, and the submission of a form assuring complete desegregation. Although the assurance form had been intended only for fully desegregated districts, or districts that have never been segregated, large numbers of completely segregated districts began to file such documents.

The problem arose first in Arkansas, where a whole group of districts filed assurances. The theory underlying the action was that the districts "promised, whenever caught . . . to clear it all up." [91] Nothing more, they pointed out, was required of districts outside the South. The Arkansas state superintendent, however, conceded that these districts were in no position to integrate completely and instantly when caught discriminating, and he was able to stop the movement in Arkansas. Soon, however, the assurance documents began to flow in from Georgia and Alabama.

[90] Foster interview, June 6, 1967.　　[91] *Ibid.*

The problem became terribly serious in Georgia, where a young assistant attorney general persuaded state authorities that all that Title VI required was a promise not to discriminate, a promise any school district could make by signing the assurance form. The state's newspapers, including the moderate *Atlanta Constitution*, joined Governor Sanders in his vigorous attack on the Office of Education for its refusal to accept the promises the state superintendent had labored to obtain from local school boards.[92] With hundreds of school districts involved and an influential governor publicly stating that Georgia school board members should "regard any suggestion that signing was not with good intent as a personal insult," the situation was very serious.[93]

The issue was finally settled in a marathon meeting in Atlanta, with Seeley and Foster arguing the legal issues involved in the assurance form with Georgia's attorney general. The state's legal official was eventually convinced by a single sentence in the December instructions to school districts stating that such an assurance should not be filed by a district that was neither desegregated nor prepared to comply fully with Title VI. This provision, accidentally included in the Instructions at the last minute, convinced the Attorney General that his assistant's argument would not hold up in a legal test. After this session the Georgia move receded rapidly, sparing the Office a major confrontation that might well have changed the basic structure of the program.[94]

While political crises were providing tests of the skill and resolve of the Office of Education, the most important development of these early weeks was buried in a mass of mundane day-to-day activities. In these chaotic weeks a new bureaucracy had come into existence, a tiny bureaucracy with highly unsettled policies, uncertain lines of control, and with no constituency, no established procedures, and no budget. From the beginning the new program was operating on uncharted ground in the midst of a much larger agency with fundamentally different goals and principles of operation. Survival and success of the program depended on the creation of an administrative institution able to bear the strains of enforcing far-reaching social changes in thousands of communities.

As the first elements of a professional staff began to emerge, the part-time dual responsibilities of most of the consultants proved increasingly untenable. During the days they could spend in Washington the professors were involved in discussions hashing out early policy problems. During the remainder of the week they were continually called at their university offices by school administrators asking for guidance in prepar-

[92] *Ibid.*
[93] Memorandum from Secretary Celebrezze to Douglass Cater, March 23, 1965.
[94] Foster interview, June 6, 1967.

ing desegregation plans. The consultants tried to provide advice based on recent Washington discussions and analysis of the relevant decisions in various southern appeals courts. As a permanent staff was assembled in Washington, however, the consultants found that the advice they gave during the week had become obsolete by their next visit to Washington. Most of the professors gradually moved away from the center of the policy-making process and specialized in advising school officials in particular regions.

The endless discussions had begun to produce some general rules of thumb for dealing with the plans coming into the Office in increasing numbers. The first substantive decision had been reflected in the December instructions. Seeley had agreed with Burke Marshall, of the Justice Department's Civil Rights Division, that all schools be required to follow the pattern established in the decisions of the New Orleans Court of Appeals, which required integration of the initial grade in each system. Discussions within the Title VI program gradually began to produce agreement on the conditions under which the Office would accept a freedom-of-choice plan. Nothing was done, however, to pull together these rules of thumb and make them available to school officials demanding advice. Each community faced the painful process of developing a plan generally based on the plan of a nearby district operating under a court order falling far behind current appeals court standards. Only after the plan was rejected could local officials obtain specific advice. The situation of the local school superintendent, who won community acceptance of a disturbing change only to have the local plan rejected on completely new grounds, became intolerable.

THE EMERGENCE OF THE GUIDELINES

The Arkansas Letters

Early in the second month of the enforcement effort a number of county school superintendents from southeast Arkansas approached Professor Foster for advice on drawing up desegregation plans. Foster was eager to encourage progress in these black-belt counties across the river from Mississippi's hard-core delta region. Foster learned of the local leadership exercised by Superintendent C. R. Underwood, who ran a small rural district with a two-thirds Negro enrollment. When Underwood called the Wisconsin law professor to tell him of a plan to bring together a number of local superintendents to adopt a common plan and begin desegregation together, Foster quickly responded. Hoping for an important breakthrough, Foster prepared a long letter which crystallized current thinking within Seeley's office. The letter was the first systematic statement of the specific requirements that faced local school authorities.[95]

In his letter to the Tiller, Arkansas, superintendent, Foster set out standards derived from decisions of the several courts of appeals dealing with school cases. Foster's earlier inclination to rely on the separate patterns of law created within each state by Federal district court decisions had given way to a general consensus among the consultants to draw standards from the appellate tribunals; this decision permitted the development of uniform national criteria and imposed on districts the more stringent constitutional protections forged by courts less oriented to local interests. For the present, Foster wrote, freedom of choice plans would be permissible, but they would not be simply accepted at face value. The Washington office would study both the genuineness of the free choice provided and the plan's actual success in producing integration. All students must be offered a choice before entrance rather than after being assigned to a Negro school. Widely used practices making it highly complicated or embarrassing for a Negro student to transfer would not be tolerated. The law professor proposed that a form letter about the plan be sent to all Negro parents, suggesting language prepared by the NAACP Legal Defense Fund.[96] Pointing to the growing impatience of the high Federal courts, Foster wrote that a plan calling for extension of the free choice system to six grades the first year would probably be accepted, while a plan opening only two classes would not. Like the Federal courts, the Office would demand far more rapid progress from the more than 1500 districts that had done nothing for a decade than had been expected of communities beginning desegregation earlier.

While demanding that school districts move promptly and build protections of Negro students' rights into the free choice system, the Foster letter provided some reassurance on the explosive issue of faculty integration. He noted that some courts had already directed "steps in the direction of nonracial hiring and assignment of teachers," recognizing the obvious influence of faculty segregation on student choices. Recognizing, however, the insistence of sympathetic southern schoolmen that "they absolutely couldn't do that part of the job this early in the game," Foster wrote that for the first year the district need only indicate some long-range commitment to the objective of faculty integration.[97]

The policy summary met a chronic need, and Foster was beseiged for

[95] *Ibid.*

[96] Letter from G. W. Foster, Jr., to Superintendent C. R. Underwood, February 11, 1965.

[97] *Ibid.*; Foster interview, June 6, 1967.

weeks by phone calls from Arkansas superintendents asking for similar guidance. "I was," he recalls, "called every hour of the day and night. I was told that copies of . . . this letter were Xerozed and moved around down there." [98] When he wrote to other superintendents, he continued to revise the letter, incorporating new policy decisions. The great sense of relief many felt when they finally were told what must be done is evident in the comment of one Arkansas superintendent: "We, like a good many other school people, had been groping our way in the dark haze of wild rumors and misinformation pertaining to the requirements of the Civil Rights Act." [99]

Although much appreciated, Foster's letters still lacked official status as Federal policy. Confusion persisted within HEW. What one Federal official told an educator in one district would be overruled by a superior in Washington or contradicted by an official dealing with an adjoining school system. By the time a district wrote up a plan and obtained local approval the rules of thumb in Washington would have changed again. Local school officials, a normally cautious group, were being forced to play an extremely dangerous game in which the penalty for mistakes was either loss of essential funds or essential local support. These men felt that it was intolerable that there were no stated rules to the game and that judgments seemed to be made by powerful but whimsical referees who disagreed with each other and wouldn't explain the rules. Indecision within the department remained so high that not a single plan had been approved three months after the program began.

The *Saturday Review* Article

Almost in spite of itself, the Office of Education soon found itself with a semi-official statement of policy prominently featured in the education section of *Saturday Review*. Encouraged by the response to his letters, Foster drew together a set of draft guidelines. Knowing Quigley's strong opposition to a formal statement of minimum standards, Foster conceived the idea of issuing the document on his own authority through publication in the magazine that had carried several of his earlier articles. Impelled by his belief that the Office was "making a tragic mistake in not giving adequate guidance to a bunch of unsophisticated people who desperately wanted guidance," Foster submitted the document without authorization.

Writing to a *Saturday Review* editor, Foster explained the crisis produced in the South by Federal failure to tell school officials what must be done. The consultants, he explained, could not cope with the job, and

[98] *Ibid.*
[99] Letter from Superintendent Samuel King to Foster, February 25, 1965.

some mechanism was needed to broadly disseminate the summary of the advice now being given.

> Frankly, I think it doubtful that anyone in HEW would dare give me permission to seek publication of the memo in light of my close association there as consultant. Nevertheless if the initiative were to come from you, where you take the position that the information is urgently needed and that you have turned to me . . . I think you can at least pry out the concession that the publication will not be repudiated. . . .[100]

The editor agreed to carry the legal memorandum, but only on the condition that it would be informally approved by the Commissioner of Education. Keppel readily agreed to publication under Foster's name.[101]

As the article was prepared for publication, the need for information became increasingly obvious. Although new commitments of badly needed Federal funds had been frozen across the South, far less than one-fifth of the concerned school districts submitted desegregation plans in the first two months. Most of the plans had come from relatively untroubled sections of Texas. Florida was the only other southern state in which more than a handful of districts had acted. In seven states with serious problems fewer than five districts had attempted to file plans.[102] With less than four months to receive approval for new projects before the end of fiscal year 1965, school officials were very disturbed. Tension was augmented by the likelihood of passage of a major new program aiding elementary and secondary schools. Lack of agreed standards within the department continued to prevent disposition of the 250 plans that had been received. "Not one has been completely acceptable," reported the *Christian Science Monitor*. "On the other hand, none have been finally rejected." [103]

The administrative crisis boiled over in North Carolina, where a disgusted state superintendent threatened that if the Federal government didn't provide some guidelines, he would. He wrote to Commissioner Keppel:

> We believe that we are entitled to official written guidelines and criteria for structuring and evaluating compliance documents before proceeding further. We do not want to be unreasonable, but it is our honest conviction that your office is obligated to provide official guidelines to school districts desperately seeking official answers.[104]

100 Foster interview, June 6, 1967; Letter from Foster to James Cass, February 22, 1965.
101 Foster interview, June 6, 1967.
102 Equal Educational Opportunities Program, "Voluntary Desegregation Plans Received," March 3, 1965.
103 *Christian Science Monitor*, March 8, 1965.
104 U.S., Congress, House, Committee on the Judiciary, *Hearings, Guidelines for School Desegregation*, 89th Cong., 2d Sess., 1966, p. 123.

In a meeting with Florida's educational leaders, the acuteness of the need was forcefully impressed on Seeley. By this time Seeley had worked over the draft of the *Saturday Review* article, and he decided to release it to the angry Floridians. Although denying that it was officially sanctioned, Seeley indicated that it closely approximated what would be required.[105]

To maximize the impact of the guidelines memo, wide distribution of reprints was arranged. The American Association of School Administrators and the Southern Association of Colleges and Schools cooperated with the civil rights-oriented Potomac Institute in getting the needed material to all school superintendents in the South.[106]

Although the civil rights movement was perhaps the natural constituency of the enforcement program, civil rights groups had remarkably little involvement in the shaping of the policy memorandum. Comments were requested from representatives of the Civil Rights Commission and the NAACP Legal Defense Fund, the long-time leader in school desegregation litigation, but neither suggested any significant change.[107] Civil rights groups remained heavily oriented toward legislative and judicial action, and it was to be some time before they began to understand the possibilities of administrative enforcement procedures.

Appearing in the March 20 *Saturday Review*, Foster's article was preceded by an introduction explaining that the memo had no official status. "Yet," the introduction concluded, "there is no doubt that it reflects directly the thinking of the officials charged with the responsibility for enforcement of Title VI as it applies to education." [108]

The ultimate meaning of Title VI, the memo explained, was the abolition of the southern dual school system, "doing away with these separate Negro and white schools." Freedom of choice plans, Foster explained, were "perhaps no more than transitional devices" ultimately to be replaced by nonracial neighborhood schools. Failure to produce effective desegregation had already produced some Federal court decisions striking down free choice plans, and the Office of Education would accept these plans only under strict conditions. Federal authorities would require elimination of complicated forms and embarrassing personal interviews. If a school in a free choice system became overcrowded, those to be transferred would have to be chosen on the basis of distance from the school

[105] Foster interview, June 6, 1967.

[106] Letter from Foster to Forrest Conner, March 11, 1965; letter from Margaret Hughes to James Cass, March 15, 1965; letter from Foster to Eleanor Ambrose, March 15, 1965.

[107] Letter from Foster to author, July 12, 1967, supplementing June 6, 1967, interview.

[108] G. W. Foster, Jr., "Title VI: Southern Education Faces the Facts," *Saturday Review*, Vol. XLVIII (March 20, 1965), p. 60.

rather than race. Southern educators learned that public announcement of the details of the local plan, a step many regarded as an invitation to disaster, was an absolute necessity. Community leaders, Foster wrote, would have to make clear "their intention to brook no disorder and to see to it that the rules are given firm and faithful implementation." [109]

The published memo spelled out the detailed administrative procedures necessary to protect the Negro student's choice. Foster suggested, for example, repeated publication of a lengthy notice for several weeks before initial enrollment of students entering the school system in order to inform the Negro community of its rights. This and other protections represented efforts to transform an ordeal filled with opportunities for intimidation to an easy and routine procedure. Most of the specifics were drawn from the body of case law, but in one significant respect the memo went beyond the decisions. Although there were no major decisions on segregated school transportation, the *Saturday Review* memo called for ending the separate and overlapping systems of school transportation characteristic of most southern counties.[110]

Although the article provided many answers, it was curiously vague on the issues of faculty integration and the central question of how many grades would have to be opened to possible integration to remain eligible for Federal aid. Foster noted that Federal courts had permitted attacks on faculty segregation under three different legal theories, but set forth no specific requirements. The ambiguous position on the number of grades reflected persisting indecision within HEW, where it was believed that some special provision would be necessary for Mississippi. The memo underlined the fact that standards would probably be changed from year to year, and Foster did speculate that the Commissioner was unlikely to approve less than the southern courts were demanding—four grades opened in the first year of integration, even in the Deep South.[111]

The elaborately distributed trial balloon produced a general sense of relief across the South. Although unofficial, the guidance was sufficient to stimulate a good deal of action. "Like a huge ship looming through fog," observed one South Carolina paper, "the outline of next fall's public school integration is beginning to emerge from a cloud of official obscurity."

Professor Foster does not claim that his guidelines are official policy. But it would be naive, indeed, to assume that they were written without official sanction. As southern reporters have discovered, Foster is the authority to whom all their questions on integration are referred. If he does not have all the answers . . . it is because no one in Washington does at this point.[112]

[109] *Ibid.*, pp. 61, 76.   [110] *Ibid.*, p. 77.
[111] *Ibid.*, pp. 77–78; Foster interview, June 6, 1967.
[112] *Charleston News and Courier*, March 21, 1965.

The favorable initial reaction and continuing local demands for official commitments from Washington led Commissioner Keppel to write to the North Carolina state superintendent, giving Foster's memo much of the force of an official pronouncement:

> The Foster memorandum while not representing rigid requirements which must be adhered to verbatim in all cases does represent a synthesis of our experience to date. . . . With few exceptions, a school district which follows these guidelines should be able to present an acceptable plan of desegregation.[113]

The article, as Foster wrote a *Saturday Review* editor, had "played a key role in the evolving policy of the Office of Education." [114] The professor's initiative made possible an end run around opposition to issuance of guidelines within HEW. In effect, there now were public guidelines.

Once the article "broke the ice," Seeley recalls, "it just became a question of formalizing it." [115] Keppel had concluded that there was no alternative to issuing official guidelines. Individual district negotiations had proved to be an administrative impossibility in spite of Quigley's skill and commitment. Very shortly after the appearance of the article Seeley and Foster began work on official guidelines, preferably issued by the President.[116]

There seemed to be serious obstacles to obtaining formal Administration approval for directions as far-reaching as those incorporated in Foster's memo. After the memo appeared Foster was told by Burke Marshall, former Assistant Attorney General for Civil Rights and then advisor to President Johnson on civil rights enforcement, that the Office of Education had put itself in a very exposed position, far ahead of other executive agencies that were studiously ignoring their Title VI responsibilities. This, in addition to the notable lack of enthusiasm of the HEW legal staff and Assistant Secretary Quigley's firm opposition to official minimum standards, created a series of potential barriers.

The decisive factors were to be strong support from Commissioner Keppel and growing civil rights sentiment within the Administration. After nursing the historic Elementary and Secondary Education Act safely through the Senate, Keppel was able to turn his attention to the civil rights program. The entire Administration was feeling the impact of another wave of national anger, this one ignited by the beatings at the

[113] Letter from Commissioner Keppel to North Carolina State Superintendent Carrol, March 31, 1965.
[114] Letter from Foster to James Cass, February 22, 1965.
[115] Seeley interview, June 17, 1967.
[116] Interview with Francis Keppel, January 5, 1967; memorandum from Foster to Seeley, March 22, 1965.

Selma bridge and the march to Montgomery. Burke Marshall and John Doar, his successor in the Civil Rights Division, returned from Selma convinced that further action was necessary. The schools, they told Foster, remained the most obvious and central symbol of segregation in the South. Now Marshall indicated that the guidelines memo, considered radical weeks earlier, was too conservative. From this point on the Justice Department was to push the Office to further strengthen the guidelines.[117]

The most basic reason for the emergence of the guidelines, however, was the reaction of the Office of Education's major constituency, the state and local education officials, to the unstructured and uncertain situation that had prevailed in the first months of the program. Accustomed to orderly dealings with sympathetic fellow educators in the Office's bureaucracy, they found intolerable a situation in which increasingly important programs were endangered by a confused, formless, and threatening program that refused to make clear its inherently disruptive demands. The education bureaucracies were simply unable to cope with a staff that still possessed neither the settled procedures nor the formal and explicit policies of a bureaucracy. Particularly in a situation involving such intense local feelings, school authorities found dealing with a disorganized, sporadic, and inconsistent program based on negotiating an individual plan for each locality unbearable.[118] The Office's constituency demanded that the civil rights program take on the aspects of a bureaucratic operation. The production of the guidelines was much more a response to bureaucratic need for certainty and predictability than to any civil rights impulse within the Office. Ironically, it was to be the very transformation engendered by this need that made it possible for a small number of people to administer a major transformation in southern education.

The 1965 Guidelines

Once Commissioner Keppel decided to issue formal rules, the procedure took little time. Working closely with the Justice Department's Civil Rights Division, under the supervision of White House aide Douglass Cater, the Office issued the guidelines three weeks after consultations began.

The decision to go ahead with the guidelines was made firm at an early April meeting at the White House. Everyone, Assistant Attorney General Doar says, agreed that guidelines were necessary. Doar pledged to

117 Foster interview, June 6, 1967.
118 The Quigley approach left the Office of Education dangerously exposed to predictable congressional claims of arbitrary bureaucratic decisions reflecting the preference of an official rather than the general requirements of the law.

have a Justice Department discussion draft prepared over the weekend, and Foster was called at his Wisconsin home to work with Seeley on the Office of Education draft. Doar assigned the drafting job for the Justice version to David Rubin, an attorney on the appellate section, who worked with occasional assistance from Doar and his deputy.[119] Although the rapidly assembled drafts could be more accurately described as the views of the individuals concerned than as formal departmental positions, the Justice draft called for tightening the rules of thumb incorporated in the Foster memorandum.

The Justice draft called for faster integration and much more far-reaching faculty integration requirements. This version called for opening all grades in two years and the provision of an immediate guarantee of any Negro student's right to transfer to a white school offering a program not available in the Negro system. While the Seeley-Foster draft supported an eventual ban of faculty segregation, the Justice document called for an immediate end to faculty segregation in all desegregated grades. Justice called for a large first step during the coming school year, while the Office of Education proposal gave the Commissioner authority to waive any requirement for a year in districts with exceptionally difficult problems. Seeley and Foster had tightened their draft by forbidding segregation in any school activities, a provision going beyond the settled law of court decisions. Rubin's draft added other provisos forbidding the practice of bussing Negroes to segregated schools outside the school district and requiring integration of the twelfth grade in every system.[120] This final requirement was intended to permit students denied their rights during the decade since the Supreme Court decision to graduate from integrated schools.

Foster now feared that Justice would "push us to adopt standards considerably more stringent than those we have tried to sell reluctant southerners."[121] While Office of Education standards were generally based on the assumption that administrative enforcement criteria should be clearly derived from decisions in the Federal courts of appeals in the South, Justice Department attorneys now urged the Office of Education to move away from rigid reliance on the case law toward a more independent judgment of "where the cases are going." In an analysis of the legislative history, Justice lawyers argued that Congress had intended just such an approach.

119 Interview with John Doar, August 10, 1967.
120 Memorandum from Foster to Assistant Attorney General Doar, April 9, 1965; memorandum from Foster to David Rubin, April 10, 1965; Foster, "Tentative Draft," April 11, 1965; memorandum from John Doar to Burke Marshall, April 12, 1965.
121 Memorandum from Foster to Carl Auerbach, April 12, 1965.

The legislative history . . . suggests that HEW is to be generally consistent with the rulings of the courts. . . . There is nothing that we have found in that history, however, which would tie HEW to any specific rate or degree of desegregation which may have been adopted by a particular court. The legislative history suggests that HEW may determine what constitutes full desegregation by applying the lower Federal court rulings in this area and the spirit of the most recent Supreme Court decisions.[122]

The issue of guidelines requirements grew in importance when the Senate gave final passage to the precedent-making Elementary and Secondary Education Act in early April. On April 11, President Johnson signed into law the measure channeling more than $1 billion into school districts containing low-income children. The program affected 90 per cent of all American school districts but directed particularly large sums of money into those very areas where the segregation problem was most critical. Keppel had carefully avoided any move to call attention to his civil rights responsibility when the act was before Congress. Now he felt free to give substance to his commitment to civil rights.

In a memo written two days after the President acted, Keppel outlined his understanding of the enforcement effort. The new act, he wrote, "makes possible a new approach in handling civil rights problems in education." "Title VI can become less of a negative threat and more of a condition necessary to progress in the future." [123] The vast new Federal financial leverage provided by Elementary and Secondary Education Act funds changed the assumptions underlying the compliance program.

The first necessity, he wrote, was to put an end to the continuing hope of southern educators that "their political leaders will find some way to avoid having to face the abandonment of the dual school system." The best way, he told Secretary Celebrezze, was through issuance of specific regulations formally approved by the President.

Reviewing the discussions of the guidelines, he saw the question of the number of grades to be opened the first year as the most "politically sensitive" issue. In spite of Mississippi arguments that compliance would not be possible if more than one grade was demanded the first year, Keppel proposed a two-grade minimum. He suggested that three years be allowed for extension of freedom of choice to all grades, with the possibility of extending the deadline in Mississippi and perhaps Alabama and Louisiana as well. Because the question of faculty integration was "extremely difficult," he called for delay of such a requirement until the second year.[124]

122 "General Legislative History," accompanying Doar memorandum to Marshall, April 12, 1965.
123 Memorandum from Commissioner Keppel to Secretary Celebrezze, April 13, 1965.
124 *Ibid.*

The job of the Office of Education, in Keppel's mind, was to fairly and energetically enforce the law, and to create standards that could be met across the South. Responding to discussion in the Justice Department about possible prohibition of free choice plans, Keppel reported that his knowledge of the situation facing schoolmen in the Deep South forced him to oppose the idea.

> As usual, we are forced to find a path between two dangers. On the one side is the danger of requiring . . . so much desegregation so rapidly that the educators and leaders of the deep South who want to accomplish desegregation will be either thrown out of office or unable to move forward. On the other side is the danger that civil rights groups and other branches of the government will protest that the Federal establishment is ducking the issues and permitting unconscionable delays in desegregation.[125]

The Commissioner of Education did not perceive Title VI as an instrument to force immediate and radical change on southern schools, but rather as a lever using the growing Federal grants to prod local school officials to move as rapidly as their communities would tolerate. His ideal was vigorous enforcement of the law, but not creation of local disruption. His central emphasis was on progress. On the touchy issue of faculty integration, Keppel supported delay because of his concern about how much the South could swallow in a single year.[126] Although deeply committed to school integration, Keppel's daily contacts with Office program administrators, state and local schoolmen, and leading political figures made him aware of the danger to the Office inherent in the creation of standards that proved to be unenforceable. Keppel's moderation and his willingness to put faith in the good intentions of southern school officials were shared by Seeley and set the tone for the guidelines soon to be issued.

Even if Keppel had been less sympathetic to the civil rights movement, there is no doubt that he would have been forced to issue some kind of guidelines. In his mid-April memo he reported that less than one segregated school district in 100 had submitted an acceptable plan, with less than two months remaining before the end of the school year. The Commissioner had still not given final approval to a single plan, and thus all planning for Federal aid programs was at a standstill in many hundreds of school districts.[127] Should this situation persist, the grant programs would be seriously impaired, hundreds of thousands of children would be denied needed programs, and public and congressional support for the Office of Education would be seriously damaged.

After Keppel's intervention, the work progressed rapidly. In the new Office of Education draft guidelines produced the next day, Seeley and

[125] *Ibid.*   [126] Keppel interview.
[127] Keppel to Secretary, April 13, 1965.

Foster agreed to the shorter deadline for desegregation of all grades, proposed by the Justice attorneys, and approved the demand for integration of four grades the first year. Differences in proposed conditions for the acceptance of free-choice plans were ironed out in a negotiating session. On the two highly important issues of faculty desegregation and the handling of districts operating under court orders, the Justice attorneys held out for a somewhat stronger requirement.[128] Ultimately, the Office of Education position was to prevail on these questions.

As the guidelines neared approval, several sessions were held at the White House to discuss the policy questions involved. Consultations were also made with Vice-President Humphrey, then responsible for coordination of civil rights activities. At the White House the points under discussion between the Office of Education and the Justice Department were argued, and the staff director of the Civil Rights Commission made a case for more far-reaching demands, particularly on the freedom of choice question. Douglass Cater, the President's aide, did not make specific decisions, but pressed for a consensus between the Office and Justice. One leading participant saw Cater's role as calling the group together and ratifying their agreements.[129]

The Office of Education position was adopted on the issues still under dispute. The urgent need, Assistant Attorney General Doar felt, was to get the enforcement process underway. Because speed was demanded if the regulations contained in the guidelines were to make an impact in the South before the end of the school year, the additional month of delay involved in the issuance of presidential regulations was not possible. Without formal support from the President, however, the Justice Department was reluctant to defend in court guidelines that used Title VI to establish standards significantly in advance of the courts.[130] Thus the pressure of time tended to blunt the trust within the Justice Department for more far-reaching standards.

The decision to remain close to judicial standards, Doar recalls, precluded any immediate possibility of a strict faculty integration requirement. The faculty integration demand in the early Justice Department draft had gone far beyond settled case law, proposing use of the general administrative authority granted by the title. "We had a situation where there was no desegregation," Doar says. "You couldn't predict exactly what the Deep South would do." The federal circuit court of appeals for

---

[128] Seeley and Foster, draft of guidelines, April 14, 1965.

[129] Seeley interview, June 17, 1967.

[130] Doar interview, August 10, 1967. The language of Title VI specifically required presidential approval of regulations. Thus an Office of Education document might have far less standing in a court test.

the Deep South had "really pussy-footed around" this sensitive question, saying a lot while demanding virtually nothing. This situation produced a sharp division of opinion within the Justice Department. The final decision, requiring nothing more than joint faculty meetings the first year, was "pretty soft," Doar concedes. The emphasis in April 1965 was on getting things started, on beginning to make progress. In a situation in which southern response was uncertain, Doar was satisfied with a cautious approach.

Although presidential assistant Douglass Cater did not overtly intervene in the policy discussions, he did establish an atmosphere in which debate took place. Several times during White House discussions he asked how much money a given decision would withhold from southern school districts.[131] While strongly supporting enforcement of the Civil Rights Act, Cater clearly wanted "something that was enforceable, that was within the political realm of possibility" for local school districts in the South.[132] Acutely aware of the financial needs of desperately poor southern districts, Cater wished to avoid any obstacle seriously impeding the flow of funds from the historic Elementary and Secondary Education Act.

When general agreement on policy was reached, Keppel pressed for rapid action. Through direct negotiations with the Justice Department and the White House, Seeley and Foster had defeated Quigley and outmaneuvered HEW program officials and the department's legal staff. Now Commissioner Keppel presented Secretary Celebrezze with a fait accompli, informing him that approval was essential to meet urgent problems.

> . . . almost 500 desegregation plans are in my office. The plans are inadequate and the districts which submitted them must be informed immediately of this fact and given adequate guidance to get the job done properly. Altogether there are about 3000 biracial school districts in the South, the great bulk of which are not moving satisfactorily to achieve compliance. In my judgment it is essential that these districts be given instructions which are written, specific and official in order to avoid a serious crisis of non-compliance and fund withholding.
>
> . . . failure to announce specific standards penalizes those who want to act in good faith and invites further delay from those who would probe further to see how little they ultimately can get away with.[133]

Given the lack of adequate manpower for individual negotiations, it was "imperative" that guidance be provided within the next week.[134]

Commissioner Keppel hoped that Secretary Celebrezze would support

[131] Foster interview, June 6, 1967.   [132] Seeley interview, June 17, 1967.
[133] Memorandum from Commissioner Keppel to Secretary Celebrezze, April 21, 1965
[134] Ibid.

an appeal for direct presidential support of the desegregation standards. Keppel explained to the Secretary that the rules could be issued either as presidential regulations or as the Commissioner's interpretation of the law. Although formal issuance of an executive order would not be possible until after the guidelines had been mailed, Keppel felt that the public endorsement of the President would greatly lessen the "pressures for downgrading the standards." [135] Once again, however, Assistant Secretary Quigley strongly objected to committing the Administration to rigid minimums. The Secretary made no request to the President, and Keppel issued the guidelines on his own authority. Just as he had predicted, the lack of public endorsement from President Johnson multiplied the difficulties of enforcement and encouraged southern politicians to hope that delay and pressure would result in lowered requirements.

The brief five-page document mailed to school districts at the end of April was a charter for the reconstruction of race relations in the schools of many hundreds of communities where the Supreme Court decision had produced no change. The main thrust of the 1965 guidelines was toward breaking the back of the die-hard resistance which had kept most rural southern districts and virtually all districts in the Deep South from the first steps toward integration.

The Federal standards posed a very serious challenge for totally segregated districts. While some of the lower Federal courts were still approving plans opening only one grade for possible integration each year, the guidelines required the opening of all grades by fall 1967 at the latest. In fact any district not extending a freedom of choice plan to every grade the first year had "the burden of justifying the delay." [136] The significance of the demand for rapid progress was greatly heightened by carefully drafted requirements on the notice to be given to Negro families and the nature of the procedures used to implement the free choice plan. School officials were warned that actual integration rather than mere theoretical opportunity for desegregation was an important test of any desegregation plan and that the Commissioner reserved the right to change the standards the following year. The guidelines reached into new areas, forbidding segregation on school buses and in school activities. Schoolmen were also warned that they must eventually face the explosive issue of faculty integration.[137]

In Washington it was clear that the first task was to begin desegregation in those large areas of the South where a rigid caste system was

[135] *Ibid.*
[136] U.S. Office of Education, "General Statement of Policies," reprinted in House Judiciary Committee *Guidelines* hearings, p. A23.
[137] *Ibid.*, pp. A20–A24.

untouched by the civil rights movement. This was the task for which political support was most overwhelming and the legal tools forged in a decade of litigation most adequate. The first guidelines demanded a local effort to end total segregation and hinted at a much more fundamental attack in future years. For the present, little change was demanded in any school system that had opened all grades in a fairly operated free choice plan, even if only a handful of Negro students had defied community attitudes to enter white schools. Although the guidelines contained the seeds of more dramatic change across the South, the first campaign was to center on those areas where the first step had not been taken.

When the Civil Rights Act became law in July, 1964, no one knew what Title VI meant for southern education. The little-noticed provision delegated to HEW and the Commissioner of Education primary responsibility for defining and ending discrimination in federal education programs. Few agencies could have been less suited, in terms of historic and contemporary state and local relationships, for this major new administrative responsibility. Only the strong personal commitments of the Commissioner of Education and an assistant secretary of HEW made possible the emergence of a significant program of enforcement.

The initial challenge facing HEW was massive ignorance of Title VI among southern educators. Awareness of the new enforcement program was spread through a series of meetings in various sections of the South shortly after the Civil Rights Act became law. In these sessions and in other early contacts Federal officials attempted to convey their determination to forceful implementation of the law, and southern schoolmen attempted to impress on HEW spokesmen the limits of local toleration for change. Working with only a sketchy understanding of the legislative history of Title VI and of the dynamics of school desegregation, Federal representatives made early analyses of such important issues as faculty desegregation and the permissibility of freedom of choice plans, which reassured worried educators but also limited in important ways the requirements that could be imposed during the first year of enforcement.

The Civil Rights Act provided that Title VI enforcement standards took effect only with the President's signature on a formal regulation. This requirement gave rise to a struggle within HEW and within the Administration as a whole over the basic contours of enforcement policy as incorporated in the HEW regulation. Those involved in the battle to determine what the sweeping prohibition against discrimination would mean in actual day-to-day administrative practice tended to crystallize into three groups defined by their differing orientations. Program officials and the HEW legal staff, primarily oriented toward maintenance of cooperative Federal-state and Federal-local relationships necessary for successful administration of grant programs, favored a general unspecific pledge of compliance, thus putting a good deal of faith in local officials and relying heavily on program officials in the enforcement process. The Civil Rights Commission and Assistant Secretary Quigley's office, primarily oriented toward the civil rights movement, pressed for a broad interpretation of Title VI powers. The decisive voice, however, was that of the Justice Department attorneys, oriented toward the courts, experienced in the politics of enforcements, and determined that the regulation accurately reflect the intent of Congress.

The regulation settled certain basic issues about the shape of compliance policy, but it soon became evident that it failed to provide adequate guidance to most school districts. After the tiny new staff established by Commissioner Keppel to administer Title VI mailed out copies of the regulation and some simple instructions to thousands of school districts, it was rapidly submerged in a morass of plans raising endless policy complexities plus constant and insistent questions from all sections of the South. Local educators were so severely threatened by the dangers of a misstep on the thin ice of community attitudes that very few submitted any plan at all, and none submitted plans considered up to current judicial standards by Office of Education consultants. Local school officials and state superintendents demanded specific guidance, and it became obvious in Washington that the only way in which the available staff could cope with its task was through creation of detailed uniform standards. The decision to issue guidelines had nothing to do with the content of policy; it was simply a response to the sheer pressure of bureaucratic need for predictability and standardization on both sides of the relationship.

The pressing need for standards put the one group that had a set of concrete criteria to propose at a tremendous advantage. Some answer had to be given to the angry superintendents lining up in the halls of the Office of Education, and the young lawyer Keppel appointed to head the compliance program solved the problem by reliance on the advice of a group of law professors specializing in desegregation law. As this group of consultants worked together, rules of thumb began to emerge—general policies based on the decisions of the higher Federal courts. The fact that administrative enforcement standards should thus be basically derivative from judicial principles was decided by default.

Once the guidelines had been informally issued through Professor Foster's *Saturday Review* article, it became completely obvious that formal standards were needed. Tremendous pressure of time for rapid issuance before the end of the school year and David Seeley's excellent relationship with a sympathetic Commissioner of Education permitted exclusion of program officials in the discussions on the guidelines. Once again there were debates between those primarily oriented toward the courts, the dominant perspective of the Office of Education compliance program, and those taking a more activist stance toward a civil rights movement again boiling over in Selma, represented by some members of the Justice Department and the Civil Rights Commission. Compromises were made on a number of secondary issues. On those questions remaining unresolved, the Office of Education position prevailed. Without the President's public endorsement, the Assistant Attorney General was not eager to pass beyond the easily protected frontiers of settled case law, and his caution was reinforced by White House concern that the regulations be enforceable.

Shortly after they were issued the guidelines became one of those rare bureaucratic documents known to a vast public and readily referred to by politicians and editorial writers. This was the shape of the future, part of the price to be paid for the southern defeat in Congress in 1964. To many in the South, Commissioner Keppel's guidelines became the official interpretation of the meaning of Title VI, an interpretation that turned out to be acceptable in most southern communities. When the rules were substantially tightened the next year, it was widely assumed that the Office of Education had exceeded its authority under Title VI. Actually the first guidelines were moderate in tone and placed very heavy reliance on the good faith of local leadership. The failure to perceive the fact that the initial requirements would be seen by an anxious public as the ultimate meaning of the law was to create very serious problems for the Office of Education when it moved to correct glaring deficiencies revealed by the first year's experience.

Great social movements are rare in American life, and even more rare is the penetration of an insistent demand for basic social change into the corridors of established bureaucratic power. After almost 10 months of effort inside the Federal establishments, those concerned with implementing the injunction of the Civil Rights Act to end discrimination in Federal education programs had gathered the resources of staff, power, and settled policy decisions necessary to begin in earnest. The guidelines provided the standard operating principles that were to enable a small group of men to desegregate, in four months time, far more districts than the Federal courts had reached in 10 years. One of the oldest and most cautious of Federal agencies had been propelled to the forefront of the national attack on the caste system of the South. The authority of the Federal government was now committed to a major step toward abolition of the separate educational systems of the South.

3

Administering a Social Revolution

The months of spring and summer 1965 provided a test of the ability of the American Federal bureaucracy to force a bitterly resisted change in a central institution of the southern social order. Publication of the guidelines shifted the arena of Federal action from the White House meeting room to a section of Tempo S, a run-down wartime "temporary" building already scheduled for demolition. In a collection of offices in this weathered frame relic, a growing staff of people from miscellaneous backgrounds attempted to cope with a mounting tide of paper, incessant phone calls, and delegations of confused or indignant local schoolmen. With basic official standards settled for the first year, the uncoordinated and indecisive negotiating operation of the first months was gradually transformed into a bureaucracy with regular operating procedures, able to handle the large and sensitive task of breaking southern resistance during the summer of 1965. The work of the Equal Educational Opportunities Program rapidly became a basic test of the capacity of American federalism to resolve the American dilemma.

The first summer's confrontation with the South began in innocence and ended in understanding. The policy discussions resulting in the guidelines were heavy on theory and speculation, but by summer's end the facts of the southern response had become clear to those involved in the compliance effort. Beginning with naïveté, optimism, and idealism, the enforcement staff was to end the season as a corps of professional school desegregators, able to realistically estimate local attitudes and accurately outline the requirements for protection of the constitutional rights of southern Negro students. The emergence of this group of men and women made possible the implementation of the first guidelines and permitted definition of the extremely important policy changes ultimately incorporated in the second guidelines. There is no better way to understand the nature of the demands imposed by Title VI enforcement on the Federal government than through the examination of the development of the bureaucracy that administered the guidelines.

102

Initial Steps

The guidelines permitted the Office to take its first decisive action, and the Commissioner promptly returned hundreds of inadequate desegregation plans. School superintendents received letters outlining their plan's weaknesses together with copies of the new guidelines. This essential first step had the immediate effect of submerging Seeley's office with demands for further explanations and specific questions about individual plans. Local concern was rapidly reflected in increasing amounts of high-priority congressional mail.

In spite of the turbulence, the first plans were finally approved in May; Commissioner Keppel signed the first batch of letters on the anniversary of the Supreme Court decision. The handful of plans accepted that day included that of Selma, Alabama. The first small step had been taken.

The existence of explicit compliance standards permitted Keppel to reactivate processing of grant applications from southern school districts. State agencies had previously been forbidden to commit Federal aid money to districts until their desegregation plans were approved in Washington. Any school district that applied for renewal of a program or a new grant had been threatened with a hearing to cut off all funds. Now that the requirements were clear, Keppel authorized processing of grants for any district certifying to state authorities that the local superintendent had been directed to submit a plan in conformance with the guidelines. The decision took some of the urgent time pressure off both local officials and the overburdened compliance program and avoided the strenuous political attacks which would have been provoked by a continued freeze on grant applications.

The guidelines made an organized enforcement program possible, but policy decisions in themselves were not to resolve the persisting administrative confusion within the growing staff. Seeley's prior experience had been as an advisor rather than an executive, and he had been unable to obtain help within the Office in pulling together the administrative side of the severely strained operation.

Seeley had been working nonstop for five months and was on the verge of collapse by late May. The pressures of political crises and unending meetings with southern educators, plus drafting the guidelines and working them through the bureaucracy, had been piled on top of the exhausting job of trying to find resources for a nonbudgeted staff handling an extremely difficult new program. Finally, under orders from his superiors, Seeley took a 10-day vacation, leaving the compliance program leaderless as the decisive summer months began.

The Establishment of an Administrative System

The guidelines made the development of a regularized bureaucratic approach to the problems of enforcement possible. The immense external pressures for decisions made absolutely essential the creation of an administrative structure with the efficiency and predictability resulting from division of labor, specialization, the creation of simple routine procedures, and the emergence of a systematic process of coordination.

Disorder in the civil rights operation caused increasingly serious problems for Commissioner Keppel. Congressmen and local officials, exasperated by waiting weeks or months in unsuccessful attempts to get answers, demanded the Commissioner's help. The enforcement program's inability to cope with its business posed a severe threat to the Office's programs and to its congressional support. By the end of May the school year was almost over, and it would soon become physically impossible for school districts to operate effective free choice periods for the coming school year. Confronted by a crisis, Keppel turned in late May to his deputy, Henry Loomis, for advice. Loomis, who was responsible for the internal administrative arrangements of the Office, immediately dispatched his assistant, Walter Mylecraine, to investigate the situation.

Seeley had long pleaded for administrative advice. While his frank, open, and good-natured manner and his deep and thoughtful commitment both to education and civil rights were priceless assets in the tasks of policy-making, gathering support within the bureaucracy, and maintaining a tolerable relationship with southern schoolmen, they sometimes limited his effectiveness as an administrator. Deeply absorbed in policy questions, Seeley had not been able to effectively organize the work of his office. Fortunately for the program, this deficiency was remedied during his vacation through the efforts of Mylecraine, a forceful administrative technician.

Mylecraine, who came to the Office with Loomis to try to help Keppel impose a measure of managerial control on the Office's sprawling, decentralized collection of programs, was appalled by what he saw. "Complete pandemonium" prevailed, with everything being done on an ad hoc basis. There was no specialization among the staff, and important southern attorneys and even congressmen were waiting in the halls to try to find someone in authority. No system had been devised to handle the numberless telephone calls and the constant arrival of unscheduled delegations wishing to negotiate with somebody.

The lack of managerial control was particularly evident in the handling of letters from local school officials. Since there was no internal specialization, mail was simply forwarded to whoever had been handling that particular district in the past. With no effective control of the flow of documents through the Office, plans were getting lost in the tide of paper that engulfed the staff, and important letters were not being answered. A situation in which one official dealt with one school district while another man of different experience handled its neighbor, and anyone free in the Office might negotiate the problems of either district should a delegation arrive in Washington, magnified the difficulties inherent in the program. No tools were available either to the program's leadership or the Commissioner of Education to find out just what was going on and to effectively direct the operation.

After a day's observation Mylecraine submitted a series of recommendations to Keppel. He called for an immediate doubling of the 30-man staff. He proposed specialization and divided the staff and the files on a regional basis with state subdivisions. Correspondence and incoming phone calls, he suggested, should be centrally controlled. Finally, he sketched a central review operation to supervise the regional negotiating teams and coordinate the work of the program. Keppel gave immediate approval to the revisions. The next day, the Commissioner ordered every operating agency within the Office to supply a quota of personnel until the enforcement crisis was past. A group of 30 cautious civil servants supplemented the original staff.

Within days Mylecraine reorganized the office space and assembled the necessary equipment for the new regional organization. With Keppel's support, a complex telephone system was promptly established, and normal procedures were suspended to obtain equipment on an emergency basis. When the office opened the next week, visitors and calls were centrally screened and forwarded to the proper person in the right regional office. Delegations were scheduled to permit some preparation. Each night policy issues were centrally reviewed, and approved plans were forwarded to the Commissioner.

During the first weeks of June, policy questions were debated in almost daily staff meetings. Keppel attended a number of these sessions and either provided an immediate decision or resolved the issue the following morning after discussion with Secretary Celebrezze.[1]

As Seeley and Foster had worked to established the standardized policies essential to rational bureaucratic procedure, so Mylecraine imposed on the staff the organizational structure and methods necessary for systematic administration of these standards. The Commissioner's support of

[1] Interview with Walter E. Mylecraine, March 27, 1967.

both policy and organizational steps and his willingness to order temporary transfer of personnel made possible the creation of the administrative
mechanism that was to transform southern education.

Neither an educator nor a lawyer, Mylecraine stormed into the chaos
in Tempo S with self-confidence, enthusiasm, and an air of command. A
first-rate management technician, he was able to bring order and coherence to the rapidly expanding program. His one significant contribution
to policy was the support he gave to Office negotiators who desired to
push for the opening of all 12 grades the first year in all desegregation
plans. Although this effort was protested by those who felt that the Office
was committed to accepting four-grade plans, later support for this policy by key staff members resulted in incorporation of this feature in the
great majority of plans accepted during the summer.

When Seeley returned his staff had been doubled and, for the first time,
he had the instruments of control and coordination essential to survive
the coming ordeal. "For the first time," he remembers, "I was able to
breathe." [2] While it had taken more than four months to approve the first
handful of plans, 352 had been cleared by the end of June.[3]

The "Johnson Amendment"

Although the guidelines had established the basic structure of compliance plans, new issues continued to arise and demand solutions. The issue
of widespread firing of black teachers, a question that had not been
discussed by the drafters of the guidelines, became the first instance of
successful civil rights group intervention in the policy-making process. It
was also the only question in which the President personally played a
major role.

A disturbing pattern of firing teachers after schools were integrated
had developed in several southern states by late 1964. Shortly after the
guidelines appeared, the question of Federal protection was raised by the
director of the Virginia Negro teachers association. Assistant Secretary
Quigley replied that there was no Federal authority in this area.

> . . . there are going to be some Negro teachers who will lose their jobs. We are
> trying to get school people to hire teachers according to qualifications, but we
> have no law to back us up.[4]

The firing of 13 Negro teachers when the Asheboro, North Carolina,
Negro high school was closed drew wide attention. A Negro congressman called for an investigation of HEW inaction, and the teachers took
their case to the NAACP Legal Defense Fund. Legal Defense Fund law-

[2] Interview with David Seeley, June 17, 1967.   [3] *Ibid.*
[4] *Washington Post,* May 19, 1965.

yers promptly drafted a memorandum of law arguing that both the legislative history of Title VI and the court decisions demanded that the Office of Education require faculty integregation as an integral part of school desegregation. Nothing in the Civil Rights Act, the attorneys asserted, limited the Commissioner's authority to forbid discriminatory firing of Negro teachers.[5] The argument was buttressed by a new Federal court decision on a teacher dismissal case in Giles County, Virginia.[6]

The public attack stimulated Keppel to circulate a memo which stated the Justice Department and Legal Defense Fund view that the Office possessed authority to prohibit racially inspired teacher firings. Unable to rebut the argument, the HEW General Counsel's office reversed itself the following day. The Office promptly announced that systematic firing of Negro teachers would violate a district's promise of "good faith" compliance with its desegregation plan.[7]

The announcement was not sufficient. Less than a week later a small Florida town gave notice to all its Negro teachers. Although most were area natives and some held master's degrees, all were to be dismissed, while less-qualified whites were retained.[8] Such actions struck at one of the few sources of middle-class employment widely open to southern Negroes and constituted a serious threat to the Negro communities. The Legal Defense Fund predicted 500 firings in North Carolina, and an official of the National Education Association estimated that more than 5000 teachers would be dismissed in the 11 southern states.[9]

In an address to the NEA annual convention, President Johnson made his only public intervention on the issue of desegregation standards. Presenting himself as a teacher on leave from a Texas school district, Johnson told the meeting of his concern about the teacher-firing issue. "I have," he said, "directed the Commissioner of Education to pay very special attention, in reviewing desegregation plans, to guard against any pattern of teacher dismissal based on race or national origin." The President also revealed that the Administration had decided to provide funds from two different programs to retrain fired teachers.[10] After the speech, the President's remarks and a summary of the Virginia Federal court decision were sent to school superintendents. A "Johnson amendment" to desegregation plans was developed, requiring that displaced Negro teachers be

[5] Washington Afro-American, May 29, 1965. NAACP Legal Defense and Educational Fund, Inc., "Discriminatory Practices in Teacher Hiring and Firing: Case Law and Title VI of the Civil Rights Act of 1964," June 1, 1965. (Mimeographed.)
[6] Washington Star, June 8, 1965.   [7] Seeley Chronology, p. 14.
[8] St. Petersburg Times, June 15, 1965.   [9] Time, June 18, 1965; Jet, June 17, 1965.
[10] Lyndon B. Johnson, Public Papers of the Presidents of the United States (Washington: Government Printing Office, 1965), pp. 718-19.

given first chance at any new job openings. School officials were warned that if the number of Negro teachers on the district's rolls fell sharply, it would raise a serious question. The Office succeeded in getting back jobs for some fired teachers and provided funds for an NEA faculty discrimination survey, thus putting educators on notice that their performance was being watched. In spite of this effort, several hundred teachers did lose their jobs, and new graduates of Negro colleges experienced difficulty in finding teaching positions.[11] The problem, however, was far less serious than had been expected earlier in the year.

A Summer of Negotiations

Before mass negotiations involving the hundreds of districts still to begin desegregation could begin in earnest, the reality and the full import of the Federal threat had to make itself felt. On July 1 the fiscal year came to an end, and the fact that desegregation plans were preconditions to local participation in the educational bonanza created by the Elementary and Secondary Education Act began to sink in across the South. The realization that the local schools might lose aid money amounting to as much as one-third or one-fourth of the current total school budget generated anxious activity and consultations in school board offices. Although the Commissioner had accepted only 352 plans at the beginning of the month, more than 1800 plans, covering the great majority of the segregated districts, were in Washington by mid-July.[12]

Each plan in this paper tide was an individual case. Within the general requirements of the guidelines, local school boards and school attorneys devised an enormous variety of ways to express the necessary promises. The guidelines were based on a fundamental assumption of the good faith of local educators, and many of the early plans justified this assumption, indicating a determination to comply. Hundreds of districts, however, saw the guidelines as a pernicious invasion of local rights and were determined to do the absolute minimum necessary to receive Federal funds. The plans submitted by such districts required careful study, policy decisions, and, often, negotiations with local representatives.

This morass of legal technicalities engulfed a staff that reached a peak of 135 during the summer emergency. The 60 professionals charged with the decisions were a disparate group that included the permanent staff of 15, commonly drawn into the program by an interest in civil rights, and

[11] Interview with David Barus, May 9, 1967; interview with Samuel Ethridge, February 20, 1967. National Education Association Press Release, December 21, 1965. (Mimeographed.)

[12] Student Non-Violent Coordinating Committee (SNCC), *Special Report*, September 30, 1965, p. 9. (Mimeographed.)

an equal group of grant program officials. The Office of Education personnel were supplemented by 10 law professors, 5 law students, and 15 attorneys on loan from the Justice Department.[13] Although both activists and program-oriented people were represented on the staff, the program was dominated by those who saw the problem in legal terms, a tendency reinforced by the legal background of both Seeley and his deputy.

Problems that generated community crises in the towns of the rural South came to Washington in the form of paper plans of all lengths and descriptions, plans that buried local disagreements in legal phrases or passed over them in generalities. Many of the documents were obviously inadequate. The basic task for staff members was to educate themselves about the essentials of a good plan and then try to convey this information to local superintendents.[14]

The most fundamental difficulty confronting the Office was the persistent failure of a large number of districts to submit any desegregation plan. In early July Keppel wrote to southern state superintendents asking their help in finding out the intentions of the several hundred districts yet to act. The Commissioner increased Federal pressure by warning that the Office would end its reservation of Federal funds for districts with inadequate desegregation plans at summer's end. As August began, with schools opening in two weeks in some areas, the effort still seemed overwhelming; 700 superintendents were informed that their plans remained unacceptable. With only weeks to go, less than one-fourth of the southern districts involved had received final approval of their plans, and there were still 400 districts that had submitted nothing.[15]

The time of the staff in Washington was largely consumed in efforts of persuasion—on the phone, by mail, and in meetings called in the states. The first requirement was to obtain a plan meeting the guidelines minimum, a freedom of choice plan opening at least four grades and providing the necessary procedural guarantees. Once a minimum plan was submitted, staff members made a strong and generally successful effort to gain opening of all grades the first year. Negotiators also attempted to convince districts with few Negro students to totally desegregate and assign all students by geographic location rather than race.[16] The plan accepted in a specific case largely depended on the skill and judgment of the negotiator in using the leeway written into the guidelines and the standards set by the directors of the regional negotiating teams.

Reality dawned very slowly in parts of the Deep South. At the end of

[13] Beis, p. 4.   [14] Interview with Harriet Ziskin, March 7, 1967
[15] Memorandum from Commissioner Keppel to chief state school officers, July 6, 1967; Seeley Chronology, p. 16.
[16] Ziskin interview.

July Keppel warned 700 local superintendents that their plans were not adequate and sent them two "model desegregation plans" based on plans that had been accepted.[17] Local schoolmen who were integral parts of their communities simply did not want to face the fact that they were being forced to think through and promise to implement what some saw as an immoral social revolution, destructive to the feelings and customs of their communities. People were being asked to plan to do immediately that which had always been unthinkable. Some continued to hope that if they did nothing they might escape. Perhaps southern political power could, once again, find a way to protect cherished convictions. As late as August 17, with some schools already open, almost 200 districts had done nothing. The problem was acute in Louisiana, where school officials were united and refused to submit plans. In Mississippi, one district in three had taken no action.[18] Once again Keppel wrote to each superintendent, threatening to begin cutoff proceedings if no plan had arrived in Washington by the end of August. The Commissioner also notified state congressional delegations of the possible loss of Federal funds in their districts.[19]

As the opening of school rapidly approached, pressure mounted not only on local superintendents but also on the Federal enforcement program. Congressmen representing the hundreds of districts whose plans were still under review exerted growing pressure for speedy decisions. Until this time southern congressmen had been surprisingly quiescent. Having given their all in the futile fight against the civil rights bill, many felt that there was little they could do to prevent enforcement of the revolutionary measure that had been rammed down their throats. With the imminent possibility of serious damage to local school programs, however, congressional offices became reactivated, and the Office of Education received large numbers of inquiries, requests for negotiations, and demands for action. At the same time the White House staff became strongly concerned by the possibility of severe disruption of the new aid-to-education program in many districts.

The crisis brought presidential intervention. President Johnson announced that he had asked HEW Secretary John Gardner "to have his men work around the clock to make the desegregation decision of the Supreme Court a reality and a fact." He expressed the hope that "we will complete the job between now and the time the school term opens." [20] The President's order forced a sharp alteration in the pace and method of processing plans. With a daily report going over to the White House and a check sheet distributed among the staff showing the number of plans

[17] Seeley Chronology, p. 16.   [18] Ibid., p. 19.   [19] Ibid.
[20] Lyndon B. Johnson, Public Papers, 1965, p. 911.

approved each day, everyone worked under tremendous pressure. The program operated two shifts every day, remaining open until 9:00 P.M. Many worked until midnight and on Saturdays and Sundays.[21]

The pressure of time brought to completion an evolution in the nature of the negotiating process. Weeks of struggling with a vast array of different plans had made it evident that the guidelines were not sufficiently detailed. Just as initial confusion had led to the drafting of the guidelines, pressure for rapid action now led to their elaboration, both to help confused school officials and to further routinize the bureaucratic process. During the summer, the program had begun providing districts with sample letters to Negro parents, sample freedom of choice forms, and, eventually, sample clauses covering key issues for incorporation into desegregation plans. By late summer, these aids had evolved into "model plans," which school district officials need only copy in their entirety and sign to be eligible for Federal funds.[22]

When political pressure failed to bring the hoped for last-minute lowering of standards, many districts joined the rush to submit model plans. Approximately half of all plans accepted in 1965 followed the standardized models. This procedure had both advantages and disadvantages. The requirements in the model plans were more strict and sophisticated, incorporating what had been learned in the negotiating process. On the other hand the probability of strict adherence was less when a school board did not thrash out its own plan but merely authorized the signing of a complex document prepared in Washington. In Texas, where large numbers of the state's many tiny school districts had submitted no plans, an organized effort rapidly gathered signatures for model plans. On paper these plans contained guarantees superior to many of the earlier plans, but, as Seeley says, "It was questionable how meaningful they were since we wrote them." [23]

Although the White House pressed for rapid action, there was no change in the minimum standards used to judge plans. The urgent deadline, however, did limit the time available for persuading recalcitrant localities to do more than the minimum required. An overworked and exhausted staff made some mistakes, but official standards were not breached. The special two-grade minimum written into the guidelines for Mississippi was extended to no other state and was approved for some Mississippi districts in late summer only after Commissioner Keppel was convinced that it was the maximum that could possibly be obtained. On paper at least, the fledgling Equal Educational Opportunities Program had broken total resistance to desegregation in almost 2000 school districts.

[21] Seeley interview, June 17, 1967.   [22] Barus interview.
[23] Seeley interview, June 17, 1967.

On the last day of August, President Johnson issued a statement summarizing the "heartening evidence . . . that respect for law remains a vigorous force everywhere in the country." Voluntary compliance, he said, had been "deeply encouraging," with almost nine-tenths of the concerned districts already committed to a plan. The President reported that almost 300 plans had been accepted the previous week and that most of them came from the states with the most serious problems. Only 135 districts had taken no action, and that number is "shrinking rapidly." [24]

> The adoption of an acceptable desegregation plan, of course, is only a beginning. The coming weeks—and years—will demand of local officials and concerned citizens much patience and dedicated effort if change is to be achieved successfully and if plans are to be translated into performance.
>
> I have directed the Office of Education to stand ready day and night to work toward solutions in the remaining communities which have not submitted plans or whose plans have not yet been accepted.
>
> I strongly urge every responsible State official, school officer, and local official who cherishes the future of our children to lose no time in working for progress where progress is needed. There is still time—and the results of your labors can mean the difference, in many cases, between full educational opportunity for all and the tragedy of lost opportunity. Certainly none of us wants to see this Nation's educational future clouded by delay, indifference, or neglect.[25]

Not only were the guidelines supported by the President, but they were also strongly endorsed in mid-August by the Fifth Circuit Court of Appeals in New Orleans. In a case involving the Jackson, Mississippi schools, the court ruled that the Office of Education was "better qualified than the courts and is the more appropriate Federal body to weigh administrative difficulties inherent in school desegregation plans." [26] This willingness to defer to the guidelines on the part of the court with jurisdiction over the states of the Deep South smothered the hope of many districts that they could avoid significant integration through lenient court decisions.

Judged by the standards of the previous 10 years, the summer's work was monumental. Judged by the goal of eliminating the system of separate segregated schools, only a beginning had been made. In communities where even discussion of desegregation had seemed impossible only months earlier, the first step had been taken. "Many areas of the South," the Civil Rights Commission reported, "shifted their position from resistance of Federal law to at least agreement to comply." [27] The most

[24] Lyndon B. Johnson, *Public Papers*, 1965, p. 957.   [25] *Ibid.*, pp. 957–58.
[26] U.S. Commission on Civil Rights, *Survey of School Desegregation in the Southern and Border States 1965–1966* (Washington: Government Printing Office, 1966), p. 23.
[27] *Ibid.*, p. 25.

important change was psychological. In many communities in which rigid local leadership had said "NEVER," the pressure of Federal money had changed the slogan to a less certain "maybe a little."

The summer's task had been a complex and sensitive one. Everyone in the Office of Education felt that it would be tragic to deny the new Elementary and Secondary Education Act funds to backward school districts offering both Negro and white students a seriously inadequate education. This feeling was echoed at the White House and powerfully represented in Congress. Thus the Office of Education had to make a convincing demonstration of determination to withhold funds but to avoid the necessity of actually cutting off massive sums of money. The task was to demand as much, but no more, than the local officials could tolerate. Thus all schools in the border states were required to open all grades at once, while a more cautious approach was taken in the Deep South. In areas where bitter segregationism was unchallenged and Federal district courts were demanding integration of only a single grade each year, local leaders were severely limited, no matter how much they wanted the money. "Local school boards," Seeley recalls, ". . . would come in and say: 'we can desegregate and we know that we've got to desegregate but we just can't possibly do it all at once; if we tried to do it all at once the whole community would fall apart.' " Seeley reports:

> Where we were convinced that the local school board would carry the thing out —at least in some degree carry it out—on one basis but simply would not carry it out on the other, we were faced with the reality that it did take local officials to carry out this plan and we didn't have Federal agents in every school district actually to implement the plan. Where . . . local officials would simply dig in and refuse to do it, this is basically the area where we agreed that some compromise would be made.[28]

The combination of pressure, persuasion, moderate demands, and the promise of huge new sums of Federal money eventually brought all but a handful of districts into compliance. Some educators were actually grateful for the opportunity to resolve local problems; others recognized that the probable alternative to compliance was a costly and futile legal battle with the NAACP or the Justice Department. The general standards and the bureaucratic machinery of the Office of Education brought desegregation in more districts in a few months than had been touched by the tedious case-by-case litigation in the Federal courts in the space of a decade.[29] A revolutionary breakthrough had been made, even though most of the plans still existed only on paper.

[28] Edward Beis, Transcript of interview with David Seeley, November 23, 1965, pp. 11–12.
[29] Civil Rights Commission, *Survey* . . . , p. 26.

Review of Local Implementation

Until shortly before school opened, the Office of Education staff was so involved in the negotiation of plans that there was very little time available to worry about the problem of forcing districts to honor their promises. A small compliance review unit was begun in early August. Until September it did little more than send form letters to those who were flooding the Office with complaints about local abuses. Surprisingly, the first major investigation was mounted in response to a lengthy complaint from the Chicago civil rights confederation, which claimed legally enforced segregation in the Chicago schools. By late September the compliance unit had a staff of 14 people, but it was very slow in launching field investigations in the South.[30]

Unless well-drawn plans were accompanied by fair and effective implementation, the Office of Education effort was virtually meaningless. Seeley was acutely aware of the need for supervision:

> What isn't realized is that almost 100 percent of the cases are not only potential non-compliers but actively trying to do as little as possible. . . . You've got to make it clear that the law is going to be enforced.[31]

The summer's experience made Office of Education staff members realize that investigation of complaints would be a major responsibility calling for a large investment of trained personnel; but such action was prevented by an intradepartment squabble over compliance procedures. At a much earlier stage, the decision had been made in HEW that complaints would be handled primarily by the department's regional offices under the coordination of Assistant Secretary Quigley.

Each complaint went to Quigley's office and was then forwarded to one of the small regional staffs, which were expected to undertake compliance investigations in addition to their regular jobs. Quigley worked hard to stimulate vigorous enforcement. He hoped to make regional program officials, many of them southerners, aware of the importance of the civil rights responsibility. His visits to the regional offices succeeded in producing temporary spurts of activity, but failed to produce an effective investigating mechanism. Basically, the regional offices had neither the staff, the specialized knowledge, nor the commitment necessary in the compliance job. Existing as intermediaries between Washington-based programs and state and local officials, it was very much to the interest of the officials in Charlottesville, Atlanta, and Dallas to avoid disruption of these relationships.

[30] SNCC, p. 28.   [31] Beis, pp. 20–21.

The regional compliance procedure was viewed with skepticism in the Equal Educational Opportunities Program, and thus an independent staff had been assembled. Because HEW was awaiting the arrival of a new Secretary in August, no one had been able or willing to clarify the roles of the two distinct investigating operations. The critical early months, when a demonstration of Federal determination to enforce the letter of the plans would have made a great difference, rapidly passed. Jurisdiction remained confused into December. Whenever Seeley attempted to send out an investigator to check reports of local violations, he would run afoul of a regional official who would insist on a written statement from HEW granting the Office of Education staff authority for a field investigation. Thus every field trip required exhaustive negotiations. "Instead of fighting segregationists," Seeley said at the time, "you find yourself fighting internal bureaucratic problems. Until it can be straightened out, I'm not disposed to continue to try to do something about it except in an emergency." [32]

During the first six weeks of the school year, Seeley's staff made only one field investigation. Although 517 complaints involving more than 150 alleged plan violations reached Washington by the year's end, only 15 significant reviews had been completed as 1966 began. In the great bulk of the cases the Office was able to do nothing more than make phone calls or write letters, generally only to local school officials. [33]

In the absence of effective review machinery, the only tool available for making Federal determination felt was prompt action to cut off funds from districts that had either submitted no plan or were blatantly violating their promises. Concern and confusion within the department, however, led to an emphasis on month after month of negotiations rather than speedy denial of funds. Threats and persuasion reduced the number of districts adamantly refusing to submit plans to 51 by the end of the year. Late in the year the remaining districts, together with one district that had submitted an inadequate court order, were called to Washington for fund-cutoff hearings. Not until early February, 1966, were the first decisions of hearing examiners announced; they directed termination of Federal aid to 16 Alabama, Louisiana, and Mississippi districts. [34] Not a single district in the South was called to account for violation of its plan. In the end funds were denied to only 38 districts in the entire South. [35]

[32] Ibid., pp. 18–19.
[33] Civil Rights Commission, Survey . . . , pp. 49–50; SNCC, p. 28.
[34] Civil Rights Commission, Survey . . . , p. 50.
[35] U.S., Congress, House, Committee on the Judiciary, Subcommittee No. 5, Hearings, Civil Rights, 1966, 89th Cong., 2d Sess., 1966, pp. 28, 41; G. W. Foster, Jr., "Who Pulled the Teeth from Title VI?" Saturday Review, April 16, 1966, p. 88.

Even where noncompliance was total, Federal authorities made clear their great reluctance to withhold money. Those districts that had openly renounced their plans or had succeeded in dragging on negotiations so long that no progress was possible during a school year already well underway evoked only admonitions from Washington. Rather than exercising the administrative sanction Title VI was designed to provide, the Justice Department turned back to the courts and initiated lawsuits against several districts violating their plans. This procedure made Title VI completely meaningless, and actually gave districts several extra months to stall.[36] A district could be sued for violating the judicially determined principles set out in the guidelines only after it was completely evident that the guidelines had been violated. All that would be added to the normal judicial process would be additional delays.

The Administration viewed the terminating of funds as a very drastic step, just as Congress had. In each instance it was necessary to prepare a legal case against the district which would stand up in court should the district take advantage of the provision for judicial review written into Title VI. This task was assigned to the HEW General Counsel's office, a staff lacking both the personnel and the expertise for large-scale enforcement.

Even before work was begun in the HEW legal staff, each case had to pass through a formidable obstacle course. After the Office of Education enforcement staff had exhausted all possibilities of negotiation and Seeley approved cutoff proceedings, his request was forwarded to the Secretary's office, where Quigley would act on it. If approved there, the case next went to the Justice Department. In late September President Johnson had given the Attorney General responsibility for civil rights coordination, and Justice attorneys were inclined to demand legal preparation adequate for a full-blown lawsuit, even when there was a clear case of obvious noncompliance. Only after this cumbersome process was completed did the local district receive a hearing notice. Pervasive fear of mistakes had resulted in a procedure that gave anybody with a question or a policy disagreement an opportunity to delay or veto enforcement action. Protracted delays forced Seeley to devote much of his energy to internal bureaucratic discussions. "Thirty-five million people," he says, "had to be brought into it and convinced for the routine case."[37]

Confusion and delay built into the process were compounded by inadequate staffing in the Office of Education. The total civil rights staff including those on loan, those involved in the grant program for desegregating districts, and all the clerical personnel, was set at slightly over 100

36 *Ibid.*   37 Seeley interview, June 17, 1967.

people. Only half were allocated to the enforcement program. With most of the available manpower involved in continuing negotiations, and with continuing jurisdictional battles within the department, the extensive field investigations necessary for citing a school district for violations of its plan became almost impossible.

Although the guidelines purported to establish Federal minimum standards, it was rapidly becoming clear that the Federal government was not prepared to support these standards with enforcement actions. In fact, the caution dominating the process was further magnified when the program incurred its first major political defeat. The confrontation between Federal and local power that arose out of the Office of Education's unsuccessful attempt to delay the flow of $30 million in aid to Chicago, while an investigation was made of local civil rights complaints, chastened the enforcement officials. The President's anger about the showdown with Mayor Daley was well known, and no one was eager to provoke a similar reaction.

The President's directive to release the Chicago funds forced a reevaluation of the usefulness of the withholding device. The Chicago situation, recalls the head of the Justice Department's Civil Rights Division, revealed that the cutoff tool was a "sledge-hammer not a scapel." "People kind of woke up after that happened." [38] The Justice Department began to closely supervise fund deferrals and became increasingly interested in enforcing Title VI through lawsuits rather than termination of Federal aid. After Chicago, inertia on the issue of administrative action against districts violating their plans became so massive that an explicit directive from Congress was necessary before the machinery for hearings was organized on a reasonably efficient basis.

In spite of grave difficulties and administrative weaknesses, however, 1965 ended with an impressive record of accomplishment for the Office of Education. Integration had increased in the 11 southern states far more rapidly than during any previous year. The final reports showed that the percentage of Negro students attending integrated schools had jumped from 2¼ per cent to 6 per cent, surpassing the achievement of a decade in a few months. Between the closing of schools in June and their reopening in September, almost one out of every 25 black students had moved from segregated to integrated education. In the border states the degree of change was less dramatic, but still significant, with students in integrated schools climbing from 58 to 68 per cent. In the entire 17-state region where segregated schools had been the rule before 1954, one Negro student in 20 moved into desegregated schools for the first time.[39]

[38] Interview with John Doar, June 20, 1967.
[39] *Southern Education Report,* January–February, 1966, pp. 28–29.

In the Deep South the major change was psychological, with only a tiny minority of the Negro students actually entering white schools. Although all but a handful of districts came into compliance, more than 99 per cent of Negro students in Alabama, Mississippi, and Louisiana remained in all-Negro schools, and the situation was not much better in South Carolina and Georgia. The important change came with the smashing of the façade of total resistance. In Mississippi, where there had been no integration in 1963, and only 57 Negroes in white schools in 1964, the fall of 1965 found 1750 Negro students crossing the color line.

The greatest numerical gains came in those states of the South that had made the most progress before the Civil Rights Act became law. In the fall of 1965 one Negro in six was in an integrated school in Texas, and the Florida rate grew from one student in 25 to one in 10. In the entire region, the Title VI program was largely responsible for the entrance of 180,000 Negroes into desegregated schools. This was a massive accomplishment, but more than three million Negro students still remained in segregated schools.[40]

Southern Attitudes

Of even greater importance to the future of southern race relations than the actual level of integration achieved was the psychological impact of the enforcement program. The repercussions varied widely. In areas that had already made significant progress, the Federal demands often provided a strong incentive for a further long step toward desegregation or, in many cases, for a decision to eliminate the dual school system in favor of a system organized on the northern model. In those districts where nothing had been done, and where the percentage of Negro students was often high, the impact was quite different. The cherished commitment to total segregation was grudgingly set aside in favor of freedom of choice and a small amount of token integration. The nature of the initial guidelines and the manner in which they were explained and enforced convinced both the citizens and the political leadership in much of the South that freedom of choice was all that the Civil Rights Act required.

Southern reaction to the guidelines had been surprisingly moderate. When the requirements had been spelled out in the spring, the response had been calm. Mississippi's Governor Paul Johnson told the press that "obedience to our laws is not optional," while Georgia school officials reluctantly conceded that they would "have to go along." A leading Birmingham newspaper called for "utmost realism" to avoid "a tragic disser-

[40] *Ibid.*, pp. 30–31; Southern Education Reporting Service, *Statistical Summary* (Nashville: Southern Education Reporting Service, 1967), p. 43.

vice to the State and its children." [41] Only in Alabama, where Governor Wallace urged school districts to challenge the guidelines in court and to refuse to open more grades than court decisions demanded, did the guidelines come under serious political fire.[42]

Most southern members of Congress held their fire. A number of congressmen and Senate staff members actually worked with school officials to help them obtain information and come into compliance. Most political leaders either avoided the issue or quietly advised schoolmen that Title VI was the law and they should try to strike the best bargains they could with the Office of Education. State attorney generals said that noncompliance probably meant not only the loss of Federal aid but also the need to finance a costly and useless legal battle with the Justice Department, acting under another title of the Civil Rights Act. A Mississippi Federal judge summed up the alternatives: "Submit a desegregation plan and keep receiving Federal money or have the court do it without the money." [43]

Seeing no alternative, many politicians deserted the tattered banner of blind resistance. Georgia's Senator Herman E. Talmadge said that southerners "realize that court decisions and acts of Congress have become the law of the land—an accomplished fact." Arkansas's Governor Orval Faubus, famous for his defiance of a Federal court order in Little Rock, commented that school boards submitting desegregation plans were "doing what must be done." In both North and South Carolina, the governors took a strong stand against violence in areas being desegregated for the first time.[44]

Lacking effective political leadership, needing the Federal money, and seeing no way out, districts in the Deep South eventually recognized that some kind of token integration would have to be accepted. Explanations from two Louisiana districts that decided to comply at the last minute are revealing. The superintendent in Beauregard said:

> We're a typical Southern community, but we see nothing logical in having to go into court. The school board knew it had to face up to it. Rather than face the court process . . . we decided to go ahead and comply.[45]

In a neighboring district, the financial concern was dominant. The school board announced:

> Faced with a certain loss of $330,000 in Federal funds or 20 percent of its 1965–1966 operating budget, board members felt it was better to desegregate partly in their own way rather than integrate all the way according to Federal plans. . . .

[41] U.S., Office of Education, "Press Reaction to Guidelines," April, 1965. This summary quotes from the *Jackson Clarion-Ledger, Atlanta Constitution,* and *Birmingham News.*
[42] *Southern Education Report,* September–October, 1965, p. 33.
[43] *Ibid.*   [44] *Ibid.,* pp. 32–33.   [45] *Ibid.,* p. 33.

The legal and economic pressures were simply too much for us. The question is whether we integrate on a full stomach and with everyone working and prosperous or whether we integrate with Ft. Polk closed, our people broke, jobless and hungry. We have to integrate come hail or high water, so why not make it as painless and peaceful as possible.[46]

Resistance to token integration had been broken, but this did not mean that the Federal goal of abolishing the dual school system was either understood or accepted. The officially sanctioned idea of freedom of choice, with its fair and democratic ring, rapidly was adopted as a powerful fallback position by those fighting for segregation. Once it became obvious that the system would produce substantial integration only in communities with relatively good race relations, those opposed to any integration took up the cause of freedom of choice, denouncing anything else as "forced integration" and righteously promising to enroll in the white schools all the Negro students who chose to come. In more than 100 districts with approved freedom-of-choice plans, community attitudes were so strong that not a single Negro student chose to enroll in any white school.[47] In hundreds of other districts only an insignificant fraction of Negro pupils challenged the system of racial separation. The fear and apathy pervading Negro communities in areas with a poor racial climate transformed the freedom-of-choice plan from a mechanism for integration to a means of legalizing segregation.

The enforcement of the school guidelines produced a crucial change in public opinion in the South. As late as the previous spring, three-fourths of the South's biracial school districts had been totally segregated. In the fall of 1964 only 139 districts had begun integration. Now all but a handful of localities were publicly committed to integration. Legal and financial pressure from Washington had inexorably worn down the front lines of resistance. Mississippi school officials, for example, had no real alternative to reshaping their attitudes when confronted with the possible loss of $75 million, a sum larger than total state expenditures on education in 1963.[48] Recognition of the new reality was strikingly apparent in public opinion surveys. When polled at the time President Kennedy first sent his civil rights bill to Congress, three-fifths of the southern whites opposed sending their children to a school with a few Negro students; by 1966, the public had accommodated itself to the new reality, and only one parent in five objected to token integration.[49]

[46] *Ibid.*   [47] Civil Rights Commission, *Survey* . . . , p. 31.
[48] Leonard Baker, "Compliance," *American Education*, Vol. I (September, 1965), pp. 24–26.
[49] Meyer Weinberg, ed., *Learning Together* (Chicago: Integrated Education Associates, 1964), p. 210; Robert L. Crain, "Urban School Integration: Strategy for Peace," *Saturday Review*, Vol. L (February 18, 1967), p. 98.

The crucial fact for the future was that the new reality to which southern education was forced to adjust was not one of complete desegregation but one of token integration. Although the guidelines contained a provision authorizing the Commissioner of Education to upgrade the requirements for the next year, the Federal intention to wipe out the whole system of separate schools was not made clear either to the southern public or to the local schoolmen and politicians who negotiated the desegregation plans. Thus a basic part of the southern reaction was the feeling that the requirements had been spelled out and the law complied with, and nothing further would be demanded. Office of Education acceptance of plans, which frequently extended over a three-year period, was taken as a Federal commitment to maintain the acceptable standards of the 1965 guidelines for at least that period. This fact underlay the bitter reaction across much of the South to the tightened requirements that were to be imposed the following year.

Even token integration was sufficient to arouse bitter and even violent resistance in a number of communities. The Civil Rights Act provided a great stimulus for growth of the Ku Klux Klan and cross-burnings, shootings, and threatening letters and phone calls were employed by the diehard segregationists. The Justice Department launched investigations of scores of incidents involving claimed harassment or intimidation of Negro students and their families. Even in Maryland, intimidation was reported to be a significant factor influencing student choices in several counties.[50] Although public opinion and southern leadership had decided to comply, the extremist groups remained unwilling to accept the slightest change. A less dramatic but perhaps more important indication of local resistance was evident in the rapid growth of the private school movement, particularly in those areas just beginning integration. New private schools began to spring up rapidly, especially in those states providing tuition grant subsidies to parents wishing to send their children to segregated private schools. A number of counties without adequate resources to support even a single system of schools now found themselves with three systems —white, Negro, and private—none of which could meet reasonable minimum standards.

Southern attitudes had changed more than had seemed possible two years earlier, but very powerful resistance to further steps remained. The outer defenses had been destroyed, but already southern forces were regrouping. Much of the energy generated by the Civil Rights Act had been spent, but the citadel of segregation remained largely intact.

---

[50] Civil Rights Commission, *Survey . . .* , p. 39.

Response to the Civil Rights Movement: A Constituency in Search of an Agency

The Civil Rights Act was passed at the crest of a great national social movement demanding Federal intervention to protect the rights of Negro citizens against local violations. The act was pushed through Congress by a very broad and ephemeral national coalition called into being by the Birmingham crisis and dissolving after passage of the act, only to be briefly reactivated by the Selma March and the fight over the 1965 Voting Rights Act. This coalition of church, labor, and civil rights groups focused on clear legislative objectives where its tactics of building and expressing a national consensus were most appropriate. This loose grouping, however, possessed neither the coherence, the continuity, nor the expertise necessary for exertion of influence in the intrabureaucratic struggle over the translation of the broad principles of the act into administrative regulations and procedures.

The coalition lost its focus after passage of the Civil Rights Act, and only the civil rights groups remained to monitor the enforcement process. None of these groups, however, had much experience with administrative politics, being primarily oriented toward the courts, Congress, or local community organization and direct action. For months the groups were curiously uninterested and ineffective in the policy-making process. Only when it became evident that enforcement would be far less vigorous than had been hoped did the movement begin to exert some effective pressure on the Office of Education.

Like everyone else, civil rights leaders failed to realize at first that Title VI would become the most important section of the 1964 law. The public accommodations provision was seen as central, and much of the movement's available resources went into programs of testing compliance in restaurants and hotels. The feeling was one of euphoria and optimism. Since Title VI had passed so easily and provided what seemed to be so clear and sweeping an injunction against discrimination in Federal programs, the Administration seemed to have no choice but vigorous enforcement.[51] While the HEW regulation was being hashed out within the bureaucracy, the attention of the civil rights groups was absorbed in the crusade against Barry Goldwater.

The first attempts to discuss enforcement policy were rebuffed. The Washington-based Leadership Conference on Civil Rights, then a confederation of almost 100 groups, had coordinated the 1964 legislative battle. When Conference officials tried to arrange meetings to discuss the HEW

[51] Interview with Harold Fleming, June 25, 1967.

draft regulation in late 1964, department officials refused to discuss the issues still being debated internally.[52] When the regulations appeared in December, an analysis by an NAACP staff member found them seriously inadequate. The approach to school segregation, the NAACP attorney wrote, nullified the intent of Congress. Congress, he argued, had not provided for gradualism but had established an enforcement tool to protect every child's right to attend an integrated school at once. Also disappointing was the failure to clearly provide for faculty desegregation as "an integral part of the desegregation process." [53]

On the last day of 1964, a mere three days before the regulation went into effect, the secretary of the Leadership Conference sent short letters to the heads of various departments, protesting the draft regulations. He informed Secretary Celebrezze that the groups in the Conference unanimously favored amendment of the regulation to avoid "unconscionable delays in granting the rights guaranteed by the Act." He objected to the decision to accept court order desegregation plans that might "be used as an occasion for delay or even subterfuge." [54] The protest was neither thorough nor forceful, and it was far too late. An Office of Education memo summed up the response: "We don't feel that the Leadership Conference has much substance or insistence." [55] The letter had no impact on policy.

In January 1965 the new enforcement bureaucracy began to emerge in the Office of Education. Even in its earliest days, it was clear that the mission of this staff was strikingly unlike that of the remainder of the Office. Although the basic task of the Office was to strengthen state and local educational programs through the infusion of Federal money, the objective of the new organization was to use the threat of powerful administrative sanctions to revolutionize race relations in the local educational systems of the South. The central constituency of the Office of Education was state and local education officials, but the civil rights goups felt that the new program should look primarily to them.

Even as the Agriculture Department sees farm groups as its major constituency and the Commerce Department is most responsive to business groups, it seemed obvious to civil rights groups that the Equal Educational Opportunities Program should be "their" office and that their advice should be listened to with great care. Civil rights enforcement, however, was a fundamentally different kind of issue. Although the

[52] Interview with Marvin Caplan and J. F. Pohlhaus, January 4, 1967.
[53] Memorandum from J. Francis Pohlhaus to Arnold Aronson, December 18, 1964.
[54] Letter from Arnold Aronson to Secretary Celebrezze, December 31, 1964.
[55] Memorandum from Commissioner Keppel to Assistant Secretary Quigley; draft by David Seeley, January 8, 1965.

claims of powerful farm and business groups are reinforced in Congress and are countered only by vague notions of the public interest or the relatively powerless consumers' groups, the civil rights movement was unable to develop continuing congressional pressure and faced the forceful opposition of southern educators and congressmen, who were accustomed to close, cooperative relationships with the Office of Education. Southern schoolmen insisted that the enforcement effort operate like other Office programs, with Federal officials dealing with the local white officials and accepting their "good-faith" promises.

The effort of the civil rights movement to influence civil rights enforcement policy is a story of sporadic skirmishes employing a wide range of tactics. Ironically, the strategy that was to prove most effective was the most indirect. This approach involved fighting in the Federal courts to expand the constitutional requirements for school desegregation, while pressing the Office of Education to incorporate the broadest judicial standards into its administrative regulations.

The most impressive initiative mounted by the civil rights groups was the School Desegregation Task Force, which was to operate in several states during the summer of 1965. In late 1964 the NAACP Legal Defense and Educational Fund, Inc., which had handled the important school desegregation cases in the South for a generation, decided to join forces with the American Friends Service Committee, which had been working in communities undergoing desegregation for 15 years. Their decision to jointly sponsor a school desegregation task force crystallized during a conference on Title VI held in Washington in early 1965. The obvious confusion in Washington suggested a need for local organization of Negro communities and for legal action to make the Federal program work.[56]

The first need was to establish contact with the Office of Education. Jean Fairfax, a veteran of the AFSC community work program, raised a number of questions about Office policy in a letter to Commissioner Keppel. She urged establishment of clear compliance standards, warning that the only alternative was confusion and evasion. She raised questions about the decision to accept court order plans, and pointed to the need for Federal action against states undermining school integration by subsidizing private segregated schools. The AFSC spokesman raised a very significant issue about the compliance program's constituency when she asked whether local Negro leaders would be given an opportunity to comment before final approval of plans negotiated with white officials.[57]

[56] Interview with Jean Fairfax, February 21, 1967.
[57] Letter from Jean Fairfax to Commissioner Keppel, January 24, 1965.

In late January Keppel and Seeley met with representatives of the Task Force. At this point, Jean Fairfax recalls, "We had the feeling that we were outsiders and we were not really wanted." The Office of Education, she observes, had traditionally seen local schoolmen as "their constituents" and had "never really been directly involved with activist-oriented people." [58] The civil rights spokesmen urged the Office to set firm conditions for Federal aid and to rigorously enforce them rather than engage in an attempt to act as a broker, demanding racial change only at the level considered reasonable by southern officials.[59] The spokesmen tried to make optimistic Federal officials realize that there would be widespread evasion in southern school systems.

During the early months, the only civil rights group to make any impact was the NAACP Legal Defense and Educational Fund, Inc. The New York organization, known as the "Inc. Fund," operates independently of the national NAACP and specializes in school litigation. Having a number of the nation's most experienced civil rights attorneys, this well-organized group's legal commentary was valued. During the drafting of the guidelines, the Inc. Fund was asked to provide legal memoranda on freedom of choice and on the requirements for notice under freedom of choice plans. One of the staff members was asked to comment on a draft of the *Saturday Review* article that was to launch the guidelines. The letter to Negro parents proposed in the article was taken verbatim from an Inc. Fund proposal. After the guidelines were issued, Professor Foster made a trip to New York to urge the prestigious organization to sharply criticize the inadequacies of the document, thus strengthening the position of the Office of Education in the face of possible southern criticism.

Generally, the Inc. Fund failed to effectively use its early opportunities to influence policy. The Fund's attorneys were accustomed to the judicial process and unfamiliar with the workings of executive agencies. Deeply involved in the judicial requirements for desegregation plans, most of which had evolved in Inc. Fund litigation, the organization was most effective when interpreting the case law to support such requirements as effective notice and faculty integration. Lacking a clear conception of administrative policy, the Inc. Fund generally supported standards consonant with the court decisions.

The first significant policy change resulting from external pressure was the mid-1965 "Johnson amendment," which attempted to protect teachers from racially motivated firing. This issue saw the Inc. Fund function-

[58] Fairfax interview.
[59] Letter from Jean Fairfax to Commissioner Keppel, February 10, 1965.

ing at its best; it submitted an impressive legal memorandum analyzing the legislative history of Title VI and the relevant court decisions. This document, together with the activities of the National Education Association, was unquestionably important in thus extending Title VI requirements.

The chances for successful influence on Federal policy were highest when a relatively narrow policy question was involved and very strong evidence could be brought to bear. Efforts to change the basic assumptions of policy had very little success. After issuance of the first guidelines, for instance, Roy Wilkins of the NAACP made an eloquent but futile protest, charging the Office of Education with disregard of congressional intent to abolish segregated education rather than merely continue the endless process of gradual change that had so frustrated Negro hopes since 1954. "Equating Title VI with any of the standards evolved in the complex body of school desegregation litigation," he wrote, would encourage "endless delay and evasion." Freedom-of-choice plans would only "place the burden of initiating change not on school boards . . . but on their victims, Negro parents and pupils." Title VI, he argued, was designed as "a new and better weapon than litigation," and it was a serious error to "entangle this new weapon in the confused variety of opinion represented in the types of school desegregation which have frustrated Negro citizens for more than a decade." [60] Wilkins' worry that Title VI might become "another in the succession of cruel hoaxes practiced on the American Negro citizen," produced no change in policy.[61]

During the summer of 1965, when desegregation plans were being negotiated and implemented in hundreds of communities, the major initiative of the civil rights movement was the School Desegregation Task Force sponsored by the AFSC and the Inc. Fund. This group of more than 20 people worked out of a base in Atlanta to spread information about Title VI, to help local Negro communities form plans to make freedom of choice work, and to inform the Office of Education, via telephone calls and written complaints, about local violations of desegregation plans. The idea was to provide a "channel between government and the individual Negro." [62] Similar work was done in some areas by field secretaries from the Student Nonviolent Coordinating Committee.

Concentrating their work in four Deep South states, Task Force members learned a great deal about the actual problems of implementing, in a hostile environment, a plan that seemed fine in Washington. Since the

[60] Letter from Roy Wilkins to Keppel, May 13, 1965.   [61] *Ibid.*
[62] Fairfax interview.

Office of Education made no field investigations until September, Task Force complaints and reports provided an invaluable source of information.

Members of the Task Force experienced difficulties in establishing working relationships with Office personnel. Many felt that staff members in Washington were being told to "keep away from the civil rights crowd." When one enforcement official was invited to attend a weekend conference on his own time and at his own expense, his superior refused to permit him to go. When the Task Force director reported on serious problems in August and appealed to Secretary Gardner for last-minute reforms, a meeting was arranged with enforcement officials, but nothing changed. Gardner never answered the letter.[63]

Of far greater immediate importance for the Office of Education was an issue raised by the initiative of a local civil rights group in the North. Although national civil rights organizations had made no attempt to obtain enforcement of Title VI outside the South, the title clearly forbade the use of Federal funds wherever unconstitutional segregation existed. Chicago's Coordinating Council of Community Organizations, involved in an extremely bitter struggle over school segregation, invoked Title VI in a carefully documented complaint alleging that the Chicago school board had intentionally fostered segregation. The complaint was the most impressive the Office had received and became one of the first orders of business for the compliance review unit established in August. Thus it was the initiative of the local civil rights group that drew the Office into the damaging confrontation to be described in the next chapter.

After the dust settled from the summer's activity, both the Task Force and the Washington office of SNCC started to prepare public reports analyzing the Office of Education's record and suggesting policy changes. Both reports were issued in the fall of 1965, and both were sharply critical.

The SNCC report, drawing both on Office records and data leaked by sympathetic staff members to supplement reports of SNCC fieldworkers in six states, harshly criticized both policy decisions and administrative actions. Asserting that integration was "still moving at a snail's pace," SNCC asked for rapid cutoff of Federal funds. The group called upon Secretary Gardner to fire David Seeley.[64]

Federal officials, the militant group argued, had left "innumerable loopholes" in the guidelines. Most compliance staff members had "little or no

63 *Ibid.*
64 Letter from John Lewis, Marian Barry, Jr., and Betty Garman to Secretary Gardner, September 30, 1965.

experience with the conniving, scheming, evasive, or downright dishonest tactics of most southern school superintendents and boards," and had naïvely relied on information provided by white officials.

> We submit that it is absolutely essential for any civil rights compliance section in the government to establish and maintain communication with active civil rights groups and local movements in every county. Some small attempts to establish these contacts have been made—but . . . Federal agency policy is to work primarily through local and state governments. . . . Government officials in Washington *must learn*, however, that compliance with civil rights legislation can only become more than token if voluntary organizations are closely involved in the process.[65]

SNCC was asking that the compliance organization look to black community organizations as its primary constituency. To make this kind of relationship possible, it was recommended that more Negroes be included on the overwhelmingly white compliance investigation staff.

The Office of Education, SNCC claimed, had actively promoted freedom of choice in the Deep South even though the plan had been ineffective even in the border states. This decision encouraged local harassment, particularly since the Federal officials had made it crystal clear that school districts would still receive funds if no Negroes chose to enter the white schools. Given this encouragement, the report charged, communities across the South had mobilized social and economic pressures and physical violence to maintain total segregation. "In most counties where no Negroes have applied for transfer to white schools *we know that fear of retaliation was the reason.*" [66]

> One of the easiest ways for school boards to comply . . . is to adopt a so-called "freedom of choice" plan. The method is simple . . . get a few Negroes to sign up to attend white schools, and then let the local citizens "encourage" them to withdraw their applications. An even better way is to reject all Negro applicants because of overcrowding, bad character, improper registration, or any other excuses. . . . But, if by chance a few Negroes slip through—go directly to the parents' employers or the local welfare agent.[67]

Even if freedom of choice were an appropriate means toward desegregation, SNCC charged, the Federal authorities had permitted unjustified delays and had failed to respond to blatant local violations. Examination of 100 accepted plans revealed that the Office of Education had permitted delays in opening all grades even when the school district had no argument to support procrastination, or when local officials weakly argued that the local "emotional atmosphere" prevented going faster than "the majority of our neighboring districts." [68] The Office was also accused,

[65] SNCC, pp. 5, 7–8, 29–30.   [66] *Ibid.*, p. 24.   [67] *Ibid.*, p. 26.
[68] *Ibid.*, p. 10.

quite accurately, of a "conscious decision" to allow postponements in districts with high proportions of Negroes.[69]

Drawing instances from field reports on county after county in Arkansas, Alabama, North Carolina, Georgia, and Mississippi, SNCC urged prompt investigation of flagrant violations of local desegregation plans. A statement from the President or Secretary of HEW stating Federal determination to enforce local promises, the group suggested, "would have an important effect upon the future actions of school board members, school superintendents and local citizens who are flaunting the law of the land." [70]

The impact of the SNCC report was small. Much of the constructive force of one of the last major appeals for integration by the militant organization that was soon to adopt the black nationalist outlook was dissipated by the call for the dismissal of David Seeley.

Although it reached many similar conclusions, the leaders of the School Desegregation Task Force received a far more careful hearing for its recommendations. In November the Task Force leaders met with Secretary Gardner to report on their summer's experience and to recommend policy changes. Like SNCC, the Task Force felt that the Office of Education had made a serious mistake in defining the constituency of the Title VI program. The failure to "seek wisdom and assistance from private groups with experience in school desegregation," the report argued, had produced "paper compliance and continued segregation." "To those of us on the outside," the Task Force observed, "it appeared that the operation was conceived as a matter between the Office of Education and school officials." [71]

Secretary Gardner was informed that the decision to certify the compliance of school districts' desegregation under court orders or under free-choice plans had placed intolerable strains on civil rights groups working for school desegregation. The Federal decision on court orders had prompted a rush of 20 Louisiana districts into sympathetic district courts. To prevent destruction of the guidelines standards, the Inc. Fund was forced to use its resources to appeal these cases to bring the court order plans up to HEW standards. Similarly, the fact that successful free-choice desegregation in the Deep South demanded a higher level of organization than most Negro communities possessed meant that any significant results generally demanded massive outside help. Full-time work of a professional community organizer able to activate Federal attention was necessary in one Georgia county to make possible the transfer of a frac-

[69] *Ibid.*, p. 15   [70] *Ibid.*, p. 29.
[71] Memorandum from NAACP Legal Defense Fund, Inc., and American Friends Service Committee to Secretary Gardner, November 15, 1965, p. 5.

tion of the Negro students to white schools. In another locality four full-time workers plus 20 volunteers were needed to surmount a maze of procedural barriers and to organize the Negro community to make and support a commitment to desegregation. The civil rights movement lacked the resources to sponsor such an effort in more than a handful of counties. Thus, the report concluded, "for most communities Freedom of Choice means freedom to remain segregated." [72]

Although the Task Force obviously favored elimination of freedom of choice, its recommendations were carefully drawn within the framework of constitutional law from which the guidelines had been derived. The Task Force called for the Office of Education to strictly limit the conditions under which such a plan would be accepted and to judge compliance not only in terms of local conformity with procedural requirements, but also in terms of the actual success of the plan in desegregating the local schools. The Task Force specifically recommended that the Office get at the problems of harassment and subtle local resistance by creating an administrative presumption of noncompliance whenever fewer than one-fifth of a school district's Negro students failed to enter integrated schools.[73]

The Task Force recommendation was designed to counter the strong southern tendency to regard the free-choice procedure as an end in itself, rather than as a means of recognizing the constitutional rights of Negro students. While most southerners maintained that a school system was desegregated if schools were theoretically open to any Negro student choosing to transfer, the Task Force spokesmen asserted that it was sophistry to certify the desegregation of any system without a significant number of Negro students actually learning in integrated classrooms. The Federal role of soliciting local promises, the group argued, had to be replaced by Federal determination to force a definite level of performance. The level suggested was far higher than any of the 11 southern states had achieved and thus would require either a drastic change in local attitudes or wide abandonment of freedom of choice in favor of a nonracial assignment plan.

The report of the Task Force also stressed the need for firm faculty integration requirements. In a series of decisions, the report asserted, the Federal courts had clearly determined that the rights of Negro students could not be fully protected unless there was integration of faculties as an integral part of desegregation plans. Since the case law was "crystal clear," the Office of Education was urged to renounce its timid posture and set out explicit requirements in this sensitive area.[74]

[72] Ibid., pp. 12–14, 28–29.   [73] Ibid., p. 18.   [74] Ibid., p. 41.

More than a year after the Civil Rights Act became law some of the civil rights spokesmen were beginning to understand the nature of the administrative process and beginning to make explicit demands for change. Until this time effective civil rights pressure had been very rare, the Legal Defense Fund memorandum of law on teacher firing being the one conspicuous exception. Although other legal opinions of the Inc. Fund attorneys had been carefully examined, the civil rights movement had not made any impact on the basic contours of policy. Now, after a summer of work attempting to make the guidelines work in the Deep South, civil rights groups could forcefully point out the radical deficiencies in the 1965 compliance standards. More important, however, than specific recommendations for change was the long-range effort to make Washington officials aware of what was happening through a barrage of complaints, reports, and personal contacts with enforcement staff members. These efforts contributed powerfully to the growing awareness of the need for policy revision.

In spite of gradually improving relationships, however, civil rights representatives strongly objected to the Office of Education's heavy reliance on local school officials and continuing neglect of local Negro leadership. During the year the civil rights movement had achieved far more in raising standards for desegregation plans through constitutional litigation than through administrative lobbying. Dealing with an agency whose primary constituency was composed of state and local officials and whose enforcement staff was primarily oriented toward the courts, the only real opportunity for broad influence came through litigation that forged more complete definitions of constitutional rights. The Equal Educational Opportunities Program had consistently rejected civil rights demands for the establishment of a special relationship between the movement and the Federal enforcement staff.

Split within the Program: The Issue of Constituency

From the very beginning the staff in David Seeley's office represented a wide diversity in background and orientation, ranging from orthodox Office of Education program officials to civil rights activists. Policy alternatives were continually debated from the varying perspectives of the local educator, of the Federal courts, and of the local Negro communities. Although the legalistic perspective was continually dominant, Seeley was able to hold the three factions together for most of a year. As the issue of constituency became increasingly obvious, those who viewed the compliance effort as an extension of the civil rights movement became seriously dissatisfied and the staff polarized.

The imperatives of the administrative situation seemed absolutely clear to Seeley. In a situation where a great deal depended upon the persuasion of reluctant southerners, it was obviously essential to "maintain an appearance of objectivity." Personal commitments were to be strictly controlled, and all officials were to conduct themselves as impartial civil servants carrying out a law of Congress and a policy of the Administration. Civil rights emblems could not be worn in the office. The kind of attitude that led one staff member to tell school superintendents that they had enslaved Negroes for hundreds of years was proscribed. One staff member was transferred to another position after a state superintendent objected to his personal approach. Staff members were told not to contact Negro leaders on the early informational trips. Normally, negotiations were conducted only with local school officials, and requests by Negro leaders to participate in these sessions were rejected.

Naturally enough, activists found these restrictions uncomfortable. Well aware that the school superintendent generally represented only the white community rather than the total community, as Office of Education procedures assumed, they wished to consult and share information with civil rights leaders. Viewing Title VI as one aspect of the national battle against discrimination, they favored coordination with the natural allies fighting on other fronts. In spite of Seeley's policy some of the activists did discuss common problems with friends or acquaintances in civil rights groups. When the arrival of a team of negotiators for a meeting with school officials was announced in a local paper, one activist recalls, he saw nothing wrong in discussions, after working hours, with a civil rights leader who called for information about the program.

A split within the program was finally precipitated by a minor issue. Unaware that the power was very rarely exercised, Seeley fired a probationary employee who was handling research materials, believing that she could not work effectively with her co-workers and the users of the research materials. The woman had played an active role in the Washington civil rights movement, and her removal was seen by the activists as an attack on freedom of expression. A majority of the staff members signed a petition asking reversal of the action, and Seeley's decision was unsuccessfully appealed to the Civil Service Commission. The program offices were picketed by the Washington branch of the Congress on Racial Equality.[75]

The division was heightened by the SNCC report, obviously drawing heavily on information leaked to the civil rights group from within the staff. The critical report, with its call for Seeley's dismissal, came during the period when the program was battered by the fiasco in Chicago. The

[75] Interview with Mordecai Johnson, March 1, 1967; Seeley interview, June 17, 1967.

leaking of damaging documents was deeply resented by those who felt that the staff member's first allegiance must be to the program and to Seeley's committed attempt to keep the ship afloat and on course in very heavy seas. While many saw the report as a dangerous blow to a badly listing program, the activists resented the Office's failure to respond effectively to the substance of the SNCC criticisms. Seeley recognized the validity of many of the SNCC arguments, but was disappointed by a situation which revealed that "some people clearly did not have loyalty to me." [76]

The stunning rebuke to the Commissioner of Education in the Chicago crisis severely threatened the entire enforcement effort. The President's intervention endangered support for the program and emboldened opposition both in the localities and in Congress. Indeed, a prominent civil rights figure in the Administration reports a general assumption within the government that the Title VI effort was finished. Survival required that the program ride out the storm by dropping anchor and lowering all sails until the gale abated.

Morale plummeted as the uncertain future and bureaucratic infighting kept staff members sitting idly at their desks while the pressing need for field investigations was not met. Some members began to use their spare time for a rapid reading program. A detailed report on widespread local violations in Baker County, Georgia, was withheld after the Chicago crisis. Flagrant local abuses made this the only place where an emergency situation had permitted Seeley to justify an investigation bypassing the regional office. The opportunity to warn local officials who were encouraging defiance that their earlier promises would be strictly enforced was lost.[77]

After nearly a year of operation Seeley was faced with the necessity of making permanent decisions about appointments of regional directors, important positions that involved a good deal of responsibility for determining enforcement strategy in regions composed of several states. Seeley's choices precipitated the resignation of a number of activists who felt that less-qualified but more cautious officials had been favored. A Negro attorney who had served as a regional director was told that unless he ended his prominent participation as chairman of the housing committee of the Washington CORE chapter he would not receive a permanent assignment. He refused. Two activist lawyers who had played a major role in the short-lived Chicago investigation resigned after the Chicago file was turned over to a staff member unfamiliar with the complexities of northern segregation.

[76] *Ibid.*   [77] Fairfax interview.

At this point the activists felt that a distinctly "Uncle Tom" atmosphere was engulfing the Title VI program. Having joined the staff hoping to speedily accomplish the civil rights objective of destroying southern school segregation, they felt that the program had mistakenly assimilated the frustrating gradualism of the courts and had been weak-kneed in the face of political attacks. Some felt that timid bureaucrats were being rewarded, while more competent activists were being held back. A number of people decided that they could do more for the civil rights movement outside the program. In the early weeks of 1966 a number of activists left the program, several for the more militant Civil Rights Commission. In spite of hirings, the total staff fell by nine between November and February. Those who fundamentally disagreed with Seeley's philosophy of operation or his definition of the constituency of the program had departed.[78]

The final months of 1965 and the first months of 1966 were the low ebb for the Equal Educational Opportunities Program. Very strong external pressures forced a rapid and fairly complete crystallization of the divergent tendencies within the staff. Once this occurred, the outcome could not be in doubt. A program run by activists and openly identifying with the civil rights movement was simply not possible within the Office of Education. Staff identification with Negro leadership would magnify the difficulties of negotiations, and the Office would be forced to cut off funds in more cases to enforce Title VI. The Administration clearly wanted money from the new education program to flow into the districts. Commissioner Keppel's emphasis was on progress not on immediate transformation, and the Commissioner could not tolerate an administrative style that would have seriously jeopardized the entire range of Office of Education relationships in large parts of the South.

The program existed within an Administration that was committed to Negro rights but also placed a very high value on consensus. The President had assigned the coordination of civil rights policy to a Justice Department which was often moderate in tone and endorsed no actions that would be difficult to defend in southern Federal courts. Operating within this context, Seeley had chosen the only path open to him in attempting to construct an impartial, professional program, gaining as much desegregation as possible without forcing hundreds of school districts out of Federal programs. The only practical alternative would have been to turn the enforcement task over to grant program officials, as many agencies had done, and see it quietly buried.

Seeley's program, though timid and ineffectual by activist standards, represented a radical break in the traditional pattern of Federal-state rela-

[78] Summary of personnel data provided by the Office of Education.

tionships. Seeley's legalistic outlook, respect for local educators, emphasis on endless negotiations, and his willingness to seek a quiet harbor during the Chicago crisis were probably critical to the survival of the program.

As the first year ended, it was clear that serious mistakes had been made, but much had been achieved. The guidelines were obviously too weak to effectively protect the rights of Negro students in hundreds of districts, and Office of Education policy makers had seriously underestimated the level of southern resistance. The distribution of authority within HEW remained confused, and the compliance investigation function had been totally inadequate. Nevertheless, the program had had remarkable success in obtaining written promises from virtually all southern school districts to desegregate more rapidly than most Federal district courts were demanding. Although no budget was provided, Commissioner Keppel had made possible the creation of a sizeable enforcement staff. Invaluable experience had been gained. By year's end, the true dimensions of the job of breaking segregation in southern schools were becoming apparent.

Revising the Guidelines

The initial guidelines included a little-noticed provision announcing that the Commissioner retained the right to revise the standards the following year. The provision had been incorporated not because major changes were expected, but because of the possible need to change the three-year deadline for opening all grades to desegregation. Even at summer's end, Seeley recalls, it had not become evident that wholesale revision was necessary. As the staff began to analyze the concrete achievements and failings of the summer, however, it became obvious that the 1965 guidelines were much more successful in theory than in practice. Local promises had been good, but performance had often fallen far short. It had been "much too much of a paper operation." [79]

The review of policy began within Seeley's office in a number of sessions dealing with problems and possible remedies. The leaders of the enforcement staff, most of them lawyers, were involved in the discussions; the review process was directed by Seeley's acting deputy, David Barus. Two kinds of problems confronted these sessions. In the first place, it was necessary to consider possible changes in the guidelines to take account of the development of case law in the past year. Second, administrative means had to be found for dealing with the inadequacies of the guidelines revealed in the complaints and reports submitted to the Office of Education by the groups that had tried to make them work.[80]

The basic parameters of policy were determined by the continuing

[79] Seeley interview, June 17, 1967.   [80] Barus interview.

assumption that the definition of "discrimination" in Title VI must be derived, at least in a general way, from court decisions defining what was unconstitutional under the Fourteenth Amendment. This fundamental assumption made it impossible to forbid the troublesome free-choice plan until it had been struck down by the courts.

In a number of important ways the context of law within which the policy review took place had been altered substantially in recent months. The courts were beginning to see freedom of choice not as a fully adequate plan for desegregation, but merely as a means to end discrimination, acceptable only if the choice was genuinely free and the plan was effective. In a major case, the Fourth Circuit Court of Appeals in Richmond upheld a free-choice plan; but two of the five judges approved the plan only on the assumption that it was an "interim measure," subject to further review to determine its effectiveness.[81]

Lawsuits attacking the freedom-of-choice plan were successful in winning strong court orders directing faculty integration. Conceding that the plan was not working effectively, some Federal judges decided that a necessary precondition for success was faculty integration to destroy the community "image" that identified schools as either "white" or "Negro" and thus superior or inferior. A Virginia district court ordered one school system to reassign all teachers so that each school would have the same percentage of white and Negro teachers by the beginning of the coming school year. A Supreme Court decision strengthened the legal argument, holding that "there is no merit to the suggestion that the relation between faculty allocation on an alleged racial basis and the adequacy of the desegregation plans is entirely speculative." [82]

Staff members reviewing guidelines policy worked not only with an awareness of the changing pattern of case law, but also with a heightened sensitivity to the administrative problems involved in the enforcement process. Techniques that seemed adequate when the guidelines were first drafted had failed to prevent widespread failures. Almost 94 per cent of southern Negro students remained in all-Negro schools, and in several states only the very slightest numerical dent had been made in the tradition of separate schools. Obviously new administrative standards and procedures would be necessary if the dual school system was to be ended. The fact that more than 100 districts with acceptable plans had remained completely segregated and virtually no district had acted on the important issue of faculty integration clearly demonstrated that initial assessments about the extent of southern cooperation had been optimistic. It was now evident that nothing more would be done than was explicitly and unambiguously required.

[81] Civil Rights Commission, *Survey* . . . , p. 13–14.   [82] *Ibid.*, pp. 16–17.

Since freedom of choice had not been struck down by the courts, the basic challenge confronting Seeley's staff and the Justice Department attorneys, who soon became involved, was to devise a set of specific administrative requirements for free-choice plans that would transform them from bulwarks of the status quo into tools for genuine desegregation. The first necessity was to provide some response to the scores of accurate complaints about intimidation by creating procedures that would make the act of choice as easy and as protected as possible.

As discussion of the free-choice dilemma proceeded, the mechanics of choice were broken down into approximately 25 "problem areas" needing solutions in the new guidelines. One issue, for example, concerned the method of making choice forms available to Negro parents. The forms had commonly been given to school children to take home. In some districts, however, Negro teachers had been pressured by school officials to mark down choices for the Negro schools. Parents had often been afraid to take back to the school principal a request for transfer to a white school. Eventually a new requirement was devised, providing that the forms must be mailed to parents from school headquarters, and parents must be permitted to return the forms by mail.[83] The extent of local resistance and the wide variety of means employed to subvert desegregation plans forced the Office of Education to regulate seemingly trivial details of the administrative process.

Ideas for tightening up the choice process came from a variety of sources, but a decisive role was played by a unique meeting held in late December by the Office of Education at the Airlie House Conference Center in Virginia. The Office called together a group including Federal officials, southern schoolmen, legal experts, and civil rights representatives to discuss enforcement policy issues before the final decisions were made. Although this session failed to produce any consensus on the basic shape of the compliance operation, it did prove surprisingly useful on the mechanical problems. A panel on freedom of choice provided Federal policy makers with criticisms of tentative ideas both from the perspective of the Negro community and in terms of the administrative functioning of the local school districts. The lawyer chairing this discussion found that "after the reasons for each of the various problem areas were discussed, there was a fair degree of unanimity as to what a reasonable attempted solution to the problem might be." [84]

The approaches developed can be illustrated by the new requirement dealing with students who returned choice forms with no choice indi-

[83] Barus interview.

[84] Deposition of David N. Barus, January 26, 1967, in case of *Demott Special District v. John Gardner and Harold Howe*, Civil Action No. PB66C94, U.S. District Court, Eastern District of Arkansas, pp. 22–23.

cated. The first guidelines directed school superintendents to assign such students to the nearest school with available space. Although this apparently reasonable procedure was drawn from court decisions, school officials now reported that it had become an administrative nightmare. The local superintendent had to determine the distance from each school of each student involved and to take time to consider space in each school, plus other factors. Thus the panel gave support to a Justice Department proposal that each student must choose and that no student could be assigned to a school until he chose. Other issues of mechanics involved such problems as the wording of the letter to Negro parents and the length of the choice periods.[85] In a variety of ways, the general outline of the initial guidelines was replaced by detailed procedures designed to limit intimidation and local evasion.

The new procedures were to improve the protections built into the free-choice plan and were to produce an irritated response from some local educators who objected to the work and expense involved. These changes, however, were almost lost sight of in the controversy stirred by the development of new requirements in the troublesome areas of faculty integration and evaluation of free-choice plans in terms of the actual progress made toward elimination of separate schools.

Faculty integration was seen by most southern whites as a serious threat to the educational system and was recognized as a crucially important change by Negro leaders. The existing pattern in which integrated schools were almost universally taught by all-white teaching staffs ratified the southern belief that Negroes were intellectually incapable of teaching in the more advanced white schools. If this pattern continued, Negro teachers would find little demand for their skills as school integration spread, and Negro students making choices would be denied the support for transfer that an integrated faculty would provide. The problem was compounded by the fact that many systems had adopted a double standard in teacher recruitment; they were perfectly satisfied to staff Negro schools with inadequately prepared teachers from second-rate Negro colleges, but found intolerable the prospect of these same teachers handling academic subjects in white schools. School officials reported that many white teachers would sooner resign than teach in a Negro school. Teacher integration was widely perceived as even a more serious assault on the social order than the "mixing" of students.

In recognition of very strong local resistance and because of initial confusion about the legislative history of Title VI, the original guidelines straddled the issue, demanding very little the first year. Although one

[85] Barus interview; interview with M. Sklar, May 15, 1967.

section of the guidelines stated that a school system must ultimately provide both for nondiscriminatory initial assignment of teachers and for reassignment to break up existing patterns of discrimination, another section had made clear that no actual integration of teaching staffs was necessary the first year.

The new guidelines were to shock southern educators with four paragraphs of explicit directives demanding a substantial start toward the elimination of segregated faculties. After a season of enforcing Title VI, Seeley and his staff recognized that it was "impossible" to eliminate the dual school system while segregated faculties remained, thus underlining for everyone in the community the racial identity of each school.[86] It was perfectly obvious that nowhere in the South would white students transfer willingly into Negro schools. If these schools were to be integrated, change in the racial composition of the faculty was an essential first step. Without speedy faculty integration, it was clear that the largest Negro professional group in the South, the teachers, would be asked to pay with their jobs for student integration.

The new urgency of the issue was matched by a new understanding of the legislative history of the law. Although an amendment to Title VI forbidding action against employment discrimination seemed to limit Federal authority, the legislative history suggested the opposite conclusion. Before Dirksen's amendment was accepted by the Administration, Humphrey specifically stated that faculty integration might be required, citing an early court of appeals decision on this issue. After agreeing to the amendment, Humphrey stated that the new language "made no changes of substance in Title VI." The history of the debate showed that the primary intention of the change had been to prevent the use of Federal power to regulate employment relationships that had no impact on those benefiting from the Federal program, such as the hiring of farm workers by a farmer who happened to be receiving an agricultural subsidy.[87]

The legal position of the Office had been further strengthened by two Supreme Court decisions indicating the Court's general support for the proposition that faculty integration could be a necessary part of the constitutional requirements for a desegregation plan. These decisions, together with several specific orders from lower Federal courts directing rapid action against faculty segregation, meant that the original guidelines standards were far behind those of the courts. Until the first Supreme Court decision, Seeley's advisor on the faculty question had still been

[86] Interview with David Seeley, December 13, 1966.
[87] House Judiciary Subcommittee, *Civil Rights, 1966*, p. 13; Slip opinion, *U.S. v. Jefferson County Board of Education*, December 29, 1966, pp. 84–86.

troubled by the Office's questionable legal authority. Shortly after the timely November decision, however, he outlined a series of necessary actions. Experience had shown the value of a firm deadline, and he proposed required integration of all faculty and staff by 1967.[88]

Well aware that a sweeping but unspecific requirement would be meaningless, administrators in the Equal Educational Opportunities Program searched for clear and easily administered standards for faculty desegregation. Litigation had not yet produced general standards, but there was some evidence that gradualism would have far less applicability than in the area of student desegregation. Federal officials had to decide whether to press for a quick and total solution or to give communities a chance to become gradually accustomed to a new and shocking situation. Although in the past the strategy of gradualism had proved more valuable to those organizing resistance than to those working for compliance, the Office eventually chose to extend this approach into the area of faculty desegregation.

Although the Justice Department had been given the responsibility for coordinating Title VI enforcement, the Justice attorneys involved in the revision process were of very little help in devising explicit faculty integration requirements. Approaching the problem from a legal rather than an administrative standpoint, the Justice draft called for a general elimination of the racial characteristics of schools. The idea was to make the broadest possible statement that would be universally applicable about the legal requirement, leaving it to the compliance program to negotiate within this general mandate.[89]

Officials in Seeley's office, profoundly skeptical about the value of general statements, were very eager to gain Justice Department assent for a standard that would be both clearly understood in the South and a practical enforceable minimum. This issue was debated at the Airlie House sessions and emerged as perhaps the most disruptive topic of the meeting. Civil rights spokesmen called for rapid and substantial desegregation in each faculty, while normally cooperative southern educators expressed grave concern. The outcome was a judgment in Seeley's office that a push for rapid faculty integration would cause more difficulty for the entire program than it was worth. Given the lack of clear judicial standards, the Office selected a strategy of politically safe gradualism.[90] By January 1966 the proposed deadline of fall 1967 for complete faculty integration was being dismissed within HEW as unreasonable and of questionable legality.[91]

[88] Memorandum from John Hope to David Seeley, November 24, 1965.
[89] Sklar interview.   [90] Barus interview.
[91] Draft memorandum from Peter Libassi to Under Secretary Cohen; drafted by Ruby Martin, January 26, 1966.

The need for specific standards still remained, however. An alternative position was developed within the department; it called for placement of at least one teacher of the opposite race into each school within a system.[92] The caution of the Justice Department, however, transformed numerical requirements into nearly useless "examples." Once again the 1966 guidelines were to strongly affirm the final goal of eliminating the racial identity of all schools by abolishing faculty segregation but to be ambiguous in concrete application. The requirement for the coming year was buried in the bland phrase "significant progress." Worried school superintendents who studied the five examples of significant progress could find a clear suggestion of a minimum standard only in the first, which called for "some desegregation . . . in each school," thus stating the one-per-school conception by indirection. The other examples were even more obscure. The legal experts' inability to understand administrative problems and unwillingness to endorse standards designed for an administrative rather than a judicial process resulted in language that created understandable confusion throughout the South. By summer, uncertainty was so widespread that the Commissioner of Education found it necessary to circulate a letter clearly setting out the minimum requirement—an average of one teacher crossing racial lines for each school in a school system.[93]

While the specifics were compromised and hidden in the guidelines, the mandate proved to be sufficiently strong, when reinforced by the Commissioner's ruling, to support a determined effort to begin faculty desegregation during the summer of 1966. Although the standards were far lower than many felt necessary, the decision to incorporate a faculty provision in the new guidelines was still an important and politically dangerous move to resolve an urgent problem. As Seeley explained in a memo drafted for Secretary Gardner:

> The new guidelines require actual staff desegregation, either by having some desegregation in every school or by some other pattern which would be equally effective. . . . Many southern school districts have said that it will be flatly impossible to undertake any staff desegregation next year. It is impossible, however, to reconcile further delay . . . with compliance with Title VI.[94]

As predicted, the new proviso generated bitter attacks on the Office of Education from all parts of the South.

[92] Seeley interview, June 17, 1967.
[93] "Revised Statement of Policy," 181.31 (b–d); Seeley interview, June 17, 1967.
[94] Draft memorandum from Commissioner Howe to Secretary Gardner; drafted by David Seeley, February 8, 1966. Commissioner Howe was particularly concerned that there be "real teeth in the business of desegregating teachers" and strongly supported some action in spite of the absence of unambiguous judicial standards. (Interview with Harold Howe, II, September 20, 1968.)

Performance Criteria

The most important single change incorporated into the new guidelines was the decision to judge the adequacy of free-choice plans by their actual results in integrating schools. To local leaders who saw the freedom-of-choice mechanism as an end in itself and all that the Constitution required, this change was seen as a clearly illegal alteration of the basic structure of the enforcement program. No single policy decision was to subject the Office of Education to more sustained and heavy abuse.

Once again Seeley's office and the Justice attorneys approached the problem from different perspectives. To the compliance staff the spectacle of hundreds of districts with almost completely unsuccessful free-choice plans indicated a serious need for an administrative move to unambiguously bring home to recalcitrant school officials that they really had to achieve a certain level of integration to receive Federal money. In administrative terms, there was simply no conceivable way in which a tiny staff in Washington could accurately assess the subtleties of local resistance used to subvert free-choice plans. Only by creating an administrative presumption of noncompliance if performance fell below a specified minimum did the problem become manageable.

None of the Justice attorneys, with their strong orientation toward the judicial rather than the administrative process, was enthusiastic about setting specific performance standards before the courts had clearly charted this troublesome area. The Civil Rights Division attorneys, responsible for handling civil rights lawsuits and for defending the Office of Education guidelines in the courts, naturally found their task easiest when the Office of Education eschewed development of independent administrative standards and adhered closely to standards emerging from the very courts in which the guidelines might be challenged. Justice staff members also brought to policy discussions a good deal of sensitivity to congressional attitudes on civil rights policy and an ability to estimate the great damage to the enforcement program, both in legal and political terms, that could result from a serious reversal in the courts.

No Selma crisis was now sweeping over the Administration, putting pressure on the Justice Department for vigorous enforcement. Indeed, the Watts riot had replaced the Selma March as a symbol of the racial revolution in the country, and the civil rights movement was on the defensive. If the attorneys responsible for litigation had made the decision, the new guidelines would have been cautious indeed. Significant progress was possible only because Attorney General Nicholas Katzenbach was sympathetic toward the civil rights movement and because he had appointed a Title VI advisor, David Filvaroff, independent of the litigators in the department's Civil Rights Division. Filvaroff came to the Justice Department from a position as a civil rights advisor to Vice-President Humphrey and supported the idea of delegating some policy discretion to the agency actually enforcing Title VI. After Filvaroff left the department, the legal mentality was to assume greater importance.

The debates on performance criteria and faculty integration revealed a new set of divisions among the policy makers. In drafting the regulations and the original guidelines, participants divided in terms of primary orientation toward the grant programs, the courts, or the civil rights groups. In the new discussions, no one represented the civil rights movement, but civil rights organizations did raise important issues by public attacks on the first year's record. The striking feature of the debate was the emergence of a powerful new orientation—an orientation of the new enforcement professionals toward the requirements of the administrative process itself.

All who were involved in the initial debates had been equally innocent of the actual requirements of dealing on a day-to-day basis with thousands of school officials. A year of experience made enforcement officials acutely aware of the need for regulations which were not simply clear in legal theory and defensible in the courts but which also set standards that could not be mistaken in communities determined to do the absolute minimum and that could be reviewed by a tiny compliance staff in Washington. Now the central policy disputes were not between those supporting moderate standards emerging from constitutional litigation and those primarily oriented toward external constituencies, but between those who conceived enforcement as a judicial problem and those who saw it as a problem of administration.

Commissioner Keppel's decision to create an enforcement staff independent of the grant programs and separate from the HEW legal office permitted the development of full-time enforcement professionals whose policy perspective was determined by their experience in attempting to overcome local resistance in thousands of communities. This experience made it obvious that mass long-distance negotiations demanded standards different in character from those used in the slow and detailed processes of the Federal courts in dealing on a case-by-case basis. Although the courts had developed no clear performance test to judge the adequacy of free-choice plans, further progress in many parts of the South depended upon some easily understood minimum.

In the absence of court decisions St. John Barrett, of Justice's Civil Rights Division, argued that HEW should hold back and wondered whether the courts would ultimately require more than a fairly operated freedom-of-choice mechanism. Assistant Attorney General John Doar shared the same doubts and argued that on political grounds it would be far more effective to prove the failure of freedom of choice in each individual district and then propose alternative requirements.[95] Seeley felt that he just "couldn't get it into their heads that we had to make signals that would cause hundreds of districts to act." [96] Caught in the pattern of case-by-case litigation and deeply concerned about the political consequences of moving outside this framework, Justice officials emphasized judicial standards and failed to appreciate the problems of exerting pressure for compliance through mass negotiations, without either widespread cutoff of funds or extensive local investigations.

Even those favoring the creation of a minimum standard of performance were by no means in agreement on what the standard should be. Even before the School Desegregation Task Force proposed that no plan be accepted unless at least one-fifth of the Negro students actually entered integrated schools, the question was under serious study within the compliance program. In late October a draft of the guidelines suggested incorporation of language permitting the Office to require submission of a new plan when a district produced "insufficient" desegregation.[97] In an early December memorandum to Commissioner Keppel, Seeley suggested that it might be necessary to force abandonment of free choice in districts with only a small number of Negro students, where separate schools were wholly unnecessary, and in areas where "local conditions of violence or economic reprisal preclude any adequate free choice. . . ." [98]

In early December two members of Seeley's staff told a regional meeting of civil rights leaders that it was "quite likely" that the freedom-of-choice plan would be proscribed in the future.[99] By January, however, HEW officials had recognized that a standard of the sort proposed by the Task Force would be an effective answer to the problem. An advisor to Secretary Gardner's assistant for civil rights wrote:

> Perhaps the most crucial provision in the new Guidelines is the 80 percent rule for school districts operating under a freedom of choice plan. The effect of this rule is that unless at least 20 percent of the Negro students in the district choose during the spring registration period formerly white schools, the school district will be *required* to take additional desegregation steps. . . .[100]

[95] Seeley interview, June 17, 1967; Foster interview, June 6, 1967; Sklar interview, May 15, 1967.
[96] Seeley interview, June 17, 1967.
[97] Memorandum from Carlyle C. Ring to Mordecai Johnson, October 28, 1965.
[98] Memorandum from David Seeley to Commissioner Keppel, November 5, 1965.
[99] *Washington Daily News*, December 2, 1965.
[100] Ruby Martin draft memo, January 26, 1966.

By the time the document was submitted to the Secretary, the idea of an explicit and inflexible figure written into the guidelines had been abandoned in favor of a requirement of "substantial" desegregation. The basic conception, however, remained the same:

> "Substantial" as set forth in the new Guidelines is a percentage cloaked in vague but flexible terms. In effect, substantial means that about 20 percent of Negro pupils must choose white schools.[101]

The idea of a firm minimum standard had been vigorously attacked by the Justice Department and also by the HEW General Counsel. Assistant Attorney General Doar dismissed Office of Education claims that rigid quotas were necessary to assure progress by stating that such standards would be "illegal" and would not be upheld in the courts. If an objective performance standard was necessary, Doar argued, the requirement should be modeled on the Voting Rights Act provision requiring the Attorney General to consider both the voting registration figures and local facts before initiating enforcement actions.[102]

The hostile attitude of the HEW General Counsel was evident in a memo he wrote in response to the report and recommendations of the Task Force. Someone, he said, should tell the civil rights groups that perhaps the progress already achieved was more important than the percentage figures of children still in segregated schools. "Could we not," he asked, "suggest that the Federal Government is something less than omnipotent, and that steady pressure wisely and firmly applied may be the most effective instrument of change?"

> The whole force of the national Government equipped with large legal powers was unable in a decade and a half to change the social habits of the people in the matter of alcoholic drink. One could cite many other instances—from birth control to highway safety—in which the law's effectiveness extends not much beyond its support in public opinion. It is a good deal to ask, as this civil rights report does, that in a year and a half we should have changed the social habits of the South in a matter deeply tinged with emotion.[103]

In the face of heavy resistance the 20 per cent minimum was dropped, and a new formulation was devised in early February. Since free choice rarely resulted in transfer of as many as one-fifth of the Negro children, the result of this figure would have been to force most southern districts to abandon the system. A compromise resulted in lowering the minimum to a level that a reasonably effective plan was likely to achieve. The new

[101] Memorandum from Peter Libassi to Secretary Gardner, February 2, 1966.
[102] Interview with John Doar, August 10, 1967.
[103] Memorandum from General Counsel Willcox to Assistant Secretary Quigley, December 13, 1965.

draft replaced the idea of "substantial desegregation" by the conception of "significant progress," which established minimums varying according to the level of integration existing in the district concerned during the current school year. The approach that emerged out of discussions with the Justice Department and two members of the White House staff stated that the Commissioner would use a series of rates of progress as a general guide for reviewing plans for noncompliance. Thus a district with an 8 or 9 per cent rate of integration would be expected to double this factor, while one with 4 or 5 per cent would have to triple its rate. Where no students had transferred, a "very substantial start" would be required.[104] The 20 per cent figure that had been proposed as a minimum was transformed to a maximum, above which nothing further would be required.[105] The performance standard emerged as a frail reflection of the initial clear minimum.

When the revised school guidelines were finally issued in March, the new policies went partway, but only partway, to meet the defects revealed in the first year's enforcement. In the crucial areas of teacher integration and performance standards, the requirements were greatly tightened, but clear and easily understood standards had not been produced. The teacher integration issue was compromised twice, largely on political grounds. Recognizing the extremely sensitive nature of this issue, particularly in the rural South, the responsible officials rejected first the idea of a 1967 deadline for total faculty integration and then the writing into the guidelines of a specific minimum figure. The guidelines only ventured an indirect suggestion that districts achieve an average of at least one teacher of the opposite race in each school. Although districts were finally put on notice that they must actually begin the difficult process of faculty integration, it was clear that the Office of Education had decided on a gradual approach.

The most significant changes came in response to the widespread failure of the free-choice plan. Less than a page and a half of general directives in the 1965 document were replaced by more than three pages crowded with specific requirements closing a number of procedural loopholes that had been used to sabotage the plan in many districts. More importantly, however, the plan was clearly labeled as nothing more than a means to the end of eliminating the dual school system, and local officials were told that such plans would be rejected if they failed to produce significant progress toward that end. Because of opposition within the Administration, the specific rates of progress were set much closer to

---

[104] "Revised Statement of Policy," 181.54; Draft memorandum from Secretary Gardner to President Johnson; drafted by David Seeley, February 8, 1966.
[105] Confidential draft of regulations, February 8, 1966.

what had been actually achieved in districts where the plan had worked effectively than to what enforcement officials considered a reasonable minimum. Nevertheless, the new requirement foreclosed the possibility cherished by many Deep South school officials that it would be permissible to use freedom of choice to keep integration at a very low level. This decision, as limited as it was, marked the first important step away from strict reliance on judicially developed standards toward standards emerging from the administrative process.

Although there was a complex process of consultation involving the Justice Department, the White House staff, southern officials, civil rights groups, and others, the basic framework of decision was constructed in HEW. The experience of the Equal Educational Opportunities Program in administering the first guidelines had created a new specialty and new administrative expertise. This specialized knowledge weighed heavily and, in the end, persuaded the Justice Department to approve requirements more specific and more independent of the court decisions (although consonant with the general development of case law) than the department's attorneys would have preferred.

The task of the White House staff was to see that there was a "consensus" between the department administering the guidelines and the department with the responsibility for coordinating enforcement programs and defending the guidelines in court. Although there was no significant public demand for more stringent Federal standards, and although the White House was fully warned of the expected intense southern resistance, the President approved the new rules after a delay of a few weeks.

Summary

Confronting the task of enforcing a revolutionary change in southern schools, the Commissioner of Education recognized very early that a staff independent of the grant programs was essential. The establishment of the Equal Educational Opportunities Program was a recognition of the fact that the most important constituency of the program officials was composed of state and local schoolmen, and that the same men could not run effective programs that depended on local cooperation and simultaneously enforce a revolution in the local social order. Given the determination to enforce the law, it became necessary to establish a new staff and to expand it as it began to define its job.

A handful of men can administer a social revolution without great difficulty if the revolution is just waiting to happen, as was the case with the public accommodations section of the Civil Rights Act. At first, Title VI officials assumed that local school districts would readily propose adequate means of complying with the new law. As it became evident that school desegregation would be bitterly resisted, it became essential for Seeley's tiny staff to organize itself and to construct a system of threats sufficiently credible to persuade local officials to undertake hated changes. The program was forced to define its goals in terms that could be understood by thousands of worried local officials and administered in a mass-production bureaucratic process. This necessity gave rise to the school desegregation guidelines.

The guidelines defined the objectives of the new program, but the chaos of the early months demonstrated the inadequacies of the disorganized administrative operation then in existence. Just as legal experts had played a leading role in sketching out the objectives of the program, an expert in administrative techniques gave the program a rational division of labor and the control of its communications essential to coping with its work load. The Commissioner helped with a large expansion of the enforcement staff. Having outlined the basic tools of policy, procedures, and manpower, the central tasks of the program then involved the development of expertise in negotiating school desegregation plans and in establishing relationships with the groups it defined as its constituency.

A summer of experience produced gradually expanding understanding of both the legal and psychological dimensions of school desegregation planning. The standardized policies and rationalized procedures of a bureaucracy were essential to administration of Title VI, and the process of bureaucratization continued as the pressure for rapid decisions in late summer produced increasingly rigorous and standardized model plans.

The summer transformed the abstract principles of the guidelines into thousands of plans molded by contacts with local school officials. The summer also saw an attempt by civil rights groups to make desegregation plans work in the Deep South, an attempt that generated a division within the staff on the issue of the program's proper constituency and the nature of its constituency relationships. The activists on the staff, those who viewed the program as an extension of the civil rights movement, saw the Negro community and the civil rights leaders as natural allies and the natural constituency of the program. Seeley and Keppel, however, recognized that such a stance would be politically impossible within the Office of Education. The only real alternative to allowing local school officials to receive primary consideration in formation of Title VI policy was to turn to the courts and to impartially enforce standards derived from Federal court decisions. This decision, however, left the program with no external supporting constituency, thus attempting to play a neutral role by balancing between school officials and civil rights groups.

The frantic effort of summer 1965 was a major achievement. Almost all southern districts promised to implement plans that would have been seen as completely intolerable a year earlier. A major psychological break-through had been achieved. Under a good deal of political pressure, the Administration held firm, and integration in the South had increased by more than 100 per cent.

In important ways, however, the initial effort was a failure. Many of the apparently impressive plans proved to be nothing but "paper compliance." Local officials commonly abused the spirit of the freedom-of-choice plan. By the end of 1965 it was obvious that the original guidelines would never be able to eliminate the dual school system.

With the broad issue of the program's constituency settled, the policy debates on the revision of the guidelines revolved about a new divergence of perspectives. In drafting the first guidelines, those officials in the Office of Education and the Justice Department who favored a neutral but firm pattern had looked to the courts and had used carefully prepared summaries of prevailing judicial opinion as a direct source of administrative standards. Although the development of case law was an important source of the revised guidelines, a year of administrative experience made the enforcement professionals of the Office of Education sensitive to the need to translate the general tendency of the legal development into the clear and highly specific bureaucratic standards very difficult to evade and easy to monitor in Washington through simple reports.

The demands of effective administration ran amuck on the shoals of the legalistic outlook of the Justice Department and the broader political realities setting the context for decision-making. On the issues of faculty integration and performance standards, the Equal Educational Opportunities Program called for precise and explicit numerical minimums, only to encounter the lawyerly objection that this was not strictly within the case law, and the practical objection that the standards would be widely seen as intolerable in the South. A compromise was reached on each issue by lowering the minimum to what was felt to be politically possible and by drafting the requirements in a vague and flexible manner easily defendable in the courts. In spite of the concessions, however, the enforcement program had won a major victory, turning what had begun as an outline for negotiations into an instrument demanding performance. No longer would conformity with procedural technicalities justify the maintenance of totally segregated schools and faculties.

The new guidelines were to provide a charter for a second summer of change across the South. When the second September under the guidelines arrived, classrooms in the states of the old Confederacy revealed that the new authority written into the revised guidelines had been sufficient to continue at an accelerated pace the revolution set in motion in 1965. The barrier of total faculty integration fell in the great majority of districts, and student integration increased from 6 per cent to 16 per cent in the 11 states where less than one Negro child in 100 had attended an integrated school when the Civil Rights Act was passed. A long step had been taken toward the destruction of the separate school systems of the South, but a longer, steeper road remained.

4

Chicago: Failure in the North

Overwhelmed by the task of negotiating desegregation plans across the South, the Office of Education staff had very little time to examine possible applications of Title VI in the North. With limited resources, Federal authorities moved strongly against southern districts that were clearly defying the Constitution, postponing consideration of the far more complex problems of the great urban school systems of the North and West.

Segregated education, however, was by no means an exclusively southern problem. The great streams of black migration meant that the educational problems born in the segregated rural schools of Alabama, Mississippi, and Louisiana festered in the segregated ghetto schools of Detroit, Chicago, and Los Angeles. As direct action protests spread from southern lunch counters into the streets of northern cities, inferior black schools became a leading target. After a 1961 Federal court decision holding racial gerrymandering of school boundaries unconstitutional, both the national NAACP and a variety of local civil rights groups took school boards to the courts and challenged school policies in boycotts and demonstrations. Frustrated at the local level, some of these organizations were hopeful that Federal intervention could break local resistance. By late August 1965 the Office of Education had received complaints from 15 northern communities alleging discrimination.[1]

Although mounting evidence indicated that the impact on educational opportunity of de facto segregation was much the same as southern school segregation, the questions posed by the northern complaints were quite different both in legal and political terms from decisions on southern enforcement. Although a number of state superintendents and local school boards were publicly committed to furthering integration, there

[1] Equal Educational Opportunities Program, "Northern school systems requiring investigation or compliance review to determine compliance with Title VI," September 16, 1965.

was very little support either in the decisions of Federal courts or in public opinion for changes in the existing pattern of neighborhood school operation. Only one state—Massachusetts—had authorized official sanctions against segregated neighborhood schools.[2] Prevailing judicial doctrine held that segregation produced by a neutral application of the neighborhood school policy violated no constitutionally protected right of a Negro student.[3] Civil rights groups were pressing the Office of Education to resolve an issue the Federal courts had barely begun to define.

THE PROBLEM IN CHICAGO

The most serious complaint came from Chicago. On July 4, 1965 the Chicago civil rights confederation submitted to Commissioner Keppel a lengthy and thoroughly documented indictment of the school board's racial policies. The complaint was particularly serious because the civil rights organization alleged that not only were the schools overwhelmingly segregated, but that the segregation resulted from intentional racially motivated decisions by the school board. In the most carefully prepared complaint received in Washington, it was claimed that local authorities had clearly violated the Constitution by maintaining segregated vocational schools and working with the Chicago Real Estate Board and public housing authorities to establish segregated schools. More than 90 per cent of Chicago Negro students were enrolled in segregated schools that were systematically inferior to white schools in such vital matters as class size, teacher qualifications, supplementary facilities, and curriculum offerings.[4] Unless Federal action broke this pattern, the complaint warned, the Chicago approach might well "become the handbook for Southern communities seeking to evade the 1954 Supreme Court ruling." [5]

The Chicago complaint forcefully posed questions of the first magnitude for the Office of Education. The document set in motion a chain of events that resulted in the most disastrous failure of the enforcement program, a failure that deeply affected the future development of the entire effort. For five days in October 1965 the Commissioner of Educa-

2 Advisory Committee on Racial Imbalance and Education, *Because it is Right— Educationally* (Boston: Massachusetts State Board of Education, 1965); Mass. Gen. Laws, ch. 15, sec. 1-I (August 18, 1965).
3 *Bell v. School City of Gary, Indiana*, 7 Cir., 324 F. 2d 209 (1963), cert. denied, 377 U.S. 924 (1964).
4 Complaint of the Coordinating Council of Community Organizations (CCCO), July 4, 1965, reprinted in *Integrated Education*, III (December, 1965–January, 1966), 11–12, 15–16.
5 *Ibid.*, p. 19.

tion delayed approval of the payment of $32 million in aid funds to the Chicago public schools, informing state and city educational officials that the system was in "probable noncompliance" with the Civil Rights Act. The action was hailed by elated local Negro leaders as a decisive step toward resolution of the long battle over segregation in the city's schools. When the Office of Education reversed itself under heavy attacks from Chicago officials, however, the possible value of Title VI as a tool against northern segregation was greatly diminished.

The Chicago incident was of profound importance to the development of national policy on an issue central to the Negro leadership in major northern cities. Failure in Chicago foreclosed the possibility of using Title VI as a tool against de facto segregation permitted by Federal courts and very seriously limited Office of Education willingness to investigate even charges of intentional official segregation in the North. The enforcement effort made serious enemies for the Title VI program in Congress, and the Administration imposed new limitations on the exercise of the authority to defer Federal funds.

On a broader scale, the outcome encouraged those who believed that enforcement of the school desegregation guidelines could be defeated by political resistance. After Chicago, the entire enforcement machinery came to a temporary halt, and many thought that the program would not survive. The confrontation seriously weakened the position of Commissioner Keppel and Assistant Secretary Quigley, and both men resigned within months. The incident revealed fundamental weaknesses in the compliance program, and it made the entire government sensitive to the political significance of Title VI. When active enforcement resumed, the leadership, policy limitations, and procedures of the program had been reshaped to meet these chronic deficiencies.

Federal officials were well aware that the Chicago complaint threatened to involve them in one of the best-known and most explosive struggles over school segregation in the country. For almost a decade the issue of school segregation had dominated the Chicago civil rights movement, and the issue had reached a climax of very great intensity in the summer of 1965. It was an issue with many meanings. It represented the frustration of the middle-class Negro parent finally able to buy a home on the far South Side only to find that he cannot enroll his child in a school with qualified teachers and with a curriculum that would prepare him for college work. The bitterness of the fight could be seen in the determination of 200 demonstrators snarling traffic at Chicago's busiest intersection. The divisiveness of the issue was reflected in acrimonious school board debates between factions opposing and supporting the General Superintendent of Schools. A tangled series of lawsuits cluttered the Chicago courts, and the dispute generated battles by small neighborhood groups physically attempting to block installation of mobile classrooms used to reinforce segregation in ghetto schools. In the summer of 1965, the conflict gave rise to a procession of 10,000 demanding action from Richard J. Daley, the nation's most powerful mayor. In its broadest terms the Office of Education was invited to step into the middle of a conflict between those speaking for 1,000,000 black people desperately in need of education and those representing the white millions, desperately afraid that the entrance of black students in their schools would mean the loss of their homes and neighborhood to the inexorably expanding Negro ghetto.

Segregation and Protest in Chicago

The struggle over school segregation in Chicago arose from gradually spreading knowledge of the facts that the city's schools were overwhelmingly segregated and that Negro students attended schools that were sharply inferior in a number of measurable ways. The problem had become critical in the mid-1950's because Chicago was absorbing the most massive tide of black migration in its history. Before World War II, fewer than one-ninth of the public school pupils were Negroes, but already the large majority of crowded ghetto schools were operating on a double-shift basis, with 76 per cent of the Negro students spending less time in school than the city's white pupils.[6] Chicago's wartime demand for labor resulted in an increase of two-thirds in Negro enrollment between 1940 and 1950, while a low white birthrate and a massive suburban migration produced a decline of almost 100,000 in white enrollment. During the next decade, one-third of a million Negroes moved into the city's South and West Sides, and almost 40 per cent of the public school students were Negroes.[7] With the black population confined by housing discrimination to slowly expanding ghetto areas, and with the school system showing slight interest in bringing Negro students into predominantly white schools with empty classrooms, the existing school facilities in Negro neighborhoods were overwhelmed.

Protest against school crowding began before World War II, when school reform groups and the Federation of Colored Women's Clubs unsuccessfully appealed for changes, and the school superintendent was publicly attacked for cooperating with the Chicago Real Estate Board in maintaining segregated schools.[8] After a 1944 National Education Associ-

[6] Robert J. Havighurst, *The Public Schools of Chicago* (Chicago: Chicago Board of Education, 1964), p. 54; Harold Baron, "History of Chicago School Segregation to 1953," *Learning Together*, Meyer Weinberg, ed. (Chicago: Integrated Education Associates, 1964), pp. 14–18.

[7] Havighurst, p. 54.   [8] Baron, p. 16.

ation investigation exposed the existence of a "political machine inside the school system," systematically intimidating teachers and administrators and engaging in a variety of unethical practices, and after the Chicago schools were threatened with loss of accreditation, a brief era of reform became possible.[9] From 1947 to 1953, the school system was run by a superintendent responsive to some Negro needs, and some primary school boundaries were altered to help relieve overcrowding.[10] This effort came to an end, however, with the 1953 appointment of Superintendent Benjamin C. Willis, who strongly believed that the business of the schools was education, not social reform.

The year after Willis' arrival, the 1954 Supreme Court decision generated a great burst of interest in civil rights in Chicago, interest that was to focus on school segregation. After the decision, Chicagoans poured into the local NAACP branch, increasing its membership from 4000 to 18,500 by 1958. What had once been merely a fund-raising mechanism for the national organization now became an active local group with a program of its own.[11] The branch's education committee soon began to receive complaints from Negro parents alleging that their children were a year or two behind children in white schools and observing that the best teachers left local schools as new neighborhoods underwent racial change.

In the mid-1950's the NAACP committee began to appear at annual school board budget hearing While studying the budget, one leader recalled, "it gradually dawned on us that they were cheating the Negro children in obvious ways." [12] In 1957, the NAACP attracted national attention with its report, "De Facto Segregation in the Chicago Schools." The group's protests were stilled, however, when the city's political machine bought enough memberships to defeat the militant candidate for leadership of the Chicago branch.

In 1961 a new legal situation, the emergence of a new local villain, and the general national energization of the civil rights movement after the sit-ins began, combined to raise the issue of school segregation to new levels of intensity. A Federal court decision forcing the New Rochelle, New York, school board to eliminate racially motivated school district boundaries rapidly led to the filing of a lawsuit against the Chicago Board of

[9] National Education Association, National Commission for the Defense of Democracy through Education, *Certain Personnel Practices in the Chicago Public Schools* (Washington: National Education Association, 1945), pp. 5, 15, 40–41; Joseph Pois, *The School Board Crisis, A Chicago Case Study* (Chicago: Aldine Publishing Co., 1964), pp. 11–15.
[10] Baron, pp. 16–17.
[11] James Q. Wilson, *Negro Politics* (Glencoe, Ill.: The Free Press, 1960), p. 282.
[12] Interview with Faith Rich, June 30, 1966.

Education. When Superintendent Willis refused to provide a community group with information on empty classrooms adjoining a West Side ghetto neighborhood with 15,000 students on double shifts, a researcher found data in old school directories indicating that the extra students could easily be housed in nearby white schools. Willis' adamant opposition to PTA and Urban League demands that this space be used made him a primary symbol of opposition for the city's civil rights groups. The battle was taken up by the new CORE chapter and by the *Chicago Defender*, the city's Negro newspaper. The national NAACP office filed a lawsuit demanding use of the empty rooms. The Negro-American Labor Council protested against segregated trade schools, and several community groups called for passage of a resolution favoring integration by the school board.[13]

One of the early civil rights efforts involved a futile attempt to bring Federal pressure to bear on the local school board through litigation in the Federal courts. Lacking the financial and organizational resources necessary to support the enormously complex effort to prove that local school segregation was, at least in part, the intended result of school board decisions rather than merely an accidental by-product of residential segregation, this effort collapsed. The complexity of the case, one law professor suggests, would be on the scale of an antitrust suit against General Motors.[14]

The first Federal intervention came in 1962 with the publication of a report on the Chicago schools prepared for the U.S. Civil Rights Commission. The report described the negative attitude of the school administration, comparing Chicago unfavorably with other systems:

> Refusal to face the issue of underutilized classrooms squarely created an impression of obstructionism that was resented in the Negro community. . . . The appearance of the mobile units at the height of the empty classroom controversy further inflamed the indignation of the Negro parents. . . .
>
> At the time Chicago contracted to purchase mobile units, Cleveland, St. Louis, and New York already had experience transporting substantial numbers of children from overcrowded to underutilized schools. Similar transportation in Chicago might have obviated the need for the purchase of many of the mobile units.[15]

[13] *Webb v. The Board of Education of the City of Chicago*, Civ. No. 61C1569 D.C., N.D., Ill. This suit was initially filed in 1961, after the *New Rochelle* decision, and it alleged deliberate segregation of students by Chicago school authorities; *Burroughs v. The Board of Education*, Civ. No. 62C206, D.C., N.D. Ill, filed January 19, 1962. This NAACP suit alleged overcrowding of a Negro school adjacent to an underutilized white school and requested redrawing of district boundaries; Rich interview.
[14] Interview with John E. Coons, June 24, 1966.
[15] John E. Coons, "Chicago," *Civil Rights U.S.A.: Public Schools in the North and West*, a report to the U.S. Commission on Civil Rights (Washington: Government Printing Office, 1962), p. 232.

Chicago's policy, the author concluded, seriously violated the rights of Negro students. "From the point of view of racial discrimination or merely that of nonracial equal protection," the report stated, "the confinement of pupils in crowded classes when other facilities are underutilized cannot be justified." [16]

The Civil Rights Commission report was one of a series of increasingly detailed and authoritative studies that stimulated further protests. The powerful Chicago Urban League began issuance of a series of research reports on the school situation. In 1963 the federation of local civil rights groups, the Coordinating Council of Community Organizations, issued the *Handbook of Chicago School Segregation,* which accused the school board of "freezing" school boundaries along the borders of the ghetto and locating mobile classrooms and new school buildings in a manner designed to "continue segregation patterns." Superintendent Willis, the report charged, had never accepted the basic philosophy of the 1954 Supreme Court decision and had even extended the prevailing pattern of segregation into a summer school program previously permitting open enrollment.[17] These findings led the CCCO to present a series of demands to the school board. When the board failed to take action, the organization went to the streets, sponsoring a successful citywide school boycott.

The lawsuit against the school board did have one favorable result. In order to temporarily end the litigation, the board agreed to sponsor a study of racial integration in the schools and to take appropriate action on the resulting report. In 1964 both this Advisory Panel on Integration and the experts directing a general survey of the public schools issued major reports that carefully documented the problems of Negro students in the city's schools. The Advisory Panel found that more than 40 per cent of Chicago's students were Negroes, but that less than one school in 10 had any significant integration. Eighty-four per cent of the Negro students attended segregated schools, and the new upper-grade centers established by Superintendent Willis were 97 per cent segregated.[18]

Claims of serious inequalities were documented by the study. Proportionately, three times as many black schools were overcrowded, and six times as many white schools had empty space. Negro areas where educational deprivation was most severe were found to have eight times more uncertified teachers than similar white areas.[19]

[16] *Ibid.*
[17] Coordinating Council of Community Organizations, *Handbook of Chicago School Segregation* (Chicago: CCCO, 1963), pp. 3, 8.
[18] Chicago Board of Education, Advisory Panel on Integration of the Public Schools, *Report* (Chicago: Chicago Board of Education, 1964), pp. 6, 14–15. A segregated school is defined as one containing less than 10 per cent students of another race.
[19] *Ibid.*, pp. 17–19.

Although the panel was able to obtain information from the school administration only by agreeing to ignore the issue of intentional segregation by the school board in the past, the civil rights groups' claims about racial gerrymandering received some support. School boundaries, the panel found, generally coincided with stable racial boundaries. The researchers, however, conceded that there were frequently reasons of student safety for using these lines—often major streets or elevated railroads. On other issues the superintendent's failure to achieve integration was more obvious. Ninety-four per cent of all schools built in the city after 1955 were segregated in the fall of 1963. Among the controversial "Willis wagon" mobile classrooms 145 out of 189 had been allotted to all-Negro schools rather than to schools where they would strengthen integration.[20]

Chicago's neighborhood school system, the researchers concluded, retarded "the acculturation and integration" of Negro migrants to the city. "Regardless of intent, the existing policies and administrative decisions by which the neighborhood school is organized in Chicago contribute to maintaining segregated schools. . . ."[21] Only strong action to support existing integration would reverse the rapid exodus of whites to the suburbs. To deal with legitimate Negro grievances, the report recommended that students be permitted to freely transfer within groupings composed of several adjacent schools and that citywide open enrollment for trade schools be established. Any student in an overcrowded classroom, the panel stated, should be authorized to transfer to an empty seat in any underused school. The panel of specialists also called for redistricting and redistribution of teachers within the system.[22]

The document was well received. The conservative *Tribune* commented that the report would "help Chicagoans . . . understand the complexity of this problem." The cautious *American* supported the proposal to cluster neighborhood schools. The editorial in the moderate *Daily News* concluded that the study "should end once and for all the semantical argument as to whether Chicago's schools are segregated." There was, the paper said, a "moral obligation to attempt remedy."[23] The school board hastened to add its endorsement, adopting the report "in general principle" within nine days of its issuance.[24] It seemed as if the panel's carefully drafted proposals to correct the most blatant abuses would indeed be implemented. As years passed without any serious effort to fulfill the school board's pledge, there was growing anger in the Negro community.

[20] *Ibid.*, pp. 62–63. [21] *Ibid.*, p. 25. [22] *Ibid.*, pp. 12, 27–34.
[23] *Chicago Tribune*, April 2, 1964; *Chicago's American*, April 2, 1964; *Chicago Sun-Times*, April 2, 1964; *Chicago Daily News*, April 1, 1964.
[24] Interview with Philip M. Hauser, July 6, 1966.

Conviction that action was urgently needed was reinforced by the findings of a comprehensive analysis of the Chicago schools sponsored by the board of education, prepared by 30 nationally recognized experts, and presented to the school board at the end of 1964. The Havighurst survey put a high priority on special assistance to the sections of the city "that most desire integration, and where there is a good chance of stabilizing an integrated community." Havighurst recommended that high schools be grouped in "clusters" providing service for "an extended neighborhood," and called for creation of three experimental high schools with stabilized integration. The city also needed a network of experimental elementary schools with stable racial quotas along the edges of the ghetto.[25]

Although the racial problem was very serious, Havighurst concluded that an even more fundamental need was for a $30 million to $60 million increase in the annual school budget. "This money," he wrote, "must be spent mainly on new things—new ways of teaching, new ways of using the time of teachers and other people working in the school system." [26] Within months of the report, the 1965 Elementary and Secondary Education Act became law, making $32 million in aid available for the Chicago schools for the very purposes noted in the report. The failure of the school board and the superintendent to begin implementation of the de-segregation recommendations of the two reports and the fear that the Federal money would be misused to reinforce segregation, however, led to a major conflict over Federal authority to use these funds as a lever to force local recognition of Negro rights.

Chicago Politics and School Segregation

If the facts of school segregation revealed a particularly serious racial problem in Chicago, the facts of Chicago politics made the issue a peculiarly explosive one. Although Federal officials were to become well aware of the issue of Negro rights in the Chicago schools, their insensitivity to the realities of the political strength of the nation's most powerful Democratic machine led them to make disastrous misjudgments.

Chicago had absorbed wave after wave of migration, with each successive group fighting for jobs, struggling to establish their own neighborhoods, and battling for recognition and power in the political machine that ran the city and disposed of vast resources of patronage in each of the 50 wards. The economic boom beginning in World War II, which made Chicago the most prosperous metropolitan area in the world, had very rapidly created a black community whose growth was "of unprecedented magnitude and speed for any one ethnic or racial group in the history of the city." [27] The dimensions of the social and political prob-

[25] Havighurst, pp. 379–80; *Chicago Daily News,* October 8, 1966.
[26] Havighurst, p. 355.   [27] *Ibid.*

lems involved are obvious when one realizes that the *increase* in Chicago's
Negro population since 1940 equaled the total population of San Francisco. The impact of this change was heightened by the net loss of
400,000 whites, equal to the entire population of Newark, New Jersey.[28]

Traditionally, Chicago political machines had incorporated new groups
by delivering patronage through the leadership structure that emerged in
ward-level political battles. Thus Democratic power in the city rested on
a coalition of ward organizations that reached their greatest strength in
Negro areas and in neighborhoods with large concentrations of second-
generation immigrants still near the bottom of the socio-economic ladder,
communities where patronage and welfare services made a great deal of
difference. As the civil rights impulse reached into Chicago in the sixties,
the central question of Chicago politics was whether the Democratic
organization could hold this coalition together or whether the bitter
Negro struggle with working class whites for housing and equal access to
the schools would shatter the Democratic base of power.

By the mid-1960's school segregation was the most potent political issue
in the city, and Superintendent Willis' arrogant rejection of civil rights
demands had made him the leading hero of those who were passionately
committed to the homogeneous neighborhood school and who believed
that stable integration was impossible.

The professional outlook of Superintendent Willis made an extremely
serious clash inevitable. In a situation in which decisions in educational
administration would inevitably have a profound impact on the future of
the city's politics and race relations, Willis clung to the ideal of the
superintendency as a professional management function in which the
primary objective was the most efficient possible operation of a gigantic
collection of educational factories. Willis was a perfect product of the
ideology of school administration that had taken root in the training of
administrators in the early 1900's, an ideology based on the mechanical
application of business methods to school systems in a profession that had
remarkably little concern with the social implications of the educational
process.[29] In fact, a researcher studying professional magazines for school
superintendents in the early 1960's found that it was evident that the
central professional issue was, "Which floor wax is longest lasting and
most economical?" [30] Given this situation, most northern superintendents
were notably insensitive to the educational significance of integration,

---

28 *Ibid.*, p. 24.
29 Raymond E. Callahan, *Education and the Cult of Efficiency* (Chicago: University
of Chicago Press, 1962).
30 Comment quoted in Gerald Grant, "Schools Need a Tough Man with Vision,"
Washington Post, July 9, 1967.

and very few took forceful initiatives in this sensitive and "unprofessional" area.[31] Willis simply represented an extreme of this general tendency, insisting that all school decisions could only properly be made by professionals and that any community pressure was wholly illegitimate.

During the first eight years of his tenure Willis had gained national recognition for his efficient and hard-driving effort to eliminate the serious double-shift problem in Chicago schools. Defining this as his central task, Willis put his immense energy into the campaign to pass the needed bond issues and to drive down the costs of school construction. In the 1950's it was a matter of little concern that most of the new schools were constructd well within the Negro ghettos, thus reinforcing the pattern of segregated education. "Big Ben the Builder" was hailed for his tireless work and his intimate involvement in every detail of the building process. In 1960, President-elect Kennedy named Willis as one of a handful of members on his education task force. Indeed, when Willis took office in 1961 as President of the American Association of School Administrators, Harvard Dean of Education, Francis Keppel, testified: "The word 'Willis' means precisely an administrative cyclone." [32] Keppel's sensitivity to the demands of the Negro revolution and Willis' arrogant refusal to recognize any possible legitimacy of these demands were to bring the two men to a bitter clash in the fall of 1965.

Although Chicago's school board is formally isolated from politics through a process of nomination of candidates for board positions by a prestigous committee of civic group leaders, the selection process carefully reflects politically significant groups in the community, and it has been possible for the mayor to obtain a nomination for someone he particularly wishes to have on the board.[33] The three great religious groupings are carefully represented, and seats are informally allotted to the craft unions, the industrial unions, Negroes, State Street business interests, real estate organizations, etc. Until the emergence of the segregation issue the board had divided seriously only on issues of employee rights and pay questions of great importance to the union representatives.[34] Community feelings about the explosive school integration question

[31] Meyer Weinberg, "School Integration in American History," *Learning Together*, p. 10.

[32] *Chicago Sun-Times*, May 29, 1966.

[33] When the Advisory Commission refused to nominate two conservative incumbents for new terms in 1968, Mayor Daley broke his pledge to choose from among the commission's nominees and reappointed both men, commenting that a new approach was needed. (*Chicago Tribune*, May 17, 1968 and May 23, 1968.)

[34] Chicago Board of Education, "Proceedings," December 14, 1960, pp. 790–870; March 22, 1961, p. 1913; April 12, 1961, p. 1916 (in the files of the Board of Education library).

polarized the board into three distinct segments, immobilizing the board as an effective decision-making instrument. Confronted by this situation, Superintendent Willis took the initiative and generally succeeded in dominating the undecided members, drawing when necessary on his fast-growing political support in the white community.

Confronting racial crises, Willis often seemed to be using professional ideology to further the racial attitudes developed during the first 25 years of his career, when he served as a principal and county superintendent in rural Maryland. The racial attitudes common in Henderson or Federalsburg, Maryland, a generation earlier could hardly have been less appropriate.

Willis' political power and his importance as a symbol for Negro protest became evident in the summer of 1963. The Birmingham crisis of that year had brought Chicago's civil rights groups together in a loose confederation (CCCO) and had stirred protests against school discrimination in many neighborhoods. After a series of explosive demonstrations, the school board approved a limited transfer program for highly qualified Negro students. When white parents complained, Willis simply refused to execute the school board's orders. After he ignored a second school board directive, Negro parents sued him and gained a court order directing him to implement the plan. Willis escaped down the back steps of the Board of Education building to avoid a summons. Finally, after losing an appeal, Willis announced his resignation. After protests began to pour in from some white neighborhoods, the school board reversed itself. The very limited transfer plan was rescinded, talented black students were again confined to segregated schools with inadequate curricula, and the board rejected the superintendent's resignation 7 to 1. One week later the great majority of Negro students boycotted the Chicago schools.[35]

Willis saw the 1963 victory as another triumph in his struggle to keep the school board out of his realm of "administration" and thus to prevent violation of his "principles and sense of professional integrity."[36] In reality, of course, the conflict made abundantly clear the impotence of a weak and divided school board attempting to control a very forceful executive with a strong political following in the city.

As "Bull" Connor symbolized the segregationists of Birmingham and provided a focus for protest, so Willis became the personal embodiment of resistance to integration in Chicago. Willis deeply resented intrusion

[35] On October 22, 1963, 224,000 of the school system's 469,000 students observed the call for a "Freedom Day," and a mass rally was held at city hall. The day after the boycott, Superintendent Willis released the racial inventory of Chicago schools, which had been demanded for years. (*Chicago Daily News*, February 22, 1964.)
[36] *Ibid.*, February 2, 1964.

on his work from any direction and treated Negro leaders as hopelessly uninformed intruders. Absolutely refusing to provide information on questions raised by community groups, Willis was prepared to put his career on the line and generate a political crisis of the first magnitude in Chicago before implementing a desegregation effort he felt was unsound. Perhaps even more than his actions, the superintendent's attitude created profound antagonism in the Negro community.

The 1965 Crisis

Neither school boycotts, scholarly recommendations, endless demonstrations, tangled lawsuits, nor the bickering of school board factions prevented a steady increase of segregation in the Chicago schools. The racial crisis reached its height in the summer of 1965, shortly before the Office of Education launched its investigation of complaints from the CCCO.

Superintendent Willis' term of office was due to end in spring 1965. As the time for board action on filling the post for the next four years approached, there was broad recognition that racial harmony required the retirement of the 63-year-old superintendent.[37] "Increasingly," said a *Daily News* editorial, "issues between the schools and the community have come to turn on the personality of Benjamin C. Willis." The *Sun-Times* stated:

> Willis has managed to alienate virtually the entire Negro community of Chicago, mostly because of his failure to unbend and listen to its grievances. . . .
> It's time the board began to assert itself and it should begin by facing up to the obvious fact . . . that "the present strife-filled situation is intolerable." It will remain strife-filled as long as Willis remains.

As the deadline approached, it seemed certain that Willis would be retired. Two weeks before the final vote, the board was divided 7 to 4 against Willis. Some 125 professors from Chicago-area colleges had made public an open letter stating that "it should be clear to every perceptive observer that *no* attempted solution can work unless the present general superintendent of schools is replaced." [38] At the last minute, however, the fear of a violent white reaction again prevailed, and the board agreed to what it hoped was a politically acceptable "compromise," giving Willis a new contract, with the unwritten understanding that he would retire at 65, a year and a half in the future.[39] The decision came as a crushing

[37] Pois, p. 110.
[38] *Chicago Sun-Times*, May 2, 1965; *Chicago Daily News*, December 16, 1965; "Professors Open Letter," press release, April 27, 1965. (Mimeographed.)
[39] Interview with Warren Bacon, July 22, 1966.

blow to civil rights leaders, who felt that Willis would doubtless find a
way to force the board to allow him to serve the full four years. The
decision ignited the largest and most sustained protest effort ever
mounted by the Chicago civil rights movement.

The Turn Toward Washington

The very day Willis was rehired, the seeds of Federal intervention
were planted. Having failed on the local level, civil rights leaders invoked
the guarantees of Federal law in an attempt to change the local balance of
power. When the news of the board's action came to a gathering of
CCCO activists that evening, many felt that years of effort had resulted in
utter failure. Meyer Weinberg, editor of *Integrated Education* and chairman of the CCCO education committee, suggested to the group that
success in the cities could come only "by making this a national issue,
involving the Federal government." Although CCCO leaders were generally highly skeptical of legalistic approaches, the failure of direct action
on the local level now made this seem like a "great idea." Weinberg was
told to go ahead. Thus began the germination of the complaint that
triggered Federal action.[40]

The same night, in another part of town, the NAACP executive board
was reaching decisions that were to greatly heighten the national visibility
of the local confrontation. In a startling departure from form, the conservative organization reflected the depth of Negro anger by calling for a
five-day school boycott, a far more drastic step than the earlier one-day
protests. The decision galvanized the local civil rights movement. In spite
of strong opposition from the news media, city and state officials, and the
Negro leaders in the Democratic machine, and in spite of injunctions
issued against the NAACP and other groups, 60,000 students stayed home
from school. The CCCO set in motion a summer-long protest against
Willis with evening vigils at the school board headquarters and marches
on city hall. In early June the police took into custody a group conducting a vigil, the first of hundreds of arrests during the summer. During the
first week, almost 450 people were arrested for blocking traffic on the
city's busiest streets.

The call for Federal action was a recurring theme. In late June, 18 local
civil rights leaders wired Attorney General Katzenbach, asking him to
investigate de facto school segregation in the city. Congressman Adam
Clayton Powell brought another element of Federal pressure to bear when
he announced plans to bring his House Education and Labor Committee
to Chicago for hearings. Powell, who now had the former editor of the

---

[40] Interview with Meyer Weinberg, June 27, 1966.

Chicago Defender on his staff, was convinced that it would be possible to document intentional segregation. He called for withholding Federal aid until the school board complied with Title VI of the Civil Rights Act.[41]

Racial polarization grew rapidly. The citizens committee set up to implement the recommendations of the Advisory Panel on Integration fell apart when several leading members resigned. The influential Citizens Schools Committee and other groups called for appointment of a new superintendent. The school board made no response whatever to a series of demands from the normally conservative business leaders of the Negro community. The white reaction was suggested in a nighttime motorcade through the loop in support of Willis. Strident statements came from both sides. The CCCO leadership promised that marches would continue until Willis was removed. Mayor Daley, who had now been drawn into the battle, falsely charged that Communists were dominating the anti-Willis marches.[42] On July 4 the CCCO complaint was sent to Commissioner Keppel.

Federal authorities were unprepared to deal with the Chicago complaint. No basic policy on northern segregation had been worked out in the Office of Education. Commissioner Keppel announced that his staff would study the complaint. Two days later he reported that the document had been turned over to Assistant Secretary Quigley. Quigley, responsible for department-wide coordination of civil rights enforcement, did not press the issue on Secretary Celebrezze, knowing that the outgoing secretary "hated controversy." Celebrezze, a former mayor of Cleveland, understood the political implications of the school issue in big city racial politics and had no eagerness to involve the department in the battle.[43] Until Secretary Gardner took office the issue was buried in the bureaucracy, and no action was taken.

Although the Office of Education stalled, Representative Powell carried out his threat to hold hearings in late July, re-emphasizing the potential Federal interest in the city's controversy. During the hearings, there was a significant passage on the subject of fund withholding in a discussion between the University of Chicago professor who had headed the school board's Advisory Panel on Integration and Adam Clayton Powell:

PROFESSOR HAUSER: I think if we can't muster enough local intelligence and morality, the Congress . . . and the administrators in the Federal Government ought to do the thing which has always worked—no program, no money.

---

[41] Chicago Urban League, chronology, summer, 1965 (in the files of the Urban League research department); Weinberg interview.
[42] Urban League chronology.   [43] Quigley interview.

CHAIRMAN POWELL: That was my policy in 1954, which is now the law of the land.
. . . I offered this amendment in 1954 on the suggestion of Thurgood Marshall.
. . . And that law applies not to the South, but to the 50 States of this Union—
that where there is segregation, Federal funds shall be withheld.

It is my purpose, personally, to pursue this as far as I can, and I think this is a
weapon that we can use in New York, Chicago, Los Angeles, and everywhere.[44]

As far as the possibility of voluntary local action, Professor Hauser
stated, the prevailing school board attitude could be best summarized by
the comment of a leading member who had recently told a television
audience that "Chicago is not yet ready for more integration." [45]

The CCCO testimony before the hearing greatly strengthened the case
for Federal action. Attempting to move from the unsettled legal issues of
de facto segregation to prove the existence of clearly unconstitutional
intentional segregation, the CCCO witnesses presented specific cases of
gerrymandering. The group concluded that only intentional racial discrimination could explain, for example, the situation of the all-white
Riverdale school. Although the school was a mere five blocks from a
Negro high school, its graduates had been assigned to a white high school
three miles away for as long as 20 years. The Riverdale school also maintained a class size half that prevailing in four neighboring Negro schools.[46]
The testimony went on to cite 21 other cases of probable gerrymandering. After the hearing this new information was submitted to Commissioner Keppel as a supplement to the original complaint.

While inaction continued in Washington, the stakes in Chicago continued to mount. Civil rights leaders proclaimed that the city had become
the "race relations arena of the country." [47] Gaining national attention
with a massive march on city hall, Martin Luther King was moving
toward his first major northern effort. In mid-July, some of the city's
business leaders issued a demand for effective integration in the Chicago
schools. "The demonstrations and arrests and the prospect of even greater
demonstrations," wrote one observer, "are believed to have inspired
major misgivings in the business community over Mayor Daley's management of the school crisis." [48] Willis' complete intractability succeeded in
uniting virtually the entire, incredibly diverse, spectrum of black leadership in a common anger. Al Raby, leader of the CCCO, underlined the

---

[44] U.S., Congress, House, Committee on Education and Labor, Ad Hoc Subcommittee
on the War on Poverty Program, *Hearings, De Facto School Segregation,* 89th Cong.,
1st Sess., 1965, p. 114.
[45] *Ibid.,* p. 102.
[46] CCCO complaint to the Office of Education, July 27, 1965, reprinted in *Integrated
Education,* Vol. III (December 1965–January 1966), 25–26.
[47] *New York Times,* July 12, 1965.   [48] *Ibid.*

national implications of the contest: "If we are successful here we believe every city in the North will then move to end de facto . . . segregation, and the South, which is ending de jure . . . segregation, will not move to re-establish de facto segregation." [49]

THE RESPONSE OF THE OFFICE OF EDUCATION

The Administrative Problem

The great issues of policy and procedure posed by the Chicago complaint and the turbulent protests in the Chicago streets confronted an agency ill-prepared to cope with them. As serious study of the complaint began, the Title VI staff was still involved in the round-the-clock push to negotiate desegregation plans with the last several hundred school districts, and the Office of Education was in the midst of chaotic preparation for the administration of the 1965 Elementary and Secondary Education Act, the first general aid-to-education measure in American history. The question of responsibility for investigations was still completely confused between Assistant Secretary Quigley's office and the Equal Educational Opportunities Program in the Office of Education. Secretary Gardner was in his very first weeks of service in a new job. All of these facts were to create difficulties in the effort to deal with the CCCO complaint, and these weaknesses were to be compounded by serious political insensitivity at several crucial stages.

Through creation of the school desegregation guidelines, the Office of Education had been able to transform the problem of dealing with thousands of local crises in the South into a manageable bureaucratic task of applying general administrative standards. In the northern situation there were no such agreed policies, and the guidance provided by the court decisions was of relatively little value. Although there were no bureaucratic standards and the question was one of extreme political sensitivity, Federal bureaucrats several times were to handle new and politically important issues as if they were relatively routine administrative questions.

In considering and trying to understand some of the major mistakes made in Chicago, it may be useful to keep in mind the different nature of decision-making in bureaucracies and in positions of political leadership. In his classic study, *Administrative Behavior*, Herbert Simon argues that, in the nature of things, an administrator operating efficiently must assume that "most of the facts of the real world have no great relevance to any particular situation he is facing. . . . Hence, he is content to leave out of

[49] *Ibid.*

account those aspects of reality . . . that are substantially irrelevant at a given time." [50] The necessity of the process of routinization had become very obvious in the chaotic early months of the Equal Educational Opportunities Program, and the desegregation guidelines constituted an official definition of what facts were relevant for administrative decision-making, a definition that made it possible for Seeley's staff to deal effectively with thousands of districts.

The reduction of an exceedingly complex human situation to a simple bureaucratic formula, necessary as it is, inevitably involves some loss of sensitivity to those aspects of the individual case unrelated to the administrative objective. The task of the administrator is to reduce problems to their essentials and to devise systematic procedures to make the most efficient use of his always limited resources of funds and personnel.

This model of bureaucratic decision-making contrasts strikingly with the ideal type of political leadership sketched by Richard Neustadt in *Presidential Power*. While the administrator's central concern is efficiency, the political leader's must be the protection of his power and authority. The President must not simplify problems or permit others to simplify them for him, but must consider all factors for possible threats to his power or reputation. A misstep can threaten not only public and congressional support for a given program but can even weaken the Administration's position on a variety of other issues. [51]

The differing perspectives of political and administrative leaders put a very heavy burden on those officials within the government who hold positions that bridge the gap between the elected leader responsible to the public and the civil servants. The President must rely heavily on the appointed top officials of the departments and on his White House staff and executive office officials to shape policy in view of the total objectives of his Administration, with sensitivity to the political implications of bureaucratic actions. These officials must search out potentially dangerous issues and bring these decisions to the President. In the case of the Chicago crisis, this machinery broke down very seriously. In a situation involving very large stakes and requiring extraordinary political sensitivity a number of important decisions were made without effective White House contact and without consideration of either alternatives or consequences.

Policy Indecision

At the time the Chicago complaint was received, the Office of Education had no policy on de facto segregation. Northern school districts had

[50] Herbert A. Simon, *Administrative Behavior* (New York: The Free Press, 1965), p. xxv. See also pp. 82–83, 88–112.
[51] Richard E. Neustadt, *Presidential Power* (New York: John Wiley and Sons, 1961).

been required to sign forms assuring the Office that they did not discriminate, but no further action was taken in Washington. Complaints slowly began to arrive from civil rights groups. Assistant Secretary Quigley's office, which had jurisdiction over complaint investigation, listed all complaints received from all sections of the country and directed temporary deferral of action on Federal grants pending investigation of the charges. No investigations were to be launched in the North, however, until Secretary Gardner took an initiative.

During the initial discussions in drafting the HEW regulation and the school guidelines, there had been no consideration of the possibility of action against de facto segregation. Indeed, this problem first arose in the interpretation of Title IV rather than Title VI of the Civil Rights Act. Northern school districts began to request grants from the funds provided by Title IV to assist local communities in the desegregation process. Since Congress had written into the same title a prohibition on Federal action to promote racial "balancing," the Office of Education confronted the problem of whether programs to integrate northern schools would fall under the rubric of "desegregation" or "racial balancing." The HEW legal staff had been unable to decide this question by late 1964.[52] In January 1965 Commissioner Keppel urged the Secretary to approve assistance for northern school districts: "The problem faced by these northern schools with mixed racial attendance areas is identical with most respects to the problems of the desegregated southern schools." [53]

The issue produced a dispute between Justice Department attorneys and the more cautious HEW legal staff. After reviewing the legislative history, the Justice Department finally came to the conclusion that "desegregation" included the northern situation. Justice attorneys informed HEW that "bussing of children was the real issue during the Congressional debates, and that as long as we do nothing to promote bussing we will incur no criticism." The HEW General Counsel, however, argued that "the narrow interpretation of the word 'desegregation,' limiting it to a change from segregation, has considerably the stronger legal basis." [54] After months of indecision, Seeley appealed to Quigley:

> I recognize that the final decision on this matter may well be as much political as it is legal. . . . I don't believe there is any excuse whatever for the Federal Government after all these months still not to know whether this assistance is available in the North. We have gotten sufficiently impatient about the matter that I have told my own staff to operate on the assumption that assistance is available in the North.[55]

[52] Letter from David Seeley to H. Edelsberg, December 10, 1964.
[53] Memorandum from Commissioner Keppel to Secretary Celebrezze, January 4, 1965.
[54] Memorandum from General Counsel Willcox to Secretary Celebrezze, January 5, 1965.
[55] Memorandum from David Seeley to James Quigley, January 26, 1965.

Permission was eventually granted to provide grants for programs designed by northern school systems.

If the issue of minor financial aid to northern school districts was a touchy one, it might be expected that Federal officials would approach the actual possibility of an enforcement action in a major northern city with far greater caution. Actually, the decision to begin serious investigation of northern complaints was made far more easily and carelessly. The decisive influence was the appointment of a new Secretary of HEW, John Gardner.

Gardner, who came to HEW in early August from the presidency of the Carnegie Corporation, brought with him abiding idealism, the strong support of the President, and very little knowledge of American politics. A former college professor who had spent a decade directing a very small staff in the cloistered environment of the nation's fifth largest foundation, he brought to the government a conviction that "for this nation, justice for the Negro is *the* social problem." [56] "The basic American commitment," Gardner wrote, "is not to affluence, not to power, not to all the marvelously cushioned comforts of a well-fed nation, but to the liberation of the human spirit, the release of human potential, the enhancement of individual dignity." [57]

In 1964 Gardner had headed the President's task force responsible for the design of the historic Elementary and Secondary Education Act. A strong mutual commitment to education led to the establishment of a close relationship of mutual esteem with President Johnson. Gardner recalls:

> One of the most exciting moments in my life was the first time I heard the President talk about education. He seemed to expand, as he spoke. He fairly lit up. It was quite a thing for a man in my line of work to realize that this man, this President of the United States, felt what he felt so strongly.[58]

When the President called a White House Conference on Education for July, 1965, Gardner was named chairman. In late July he presided over a session in which major discussions were devoted to such topics as "Extending Educational Opportunities" and "Education in the Urban Community;" this conference heard the New York State commissioner of education condemn racial segregation and call for strong Federal action to mobilize the resources of the nation in an attack on this educational problem.[59]

Very shortly after the conference Gardner was named Secretary of HEW. The Republican foundation officer took the position on the

[56] Article from *Time*, reprinted in *Congressional Record*, January 17, 1967, p. S376.
[57] *Ibid.*, p. S375.   [58] *Newsweek*, February 28, 1966, p. 23.
[59] White House Conference on Education, 1965, printed by the Senate Committee on Labor and Public Welfare, 89th Cong., 1st Sess., 1965, pp. 199–200.

understanding that he would devote his efforts to creating some kind of administrative control over the conglomerate department with responsibility for most of the innovations of the Great Society. "You take care of the department," the President reportedly told him, "and I'll take care of the politics." [60]

When the new Secretary took office in August, one of the first issues presented to him by Assistant Secretary Quigley was the question of beginning formal investigations of civil rights complaints against northern school systems. The rapid approach of the school year meant that Quigley's policy of deferring action on grants until local complaints were investigated would soon begin to seriously pinch a number of northern school systems. Obviously, either investigations would soon have to be launched or the money would have to be released. Confronting these alternatives, the Office of Education favored release of the money, while Quigley's office held firm for investigations.

Keppel and Seeley, sensitive to the volatility and complexity of the northern situation, argued that the system of automatic deferral should be dropped completely, but Keppel failed to persuade Gardner.[61] Quigley, whose primary concern was with racial justice rather than with the programs and constituencies of the department, believed that "the Civil Rights Act applies just as well in Illinois as in Mississippi." "Any other position," he held, "is not only indefensible but it's going to be politically embarrassing." In spite of Keppel's reluctance, Quigley pressed the idea of investigations.[62] Quigley and his assistant argued that the department could not treat northern complaints differently than those from the South. Gardner, Quigley recalls, "seemed to have no trouble in deciding to go ahead." "This was not a politician." [63]

The first serious failure to estimate the political implications of enforcement in the North came at this very early stage, and clearly the responsibility was Secretary Gardner's. In appointing an administrator to do a job that demanded significant political abilities, President Johnson was moving to pull together an ineffectively run department, but he was also running the risk of political missteps. That a step which seemed equitable and educationally sound might result in a political setback jeopardizing the entire enforcement program seemed not to have occurred to the Secretary. Quigley, a former congressman, "sensed the potential for fireworks, but . . . was willing to take the calculated risk." [64] By relying on Quigley's judgment and his own intuition rather than carefully reviewing the nature of the problem and the likely political repercussions,

[60] *Newsweek*, February 28, 1966, p. 30.
[61] Interview with David Seeley, November 21, 1967.
[62] Quigley interview.   [63] *Ibid.*   [64] *Ibid.*

Secretary Gardner seriously endangered the power of the Administration.

Convinced that there would be investigations, Commissioner Keppel proposed a compromise. Keppel accepted Seeley's suggestion that the Office of Education agree to follow Quigley's approach in a few northern cities, for which the enforcement staff already possessed some data. In return Quigley would agree to take the other cities off the automatic deferral list. It happened that those cities for which information was available were Boston, Chester, Pennsylvania, San Francisco, and, most importantly, Chicago.

In agreeing to this compromise, Keppel made a serious error. Relatively little information had been processed by HEW on any city and the only field study had been a brief visit to Boston by a team checking into a complaint submitted by the local CORE chapter. Thus only a relatively weak bureaucratic argument could be made for selecting most of these cities.[65] Overbalancing any possible advantage of efficient procedure was the fact that each of these localities had seen serious and well-known struggles over school segregation, and each had an important faction prepared to attack any Federal action. Accepting the bureaucratic rationale, Keppel apparently passed over without consideration the politically safer route in testing Federal power in one of the relatively unimportant localities complained against, communities such as East St. Louis, Illinois, Bridgeport, Connecticut, and Pasco, Washington. Thus the first group selected for investigation included Chicago, the scene of the nation's most bitter struggle over school segregation, Boston, the city where defense of the neighborhood school had made a pudgy and obscure woman schoolboard member a dominant figure in local politics, and Chester, the bleak Pennsylvania city where a CORE campaign had produced local violence. Rather than testing its power where it was most likely to prevail, the Office of Education had chosen the least favorable circumstances.

The investigations were begun before the Office of Education and HEW had reached any internal decisions about the applicability of Title VI to de facto segregation. Secretary Gardner's announcement clearly reflected the uncertainty. First Gardner boldly stated that if violations were found the local school district "will be required to take prompt and effective remedial action. . . ." Then, however, he conceded that HEW did not know what would be a violation. Admitting that the department's authority was unclear, the Secretary said that the studies by the investigating teams would "determine what can and cannot be done under the

[65] No one in HEW at this time had any understanding of the immense factual documentation which would be necessary to prove discrimination in a major northern school system.

law to meet the problem of unequal educational opportunities in the schools of our cities." [66] Thus the investigators were to be sent out into the midst of boiling local controversies, not with clear policy directives, but in the hope that they would define the authority under which they were operating.

Field Investigation in Chicago

The original plan was to establish an investigating team, including representatives of the regional HEW offices and of Seeley's and Quigley's staffs, for each of the four cities. A hurried and disorganized effort was made to assemble teams within the Boston and Chicago regional offices. In both cases HEW regional attorneys were interrupted during their vacations with the information that they had been named to head investigating teams, but neither chairman received specific instructions from Washington. Little was done until a member of Quigley's staff took the initiative.

With the resources available, it was possible to launch only one serious investigation at a time. The Federal officials chose to begin in Chicago. Two factors proved to be decisive in this critical choice. In the first place the Chicago civil rights confederation had unquestionably submitted the most "detailed complaint." Those who read the Chicago document were deeply impressed by the thoroughness of the documentation and the seriousness of the charges. Many complaints were simply short and unspecific letters, but the Chicago document made explicit claims and gave specific examples. The complaint clearly posed major and particularly urgent questions for Federal policy. A second major consideration was the fact that the Office of Education compliance staff had done some preliminary studies of the complaint, and the situation "seemed pretty clear." On first investigation, the evidence cited on segregation apprenticeship programs and on some of the school boundary decisions seemed extremely damaging.[67] Thus Federal investigators entered Chicago.

The Political Setting in Chicago

While there were significant administrative reasons for first examining the Chicago complaint, the decision to explore the dimensions of possible Federal power initially in the context of the racial crisis in Chicago depended on monumental political naïveté. Any Federal enforcement effort in Chicago would have to confront three extremely severe political obstacles. In the first place, it could not be expected that Mayor Daley would passively permit the use of uncertain Federal power to decide the

[66] Secretary Gardner press release, August 26, 1965.
[67] Interview with David Seeley, September 14, 1966.

most serious local racial issue without protest. The entire American political system is based on powerful local influence on Federal administrative actions; and Chicago had the most concentrated political power of any major city, in the hands of an extremely shrewd politician convinced that racial change must be worked out gradually. In the second place, an attack in Congress was certain. Illinois's Senator Dirksen, who had been of decisive importance in passing the Civil Rights Act, had been convinced that it would not apply in the North. Chicago power was perhaps even more impressive in the House, where its eight or nine members, together with downstate Democrats, exactly followed orders from the head of the Cook County Democratic machine, Mayor Daley. Since these were normally completely dependable votes for a Democratic Administration, angering Mayor Daley could seriously jeopardize the President's program.[68] A third factor arising from state politics was the fact that the state superintendent of education was a Republican elected on a conservative platform, who, in the context of Illinois politics, could naturally be expected to exploit a conflict between the Johnson Administration and Chicago authorities.

None of the other cities that might have been investigated would have involved political dangers of such magnitude. In New York, the state commissioner was committed to furthering integration, and in California state authorities directed that priority be given to integration programs in spending funds from the Elementary and Secondary Education Acts, but complaints from these states were passed over. Although the Massachusetts state legislature had recently passed a racial imbalance act, requiring the withholding of state aid from districts with segregated schools, the chance of working together with state officials to break segregation in Boston was neglected because Office of Education officials felt that the "original Boston complaint was very minor." [69] In the weeks to come HEW and Office of Education officials were to learn a great deal about politics as practiced by Illinois educators and politicians, and were to come to understand the strength of the Mayor Richard J. Daley's machine.

Daley was at the controls of a machine unmatched in this generation in any American city. While patronage has rapidly diminished in most city governments, one Chicago politician estimated that Daley directly controls some 30,000 state, city, and county jobs, positions allotted to ward and precinct organizations in accordance with their voter turnout. Partic-

68 Leo M. Snowiss, "Chicago and Congress, A Study of Municipal Representation" (unpublished Ph.D. dissertation, Department of Political Science, University of Chicago, 1965), pp. 378–79, 335.
69 Seeley interview, September 14, 1966.

ularly in the inner-city districts, including the Negro wards, the strength of the machine depended directly on the tangible incentives offered by jobs and various services in the form of political intervention with government agencies on behalf of local voters. Patronage jobs were available in each of the thousands of precincts with significant Democratic strength, and a massive and expensive election-day organization composed both of patronage employees and paid helpers worked diligently to bring out the Democratic voters in order to achieve the results necessary if patronage employees were to retain their jobs.

Daley had put together a potent organization by effectively distributing tangible rewards in the inner-city areas while working closely for Chicago business interests to foster the rebuilding of the Loop and by showing a willingness to make major reforms when demanded by the middle-class white voters on the periphery of the city. Thus, while tolerating the connection of one ward leader with rackets, the organized system of taxing patronage employees for political campaign funds, and the practice by which ward leaders grew rich selling insurance to companies needing government favors, Daley responded to a police scandal by bringing in a nationally known police expert and giving him a free hand to root out corruption in the police department. "Good government is good politics," the Mayor was fond of saying, "and good politics is good government." [70]

By skillfully blending the roles of traditional and ruthless machine politician and reformer heartily committed to a better Chicago, while muting divisive issues, Daley had created an organization able to completely control nominations for office in most parts of the city and thus able to dictate the actions of their incumbents. The vote-gathering potential of this organization, in the key swing state of Illinois, made Daley an important factor in presidential elections and an important ally for any Democratic President. The one serious threat to the continued dominance of the machine was the possibility of division within the ranks. When a popular Polish Democrat turned Republican to oppose Daley in the 1963 election, the Mayor was seriously threatened by loss of votes from the massive Polish community. In 1963 Daley actually carried only 49 per cent of the white vote and was elected only because the machine delivered more than 80 per cent of the Negro vote. Daley was eager, therefore, to avoid involvement in a racial conflict that could permanently

[70] Edwin A. Lahey, "King Richard of Chicago," *Chicago Daily News*, July 11, 1966–July 15, 1966; Snowiss, p. 46, and Wilson, p. 56; Lucille Edley, "Strategies and Techniques of Politics, A Study of Ten Selected Precinct Captains from Chicago's Third Ward" (unpublished M.A. thesis, University of Chicago, Department of Political Science, 1955), p. 8.

shatter his coalition. The Office of Education was to take drastic action on the one issue that seemed most dangerous to the Mayor.

HEW officials might well have profited by a study of the experience of other Federal administrators in dealing with the local power represented by Mayor Daley. The experience of the Office of Economic Opportunity and the Labor Department in administering the War on Poverty in Chicago was a case in point. The local operation of the Neighborhood Youth Corps, a program intended to provide temporary work for high school dropouts or potential dropouts from poor families enrolled 1700 young people from families earning more than the poverty standard. In fact, no check of the economic background of the applicant was made. Eventually the Labor Department suspended the ineligible participants. A month after this action, under attack from Chicago and other cities, the program rules were changed by Secretary Wirtz to permit local officials to alter Federal standards.[71] Similarly, although the poverty program's Operation Headstart provided that no more than 15 per cent of the children enrolled could come from families earning more than Federal standards allowed, Chicago enrolled 27½ per cent from such families and failed to keep any financial records on another 20 per cent of the students.[72] On a third issue, the Chicago Democratic machine never had any intention of complying with a Federal requirement that groups of poor people rather than just political leaders have an important role in determining how antipoverty funds were to be spent. Daley, in the words of one local observer, felt that it "would be a little goofy to use antipoverty money to finance militant groups that will wind up in a picket line at the City Hall." The Mayor used his organization to keep "unsafe" people out of the policy-making machinery.[73] When the acting director of the regional poverty program office attacked the Chicago machine, he was rapidly demoted and replaced by a member of the local political organization.[74] On issues with possible bearing on Chicago politics, the Mayor was often able to exercise extremely strong influence on Federal agencies. Had Secretary Gardner and Commissioner Keppel been fully aware of the political power wielded by Mayor Daley, they would surely have proceeded more warily.

The Chicago Study

The investigation began slowly. Alvin Cohen, HEW regional attorney in Chicago, was informed by phone that he had been named chairman of the team to study the Chicago complaint. Since he received no specific

---

[71] *Congressional Record*, March 15, 1966, p. 5574; *Chicago Daily News*, March 5, 1966.
[72] *Congressional Record*, March 22, 1966.
[73] *Chicago Daily News*, July 15, 1966.   [74] *Ibid.*, April 11, 1966.

instructions, Cohen simply informed Superintendent Willis and then finished his Florida vacation. After his return in September Cohen set out to organize the team and "figure out the magnitude of the job." This problem was serious because the team lacked anyone knowledgeable about the operation of a large urban school system. In addition to the regional attorney, the team was composed of a civil rights specialist from Quigley's office, a regional vocational education specialist, and two lawyers from Seeley's Title VI program.[75]

Most of September was spent acquiring enough knowledge about the Chicago school system to permit the phrasing of intelligent questions to school officials. With no deadline for its study and no guidance from Washington about what to look for, members of the team informed themselves by reading some of the recent reports on the Chicago schools. The Chicago school system, Cohen recalls, was a "hell of a large place," and its incredible complexity posed exceedingly difficult problems for enforcement officials. Since Superintendent Willis was unwilling to supply information unless the Federal officials knew exactly what to ask for, it was September 23 before Cohen was prepared to make a formal request for data.[76]

In a five-page letter to Willis, Cohen outlined the data needed by the team. The list covered 43 issues including class size, school capacities, and teacher qualifications in various sections of the city. The team wanted to know about transfer plans, mobile classrooms, school-budgeting, and the level of faculty integration. "May we suggest," the regional attorney wrote, "that the material presently available be forwarded to us at the earliest possible date, and the remainder be forwarded as soon as it becomes available. Please let us know within the week when we might expect to receive the remainder of the information." While school officials were assembling the data, the letter announced, the team would begin to visit a "representative sample of schools selected by us." [77]

A serious investigation was finally underway. Two members of the team met with Willis, who was "perfectly correct" and soon began to forward some of the readily available data. At this point Cohen "felt that we were going to be able to make considerable progress rather rapidly." [78] This belief was never to be tested, however. Less than a week after this meeting, Commissioner Keppel deferred action on Federal funds without consulting the regional team, thus bringing to an end serious investigation of the facts of the local controversy.

[75] Interview with Alvin Cohen, July 11, 1966.   [76] *Ibid.*
[77] Letter from Regional Attorney Cohen to Superintendent Willis, September 29, 1965.
[78] Cohen interview, July 11, 1966.

Policy Confusion in Washington

Many of the difficulties of the investigating team in Chicago were rooted in the inability of Federal officials to resolve chronic indecision about the meaning to the Title VI prohibition of discrimination in the North. The legislative history of the title clearly indicated that Federal funds could be denied to school systems violating the Constitution through demonstrable intentional segregation, and the title also seemed to prohibit involuntary bussing of students to achieve "racial balance." Beyond these very general conclusions, however, there was a good deal of room for debate.

Believing that enforcement standards should be coherent with current Federal court decisions, both Seeley and the HEW General Counsel held that Title VI had a very limited application in the North. The prevailing judicial doctrine offered very narrow grounds for Federal action:

> It seems that the courts in the Gary and Kansas City cases were more than willing to allow this entire matter to be handled by the school boards, relying on the boards' judgment and good faith in spite of a long history of segregated schools in both cities. In both of these cases, the courts seem to have applied the principle that, as long as there was a rational relationship between what the school board did and a legal end to be achieved, the courts' inquiry was concluded.[79]

Since the Supreme Court had refused to hear a case on these issues, the Chicago region Federal court of appeals decision upholding a highly segregated neighborhood school system was the primary judicial precedent for the courts with jurisdiction over Chicago. Some broader interpretations of local responsibility to provide equal educational opportunity had been handed down by certain Federal district courts, particularly in the East,[80] but these decisions would be far less persuasive in supporting action in Chicago than in the districts where the decisions were fashioned.

Working within this legal context, Seeley warned Keppel that "most of these northern city problems are very complicated and we can't predict how long it will take to come to concrete conclusions on all the issues." Citing the *Gary* case, Seeley argued that it was unclear what evidence the courts would require to prove discrimination.[81] Seeley's basic belief was that, in the absence of a clear showing of intentional official action by a northern school board to promote segregation, Title VI was an inade-

[79] Oliver Schroeder, Jr., and David T. Smith, eds., *De Facto Segregation and Civil Rights* (New York: William S. Hein and Co., 1965), p. 12.
[80] *Matter of Skipworth*, 14 Misc. 2d 325; *Blocher v. Board of Education*, 229 F. Supp. 709.
[81] Seeley Memorandum, August 20, 1965.

quate tool, and the problems could be better handled by voluntary incentives for local desegregation efforts. In August 1965 in fact, the Office of Education had received a study it had commissioned on the problems of de facto segregation, which concluded that financial assistance rather than withdrawal of Federal aid funds would be the most effective policy.[82]

In a memo written less than 10 days before the decision to defer funds for Chicago, the HEW General Counsel suggested very strict requirements for evidence to justify fund-withholding decisions in the North. He saw two possible grounds for Federal action. In the first place, the investigations would have to prove that local officials had either deliberately gerrymandered school boundaries or had permitted these lines to become "so obviously inappropriate educationally as to lead to a finding of racial motivation." Alternatively, evidence could be gathered to prove that racial considerations were involved in the provision of demonstrably inferior education for Negro pupils.

> Evidence to support a conclusion of racial motivation will ordinarily have to derive from patterns of action over a considerable period of time and will have to take into account an appraisal of the alternative courses of action which were realistically open to the school authorities. . . .
>
> The ultimate question . . . is the present motivation, and a school district which is now utilizing its available resources in a reasonable effort to redress racial inequalities is not in violation of Title VI.[83]

If this interpretation prevailed, Title VI would have limited applicability even in a case in which school officials had historically segregated Negro students intentionally but were now making some efforts to improve.

Only a week before Chicago funds were deferred, Keppel received another memo from Assistant Commissioner Seeley recommending that the Office limit its concern in the North to provable intentional segregation through gerrymandering, faculty segregation, and other devices. He warned of the practical difficulties involved in an assumption that either unequal facilities and programs or simply de facto segregation violated Title VI:

> The possibility of a "boomerang"—either in the courts or from Congress—if we launched forth with a seemingly "strong" position is not to be discounted, and practically speaking the "strong" position . . . would not enable us to do much more in actuality. . . . (Are we likely, for instance, to cut off Chicago's funds until they eliminate de facto segregation?)

In his memo Seeley pointed out the crucial fact that the Office had not defined any concrete and realistic goals to be accomplished in Chicago

[82] Fleming interview, Letter from Harold C. Fleming to Commissioner Keppel, August 20, 1965.
[83] Willcox Memorandum, September 22, 1965.

and underlined the need to consider basic questions about the fund-withholding process and the meaning of Title VI in the North before taking action.[84]

While Keppel and Gardner received cautious advice from the HEW legal staff and the Equal Educational Opportunities Program, the man responsible for department-wide coordination of civil rights activities and for field investigations held a radically different view of Title VI. Assistant Secretary Quigley had developed a conception of Title VI as an instrument for using Federal power to eliminate any trace of segregation, whatever its origin. "Title VI," he wrote in September, "applies to discrimination in any form it appears—obvious, subtle, official, unofficial, by law, and in fact." The neighborhood school policy and the practice of teacher seniority, he argued, must not be allowed to excuse the denial of educational opportunity inherent in segregated schools.[85]

Policy differences within the department were not resolved. The investigating team in Chicago requested a range of information that would support proceedings on either theory. It was to be the Chicago debacle itself that was to resolve the policy question by making the Quigley interpretation completely untenable politically.

The Decision to Defer

Ironically the decision to defer action on Federal grants to the Chicago schools arose neither from the findings of the investigators nor from a policy decision about northern discrimination. In fact, events outside of HEW created a deadline for action. With the passage of a supplemental appropriations bill by Congress in September, the funds for the first year of the Elementary and Secondary Education Act finally became available, and Chicago would soon apply for its $32 million entitlement.

The HEW officials could gain maximum influence from the huge new sum of money by denying it at the outset while the prospect was particularly tantalizing and local officials had not yet come to regard the aid as simply a customary and automatic part of their budgets. Although final *withholding* of funds would require sufficient information to prove a violation in a formal hearing, the existing Office of Education procedures permitted Commissioner Keppel to *defer* action, delaying funds while investigating a complaint. Thus when Congress provided the initial appropriation for the new program, there was a need for a very rapid decision on the exercise of this authority in Chicago.

The urgency of the situation was greatly increased by reports about the nature of Superintendent Willis' plans for use of the Federal money.

[84] Memorandum from David Seeley to Commissioner Keppel, September 23, 1965.
[85] Memorandum from Assistant Secretary to Secretary Gardner, September 14, 1965.

The Elementary and Secondary Education Act directed that the funds be used for programs designed to meet the educational needs of children in areas with concentrations of families with annual incomes of less than $2000. The programs, the law specified, must be directly related to the correction of the educational deficiencies in these areas. Although the money was Federal, the chief responsibility for judging the adequacy of a district's plans was delegated to the state superintendent. In Illinois, where the state superintendent was known to be sympathetic to Willis' outlook and where the Chicago schools had always enjoyed a large measure of freedom from state supervision, this meant that Willis would get almost anything he asked for. Information received in Washington, including an analysis by a member of the CCCO research committee, indicated that two of the three areas tentatively designated by Willis as "target areas" were white and that they included some census tracts with an $8000 median income. Willis also indicated the probability that some of the money would be used for mobile classrooms, the "Willis wagons" which were condemned as the symbol of Chicago's refusal to integrate and which had touched off confrontations in the streets in several Chicago ghetto neighborhoods.[86]

When Assistant Commissioner Seeley informed Keppel of the probable use of the new aid program in Chicago, the Commissioner became seriously concerned, as did Assistant Secretary Quigley. Both men, Seeley recalls, were very much afraid of misuse of the program, and there was a "horrible fear of embarrassment" for the Administration when angry civil rights groups charged that, far from the stated intentions of the President's program, the funds were being used to consolidate inferior segregated education.[87] Keppel and Seeley had both become angry at Willis' recalcitrance when asked to cooperate in providing information. The issue was brought to a head, however, not by a civil rights issue but by Office of Education determination to avoid perversion of the historic new Federal aid program during the first year of its administration.[88]

On September 30 Commissioner Keppel wrote to the Illinois Superintendent of Public Instruction, Ray Page, directing him to defer further grants to the Chicago schools. Incredibly enough the final decision to send the letter that transformed the Federal-state conflict from a latent test of wills to an extremely important direct confrontation was triggered by a false report in the *Chicago Tribune*. The September 28 *Tribune* carried a report that the state superintendent had already approved Chicago's spending plans. "Chicago has some very splendid plans," Superin-

[86] Interview with Mrs. Phyllis McClure, October 25, 1966; *Chicago Daily News*, October 1, 1965.

[87] Seeley interview, November 21, 1967.   [88] Keppel interview, January 5, 1967.

tendent Page was quoted as saying. "We want to give them the green light so they can move ahead." The *Tribune* indicated that Page had already forwarded the necessary documents to Keppel.[89] Knowing that the *Tribune* was a staunch supporter of Willis' policies and assuming that its reporter had advance information on Page's plans, Keppel feared that Page was conspiring with Willis to present the Office of Education with a fait accompli,[90] thus forcing Federal officials to either accept maladministration of the new program or engage in a battle to reverse the state decision, a battle which would inevitably bring the dreaded accusations of "Federal control of education." It seemed to HEW officials that Page was moving fast to make Federal review impossible.

Confronting this dilemma, the Title VI deferral process appeared to be a means to delay any action while gaining a full study of the charges against the Chicago school system. Although Keppel was generally opposed to extension of the southern deferral practice to the North, the special facts of the Chicago situation made him inclined to follow the course urged by Quigley. In a memo to Secretary Gardner, Commissioner Keppel informed him that the Chicago investigation had progressed far enough to justify deferral. Actually the investigation was barely underway, and deferral was proposed to protect the Elementary and Secondary Education Act program. As the Commissioner pointed out in another part of the same memo, this extension into northern cities of a procedure originally intended for use in cases involving legally separate schools clearly violating the Constitution was generally questionable. While assuring Gardner that the Office had sufficient information on the Chicago complaint to justify the action, Keppel conceded that "the notice will still have to be general, and will have to indicate that further investigation will be necessary." [91]

Like many decisions in any bureaucracy Keppel's decision to send a letter to Superintendent Page was taken under pressure of time, which made full consideration of all possible alternatives and their implications impossible. Reacting to what he saw as a serious threat to the program with which he was most closely identified, and a threat that demanded very rapid action, Commissioner Keppel committed the Office of Education to an important role in an explosive situation without having an opportunity to examine in intimate detail the work of his investigating team or to consider the possible political implications. In fact, Keppel hoped and expected that the state superintendent would avoid publicizing

[89] *Chicago Tribune*, September 28, 1965; *Chicago Daily News*, October 1, 1965.
[90] Keppel interview.
[91] Draft memorandum from Commissioner Keppel to Secretary Gardner, undated, September.

the Federal action and quietly permit the investigation to continue while Chicago accepted an uncertain delay on its application for more than $30 million of new Federal funds. As Quigley recalls the decision, Keppel did not want to disapprove the entire Illinois plan and thus directly defy the customary pattern of Federal-state relations in education, and the letter was "his way of saying, 'We want you to hold up approval of this plan.' " [92]

Everyone involved in the Chicago decision had at least some vague awareness of potential political dangers, but it was not clear to anyone who had the responsibility to weigh the potential threat to the Administration against the possible gains. Assistant Secretary Quigley, the highest Administration official regularly involved in the details of the case, made no attempt to strike this balance; he saw his primary responsibility as full enforcement of a law that he believed was intended to eliminate any vestige of segregation in all institutions receiving Federal funds. As the official responsible for civil rights enforcement in HEW, Quigley was perfectly willing to take the risk of a political attack. For a former congressman who considered himself a "political animal," however, Quigley was remarkably insensitive to the tactical problems involved in extending enforcement activity to the North. The fact that Chicago was investigated first, he says, was "happenstance—about the way the bureaucracy works." [93]

Quigley and the other officials involved also failed to anticipate the likely reaction to this move in Congress. When Title VI had been debated in Congress, few had been aware of the possible application of the sanction in the North, and Congress was certain to demand a justification of what many would see as an arbitrary or even illegal extension of Federal power. The fact of the matter, however, was that the Office of Education was totally unprepared to make an effective defense of its action. "Nothing had happened in Chicago when the letter was sent," reports a member of the investigating team. "The Department had absolutely no evidence whatsoever." [94] While the civil rights complaints and various studies of the Chicago schools indicated striking discrepancies between white and Negro schools, the Office of Education had gathered no data which proved the crucial question of intent to segregate.

The Assistant Secretary, the Commissioner, and Secretary Gardner confronted a situation different in absolutely critical legal and political respects from the southern situation; but their insensitivity to the magnitude and implications of these differences permitted the extension of a bureaucratic procedure devised for a situation in which a clear presump-

[92] Quigley interview.   [93] *Ibid.*   [94] McClure interview.

tion of local violations justified deferral without a hearing into a context where the law was unsettled and where deferral pending an investigation would involve a delay of months, effectively denying the funds completely to the local schools. The political difference was even more serious. Most of the troublesome southern districts were in politically unimportant rural areas, and most southern congressional protests could safely be discounted both on the grounds that the southern viewpoint had been decisively defeated by large congressional majorities and on the grounds that the protesting southerners never voted for Administration programs anyway. Chicago, on the other hand, was of decisive importance in the politics of a state that often helped decide presidential elections and the home of the most powerful Democratic machine in the country. A protest from Chicago would be heard instantly in Congress and could deny the Administration a needed margin of victory on crucial legislation. Illinois Senator Dirksen held a veto power over all civil rights legislation, and his reaction to an enforcement effort in Chicago could be predicted with certainty.

In the hectic period between the September 28 *Tribune* story and the September 30 dispatch of the letter to Illinois, no one took responsibility for judging the issues in terms of their overall advantages and dangers to the entire program of the President, and the President was not given an opportunity to make the decision himself. Keppel hoped that the entire affair could be handled quietly without publicity by Federal, state, and local education officials, and he failed to realize the full significance of the step. Quigley failed to accept the legal distinction between the northern and southern situation and thus failed to demand the necessary tactical calculations and legal preparation before extending the deferral policy to the North. Secretary Gardner was informed of the action but failed to realize its significance.

No one in HEW was sufficiently aware of the implications of the decision to insist that the President be consulted. Keppel had assumed that there would be some clearance at the White House level, but Quigley felt that none was necessary. As the letter was being dispatched, Keppel called Douglass Cater, the White House staff member with jurisdiction over HEW, giving him an opportunity to object.[95] Cater failed to discern the significance of the letter and did not take the issue to the the President. The letter was sent without the approval of the President, who was notoriously eager to be involved in every significant action of his Administration. Due to a series of failures of perception at each stage of the linkage between the President and the bureaucracy, the President was bypassed.

[95] Seeley interview, November 21, 1967.

The Letter to Springfield: Federal-State Conflict Begins

The Keppel letter was hand-delivered to Superintendent Page in Springfield on October 1. "Preliminary investigation of certain of the complaints . . . ," Keppel wrote, "indicates probable noncompliance with the act and the regulation, and brings into serious question the assurance of compliance made by the Chicago school authorities. . . . We believe that these latter complaints can, with the full cooperation of the Chicago school authorities, be fully investigated in a relatively short time and that they can and must be satisfactorily resolved before any new commitments are made of funds. . . ." [96] At the same time Keppel sent a note to Willis, enclosing a copy of the letter to Page. "Members of the Departmental staff," he wrote, "will be in touch with you further very shortly in an effort to resolve these matters as quickly as possible." [97] Keppel made no attempt to personally contact either of these two powerful educators.

Perhaps the most striking manifestation of the bureaucratic rather than political approach to the Chicago situation was the insensitive manner in which the Office of Education dealt with the Illinois officials directly administering the Federal aid programs in the state. Office of Education policy had always been one of deferential respect for state superintendents, an approach that Commissioner Keppel expressed in one of his speeches:

> In education we look to the States not merely as a matter of law or precedent, but as a matter of practical soundness and necessity. In this Nation of 50 States with vast and independent enterprises for education, the Federal Government can help as a partner . . . and a somewhat junior partner at that.[98]

In the context of this traditional relationship, exercise of Title VI enforcement powers, particularly in an area in which the law was unclear, radically altered the Federal-state relationship and threatened to transfer a good deal of power from the state departments of education to Washington. The cavalier manner in which Keppel informed Page made the dimensions of this change evident.

State Superintendent Page first learned of the Federal action from a newspaper reporter. The explosive news had leaked out of the Office of Education even before the messenger arrived in Springfield with the letter. When Page received the letter, he found no explanation of the nature

[96] Letter from Commissioner Keppel to State Superintendent Page, September 30, 1965.
[97] Letter from Commissioner Keppel to Superintendent Willis, September 30, 1965.
[98] Quoted in David D. Henry, "Some Observations on Federal Relations to Education," *Illinois Journal of Education*, Vol. LVII (February 1966), p. 53.

of the charges against the Chicago schools or of the likely delay in spending approximately half of the state's allotment under the biggest education program in American history. Accustomed to relationships between Federal and state professionals, with administrative decisions centered at the state level, the letter raised the specter in Springfield of a direct Federal-local relationship in which the state was bypassed. State officials were naturally very reluctant to see the Office of Education transformed from a passive source of funds to a powerful source of influence on the most politically sensitive question in education.

Superintendent Page, a Republican politician elected to office in 1962 after successfully coaching winning basketball teams at Springfield High, reacted indignantly to the Keppel letter. He promptly dispatched an open letter to the Commissioner stating that he had been willing to examine the CCCO complaints on his own initiative and that he believed that this was a state, not a Federal, responsibility. He demanded details:

> You have not advised what these complaints contain and have not furnished the office of the superintendent of public instruction with a copy. No investigator from your office has called upon me and I am completely uninformed as to the specific charges. What noncompliance is alleged? Is not the State office of education entitled to complete information on these matters? . . .[99]

Page's response guaranteed that the issue would not be quietly settled within the education profession but would generate a test of Federal power. Keppel had made a startlingly careless infringement on the prerogatives of the state education agency. Under pressure for a rapid decision to prevent possible misuse of aid funds, Keppel had decided to gain time for negotiations by extending the southern deferral procedure to Chicago, but nothing had been done to explain either his approach or his objectives to threatened state officials. Keppel appeared to be eagerly reaching out to the very limits of his authority and arrogantly ignoring legitimate state prerogatives. In his next campaign, Superintendent Page was to make much of his struggle to turn back the attempt to institute Federal control of the schools. "Local control of education," he said, "must be preserved and never reduced to a mere 'housekeeping' operation."[100]

The Federal threat was particularly severe because the Illinois superintendent's office was both feeble and highly partisan. It had little influence over educational policy and still had large numbers of patronage employees on its staff. Even before the Federal intervention, the Superintendent had difficulty exercising any control over the massive Chicago school

[99] *Congressional Record*, October 11, 1965, p. 25593.
[100] Ray Page, *Illinois Journal of Education*, Vol. LVII (February 1966), 1.

system. The Cook County bloc of Democratic legislators, representing the Chicago machine in Springfield, had historically traded their support on statewide education legislation for extensive delegations of authority and special provisions for the Chicago schools.[101] Thus the Office of Education had chosen a case where state authority was tenuous, even if the state superintendent had desired to actively enforce the Civil Rights Act.

Illinois is a conservative state, and there had been little statewide concern about the issue of school segregation. The one relevant achievement was the passage in 1963 of the Armstrong Act forbidding school districts to locate new schools in a manner promoting segregation. The local boards were also vaguely directed "as soon as practicable" to

> change or revise existing units or create new units in a manner which will take into consideration the prevention of segregation, and the elimination of separation of children in the public schools because of color. . . .[102]

The enforcement procedure, however, was highly complex and Superintendent Page had shown no inclination to enforce the law. Federal officials could have picked few northern states where state officials were less eager to become entangled in the race issue.

The angry reaction to the Keppel letter was grounded not only in Illinois conservatism, but also in the state's need for more school funds. Illinois' poorly developed regressive tax structure left the state close to the end of the list in terms of its effort to support public schools. A major study concluded that the state needed to rapidly double educational expenditures.[103] The new Federal aid was eagerly accepted, and there was no disposition to give up half the money without conclusive proof that Chicago was violating Title VI.

Even before Keppel's action at least one Illinois official had made this position clear. When the HEW regional attorney had asked the man administering the new program directed at poor children how he could approve Chicago's plan in spite of the city's segregated schools, the state official had pointed out that neither the courts nor HEW had made a formal finding that segregation existed in Chicago. He pledged that if the investigating team "finds and states that segregation does exist," he would

---

[101] Nicholas A. Masters, Robert H. Salisbury, and Thomas H. Eliot, *State Politics and the Public Schools* (New York: Alfred A. Knopf, 1964), pp. 100–102, 107, 168, 177.

[102] CCCO complaint, *Integrated Education*, p. 11.

[103] William P. McLure, *A Study of the Public Schools of Illinois* (Springfield, Ill.: Research and Development Department, Office of the Superintendent of Public Instruction, 1965), pp. 1, 91.

guarantee that the funds would be withheld.[104] Failing to gather the necessary proof before acting, the Office of Education made no real test of the willingness of state officials to take responsibility for enforcement.

The immediate cause of the Federal-state confrontation was the dread of Federal subsidization of more Willis wagons. Thus the Commissioner of Education permitted the power of the Office of Education under Title VI to be tested in a controversy arising from the implementation of another law that provided him with another remedy. The 1965 Elementary and Secondary Education Act specifically granted the Commissioner authority to override state recommendations and refuse to fund plans that did not demonstrate a direct relationship to the educational needs of children in poor areas. Moreover there was potential state sympathy for Federal efforts to obtain more information from Willis, whose reluctance to share his plans even with state officials was to force the Springfield office to twice withhold funds during the first year of the new program until Willis finally corrected defects in Chicago planning.[105] When Keppel acted, the state had not effectively reviewed the Chicago plan and would have been hard-pressed to defend Willis' projects.

Action by Keppel under the aid program, however, would have posed a variety of dangers. It would have seriously threatened the normal pattern of very loose Federal supervision and very rare Federal interventions. Were Washington to reject the plan of one of the nation's most important school systems and interfere in state administration in the first year of the new program, those who had warned that the education bill meant Federal control of the schools would have evidence for their claim. Such a step would pose a threat to the whole network of cooperative relationships with state officials in a variety of grant programs.

Action under the Civil Rights Act had the important advantage that civil rights enforcement was separate from the grant programs and had a discrete regulatory scope. Most school districts had no reason to fear civil rights enforcement, and the people operating the aid programs would not be involved and could thus conserve their valuable relationships. In fact after the Chicago incident disrupted relations between Commissioner Keppel and Illinois officials, it was the director of a major operating agency within the Office of Education who re-established contact with State Superintendent Ray Page and proposed that Page be represented on any further investigating committee in Chicago.

After a lengthy conference with attorneys, Page made clear his reaction to the Federal action. Even while rebuking Keppel for ignoring his

[104] Interview with Noah S. Neace, July 28, 1966.   [105] Neace interview.

office, he tempered his anger with a statement of his willingness to act against proven violations in Chicago:

> I don't want any child in Chicago to be deprived of what is rightfully due to him. I also do not want any violations to exist. If they do, let's get them straightened out and get the money.[106]

Page had hit the Office of Education where it was weakest by demanding information that Federal officials simply did not possess.

Chicago Reaction

While state criticism put Commissioner Keppel in an uncomfortable position, Chicago official reaction was to be decisive. Superintendent Willis, "bristling with anger," quickly sent off a telegram demanding details. "What," he asked, "is the probable 'non-compliance'? . . . When will you let us know?" [107] The most vitriolic reaction, however, came from Congressman Roman Pucinski, the Chicago delegation's representative on the House Education and Labor Committee. Pucinski immediately destroyed Keppel's hope of keeping the civil rights investigation separate from the issue of Federal control of education. "This," he said, "is a power play by the Office of Education to influence local school districts. . . . When Congress wrote the aid-to-education act it put in specific safeguards to prevent just this type of thing." He warned that "Congress won't appropriate another nickel for education programs" if Federal officials were to engage in such "arbitrary and dictatorial" acts.[108] Chicago officials were to press very hard and successfully the charge that the action turned not on the question of segregation but on the issue of preserving the freedom of local schools from arbitrary Federal intervention.

While the superintendent and the Daley machine were obviously disturbed, there were significant forces in Chicago supporting the Federal action. Negro leaders were elated, and moderates showed an early willingness to support Keppel's move if convincing documentation of the charges was forthcoming from Washington. "I feel wonderful," said Al Raby, leader of the city's civil rights confederation, "I hope that this is the first step toward building a school system that will make every Chicagoan proud." The Negro community's representative on the school board announced that "it is high time some outside stimulus was provided to encourage the board to take action against segregation." [109] The moderate reaction was expressed by the *Chicago Daily News*:

---

[106] *Chicago Daily News,* October 2, 1965.   [107] *Ibid.*   [108] *Ibid.*
[109] *Ibid.*

. . . it must be conceded that Chicago, through a stubborn and contrary school superintendent and a school board without the courage to either fire him or bring him into line, blundered into this mess on its own hook. . . .

The federal Office of Education has as yet given no bill of particulars. . . . It invites charges of arrogance and arbitrariness by that failure.

But the fact remains that Chicago's best chance to get the federal monkey off its back is to do what it should have done long since—set its own schoolhouse in order.[110]

While the conservative majority on the school board opposed the Federal action at once, members of the more liberal bloc were eager to learn the specific complaints and to consider the remedies the Office of Education might suggest.[111] In the absence of details from Keppel, however, both the sympathetic board members and the civil rights leadership were unable to defend effectively the Federal authorities.

The public criticism of Keppel's action confronted the Office of Education with basic questions both about the facts of the case and about the extent of the Office's legal authority. The questions being raised most incessantly were: Why has the money been deferred? What evidence do the Federal officials have? What was necessary to have the funds released? Both the local opponents and the moderates demanded answers to these questions. Local critics also strongly pressed a second kind of question, asking whether there was any authority under Title VI to desegregate northern schools and whether Commissioner Keppel had observed the procedural guarantees Congress had written into Title VI. Lack of preparation to effectively answer either question meant that potential moderate support for the action was forfeited.

Silence in Washington

Federal officials, believing that the controversy would be quietly resolved within the education profession, had failed to prepare any plausible documented explanation for the press. The published explanations were sketchy in the extreme. An informant told the *Washington Post* that the move was based on evidence of "patterns of discrimination" in the way Chicago elementary school children were funneled into segregated high schools and on data showing the existence of programs of unequal quality in Negro and white schools.[112] No details were made public. A "high ranking spokesman," probably Assistant Secretary Quigley, outlined the issues to a Chicago newsman in a manner indicating that the Office had nothing but the civil rights group's complaint. He cited five major issues:

110 *Ibid.*, October 5, 1965.
111 *Ibid.*, October 2, 1965; see comment of school board member James Clement.
112 *Washington Post*, October 3, 1965.

1. Increasing segregation.
2. Increasing numbers of totally segregated schools.
3. Larger school size in Negro schools.
4. Inferior facilities in Negro schools.
5. More noncertified teachers in Negro schools.[113]

None of these issues, even if evidence was available, involved a clear violation of the Constitution in the absence of evidence proving the intent of the school board to discriminate. No detailed support for the action came out of Washington, and even those officials providing vague justifications would not permit the use of their names.

Although the process of collecting data in Chicago had just begun and the Office was far from the preparation of a comprehensive case against the Chicago school authorities, the failure to respond was unnecessary. Had the officials involved realized that their action would be publicly challenged, there would have been little difficulty in supporting the charge of "probable noncompliance" by drawing on abundant information available in scholarly studies and in the public record of the battle between the board of education and Superintendent Willis. Careful use of this data, and a statement of the major objectives of the investigation then underway in the city, could have taken much of the initiative away from Willis and his supporters.

The problem that initially arose from the failure to prepare for a public dispute was exacerbated by a White House directive to HEW ordering official silence on what had now become a serious political issue. Although Commissioner Keppel and Assistant Commissioner Seeley were eager to try to correct what they saw as a general misunderstanding of the background and meaning of the letter to the state superintendent, they adhered to the ban on publicity. A Chicago correspondent spent a frantic evening on the phone attempting to obtain information from Seeley, Keppel, and one of Keppel's top assistants, but Keppel absolutely refused to talk to him.[114] Seeley recalls these days as a time of "deafening silence." [115] Keppel felt extremely restive but, knowing that the President was very angry, remained quiet.[116]

The Chicago Attack

The dimensions of the local onslaught grew quickly, spreading reverberations on Capitol Hill, at the White House, and in HEW. The leaders

[113] *Chicago Daily News,* October 2, 1965.
[114] Interview with Charles Nicodemus, September 15, 1966.
[115] Seeley interview, September 14, 1966.
[116] Keppel interview.

in assailing Keppel's action were Willis, Congressman Pucinski, and later Mayor Daley. Willis promptly took the offensive at a press conference:

> While I am sorry this happened to Chicago, perhaps it is a blessing in disguise. . . . It may serve to alert the public to capricious and autocratic actions emanating from the federal education offices.[117]

The *Chicago Tribune* fulminated:

> The unspecified complaints apparently consist of nothing more than various charges made by . . . a self-appointed civil rights group whose principal mission seems to be to conduct street demonstrations and otherwise harass Supt. Benjamin C. Willis and the school board. . . .
>
> The Office of Education is making an example of Chicago to frighten other cities into accepting federal control peaceably. If the will to resist can be overcome, the Office of Education will reign supreme and the constitutional authority of state and local governments over education will be reduced to a scrap of paper.[118]

Sniping against "arrogant bureaucrats" in Washington is an almost daily assignment for the *Tribune* editorial staff, but there was something unusually potent about this attack. Tying the civil rights enforcement issue directly with fears of Federal infringement of local control of education, a principle basic to American political ideology, the editorial demonstrated the depth of Keppel's miscalculation in believing that the two issues could be kept separate in the city where segregation had been the leading educational issue for years.

In Washington, Congressman Pucinski took advantage of his position on the committee controlling education legislation and appropriations ceilings to open another front in the war on the Office of Education. Claiming that Keppel had directly violated the procedural protections written into Title VI, Pucinski asked the Attorney General to investigate the action.[119] As self-designated representative of the Chicago delegation, Pucinski called Keppel and began to arrange a meeting between the delegation and the Commissioner. Keppel was surprised by Pucinski's bitter attacks and irritated by the constant badgering of his office and the White House. The Commissioner told Pucinski that he "never thought this would get into the newspapers." [120] Pucinski also harassed Quigley. After talking with Daley and Willis, Pucinski called the White House to make a protest.[121]

It was obvious at the White House that Mayor Daley was angry. Chicago congressmen were simply local representatives of the Mayor and

[117] *Chicago Tribune*, October 3, 1965.   [118] *Ibid.*, October 4, 1965.
[119] *Chicago Daily News*, October 2, 1965.
[120] Keppel interview; *Chicago Daily News*, October 4, 1965.
[121] Nicodemus interview.

would never attack a major Administration figure without Daley's knowledge.

Disturbed by the controversy, the President transferred management of the issue from Douglass Cater, his education specialist, to Joseph Califano, Jr., his leading advisor on domestic affairs. Angered that an important step had been taken without his approval, President Johnson ordered Califano to review Keppel's action. Both Pucinski and Senator Dirksen had demanded a Justice Department examination of the legality of the action, and now the White House asked the President's legal advisors for an analysis of Title VI authority. A high Justice Department official remembers that the report sent to the White House indicated "some doubt about the legality" of the action, which was seen as a "questionable use of power." Because the law was unclear and the evidence necessary for a hearing had not been assembled in Chicago, the Justice Department questioned both the legality and the wisdom of holding back urgently needed funds.[122]

The President entered directly into the crisis on October 3, when he traveled to New York to sign the new immigration bill before the Statue of Liberty. Among the crowd of invited guests were Mayor Daley and his wife. Before the ceremony Johnson kissed Mrs. Daley and greeted the man he had earlier described as "my longtime devoted friend and as great a political leader and city administrator as there is in the world. . . ."[123] When Mayor Daley expressed confusion about the Office of Education action, the President told him that he should have brought his problems directly to the top and assured him that the White House was looking into the question.[124]

The next day a number of HEW officials were called together for an urgent Sunday afternoon meeting before key officials went on to the White House for a session with the President. Keppel, Quigley, Seeley, several of those involved in the Chicago investigation, as well as the Under Secretary and the HEW General Counsel took part in the session. Keppel, who had opposed action in the North but was taking the brunt of the attack, was particularly disturbed. He was planning to leave the Office in the near future and expressed his fear that he would be remembered as the Commissioner who tried to institute Federal control of education.[125]

[122] Doar interview, August 10, 1967.
[123] L.B.J., *Public Papers* . . . , 1965, statement on June 3, 1965.
[124] Charles Nicodemus, Washington correspondent for the *Chicago Daily News*, learned the story of this discussion from two different people who overheard the conversation. (Nicodemus interview, September 15, 1966.) See also, Stephen K. Bailey and Edith Mosher, *ESEA, the Office of Education Administers a Law* (Syracuse: Syracuse University Press, 1968), p. 152.
[125] McClure interview.

No one knew what to do. Keppel sent a group of lawyers, including Seeley and the two attorneys from the Chicago investigation, into a corner of the room to draft a two-paragraph statement summarizing the legal authority for what he had done.[126]

During the meeting, one lawyer proposed an alternative approach, suggesting that Keppel justify his action under the authority granted by the Elementary and Secondary Education Act. Since the Commissioner's primary concern was with the misuse of funds in Willis' plans, it seemed that the action could be supported by the language giving the Commissioner authority to withhold funds where local programs did not give "reasonable promise of substantial progress" toward meeting the educational needs of poor children.[127] Keppel was not familiar with this authority, however, and no one had a copy of the act. When Keppel asked the General Counsel about this possibility, he was told that the HEW legal staff would not defend such an action in court.[128] Keppel recalls that he felt that such a step would fool no one, because the Chicago controversy was obviously over a civil rights issue.[129]

The HEW meeting adjourned, and Keppel went on to the White House. The President was obviously angry over the politically explosive and legally questionable action taken without his knowledge. He repeated to Keppel angry comments made to him by Mayor Daley. While he did not directly order HEW to surrender to the Chicago officials, he made it absolutely clear that he wanted this issue settled and settled quickly.

In Chicago criticism continued to mount. Superintendent Willis renewed his tirade, berating the Office of Education as "despotic, alarming, and threatening," again demanding an explanation of the Federal action. A powerful conservative Negro leader, the president of the large National Baptist Convention, was convinced to protest Keppel's action.[130]

At his Tuesday morning news conference Mayor Daley let loose with a fierce blast at the Office of Education. The Mayor, who usually speaks softly and mostly in platitudes, lashed the Administration, charging that Keppel's action would "cause any American citizen to take another look at the concept of Federal aid to education." The whole conception, he said, had been done "irreparable damage" by the interference of Federal officials. If one of his administrators had made such a blunder, Daley said, he would have fired him. Drastic Federal action, without explanations to local officials, was "something that shouldn't happen in government." [131]

While local officials were focusing tremendous pressure on Washington, those in the city sympathetic to the Federal action did not make them-

126 Ibid.   127 P. L. 89–10, Sec. 205 (a) (1), Sec. 210.
128 McClure interview.   129 Keppel interview.
130 Chicago Daily News, October 4, 1965.   131 Ibid., October 5, 1965.

selves felt. Taken by surprise by Keppel's letter and not knowing the grounds of the action, potential defenders were in a difficult position. By the time the government reversed itself, Chicago support was just about to crystallize. A group of four liberal members of the school board were in the process of preparing a telegram supporting Keppel's action, and the civil rights confederation had nearly completed a detailed statement justifying the fund deferral.[132] The Office of Education had acted in such secrecy and was to be reversed with such speed that the potential local constituency supporting civil rights enforcement never had a chance to organize itself.

Settlement in Chicago

Mayor Daley did not have to wait long. The very morning of his news conference HEW Undersecretary Wilbur Cohen flew to Chicago to negotiate a settlement with the president of the board of education. Interpreting President Johnson's comments as a directive to get out of Chicago at once, Secretary Gardner sent Cohen, known as a good negotiator, to rescue what he could. Cohen obtained very little in day-long talks with Frank Whiston, the dour and loyal Willis supporter representing Chicago.

At 5:00 that night, after clearing the details with HEW headquarters, the two men emerged with an agreement. HEW was to release the funds and withdraw its investigators for two months. In exchange, the school board merely agreed to reaffirm two earlier ineffective resolutions and to investigate school attendance boundaries.[133]

On paper, Chicago had made some concessions, but past performance by the school board suggested that nothing would be done. In fact, Chicago officials treated the agreement as a total political victory. The school board president embarrassed HEW by implying at a press conference that the Office of Education had reversed itself because of Mayor Daley's discussion with the President.[134] Representative Pucinski proclaimed that the Mayor "has done the people of the nation a service by standing firm against intolerable Federal intervention." The congressman saw the agreement as "an abject surrender by Keppel—a great victory for local government, a great victory for Chicago." The agreement was meaningless, a mere "face saving device." [135]

In Chicago, a town pervaded by politics, where "clout" is a basic unit of political analysis and where legal technicalities are of little interest, this

---

132 Bacon interview, July 22, 1966; Interview with Albert Raby, July 26, 1966.
133 *Integrated Education*, Vol. III (Dec. 1965), pp. 18, 35–36.
134 *Chicago Daily News*, October 6, 1966.   135 *Ibid.*

became the generally accepted interpretation of the incident. Civil rights leader Al Raby saw the reversal as a blatant political surrender.

> We are shocked at this shameless display of naked political power exhibited by Mayor Daley in intervening at the highest level not to bring Chicago into compliance with the Civil Rights Act, but to demand Federal funds regardless of how they are to be used.
>
> Mayor Daley ostensibly supported the Civil Rights Act and all the Democratic Congressmen from Illinois . . . voted for it.
>
> Yet they are the first to squeal like stuck pigs when the bill is enforced in the North.[136]

While Mayor Daley's activity and the political power of the Chicago machine both locally and in Congress forced the President to examine the issue, these facts are not sufficient to explain the disastrous Federal retreat. President Johnson was the same man who had passionately appealed to Congress and the nation for sweeping civil rights legislation only months earlier and the same man who was to call for Federal open-housing legislation a few months in the future. The political insensitivity and the careless miscalculations of his administrators, however, left the President no real choice in this situation.

The Catalogue of Errors

In the months preceding the October crisis the various high officials standing between the President and the day-to-day operations of the Office of Education civil rights bureaucracy had taken a series of false steps. Each time, from the perspective of the man making the decision, there were plausible administrative reasons. Persistent failure to evaluate the consequences in terms of the overall power of the President to support civil rights enforcement, however, gave rise to a confrontation in the worst possible location, against the strongest Democratic machine in the country. It left the President to face the prospect of certain reprisal in Congress and possible reversal in the courts.

The series of decisions leading toward the final confrontation included:

1. The initial decision to investigate complaints in Chicago and other racial trouble spots before considering complaints from a variety of smaller towns.

2. Sending the first investigating team to Chicago.

3. Failure to reach agreement either within HEW or in the entire government on the applicability of Title VI powers in the northern context.

---

[136] *Ibid.*

4. The careless extension of the southern deferral procedure into a radically different legal and political situation.

5. The failure to explain Federal intentions to Willis, Daley, and Page before the dispatch of the Keppel letter.

6. The failure of a White House aide to alert the President.

7. HEW dispatch of the letter without explicit presidential approval.

8. The White House directive forbidding public explanations of the move.

Clearly the release of funds to the Chicago schools was much more the product of administrative inadequacies and misjudgments than of any lack of will to enforce the Civil Rights Act.

Because the Chicago complaint was most thorough and most urgent, it was acted on first, and there was no serious consideration of alternatives. Persisting policy disagreements meant that the investigators were ineffectually spread out over a range of possible topics of study. Operating in a vacuum, the team in Chicago was sketching out a research program that would require years to complete, even as a vital deadline loomed weeks in the future.

HEW officials permitted their decision to be precipitated by what turned out to be a false report in the *Chicago Tribune*, taking as fact the report that Superintendent Page intended to immediately approve Willis' plans for misusing the funds provided for education of low-income children. Rather than taking this issue to the Mayor or Page, explaining their relatively modest plan to temporarily hold up final approval of the grant until an acceptable Chicago plan was prepared, Keppel's letter came as a surprising and shocking rebuff to state authority in education programs. Mayor Daley's celebrated special relationship with the President was made to seem so insubstantial that he was not even given the courtesy of an explanation before the Administration took an unprecedented action [137] fundamentally affecting the most sensitive issue in Chicago. The President confronted a situation in which his Administration had been committed publicly without his knowledge or consent, a situation challenged by his legal advisors, without even a prepared statement of the reasons for the action.

Inside the bureaucracy it had seemed reasonable to investigate the best complaint first, reasonable to send the first team to the city where the most information was available, and reasonable to send a letter indicating

[137] There had been a brief withholding of Federal money for a Manpower Development and Training Act project in Boston, but funds had been released before the action became public. The sum of money had been small, and the action had been taken before the Elementary and Secondary Education Act gave the Office of Education significant leverage over local school systems.

the same kind of action that had been taken many times in southern districts. From the President's chair, all these "reasonable" administrative steps added up to a political disaster. Rather than quietly testing its power and establishing a precedent in a favorable situation, the Office noisily displayed its impotence before the country.

The Aftermath

The outcome was predictable. In Washington, everyone who had gotten burned fingers set out to make sure that it didn't happen again. Although he had escaped public criticism, Secretary Gardner was clearly responsible; the day funds were released in Chicago, Gardner set an assistant to work investigating the HEW civil rights operation. Within months Gardner was to approve a major reorganization and to bring in a new man to coordinate departmental activities. Keppel carried out his previous plan to retire, only to have his departure attributed to the President's displeasure over Chicago. Assistant Secretary Quigley also left the department. Morale was damaged in the Title VI program, and enforcement actions came to a virtual standstill across the country. The Justice Department launched a study of Office of Education deferral procedures, and the Attorney General issued guidelines forbidding deferrals without hearings in the North. In the future the Justice Department was to carefully supervise all deferral and cutoff actions as the President's representative. Only the commitment of Secretary Gardner, the new Commissioner of Education, and, ultimately, of the President, prevented quiet snuffing out of the Title VI effort.

The Chicago school authorities were true to form, doing nothing substantial to honor the agreement made with the Office of Education. The Office of Education was so eager to avoid any appearance of interference that Chicago school authorities were not even asked to send any information to Washington during the two months which had been granted to the school board. When the Chicago CCCO submitted yet another complaint to Washington, Federal officials recommended that the civil rights group attempt to work the problem out with Superintendent Page.[138]

After the crisis, relations with Page were re-established, not by the Commissioner or by the civil rights program, but by a director of one of the Office's major operating programs. When Page was told that the CCCO had been directed to come to Springfield, the state superintendent said that he would handle the matter if he would not be undercut by the Federal office. When Page asked that his office be represented on any

---

[138] Memorandum from David Seeley to Commissioner Keppel, October 21, 1965.

future investigations, Keppel made such a recommendation to Secretary Gardner.[139]

Although the Chicago school board did appoint a committee to examine the school boundaries, the most important point of the agreement, the committee quickly demonstrated its inclination to make only a superficial study. Rather than undertake the extremely complicated job of examining all boundaries for evidence of intentional segregation, the committee chose to consider only written complaints submitted together with evidence, thus shifting the entire burden to civil rights groups. The committee chairman told an HEW official that little could be gained by examining the history of boundary lines, thus blithely ignoring the very question crucial to a determination of the existence of intentional segregation.[140]

One month after the Chicago agreement, it was evident that nothing would be done in Chicago unless Federal pressure was exerted. Seeley commented that retention of "any vestige of utility in Northern discrimination cases" would be impossible if Chicago was allowed to totally ignore its agreement. Such an outcome, he pointed out, would gravely threaten the credibility of Federal demands in the South as well.[141]

Another month was permitted to pass, however. When the truce period was over, the school board reported that it had received only one complaint on the boundary question and that this document had been assigned to a school official for study. On the basis of this record of progress, the board asked that HEW extend the October agreement for another two months.[142]

In Washington, the document was rapidly circulated to top HEW officials and, in the words of one observer, "greeted with shaking heads and grimaces." Secretary Gardner ordered a staff evaluation of the report within 48 hours.[143] The report failed to indicate any measurable progress, destroying the argument that HEW had withdrawn from Chicago only in exchange for local action. Chicago intransigence forced the department to either demonstrate continuing Federal concern or simply make a public admission that civil rights enforcement could be defeated by political pressure.

On December 29 Gardner announced that HEW would not permit an extension of its agreement with the school board and that Federal investi-

[139] Memorandum from Arthur L. Harris to files, October 26, 1965; memorandum from Keppel to Secretary Gardner, October 29, 1965.
[140] Memorandum from Alvin Cohen to David Seeley, October 29, 1965.
[141] Seeley Memorandum, "Next Steps in Chicago," November 12, 1965.
[142] Letter from Frank Whiston to Under Secretary Cohen, December 13, 1965.
[143] Chicago Daily News, December 15, 1965.

gators would return to Chicago. Gardner took sharp issue with the failure to study the school boundaries and stated that HEW needed an "overall city-wide study of data" on assignment policies. "It is reasonable," he wrote, "to expect that the board and the superintendent will make available the information necessary to assess the extent of compliance." [144]

Appearing on national television, Secretary Gardner made the circumstances of the investigation clear. Federal funds would be withheld only if the team found firm proof of deliberate segregation planned by school officials. The Secretary went on to tell of his high regard for the Mayor and the school board president. "We will treat Chicago with all the respect due a great city," he said, "and we are confident we will get every cooperation while there." [145]

Much had been learned. The new team went to Chicago with a directive to limit their study to clearly unconstitutional intentional segregation, and money would not be delayed until definite proof had been obtained. In fact high Justice Department officials revealed to a press conference, just a day before Gardner's letter announcing the dispatch of an investigating team, that the funds would never have been deferred in Chicago if the Office of Education had been operating under the Attorney General's new interpretation of the law.[146]

Both Office of Education attorneys involved in the first investigation were to resign after they decided that the new effort was simply an empty face-saving gesture. Both were angry that a man whose previous experience had been in the handling of Arkansas cases, who they felt was completely unfamiliar with the northern urban problems, and who was a member of the more conservative faction within the Office, was put in charge of the local study. Commissioner Harold Howe, II, Keppel's successor, was determined to maintain friendly relationships with Willis, and activists on Seeley's staff were angered by the "Dear Ben" letters that came out of Howe's office. When some clear-cut examples of discrimination were summarized, together with supporting evidence, the memo was quietly buried in the bureaucracy. Both lawyers decided that Willis and Howe were "playing footsie" and that the new study was merely a "superficial investigation to save face." [147]

In Chicago, the team of HEW analysts was received with promises of cooperation. When Seeley explained their intentions to the school board,

[144] Letter from Secretary Gardner to Frank Whiston, December 29, 1965; *Chicago Daily News,* December 30, 1965.
[145] *Chicago Tribune,* January 3, 1966.
[146] *Chicago Sun-Times,* December 28, 1965.
[147] McClure interview; interview with William Copenhaver, December 30, 1966.

the board president promised full cooperation.[148] Mayor Daley was un-
worried:

> This is an attempt to sift accusations from real facts and another attempt to find
> out how the schools are doing. No one should be concerned. If there is anything
> to be corrected, there will be corrections. The members of the board of education
> have responded in the past to suggestions that have improved education. This will
> continue.[149]

Seeley told the board that there was no danger of loss of Federal funds as
long as the board cooperated.[150]

Superintendent Willis remained unreconstructed, however, and his attitude rapidly generated a test of will over information needed for the
study. Willis estimated that it would take six months to gather the information requested by the Office of Education. By early February Willis
was ordering principals not to answer questionnaires sent to them by the
Census Bureau at the request of the Office of Education in connection
with a nationwide study. The Chicago school board did over-rule Willis,
however, in order to conduct a survey of racial distribution of teachers
within the school system.[151] The early weeks of the study indicated that
segregation persisted in the Washburne Trade School apprenticeship program, but Willis provided only a letter in which he stated "very generally
the fact that the schools are participating to some extent in the Mayor's
announced program seeking less discrimination in building trades appren-
ticeships. . . ."[152] The school board voted to disband its committee on
school boundaries and to refer all questions to Willis' office. It became
evident that Willis would simply not release data on such crucial issues as
school capacities, school expenditures, and teacher qualifications. He even
forbade school officials responsible for such information to discuss methods of gathering data with Federal officials.[153] By early April Willis was
publicly attacking the investigation in a major address:

> I find it difficult to believe that an employee in a Washington bureau whose knowl-
> edge of Chicago is what he can see from the Hilton hotel can judge what we need
> in public education in Chicago better than our able and high level career pro-
> fessionals.[154]

After several weeks of meetings with community groups having complaints and after obtaining the information that Willis and the school

148 *Chicago Daily News*, January 4, 1966.
149 *Chicago Tribune*, January 4, 1966.
150 *Ibid.*, January 5, 1966.   151 *Ibid.*, February 9, 1966.
152 Memorandum from Seeley to Peter Libassi, January 19, 1966.
153 Memorandum from Seeley to Commissioner Howe, March 10, 1966.
154 *Chicago Tribune*, April 5, 1966.

board would provide, the team withdrew to Washington to analyze the available data. There was no inclination to risk another confrontation with Willis by demanding information he was unwilling to provide. In Chicago local attitudes were made evident in the school board's refusal to provide aid to help stabilize integrated schools and in Mayor Daley's refusal to appoint another Negro to the school board.[155]

The report on the Chicago schools was not to emerge from the Office of Education until January, 1967, almost a year and a half after the study began. During the intervening months, both Secretary Gardner and Commissioner Howe emphasized the complexity of the issues in the North and the uncertainty of Federal authority. In late April Secretary Gardner told interviewers on "Face the Nation" that, although the department saw Chicago as "the most unfortunate situation educationally," the problem "probably cannot adequately be dealt with by Title VI." [156] Commissioner Howe proclaimed that northern-style segregation was "beyond the clear purview of the Civil Rights Act." [157]

Willis was obviously a central obstacle, and HEW officials decided to stall until his scheduled departure in the fall. It became "more and more evident," Seeley said, that progress would not be possible until a new man sat in Willis' chair.[158] When the Chicago board of education named James Redmond to succeed Willis, the strategy of the Office of Education was established by Commissioner Howe. Redmond was an old friend of Howe's and was considering an offer to become Howe's associate commissioner for elementary and secondary education at the time he took the Chicago job.[159] Within a relationship of friendship and mutual trust, Howe and Redmond were able to work out an agreeable strategy. "I was in touch informally with Jim Redmond about these problems very shortly after he became superintendent," Howe recalls. In private discussions, Howe tried to "arm" Redmond for the informal discussions with his board members necessary to persuade the majority to go along.[160] In this way the Office of Education was able to avoid another confrontation with Chicago political power, while Redmond was able to use the leverage provided by Federal concern to further his effort to convince the school board to do something about school segregation in the city.[161]

The Chicago report was finally released in a January 9, 1967, letter

[155] *Chicago Sun-Times,* April 29, 1966; *Chicago Daily News,* May 6, 1966.
[156] Television interview of Secretary Gardner, "Face the Nation," CBS, April 24, 1966.
[157] Quoted in speech by Edwin C. Berry, "Title VI in the Metropolis," May 30, 1966. (Mimeographed.)
[158] Seeley interview, June 17, 1967.
[159] Interview with Peter Libassi, April 26, 1967; *Chicago Daily News,* May 13, 1966.
[160] Howe interview, September 20, 1968.   [161] Libassi interview.

from Howe to Redmond. The report had been privately approved in advance by Redmond, the Justice Department, and the White House.[162] In his letter Commissioner Howe wrote:

> Our report outlines serious conditions in the Chicago schools which, in our view, may involve violations of Title VI of the Civil Rights Act. We believe that the constructive way to proceed is to seek your cooperation in moving rapidly to correct the conditions outlined in the report.[163]

The 17-page report was an exercise in generalizations, containing little of substance. The study team was "impressed with the complexity involved in sorting out the factors underlying the establishment of a particular boundary or group of boundaries. . . ." The report stated, very tentatively, that it "probably would not be possible to explain fully the selection and establishment of certain of the sites and boundaries which we have studied to date by factors which do not include race." The document noted the very high level of faculty segregation revealed by the teacher head count and concluded that the school board had made no significant effort to equalize the quality of teachers at white and Negro schools.[164]

The Federal report concluded with a series of recommendations. Chicago was asked to hire specialists to design a plan "drawing on a wide range of administrative remedies" to fight segregation. The board was also asked to increase the proportion of experienced teachers in Negro schools and to institute special incentives for attracting teachers to inner-city schools.[165] Commissioner Howe relied on Redmond's "cooperation" to accomplish these changes.

Not a Federal ultimatum, the report was an attempt to give some support to those elements in Chicago favoring change. The careful planning of the move was evident when Superintendent Redmond applied for a Federal grant to bus teachers into "difficult" schools only three days after the document became public.[166] The board also approved requests for Federal funds for experimental programs designed to keep middle-class white families in Chicago, for recruiting teachers for ghetto areas, and for financing an exchange program with suburban schools.[167]

It rapidly became evident, however, that any significant change in

[162] *Ibid.*
[163] Letter from Commissioner Howe to Superintendent Redmond, January 6, 1967.
[164] U.S., Office of Education, "Report on Office of Education Analysis of Certain Aspects of Chicago Public Schools Under Title VI of the Civil Rights Act of 1964," January, 1967, pp. 9, 14.
[165] *Ibid.*, "Recommendations," pp. 3–4.
[166] *Chicago Daily News*, January 12, 1967.
[167] *Chicago Sun-Times*, January 11, 1967.

Chicago would depend on Federal money. The financially strapped school board made no allotment for compliance in its new budget, and the school system did not even hire experts to propose solutions until a Federal grant was made available. In spite of local civil rights complaints that nothing was being done and that school officials were unwilling to consider the segregation problem in determining locations for new schools,[168] Commissioner Howe strongly supported Redmond after a meeting with him in Washington:

> No large city has solved the problem of de facto segregation. Every one has lived with it. Clearly, there is a willingness in Chicago to consider this problem in a very real way. There is no quick solution to these matters.[169]

The Office of Education report requested a progress report from the Chicago authorities by April 1. In late August Superintendent Redmond submitted to the board of education a sweeping plan to increase pupil and teacher integration. On the boundary question, the Redmond proposal called for recognition of the positive value of integration, for bussing of students to achieve racial balance, for exchanges with the suburbs and the huge Catholic school system, and for the establishment of stable racial quotas in integrated schools. All these immediate steps were to be supplemented by selection of school sites to promote integration and the establishment of a metropolitan educational council. Long-range plans called for a major effort to change teacher assignment policies to equalize teacher qualifications across the system, a feasibility study for the establishment of "magnet schools" in specialized fields to draw white students into the inner-city and the construction of massive educational parks along the city's lakefront. All of these steps were to depend on the availability of Federal assistance.[170]

The board of education promptly accepted the report in principle by an overwhelming vote.[171] In earlier years, however, the board had also accepted in principle other major reports on integration in the Chicago schools, only to refuse to take any steps toward implementation. Moreover, the current board had fewer liberal members than earlier boards. "It is not," pointed out the CCCO, "a *plan of action to desegregate* the Chicago public schools. Not a single practice of the school system changed as a result of the school board's adoption of the Redmond-Board Report 'in principle.' " [172] The civil rights group was sharply critical of

168 *Ibid.*, January 19, 1967.   169 *Chicago Tribune*, February 8, 1967.
170 Text of Redmond Plan, reprinted in *Chicago Tribune*, August 24, 1967.
171 *Chicago Tribune*, August 24, 1967.
172 CCCO, "Redmond Report," September 8, 1967, p. 1.

the failure of the Redmond report to propose specific immediate remedies to the most serious abuses and stated that the Office of Education was "a partner to de jure segregation in Chicago's schools." [173]

Even a very limited effort to begin compliance with the Redmond plan generated intense political opposition. In December 1968 Superintendent Redmond proposed bussing 5000 primary-school children in areas undergoing racial transition. By bussing both white and black students in two neighborhoods, the plan hoped to relieve overcrowding, stabilize the racial balance, and prevent white migration from areas with changing populations.[174] HEW also donated Federal land on the North Side as the site for the first integrated magnet school, to be constructed when the board of education provided the necessary funds.[175] The proposal, however, brought a bitter white protest and produced lengthy delays in the school board.[176]

The plan was eventually reduced to a token 249 students and operated in only one section of town. The superintendent was denied the right to assign transfers, and the board required fearful black parents to sign permission forms.[177] Even this slight effort to transfer black students from inadequate and overcrowded schools, under a system which guaranteed that very strong white majorities were to be maintained in the receiving schools, generated active and bitter community and political attacks on the school system and HEW.

The Daley machine, which had swept the Mayor to his greatest victory early in 1967, was in a stronger position than ever both locally and nationally. In all likelihood the role of the Office of Education would be limited to the exertion of marginal pressure on the school board in favor of implementation of the Redmond plan. This pressure, together with the availability of millions of dollars of Federal grants to take the financial burden for unpopular measures off the local school system, could possibly be significant in reshaping the Chicago schools. Unless the Chicago authorities prove completely intransigent, however, there is no will in Washington for another confrontation. The basic decisions in Chicago will be taken by the Chicago board of education. In the fall of 1968 HEW was not even monitoring Chicago's performance under the Redmond plan.[178]

[173] *Ibid.*, p. 15.   [174] *Chicago Tribune*, December 27, 1967.
[175] *Chicago Tribune*, December 22, 1967.
[176] Henry W. DeZutter, "When Folks Get Together to Talk About Bussing," *New Republic* (March 2, 1968), pp. 13–14.
[177] *Chicago Tribune*, March 12, 1968.
[178] Interview with Mrs. Ruby Martin, September 23, 1968.

The Impact of the Chicago Fiasco

When Secretary Gardner sent a team of investigators to Chicago, he expressed the hope that their study would provide answers about the extent of Title VI authority in the North. It did. The Chicago incident answered a number of unresolved policy questions, but the results were political rather than legal answers.

After Chicago, discussion of using Title VI to combat de facto segregation ended. Future studies were to be strictly limited to the far more difficult issue of intentional segregation, and little attention was given to even this question until angry southerners succeeded in passing an amendment to the Elementary and Secondary Education Act demanding equal treatment of violators in all states.

An extremely significant legacy of Chicago was a deep suspicion of the Office of Education among big-city northern Democrats. The following year the House of Representatives was to adopt amendments restricting enforcement authority, and Congressman Pucinski was to be a leading supporter. Amid continuing congressional criticism, HEW officials expressed uncertainty about the usefulness of Title VI enforcement in the North. Suspicions aroused in Congress were sufficient to provoke a heated attack on Commissioner Howe when a draft bill to aid northern districts voluntarily desegregating leaked out of the bureaucracy. In late 1967 Illinois Senator Dirksen was to lead an attempt to forbid any Federal aid to cities, such as Chicago, for bussing Negro students to white schools.

The Chicago incident was universally seen in the South as a political test of strength and proof that civil rights enforcement could be beaten politically.[179] Even after the Attorney General ruled that such deferral action was not permissible in the future in the North, a coalition of southerners and northerners in the House of Representatives underlined its disapproval by overwhelmingly passing a 1966 amendment designed to strip the Commissioner of Education of his authority to defer Federal grants before holding a formal hearing and presenting proof of school district violations. Only the resistance of Senate liberals preserved this power for the Office of Education, a power that had been a crucial tool in obtaining compliance in the South and that had been used with so little sensitivity in Chicago.

After Chicago two years were to pass before the beginning of any attempt to investigate northern complaints. During this period Commissioner Howe made moving speeches about the ghetto schools of the

[179] Secretary Gardner's civil rights advisor estimated that it took 1½ to 2 years for the enforcement program to recover from the damage inflicted by the Chicago disaster. (Libassi interview, July 25, 1968.)

North, but denied that the Office of Education had any authority to deal with these vast educational crises.

No effective remedy was provided for past abuses of local power which fostered segregation, abuses later made evident in a Federal court decision finding Chicago guilty of segregation in its public housing program. An earlier hope that HEW would use the administrative discretion provided by the broad injunction of Title VI against discrimination in Federally assisted programs to prohibit de facto segregation vanished in the first days of October, 1965. A high price had been paid for the political education of the administrators responsible for enforcing the Civil Rights Act.

5

Virginia: Desegregating the Old Dominion

The legal formulations and the administrative details so endlessly debated in Washington gain meaning only as they are perceived and acted upon in thousands of school board offices in courthouse squares across the South. The Federal effort becomes real only when the school bus that picks up the children of the peanut or tobacco farmer begins to carry both white and black students, and when Negro teachers overcome deeply rooted stereotypes of intellectual inferiority in the high school that dominates the life and even the geography of many towns. To begin to understand the change, it is necessary to leave the drab corridors of the crowded Washington offices, to leave the world of forms and bureaucracy, and to enter into the quiet informality of sleepy little communities caught in the grips of fundamental social change.

No single state can represent all of the many patterns of response to the revolution demanded by the school desegregation guidelines. In the South there has been no Chicago, no single incident that summarizes the clash between Federal power and local resistance. In each state both the racial tradition and the quality of recent political leadership have shaped local reactions.

Although every state had unique features, the presence in Virginia of several well-defined regions with distinct histories and sets of attitudes makes it possible to view within a single state a spectrum of responses almost as broad as can be found in the entire 17 southern and border states affected by the Federal regulations. The diversity of the state includes, not only the exploding Washington suburbs and the cosmopolitan port city of Norfolk, but also the backward agricultural counties of the Southside and the Eastern Shore, with their Negro majorities and rigid racial separation. Southern Virginia lies within the plantation tradition, while the Shenandoah Valley, stretching west of the Blue Ridge, and the mountain country of the southwest were settled by independent farmers who never developed the rigid racial attitudes that dominated the Southside. The state as a whole is in the midst of the political and economic transformation that has swept through much of the South. It retains strong elements both of southern traditionalism and a newer, nationally oriented, and pragmatic desire for progress.

Racial change is fundamental to the turbulent readjustment now underway in Virginia, and it has been greatly accelerated by the enforcement of Title VI. In a state where the governor closed all public schools with any Negro students in 1958 and where only 102 Negro students sat in white classrooms when President Kennedy took office, two years of enforcement brought one-fourth of all the black students into white schools,[1] a higher level than prevails in many northern cities. Only a few years earlier, such change was inconceivable.

An analysis of the social revolution in Virginia public education must, of course, focus on the decisive role of national pressure on local leadership exerted through the massive intervention of the Federal executive branch. This transformation, however, required more than a mere commitment by the national Administration. American bureaucracies must operate within a federal system characterized by pervasive localism. Not only do state and local governments possess extensive formal powers, but the members of Congress who control both legislation and funds for national programs remain strikingly sensitive to local concerns. Within this system, Federal administrators have very strong incentives to respond to local demands. Thus it is a general political fact that basic and peaceful social change must draw upon some elements of local support.

In trying to understand the sweeping changes in southern education, it may be useful to consider the school desegregation guidelines as one part of a many-sided revolution. First came the revolution in the law, denying the political elite the right to use the instruments of state authority to blatantly enforce caste separation. This judicial change was symbolically of vast importance, even though its practical impact was limited by the caution and the inefficient procedures of the courts. This change made it possible for Negro litigants to insistently press the courts for legal remedies adequate to produce actual desegregation.

Second came the transformation of politics, barriers to Negro political participation were struck down, and rural domination was diluted as state legislatures were restructured by reapportionment decisions. For the first time in 75 years the black vote became a factor to be reckoned with across the South.

Third came the revolution in public expectations of the schools. In the midst of the unprecedented prosperity of the 1960's, southerners were

[1] *Southern School News*, May 17, 1964; Office of Education, National Center for Educational Statistics, enrollment tables, December 6, 1966.

coming to see the close relationship between education and continued economic progress. One symptom was the enthusiastic support for the creation of new colleges. Communities came to realize that school quality strongly influenced plant locations, and thus local prosperity.

In the decade after the Supreme Court decision, public objections to token integration had declined dramatically in many sections. While there was no enthusiasm for integration in the white communities, the schools were now seen much more as the key to progress than as the bastion of racial purity. Thus in several basic respects the South had changed substantially since the beginning of the struggle to enforce the Supreme Court decision.

The new situation made possible relatively easy enforcement of the first set of school guidelines in much of the South and in most of Virginia. The political leaders and the public were willing to accept general token integration. When, in the second year, the Federal objectives were expanded toward a total abolition of educational segregation, however, opposition increased very rapidly. As the normal patterns of federalism began to reassert themselves and national support for civil rights enforcement faded, enforcement objectives were compromised. By the third year, the Federal initiative had reached a virtual standstill. In those areas where local opinion and local leadership were willing to move, segregation had been abolished. Very little happened in the centers of resistance until the Supreme Court intervened in 1968.

Even if no further progress was made, however, the school guidelines had forced revolutionary changes in race relations. By September 1967 whole sections of the state had abolished separate school systems, and everywhere the long-dreaded prospect of student integration and the shocking idea of some faculty integration were facts.

THE BEGINNING

Virginia's Defiance

The rapidly changing Virginia of the mid-1960's was particularly striking when viewed against the background of the bitter-end struggle against the first steps toward integration in the late 1950's. It was a Virginia governor, a product of a political organization that prided itself on gentlemanly self-respecting southern conservatism, who took the radical step of locking up school buildings for 13,000 children in late 1958 to forestall the contamination of token integration.

Virginia's initial reaction to the 1954 decision had been calm. The governor called for peaceful compliance. Opinion rapidly polarized, however, as Negro leaders rejected attempts to find a formula that would actually perpetuate the status quo and as the militant black belt segregationists pressured Governor Thomas Stanley. The governor responded by appointing a policy planning commission, excluding representatives of the state's urban "moderate-liberals" or of the politically impotent Negroes, still kept from the polls by the poll tax. Thus, while the border states and even some parts of the old Confederacy set about planning for integration, Virginians planned their resistance.[2]

A statewide anti-integration group, the Defenders of State Sovereignty, rapidly emerged as a political power. Eschewing blatant racism in favor of legalistic arguments, the Defenders called on Virginians to preserve the sovereignty of the cavalier commonwealth by striking from the state constitution provisions requiring the maintenance of public schools and forbidding state support of private schools. These changes would open the road for the creation of a publicly supported system of white private schools, giving whites an easy way to avoid integration and perhaps destroying public education in Virginia.[3] In six Southside counties local officials underlined their willingness to abandon the public schools by adopting school budgets on a month-to-month basis, on the condition that the schools remained totally segregated.[4] The same attitude was echoed in the 1955 report of the Governor's commission:

> . . . the overwhelming majority of the people of Virginia are not only opposed to integration . . . but are firmly convinced that integration . . . without due regard to the convictions of the majority of the people . . . would virtually destroy or seriously impair the public system in many sections of Virginia.[5]

The rising tide of segregationist sentiment was greatly stimulated by the belligerent stand of Prince Edward County. This Southside county, with a majority of black students, was one of the original districts involved in the 1954 Supreme Court decision. Within hours of the Court's 1955 implementation decree the Prince Edward county board voted to end financing for public schools and set in motion a massive private school campaign as soon as integration began.[6]

Recognizing diverse local conditions, the Governor's commission recommended that each locality be allowed to decide whether or not to close its schools when integration took place. In areas in which schools closed the commission called for state tuition grants to help parents send

---

[2] Robbins L. Gates, *The Making of Massive Resistance* (Chapel Hill: University of North Carolina Press, 1964), pp. 28–43. In Virginia, "black belt" refers primarily to the cluster of counties with Negro majorities.
[3] Gates, p. 49.   [4] *Ibid.*, p. 47.   [5] *Ibid.*, p. 44.
[6] Benjamin Muse, *Virginia's Massive Resistance* (Bloomington, Ind.: University of Indiana Press, 1961), pp. 12–14.

children to private schools. Under the plan, no child could "be required to attend an integrated school." [7] The report was widely approved, and the necessary amendments to the state constitution were adopted in a referendum in January 1956. The state's severely limited electorate endorsed the changes by a 2 to 1 margin.[8]

Nothing now seemed to stand in the way of a program giving each community freedom to decide whether to resist or comply with court-ordered integration. This program, however, was to dissolve in a deepening well of segregationist feeling. James J. Kilpatrick, the young editor of the influential *Richmond News Leader*, papered the state with powerfully written editorials advocating the legally absurd but emotionally satisfying doctrine of interposition. His passionate appeals, laced with historical argumentation, discourses on the nature of the Constitution, and even quotations from Jefferson, stirred the state's profoundly conservative political leadership.[9] The organization of Senator Byrd, built on courthouse political machines and strongest in the Southside, became a leading force in the growing movement to force segregation even on those communities willing to accept token integration.

When the Assembly convened the local option plan was passed over, and much effort was spent in forging an interposition resolution. Deciding that the Supreme Court decision was actually an illegal amendment to the Constitution, the Assembly announced that Virginia had "never surrendered" its power to maintain separate schools.[10] The Assembly pledged:

> . . . to take all appropriate measures, legally and constitutionally available to us, to resist this illegal encroachment upon our sovereign powers and to urge upon our sister states . . . their prompt and deliberate efforts to check this and further encroachment by the Supreme Court . . . upon the reserved powers of the states.[11]

Of the 140 legislators, only 10 opposed interposition, most of them coming from the Washington suburban area.[12]

Having resurrected an ancient and discredited doctrine, the leaders of the Byrd Organization proceeded to claim leadership in the entire South. Senator Byrd called for uniting the southern states in "massive resistance." In Washington the effort bore fruit with the issuance of the "Southern Manifesto," signed by approximately 80 per cent of the members of Congress from the 11 southern states.[13] The manifesto made resistance to the Federal courts respectable across the South.

Massive Resistance proved to be political salvation for the Byrd Organ-

---

[7] Gates, pp. 67–68.   [8] *Ibid.*, p. 85.   [9] Muse, p. 20, and Gates, p. 105.
[10] Muse, p. 21.   [11] *Ibid.*, p. 22.   [12] Gates, p. 114.   [13] *Ibid.*, p. 118.

ization. After dominating state politics for three decades, the "museum piece" political structure seemed to be in trouble in the mid-1950's. Committed to honest government by an aristocracy of Virginia gentlemen, a government providing an absolute minimum of public services, the Organization had been threatened by a progressive Republican candidate for governor in the 1953 election. In the 1954 legislative session, the organization had lost control of the Assembly on a major issue for the first time in years.[14] Just when basic political change seemed at hand the school issue emerged, permittting the organization to use racial fears to extend its clear domination of state politics for another decade.

The issue was brought to a head by Federal court decisions in the summer of 1956, which ordered the admission of Negro students to some schools in Charlottesville, where the University of Virginia is located, and Arlington, a prosperous Washington suburb. The high probability that these schools would be peacefully integrated and the facade of total segregation throughout the South would be breached was intolerable to Virginia segregationists.

Governor Stanley called a special session of the Assembly, a session devoted to creating the legal framework of Massive Resistance. Rejecting local option, the governor told the assembled legislators that he could not "recommend any legislation, or action, which accepts the principle of integration of the races in the public schools." [15]

The nature of Virginia's response was settled when Senator Byrd returned from a European trip. At the large picnic that had become an annual function at his Berryville orchard, Byrd announced that Virginia must fight "with every ounce of energy and capacity." [16] "Let Virginia surrender to this illegal demand," he told the gathering of neighbors and Virginia politicians, "and you'll find the ranks of the South broken. . . . If Virginia surrenders, the rest of the South will go down too." [17]

With Byrd's decision to lead southern resistance, Assembly approval of the Massive Resistance program became inevitable. The dominant attitude was expressed by a Southside Congressman: "We cannot allow Arlington or Norfolk to integrate. If they won't stand with us, I say make them stand." [18] During its four-week session, the Assembly enacted 23 laws designed to prevent school integration and to harass the NAACP.

The legislative program was many-sided. Taking advantage of the fact that Federal courts insist that anyone claiming Federal rights must first exhaust all procedures provided by state law to obtain the rights involved,

---

[14] James Latimer, "Virginia: A Sense of the Past," *States in Crisis,* James Reichley, ed. (Chapel Hill: University of North Carolina Press, 1964), pp. 15–16.
[15] Gates, pp. 125–27, 129.   [16] Latimer, p. 17; *Washington Post,* October 21, 1966.
[17] Muse, p. 29.   [18] Peltason, *Fifty-Eight Lonely Men,* p. 45.

the Assembly created complicated, difficult, and embarassing procedures for pupil transfer to discourage and delay black parents. Hatred of the NAACP was reflected in new laws setting up investigating committees and requiring the group to register with state authorities.[19]

The Governor's plan for withholding funds from schools that integrated touched off the most serious battle. State aid was 42 per cent of total school expenditures in Virginia, and this change would give the governor unprecedented power over local school divisions. Over-riding objections from the state board of education, Organization stalwarts passed the bill. "Any integration," thundered State Senator Mills Godwin, Jr., "is the key which opens the door to the inevitable destruction of our free public schools. Integration, however slight, anywhere in Virginia would be a cancer eating at the very life blood of our public school system." [20] Men who were later to invoke the slogan of local control of the schools in fighting desegregation requirements showed slight concern about infringing on local prerogatives to maintain segregation. Ironically, Godwin was to be elected governor in 1965, just as the school guidelines began to transform Virginia education.

The school-closing plan passed only because of over-representation in the Assembly of the rural Byrd machine strongholds. Had the Washington suburbs been fairly represented, an alliance of northern Virginians, Republicans, and urban representatives would probably have prevailed.[21] The political voicelessness of much of the Negro fifth of the Virginia population helped to allow a reactionary political elite to use the authority of the state government to impose its views on a divided public.

After President Eisenhower's dispatch of paratroopers to Little Rock in 1957, the Byrd Organization restored its unchallenged position in state politics. Lindsay Almond, who had argued the Virginia position before the Supreme Court, swept to victory over a moderate Republican, carrying almost two-thirds of the vote in the gubernatorial contest.[22] Almond's position was clear:

> We will oppose with every faculty at our command, and with every ounce of our energy, the attempt to mix white and Negro races in our classrooms. Let there be no misunderstanding, no weasel words on this point. . . . We will not yield as long as a single avenue of resistance remains unexplored.[23]

The Collapse of Massive Resistance

The extreme position taken by Virginia officials invited attack, and the NAACP answered with the most ambitious program of school litigation undertaken in any southern state. The 27,000-member Virginia chapter

[19] Muse, pp. 31–32.   [20] *Ibid.*, p. 30, and Gates, pp. 170, 174.
[21] *Ibid.*, pp. 184–85, and Muse, p. 31.   [22] *Ibid.*, p. 43.   [23] *Ibid.*, p. 42.

was the strongest in the South, and Thurgood Marshall's NAACP Legal Defense Fund was encouraged by the existence of large areas of predominantly moderate opinion to focus its energy on the struggle to dismantle Massive Resistance.[24] The ensuing battle was short but intense. Because the Assembly had made no pretense that it was doing anything but attempting to frustrate execution of the Supreme Court decision, the Legal Defense Fund was in a strong legal position in the short and intense court battle.

> The only hope segregationists had was that the . . . district judges would refuse to take judicial notice of the purpose and impact of the several anti-integration laws, considering each law in isolation and taking each at its face value. Segregationists wanted the judges to assume, for example, that the placement board would not discriminate against Negroes, and that the threat to close integrated schools was not designed to keep them segregated. . . . But with one exception, the district judges were unwilling to ignore the obvious purpose, design, and intentions of the massive resistance laws.[25]

Eventually, the vigor of the NAACP and the sense of responsibility of the Virginians serving as Federal district judges brought the ponderous edifice of Massive Resistance tumbling down. In the process, however, the NAACP was forced to fight a protracted legal battle under harassment from state authorities. Nevertheless, Legal Defense Fund attorneys continued to win the decisive legal encounters. As schools prepared to open in the fall of 1958 the state had exhausted the possibilities for delay, and school boards in three sections of the state were under court order to desegregate.[26] Governor Almond had promised to close the schools rather than permit integration, and now he faced the decision.

The day the Fourth Circuit Court of Appeals rejected a final attempt to delay integration in Warren County, the Governor took control of the school and shut it down. A week later he closed two schools in Charlottesville and then barred the doors of all the high schools in Norfolk, the state's largest city.[27] For a semester these schools remained closed. In Norfolk, children of military personnel stationed at the city's large bases were locked out of schools that had been built with Federal money, an action that generated a surge of protests in Congress.

Philosophic statements about state sovereignty and the attempt to find a "legal" way to avoid the Supreme Court decision were fine with most white Virginians, but closed schools were another thing. With 13,000 children suddenly locked out of public schools, and only a fraction of them able to find places in private classrooms, opinion began to change. By a small margin, the state PTA turned against Massive Resistance, and

[24] *Ibid.*, pp. 47–48.   [25] Peltason, pp. 209–10.
[26] Muse, p. 48, and Peltason, p. 213.   [27] *Southern School News*, May 17, 1964.

the Committee to Preserve Public Schools drew growing support in the Washington suburbs. In Norfolk the school closings were widely resented, and the city's teachers refused to work in the segregationist private schools.[28]

Governor Almond was the captive of a segregationist political organization trying to lead a deeply divided state. Senator Byrd saw the issue as Virginia's "greatest crisis since the war between the states." Unless the Old Dominion stood firm, the NAACP would "bring Virginia to its knees first and then . . . march through the South singing hallelujah." The battle was one to save the school system and to "preserve the sovereignty of our Commonwealth which is our most sacred heritage." [29] Kilpatrick's *Richmond News Leader* echoed the Senator and urged the rapid establishment of private schools in threatened communities across the state.[30]

Senator Byrd's stirring words were no longer enough. The debate turned from one of integration versus segregation to one of maintaining public education versus closing the schools. Moderates who would not support integration began to coalesce in favor of keeping schools open even if token integration was required. The Virginia Education Association, the white teachers' group, demanded a special session of the Assembly to reopen the schools. In Norfolk, for the first time in the South, white parents sued state authorities, claiming that closing the city's high schools while other Virginia schools remained open violated the equal protection of the laws clause of the U.S. Constitution.[31]

In January the years of struggle in the courts came to a head. On January 19, Robert E. Lee's birthday, decisions on crucial lawsuits were handed down by both the state supreme court and the Federal district court in Norfolk. The Virginia high court held that school closing and withholding of state education aid violated the state's constitution, while the Federal judge ruled in favor of the Norfolk parents.[32] Virginia's elaborate legal defenses against token integration were smashed beyond repair.

The Governor remained under terrible pressure. Although the legal structure of Massive Resistance was in tatters, Senator Byrd advised Governor Almond to interpose the sovereignty of the state against the Federal court and force the Justice Department to throw him in jail. Unless President Eisenhower was willing to imprison a prominent governor the year before a presidential election, the Supreme Court decision would be a dead letter in the South. If the governor were arrested, Byrd promised heroism in the state and leadership of the organization that had shaped

[28] Peltason, p. 214.   [29] Muse, p. 66.   [30] *Ibid.*, p. 72.
[31] *Ibid.*, pp. 86–88, 91, 93–94.   [32] *Ibid.*, pp. 124–25.

Virginia politics since the 1920's.[33] At first Almond seemed inclined to take this course, telling a statewide radio audience that he would "not yield to that which I know to be wrong. . . ."[34]

In the end, however, Almond's respect for the courts prevailed and he conceded defeat. In an address to the Assembly he signaled Virginia's submission:

> It is not enough for gentlemen to cry unto you and me, "Don't give up the ship!" "Stop them!" "It must not happen," or "It can be prevented." If any of them knows the way through the dark maze of judicial aberration and constitutional exploitation, I call upon them to shed the light for which Virginia stands in dire need in this her dark and agonizing hour. No fairminded person would be so unreasonable as to seek to hold me responsible for failure to exercise powers which the state is powerless to bestow.[35]

Under Almond's leadership, the Assembly rejected the segregationist proposal to close all Virginia schools and repealed the most extreme of the Massive Resistance laws. Reluctantly, and with bitterness, the state leadership accepted token integration. At the same time the Assembly made certain that no white child would be forced to attend an integrated school by repealing the state compulsory attendance law and providing tuition grants to finance private education.[36]

Integration Before the Civil Rights Act

Almost five years after the initial Supreme Court decision, integration began in Virginia. In early February 1959, 21 Negro students walked peacefully into white schools in Arlington and Norfolk.[37] Nothing had changed in the Southside, however, and Prince Edward County abandoned public education. Most of the county's white students enrolled in long-planned private schools, while the Negroes were left with no schools at all.[38]

To keep integration to a minimum across the state, Virginia relied on its pupil-placement board. The board was directed by the Assembly to assign all pupils to schools in accordance with three vague criteria:

1. Orderly administration of the public schools.
2. Competent instruction of the pupils enrolled.
3. Health, safety, education and general welfare of such pupils.[39]

Until August 1960 the board assigned all students to schools of their own race. The only Negro children entering white schools were those who

---

33 *Washington Post*, October 21, 1966.   34 Latimer, p. 19.   35 Muse, p. 133.
36 Peltason, p. 217.   37 Muse, pp. 137–38.   38 *Ibid.*, pp. 151–52.
39 U.S. Commission on Civil Rights, *Civil Rights U.S.A., Public Schools, Southern States*, staff reports (Washington: Government Printing Office, 1962), p. 163.

had been through the entire process and then successfully appealed to the Federal courts. During the second year of desegregation, only 103 Virginia Negro pupils received the integrated education guaranteed them by the Constitution.[40] Even after the state board began to grudgingly relent, only a tiny trickle of Negro students found their way through the complicated process. In the third year fewer than one in 1000 blacks sat in white classrooms.[41]

After the first three years integration increased at a somewhat more rapid rate, particularly in northern Virginia. Several communities there exercised their option to end control by the state pupil-placement board and adopted some kind of modified geographic student assignment plan.[42] By the time the Civil Rights Act emerged from Congress, the NAACP had succeeded in gaining entry for 3700 Negro students in 282 schools. Integration was still strictly at a token level in most areas, however, and the promise of the 1954 decision remained empty for more than 98 per cent of the black children.[43]

In the early 1960's the power of the executive branch first began to make itself felt in Virginia. Under Attorney General Kennedy, the Justice Department fought and won a case requiring Prince George County to integrate children of Negro servicemen.[44] Administration officials became deeply concerned with the continuing defiance of Prince Edward County and played a leading role in setting up integrated private schools there until the Supreme Court ordered reopening of the public schools. After 1962 HEW began negotiating agreements to desegregate Federally subsidized schools operated on military bases by local school systems.

After passage of the Civil Rights Act, but before the issuance of the guidelines, HEW and Office of Education officials made some attempt to convince other school divisions receiving impacted areas aid to submit desegregation plans for the fall of 1964. The substantial progress registered when schools opened in September, however, was still very largely the product of Legal Defense Fund litigation. Integration tripled in the fall of 1964. One black student in 20 was in a desegregated school.[45]

During this period the hopes of the NAACP to achieve a decisive breakthrough in the courts were frustrated. Legal Defense Fund attorneys argued for abandonment of the freedom-of-choice plan. The Su-

40 *Ibid.*; Southern Education Reporting Service, *Statistical Summary*, 1967, pp. 42–43.
41 *Ibid.*
42 Civil Rights Commission, *Public Schools, Southern States*, 1962, pp. 202–8.
43 *Statistical Summary*, 1967, p. 43.   44 *Southern School News*, May 17, 1964.
45 U.S. Commission on Civil Rights, *Public Education*, 1964 Staff Report (Washington: Government Printing Office, 1964), pp. 250–54; *Statistical Summary*, p. 43. These figures include approximately 1500 Negro children enrolled with only a handful of white students in Prince Edward County.

preme Court decision, they insisted, required affirmative action by local officials rather than a plan that put the burden of change on the Negro child and his parents, subjecting the transferring students to community pressures. The Federal appeals court upheld free choice, and the impressive legal effort of the civil rights group seemed to be at a dead end, at least for a time.[46]

Even as the NAACP cases ground their way through the courts, the school guidelines were being developed in Washington. Virginia schoolmen were slowly becoming aware that participation in the huge new Elementary and Secondary Education Act programs would depend upon compliance with the Civil Rights Act. As substantial further progress through the judiciary seemed blocked, the Federal commitment expressed in the guidelines was to provide the force needed to sustain the momentum of the process begun by the courts and the NAACP.

Title VI Enforcement Begins

The initial confusion in Washington over the meaning of the Civil Rights Act for southern education was mirrored in Virginia. Educators had been called to meetings during the summer of 1964 to make them aware of the new law, but the question did not seem extremely important. After all, most school divisions received only a few thousand dollars for vocational training, scientific equipment, and audio-visual equipment. This sum was too small to constitute a strong lever for social change. School boards could simply vote to withdraw from Federal programs.

The first concrete information came at the end of 1964, when the HEW regulations and instructions were mailed to school superintendents. While providing very little specific guidance for desegregation plans, the documents did make clear the fact that no new Federal grants would be approved and no existing programs renewed until a desegregation plan was approved in Washington. This requirement, together with the vision of tremendously expanded Federal aid, began to make the drafting of desegregation plans a real and urgent local problem.

The first task for the Office of Education was to obtain a civil rights compliance pledge from the state department of education. In a state where politicians and educators were eager to avoid any connection with the divisive desegregation struggle, this was a difficult task.

Education in Virginia was preeminently a local responsibility. Power was centered in the school divisions. The weak and ineffectual state department offered little leadership in any area. Like the Federal grant program administrators in Washington, the officials in Richmond relied on

[46] *Richmond News Leader,* October 19, 1964, April 8, 1965; *Richmond Times-Dispatch,* August 15, 1964.

persuasion within a framework of cooperative professional relationships, and, like many Federal bureaucrats, they were anxious to avoid entanglement in an issue that could disrupt or destroy these relationships. This natural timidity was reinforced by the fact that both the state superintendent and the state board of education were appointed by the governor, making the Byrd Organization politically vulnerable if the department did anything more than was absolutely required. Thus it was not surprising that the first two drafts of a compliance pledge submitted by the state board were rejected as inadequate in Washington. The state nondiscrimination plan was not finally approved until May 1965.[47]

The state plan implied no active participation in the desegregation battle. The state merely agreed to end discrimination within the department itself and to inform local school divisions of their responsibilities under Title VI. The department assigned an assistant state superintendent to the job of explaining the Federal standards to concerned local schoolmen. From the beginning, however, state officials saw themselves as neutral bystanders, relaying information, but not involved in Federal or local decisions.

Although the governor plays a central role in Virginia political leadership, neither he nor any other prominent politicians offered much advice to local authorities. After the destructive and futile Massive Resistance campaign, there was no enthusiasm for another quixotic assault on the Federal government. State leaders felt that the battle against the Civil Rights Act had been fought and lost in Congress, and now they were staying out of the issue.

General unwillingness to act was strengthened by uncertainty about the political future. In 1964, ratification of a constitutional amendment struck down the state poll tax as a qualification for voting in elections for Congress and the President, and this device for holding down the electorate in state and local elections was under heavy attack in the Federal courts. The Supreme Court's reapportionment decisions had led to a redistricting of the Assembly, eliminating the solid segregationist majority. Finally, as implementation of the school guidelines began in the South, Congress was considering the President's Voting Rights Act, which was to deny to Virginia officials the possibility of creating new devices to minimize the Negro vote. Virginia politicians, operating in a political system in transition between a white oligarchy and a more representative government, were necessarily somewhat responsive to greatly increased black political power.

In the absence of state leadership pressures for decision focused di-

47 *Richmond News Leader,* May 5, 1965.

rectly on confused local school superintendents and school boards. Because most of the major cities were already desegregating under court orders, and were therefore exempt from the Office of Education guidelines, the brunt of the Federal pressure was concentrated on rural schoolmen. The superintendent's position was most difficult of all, generally combining heavy administrative responsibility for the schools with very little local political power. Feeling the demands from Washington and acutely aware of the need for school funds, the superintendent risked his community relationships and even his job if he moved far ahead of public opinion. Similarly, the rural county school boards enjoyed little independent power, generally existing as adjuncts to the courthouse political organizations that made up the backbone of the Byrd Organization. In most counties members of the board were appointed by and were responsive to the local courthouse branch of the Byrd Organization. In the early months of 1965, the men in the local school offices floundered in uncertainty.

Richmond officials began to hold up new project applications in January 1965. When Virginia educators asked Washington what they must do, however, they were told that there were no general standards. Each district was expected to draft its own plan, moving as rapidly as possible. Many division superintendents drove to Richmond to spend hours discussing a plan with the assistant state superintendent, but he had no way of answering their urgent questions about whether a given solution would be accepted. State officials were unable to provide the standard plan continually requested by local superintendents.[48]

Lacking official standards, both the state government and the Office of Education tried to fill the policy vacuum through informal channels of communication and advice. Typically, the Virginia initiative came from the Governor's office. When Governor Albertis Harrison realized in the spring of 1965 that a large number of school divisions would find themselves in an impossible financial squeeze if the flow of Federal money ceased, he turned for help to the prestigious law firm of Battle and Battle, led by two sons of a former governor. The firm gave top priority to representing the state department of education and the various school divisions in negotiations with the Office of Education.

William Battle, who handled most of the work, was a leading representative of the new breed of Virginia politicians fighting for leadership in the state's Democratic party. Although Senator Byrd supported Nixon in 1960, Battle had managed the Kennedy campaign in Virginia and was rewarded with an appointment as Ambassador to Australia. An excellent

48 Interview with Harry R. Elmore, March 2, 1967.

negotiator, Battle could communicate effectively with both local educators and the Federal enforcement officials. Battle's first assignment was to find out what was going on in Washington. After meeting with Governor Harrison and the Virginia attorney general, he discussed the problems of Virginia school officials with officials ranging from Commissioner Keppel to Seeley's assistants.[49] By mid-April the Battle brothers were passing on the rules of thumb that were emerging in the Office of Education for local school officials.[50]

The Federal enforcement program responded to local confusion by trying to channel policy guidance through one of its legal consultants, Edward Mearns, Associate Dean of the University of Virginia Law School. During the early months of 1965, Mearns spent part of each week in Washington as a member of the team of specialists in desegregation law which reviewed plans submitted to the Equal Educational Opportunities Program. During the remainder of the week he was available to advise Virginia school officials. After it became known that all of the state's desegregation plans would pass through his office he was beseiged by school superintendents eager to learn what the law required and how they could design plans to cope with the particular administrative problems of their local school systems.[51]

Mearns joined the Battles and state officials in their early meetings with groups of local schoolmen. At the first of these workshops, he made clear that Professor Foster's *Saturday Review* memorandum spelled out the requirements of Title VI. School officials learned that the price for continuing eligibility for Federal funds would not be intolerably high. Even if they produced no integration, Mearns said, freedom-of-choice plans would be accepted if they were carefully designed to provide a genuinely unencumbered choice for Negro students. Reflecting the early view within the Office of Education, Mearns suggested that such plans would be accepted for some time, although more stringent and positive requirements might be proposed after five or 10 years.[52]

Perhaps the two most important facts communicated at the early meetings were that compliance standards would not be "impossible" and that there was no real way to escape desegregation. Any school division, Battle explained, could give up Federal funds and thus avoid submitting a deseg-

49 *Richmond News Leader,* March 29, 1966, and July 23, 1966; interview with William Battle, March 15, 1967; interview with Richard Harris, March 2, 1967; Elmore interview.
50 *Richmond News Leader,* April 29, 1965, and May 1, 1965.
51 Interview with Edward Mearns, April 21, 1967; *Richmond News Leader,* January 22, 1965.
52 *Ibid.,* April 22, 1965.

regation plan to the Office of Education. In practical terms, however, nothing would be gained because the school board could then simply be taken into Federal court by the Justice Department acting under authority granted by Title IV of the Civil Rights Act. The Virginia attorney general's office gave local school officials the same advice.[53] Thus there was only one real choice for most school boards, and it was the choice consistent with the growing tendency to remove race from state politics and consistent with increasing local demands for better schools.

The issue was so delicate that only a handful of the state's 138 school divisions submitted plans before Commissioner Keppel acted to provide formal and explicit standards in the school guidelines. In spite of a great deal of effort the consulting system was not successful. Dean Mearns' efforts to help superintendents develop plans ran afoul of an increasing divergence of approach between the law professor-consultants and the full-time employees of the growing enforcement bureaucracy in Washington.

Mearns devoted a great deal of time to fashioning individual plans based not only on the evolving Office of Education standards, but also upon judicial requirements and the facts of the individual situations. Knowing the school districts and the local school officials, Mearns favored plans flexibly shaped on a case-by-case basis to take into account community problems, difficulties of school administration, and the good faith of local officials.

At the same time, the pressures of its work load were forcing the Office of Education to veer away from the case-by-case approach toward uniform, general, and relatively inflexible minimum standards. The only way a small staff of civil servants could process thousands of plans was by creating detailed requirements, allowing a lower-level bureaucrat, without legal training, to sit at his desk and check for inclusion of certain standard features. This meant that the area of discretion was constantly narrowed. Mearns found that the commitment he made to local officials based on his professional judgment were being undercut by the continuing development of new detailed criteria. Time after time plans that Mearns had helped draft were rejected because of new policy decisions in Washington or because of failure to include minor details to conform with the particular language pattern that had gained administrative approval. Mearns came to regard Seeley's office as a bureaucratic machine with little sensitivity either to lawyerly craftsmanship or to individual community problems and stopped his weekly trips to Washington. Washington officials, who were trying to construct standards that would resist

[53] Ibid., and Harris interview.

intensive efforts to find loopholes, felt that Mearns was oversensitive to local feelings.

Mearns was attempting to bridge a widening gap between two different conceptions of the best enforcement strategy. He believed that any reasonable plan should be quickly accepted in order to get change started and to tie the districts into the enforcement machinery. Federal officials, on the other hand, were increasingly concerned about maximum immediate change and possible local subversion of plans. The bureaucracy demanded that well-meaning local officials make the very same detailed written promises that were demanded of bitter-end segregationists in Mississippi. As the Office of Education began to require plans more comprehensive than most court-ordered desegregation plans and in advance of what many communities were ready to accept, the cooperative relationship envisioned by Mearns was necessarily replaced by an adversary relationship. The Federal program could realize its ends only by assuming the essential attributes of a bureaucracy and moving rapidly to take advantage of the momentum for change expressed in the Civil Rights Act.

Relationships between Virginia and Federal officials were further exacerbated by the fact that the two men first responsible for the Equal Educational Opportunities Program division with jurisdiction over the state belonged to the activist faction within the program. Identifying with the civil rights movement, they had little confidence in good-faith promises from southern schoolmen. One staff member told Mearns that "there isn't a good white school superintendent in the state of Virginia." [54] The belief grew in Washington that Mearns was "selling the program out" by not pushing local districts hard enough. The efforts of a dedicated law professor, committed to integration, were caught between the diverging perspectives of local schoolmen and of the new civil rights enforcement bureaucracy.

A Summer of Negotiations

As summer 1965 began, a financial crisis loomed before Virginia schools. Only four of the state's 138 school divisions had been found in compliance in May. In a state ranking close to the bottom of the list in terms of support for education, any possibility of losing more than $20 million in Federal aid then flowing into the state, plus many millions expected from the Elementary and Secondary Education Act, promised disaster. To cope with this danger, state authorities again turned to the Battle firm to help review local plans, explain the legal situation to recalcitrant local authorities, and represent the school divisions in negotiations.[55]

[54] Mearns interview.   [55] *Richmond News Leader,* May 1, 1965.

In meetings across the state with school boards and boards of supervisors Battle again explained that there was no real alternative to compliance. Refusal, local leaders were told, would only buy a little time at the cost of an expensive court fight with the Justice Department as well as loss of needed money.[56]

School officials beginning negotiations generally wanted to be certain that they were not taking a political risk by doing more than was necessary. The Battles met this need by keeping in close touch with developments in the Washington office and informing local officials which issues seemed to be negotiable and which of the Federal requirements were rigid. Working within the framework of the guidelines, the attorneys concentrated on winning approval for plans recognizing the physical and administrative problems created in some school divisions by various specific requirements.[57] By concentrating on those issues that were not seen as central to the enforcement program the Battle firm, sometimes taking an issue to Keppel himself, was able to win concessions and to provide needed communication between Washington and the school divisions.

The summer's toughest issue was the question of the number of grades to be integrated. Initially, the Federal plan had been to settle for the opening of four grades to possible integration through freedom of choice during the first year. This figure had been passed on to a great many local school authorities and incorporated in many desegregation plans. The wording of the guidelines was ambiguous, however, saying that the burden of proof for not opening all grades rested with a school system. During June Federal officials made the decision to demand opening of all 12 grades wherever it was at all possible and to delay action on districts that refused to go along. Communities that had reluctantly submitted plans they believed to be adequate were now confronted, after the end of the school year, with an insistent demand for much more.

The Federal staff members assigned to deal with Virginia districts spent most of the summer in negotiating by letter, phone, and personal conversation with local superintendents, often focusing on the number of grades. Staff members were well aware of the extreme regional differences within the state and adopted different kinds of tactics in different counties. Southside counties were pressed to open as many grades as possible to freedom of choice, while some northern Virginia divisions were put under strong pressure to move toward outright abolition of segregated schools.[58]

As the summer months passed, negotiations developed into a war of

56 Battle interview.
57 Mordecai Johnson interview; Ziskin interview; and Battle interview.
58 Ziskin interview.

nerves, with local school people and Federal enforcement officials trying to outwait each other as the stakes continued to rise. The bureaucratic stalling was a crucial lever in the effort described by one participant "to talk people out of the guidelines and into something a little bit stiffer." [59] Even though classes began in mid-August in a number of school divisions, very few Virginia plans had been accepted at the beginning of the month.

The evolution of new requirements generated a predictably hostile local reaction. The Federal staff, in the words of one participant, was "trying to tackle one of the most severe social problems in the country before they organized their own office." William Battle found it virtually impossible to obtain written acknowledgement of an agreement negotiated by telephone.[60] Changes in Washington meant that a plan identical to one accepted in a neighboring district earlier in the year might well now be found unacceptable. The difficulties of this situation were compounded by what was frequently perceived as the arrogant attitude of the Office of Education enforcement staff.

Long-distance negotiations were difficult, and for many superintendents the situation came to a head in mid-August at a big session with a team of Federal officials in a Richmond ballroom. Less than 10 days before schools opened few of the worried local officials knew what their status was. Everything had to be settled quickly. The enforcement staff members brought with them the newly developed model plans, spelling out the explicit language desired in a plan. With something concrete to discuss, superintendents were able to sit down with Federal officials and a state lawyer to work out an agreement that would definitely be accepted.

The summer's test of wills ended in a Federal victory. Virginia political leaders refused to become involved in the issue, and most local boards concluded that they had no alternative to compliance. Most divisions did begin freedom of choice in all grades in September. A few systems finally consented to move beyond free choice toward abolition of separate schools. The Administration's firmness against the late-summer southern political attacks permitted Federal negotiators to insist on thoroughgoing compliance with the procedures established in the first guidelines.

The extremely important breakthrough toward completely integrated school systems in a few districts was largely due to local fears of administrative chaos. Early in the year a number of school divisions had made plans for the coming school year on the basis of free-choice mechanisms failing to meet guidelines standards on such basic matters as the length of the choice period or the adequacy of the notice sent to Negro parents. In

[59] *Ibid.*   [60] Battle interview.

mid-August superintendents from these divisions learned that their plans would be rejected unless they reopened the transfer period at the last minute.

At best, the free-choice system is difficult to administer, particularly where a relatively good racial climate makes transfer to white schools less difficult for black students. Unpredictable sudden changes in enrollment at various schools could wreck months of work in developing detailed plans for teacher assignments, class assignments, and even transportation. Faced with this prospect, some school systems in moderate parts of the state were willing to promise abandonment of freedom of choice in a future year in exchange for Federal approval of an inadequate free-choice system during the coming school year. Near the end of the summer Winchester, a small northern Virginia city near the West Virginia border with a low black population, finally agreed to such a plan. Before negotiations ended, more than 10 districts were persuaded to accept this arrangement.

Federal negotiators made this highly important breakthrough toward total integration by arguing that not only would local officials escape the future inconvenience and expense of the freedom-of-choice system, but they would also end a divisive community problem standing in the way of development of the schools. In areas with small numbers of Negro students, the cost of maintaining separate and inefficient schools was high. One Federal representative got the "strong feeling" that some superintendents "wanted to be pressured into it," using the Office of Education as a scapegoat for resolving an emotional issue and creating a united and efficient school system in place of duplicate facilities.[61]

Accomplishments of the First Guidelines in Virginia

When schools opened in September, the records showed very significant changes. While fewer than 60 per cent of Virginia's school divisions had begun integration in the previous decade, the process was now underway in every district with students of both races. More than twice as many Negro students found themselves in integrated schools, 11 per cent of the total black students. Because there were regions where local opinion permitted freedom of choice to function with some effectiveness, and because of the preparation of Virginia communities for integration produced by NAACP law suits, the state ranked third in the South and ninth in the 17-state area in percentage of desegregation. The existence of areas of serious resistance, however, was indicated by the fact that integration

[61] Ziskin interview.

had increased only 100 per cent in Virginia while it was up 200 per cent in the South as a whole.[62] The next year the areas opposed to change were to become a serious problem.

Perhaps the most important achievement of the first year was psychological. While almost nine out of 10 Negro students remained in segregated schools, Federal power had destroyed the belief of Southside leaders that they could completely escape enforcement of the 1954 Supreme Court decision. In small rural counties with Negro majorities, the first grudging steps were taken toward recognizing the constitutional rights of black children. A small opening had been made in the ancient wall of caste separation in counties ruled from an old red-brick courthouse where nothing much had changed since the Confederate memorial out in front had been built. At the other end of the state, an equally important change was reflected in the fact that local educators were seriously considering the reorganization of entire school systems on a wholly nonracial basis.

The change would have been impossible without the lure of money from the Elementary and Secondary Education Act. Directing funds into areas with high concentrations of poor children, the new program focused money in the state's poorest districts and the districts with the highest proportion of Negro students. Thus the program offered maximum inducements to the very districts most hostile to the guidelines. In some Southside counties, the Federal funds amounted to as much as one-third of the existing school budget. Across the state the program represented an increase of almost one-tenth in school funds.[63] Because the Byrd Organization had been exceptionally niggardly in its support of public education, the need for this money was desperate.

For a variety of reasons, the changes demanded by the first guidelines proved to be tolerable in Virginia. By summer's end die-hard total segregation was at an end in the state, and the most racially progressive sections were considering moves toward total desegregation. In most parts of Virginia, however, only token integration had been accepted. The battle to break the freedom-of-choice system was yet to come. It was to be a far more difficult struggle.

VIRGINIA AND THE SECOND DESEGREGATION GUIDELINES

In Virginia the first year of enforcement went remarkably well. In spite of administrative confusion and the sensitivity of the issue, all school divisions eventually submitted acceptable desegregation plans. No Federal funds were withheld, and the Federal requirements did not emerge as a significant political issue in the 1965 state election.

[62] *Statistical Summary*, p. 43.   [63] *American Education*, Vol. I (April, 1965), p. 3.

The issuance of greatly strengthened guidelines in early 1966, however, raised the price of Federal aid from token integration to a restructuring of the entire educational system on nondiscriminatory lines. This was more than could be easily accepted, and the change generated damaging attacks on the enforcement program. Both the Governor and the South-side congressmen moved from a position of neutrality to one of outright opposition. In the Southside, a number of districts totally defied the new requirements, and a showdown over Federal power became inevitable.

Virginia schoolmen, like most southerners, believed that the initial guidelines had spelled out the full requirements of Title VI. The prevailing opinion was that the Constitution required "desegregation" through procedures allowing student transfers across racial lines, but not "integration" through affirmative local action to abolish separate schools. Virginia educators felt that they had negotiated long-term agreements along these lines with the Office of Education. They were incensed by the new demands for faculty integration and for a certain percentage of actual integration rather than merely a fairly run, free-choice process. Without passage of any new Federal law, school systems with almost one-tenth of their black students in integrated schools now suddenly learned that their free-choice plan would be worthless unless it brought twice as many Negroes into white schools. More backward districts were told that their progress must be even more dramatic. The directive demanding substantial faculty integration seemed impossible to superintendents working in communities convinced that no Negro could be intelligent enough to teach children of the "superior" race.

Virginia's best-known journalist, James J. Kilpatrick, promptly denounced the new guidelines as an "arrogant edict" with a "harsh, pre-emptory, commanding" tone.

> It is impossible, in a short summary, adequately to convey the autocratic spirit of these regulations. . . . And underlying the whole statement is the explicit threat: Obey, or give up the Federal money.[64]

The new Federal standards posed such a basic threat to the racial status quo that the issue could no longer be kept out of politics. The Virginia confrontation was part of a major struggle across the South.

The nature and the outcome of the ensuing battle over the future of Negro-white relationships in the Old Dominion cannot be understood without a knowledge of the social and political context in which it was fought. Several factors are of central importance to understanding both the intensity of local resistance in some areas and the reasons for the ultimate limited Federal victory. They are (1) the spread of militant

[64] *Richmond News Leader,* March 17, 1966.

segregationism after 1964, (2) the educational revolution in Virginia in 1966, (3) the rise in Negro voting, and (4) important shifts in Virginia political leadership.

The Growth of Extremism

In a state with many convinced that the alterations demanded by the 1964 Civil Rights Act were unnatural changes in the proper order of things, enforcement of the new law spurred the growth of resistance groups. Virginia was under pressure with no parallel since Reconstruction. Even as the Ku Klux Klan had first appeared during Reconstruction, so the "new reconstruction" greatly increased the minority attracted to openly racist organizations.

One impact of the passage of the Civil Rights Act was the rebirth of the Virginia KKK, dormant since the 1920's. The weird rituals of cross-burnings and racial harangues became commonplace in the piney forests of the Southside and even reached into the suburbs of Richmond. During 1966, as the new guidelines were being implemented, the Virginia Klan was the fastest growing in the South, with membership scattered in 100 klaverns around the state. In spite of restrictive state laws, only three other southern states could claim more followers of the Imperial Wizard by the end of the year.[65] Its newspaper, the *Fiery Cross*, was widely circulated, as were ominous calling cards informing the recipient that "you are being watched by the Knights of the KKK." Scores of rallies were held in the very districts having most trouble with the school integration question. At one rally, the message was: "You will be condemned to hell if you send your child to an integrated school." At one school-board meeting, the local klavern appeared in full regalia on the evening the local desegregation plan was under consideration.[66]

The mushrooming of the KKK was dramatic but of no statewide political significance. A broader wave of reaction did, however, find expression both within the remnant of the conservative Byrd machine and also in the Conservative party, a new grouping further to the right. The new party appeared in 1965 when Mills Godwin, Jr., the Byrd Organization nominee for governor, responded to the fact of growing urban and Negro voting strength by leading the Organization in a somewhat more moderate direction. Disgusted reactionaries responded by setting up a firmly segregationist third party. The new party made a surprisingly strong showing, capturing 80,000 votes and denying Godwin a clear majority in its first campaign. In the 1966 elections the Conservatives

---

[65] *Ibid.*, January 31, 1967.
[66] Virginia Council on Human Relations, *Newsletter*, Vol. II (July, 1966), 3–4; *Ibid.*, "Memorandum," November 10, 1966.

hammered very hard on the school issue, denouncing the Democrats as a "foul and filthy party" secretly plotting with black leaders to destroy the constitutional freedom of white students. One leader warned that President Johnson was planning to take children from their mothers and place them in "compounds" to "train them to be good socialists." [67]

The Conservative party was a reminder to Organization politicians of their vulnerability from the right. In the critically important 1966 Democratic primary, in which two Senate seats were decided, the Conservatives claimed that the Byrd Organization had sold out to Negro and labor "bosses" and called for a boycott of the primary. Although the Organization responded with tactics such as a last-minute appeal for white votes to offset Negro political power, the Conservative defection was enough to account for the defeat of long-time Organization stalwart, Senator Willis Robertson.[68]

The general-election campaign took place amid a wave of racial reaction reflected in primaries from Maryland to Louisiana. The mood was most pronounced in the extravagant rhetoric of the Conservatives. Denouncing the school guidelines, one Conservative candidate claimed that the Democratic party had "sold my children into slavery to HEW." Byrd Organization support for President Johnson in the 1964 election, claimed another, "started the total destruction of our liberties." [69]

Far more significant than the Conservative position, which was ultimately endorsed by only 8 per cent of the electorate,[70] were the attitudes of the state's political leadership. The leadership of the Byrd Organization firmly opposed the new regulations and launched a many-sided attack on Federal authorities in Washington. The new political situation produced by a vastly expanded Negro vote, however, meant that statewide Democratic candidates avoided extensive public discussion of the issue.

Most resistance took the form of protests to Federal officials. In early May both of the incumbent, Organization-sponsored senators signed a southern appeal to President Johnson calling for revocation of the controversial sections of the new guidelines. When 28 southern congressmen, led by a right-wing Alabamian, carried their protest to Commissioner Howe, the delegation included Watkins Abbitt, a Southside congressman and state Democratic chairman.[71] Governor Godwin made his position known through trips to Washington to confer with Secretary Gardner,

[67] *Richmond Times-Dispatch,* May 21, 1966, and May 22, 1966; *Richmond News Leader,* September 16, 1966.
[68] *Richmond News Leader,* July 13, 1966.
[69] *Ibid.,* September 16, 1966, and September 27, 1966; *Washington Post,* September 18, 1966.
[70] *Richmond News Leader,* November 11, 1966.   [71] *Ibid.,* June 1, 1966.

through his support of southern governors' protests to the President, and through the release of public letters challenging specific actions. In September the most powerful Organization representative in Congress, Rep. Howard Smith, used his chairmanship of the House Rules Committee to investigate Commissioner Howe's administration of the school guidelines, relying on information provided by the state attorney general.

Only two factors seem to account for the fact that conflict over the new guidelines did not develop into a total Federal-state confrontation—the changing mood toward public education and the sudden appearance of effectively used Negro political power. Without these basic changes enforcement of the guidelines would have stirred the same bitter resistance that was evident when HEW threatened to withhold Medicare funds from Virginia's segregated mental hospitals.

Although the state's nonaccredited and backward mental hospitals desperately needed the new funds, the Organization of old-timers, who controlled the state board, balked. The board was quite prepared to forego both new and existing Federal aid programs rather than agree to assign each patient to the hospital nearest his home and to assign roommates without regard for race. Governor Godwin at first supported the board. During the months of controversy, Virginia took every possible step to delay and dilute Federal requirements and went to the very brink of sacrificing millions of dollars needed to maintain even the existing, seriously inadequate, standards of mental health care. In the entire nation Alabama alone had resisted more stubbornly. Only after months of confrontation testing Federal determination did the Governor quietly settle the issue.[72]

The fact that the schools were spared a similar statewide stance of defiance cannot be atributed to a lack of broad opposition to the guidelines. In fact the critical attitude of the Organization leadership was shared by the white education establishment. During 1966 both the Virginia Education Association and the Virginia Association of School Administrators lent their prestige to the attack on the guidelines. Ignoring a plea against a "professionally unwise" step to "reopen the whole question of compliance," the administrators overwhelmingly approved a resolution denouncing "guidelines and regulations which violate sound principles of public administration." The Office of Education was accused of employing professionally unqualified enforcement officials and of using its aid programs "as a bargaining instrument to achieve a prescribed numerical balance of pupils and faculties irrespective of the effect the attainment . . . may have on the quality of education." [73]

[72] *Richmond Times-Dispatch*, August 27, 1966; *Richmond News Leader*, January 25, 1967; *Washington Post*, September 8, 1966, January 25, 1967, and January 26, 1967.
[73] *Richmond News Leader*, November 2, 1966.

Opposition to the guidelines was broadly based and respectable. The state's political and educational leaders reflected general public indignation over what were seen as illegal demands for "racial balancing" and "forced integration" of teachers. There was a decisive difference from the mid-1950's, however. Race no longer dominated all other public issues. Many Virginians had had enough of futile resistance and were moving beyond an obsession with race toward a more general commitment to the economic progress of the state and to the effort to bring long-neglected public services up to national standards.

The Educational Revolution

In the mid-1960's it was far more profitable for a Virginia politician to devote his energy to the battle for educational improvement than to the fight against school integration. Other southern states had had their "education governors," and Virginians elected one in 1965, Mills Godwin, Jr. A former "Massive Resister," Godwin had adapted the Organization to the new circumstances, winning the election with crucial Negro and urban support. In his stirring inaugural address Godwin called for a bold response to the people's dreams of better public services. The first great task, he said, was the "advancement of learning."

> Knowledge is the greater equalizer of our time. . . . With it . . . comes an atmosphere of mutual respect. . . .
> We can take no rest until all our public schools—not just some—will compare with any in the nation . . . ; until all our sons and daughters—not just some—have the same chance to train their minds and their skills to the utmost.[74]

Speaking to a reapportioned Assembly in the changing political atmosphere, symbolized by the mortal illness of Senator Byrd, Godwin called on the Organization to face the twentieth century.

Godwin rejected the traditional Byrd obsession with austere government and used the power of his office to lead a successful struggle to expand the state's narrow tax structure and to channel the bulk of the new money into the schools. The new state sales tax provided revenue for an increase of almost 50 per cent in the state budget, with the bulk of the increase earmarked for education.[75] Minimum teacher salaries were raised sharply, a community college program was initiated, and funds were granted for programs never before receiving state aid. The great popular response indicated that Godwin had found a way to identify the Organization with a set of accomplishments having a broad appeal in a changing Virginia.

The fact that the Governor had tapped a powerful desire for change

74 *Congressional Record*, June 22, 1966, p. A3340.
75 *Richmond News Leader*, March 4, 1966, and March 11, 1966.

became evident when the movement for educational reform continued to gain momentum even after the Assembly went home. The state board of education shook off its normal lethargy to begin facing the problem of the thousands of Virginia teachers without college degrees, and the need was recognized for much more aggressive state leadership for the small and backward systems in rural Virginia.[76] Godwin was not satisfied with Virginia's climb, in a single year, from very near the bottom of the list to a median point in terms of state effort to support education. Continuing to press the issue, he urged that Virginia not be satisfied with catching up with surrounding states, but attempt to move into a position of leadership. In an unprecedented series of Governor's Conferences on Education, prominent figures from each region of the state were drawn into day-long sessions with the Governor to consider the impact of education on Virginia's development.[77]

Public support for improvement of Virginia schools created a serious dilemma for state political leaders trying to deal with the revolutionary changes demanded by the school guidelines. While many saw the guidelines as arbitrary and illegal, they lacked the certainty of the mid-1950's that race was the primary issue. If forced to make a choice between better schools and segregated schools, the tendency was to reluctantly accede in disruption of the existing pattern of race relations in order to maintain the impetus of educational progress. The sheer size of the new Federal program made it obvious that Virginia's effort to overtake school systems in other states demanded full participation in Elementary and Secondary Education Act programs. In practical terms the only real alternatives for the state leadership were either to quietly accept the guidelines as written or to try to weaken enforcement policies, without pushing so hard that large amounts of money would be lost.

Federal aid to education no longer was anathema to Virginia politicians. In fact, in his successful effort to unseat Senator Robertson in the 1966 Democratic primary, William Spong boldly proclaimed his support of Federal involvement and denounced continued Organization opposition.[78]

Changing attitudes within the state were also evident in the effort to remove the surviving vestiges of Massive Resistance legislation. The pupil-placement board, created to delay integration as long as possible, was rendered useless by adherence to the guidelines and passed into history in June 1966. Denouncing Federal "economic blackmail," its chairman departed with the sad conclusion that Virginians had "decided that federal

[76] *Ibid.*, March 3, 1966.
[77] *Richmond Times-Dispatch,* June 18, 1966, and October 6, 1966; *Richmond News Leader,* October 5, 1966.
[78] *Richmond News Leader,* June 20, 1966.

money was more important." [79] Public education forces were also leading aggressive battles against the suspension of compulsory attendance laws and the tuition grant subsidies that encouraged the establishment of private schools.

The attack on the tuition grant program was turned back, however, both in the 1966 and 1968 legislative sessions. The issue was an uncomfortable one for Virginia politicians committed to public education but opposed to what they saw as "forced integration." The subsidies were justified in terms of the freedom-of-choice rhetoric so often used in the state. One newspaper commented:

> . . . it is undeniable that the program continues to serve a worthy purpose in Southside and rural counties where the primary intention of white parents is to see that their children get an education among their own peers. . . . These people, humble folk most of them, consider that their parental duty to educate their children is too important to relinquish to Federal authority. . . .[80]

The impact of the program was to enlarge the alternatives for the individual white parent while diminishing support for local and state efforts to strengthen public education. Because it made possible the creation of a system of schools competing for both public funds and interest while undermining the possibility of successful integration, the private-school movement represented perhaps the most important kind of local resistance to the guidelines.

After the 1964 Civil Rights Act became law, the tuition grant program provided the framework for rapid creation of an alternative, publicly supported white school system. In the fall of 1964 there were 12 segregated private schools in the state enrolling 5700 students.[81] The great burst of growth came in 1966, when the new guidelines made perfectly clear that local recalcitrance resulting in continued segregation would no longer be tolerated. In rural areas where many people felt that even a little integration was intolerable, 15 new private schools were suddenly established. The new schools took 1300 more students out of the public systems, threatening community support in the very counties where Federal money was most needed and integration was most difficult.[82] Two of the leading tuition-grant counties ranked far down the list in terms of local effort for education, and one county fell from eleventh to ninety-first position in the state after a private school movement took hold.[83]

The seriousness of the threat was very clear to school officials who had

[79] *Ibid.*, June 22, 1966.   [80] *Ibid.*, October 26, 1966.
[81] Civil Rights Commission, *Public Education*, p. 277.
[82] *Richmond News Leader,* November 1, 1966.
[83] *Richmond Times-Dispatch*, October 25, 1966.

before them the vivid examples of two Southside counties, where virtually all white students had transferred to private academies. Local willingness to accept distinctly inferior education offered in makeshift quarters,
in preference to integrated schools, confronted some local educators with
the fearful choice of either abandoning the great progress made possible
by Federal aid or risking the future of the public school system itself.
The state department of education's willingness to accredit weak private
institutions increased the problems of local public school administrators.
Only in three Deep South states was the private-school threat more serious than in the Old Dominion.[84]

Most Virginia politicians, however, were reluctant to take any action
that could be interpreted as even indirect support for Federal desegregation proceedings. Once again the hope for relief from an effort to circumvent enforcement of the civil rights law rested with the Federal
courts. By late 1967 tuition-grant programs in three other states had been
struck down as unconstitutional, and in mid-1968 the Virginia NAACP
renewed its legal attack on the state program.

Eventually the movement for educational advancement in the state
began to have some impact on the private-school challenge. The gradual
effort by the state department of education to provide some leadership
necessarily involved a commitment to enforce some kind of minimum
statewide standards. In the fall of 1967 the state board of education ended
its practice of unconditional accreditation of inadequate high schools
across the state by warning 18 schools, including six private academies,
that their accreditation was in danger.[85] Thus the contradiction between
decent education and the local desire to create a duplicate school system
to perpetuate segregation began to make itself apparent.

The Emergence of Negro Political Power

The surge of support for public education in Virginia only partially
explains the lack of rigid and united state resistance to Office of Education integration requirements. An equally important factor was a basic
change in the political setting in which the decisions were made. In the
mid-1950's the Byrd Organization found irresistible political advantage in
arousing latent racial feeling. The race issue drew back into the Organization fold voters otherwise inclined toward the GOP or the moderate-
liberal Democratic faction. The risks were diminished by the fact that a
poll tax system administered by local Organization members tended to
keep the total vote, and particularly the black vote, relatively small. By
1966, however, the political realities were basically altered by Federal laws

[84] Civil Rights Commission, *Southern School Desegregation, 1966–67*, pp. 114–15.
[85] *Richmond News Leader,* December 1, 1967.

and court decisions that suddenly made the Negro vote a major factor in Virginia politics. Realizing that an alliance of blacks and moderate whites might now destroy the Organization's hold on the Democratic party, conservative leaders sought to avoid actions that might crystallize this alliance.

The practical necessity of a new racial stance coincided with the most important transfer of leadership in the history of the Organization. Just days after the 1965 state election Senator Harry Byrd's resignation ended his four decades as the dominant figure in Virginia politics. During the 1965 election the need for an accommodation with Negro leadership had persuaded the Organization gubernatorial candidate, Mills Godwin, Jr., to move away from the Senator's rigid positions. Faced with a Negro campaign to add 50,000 new voters to the existing black registration of 144,000, with the limitations placed on state authorities by the new Voting Rights Act, and with predictions of a Negro vote amounting to more than one-tenth of the entire electorate, Godwin moved to the left. The former Massive Resister carefully balanced his denunciation of "crime in the streets" with a call for "full equality under the law." He pledged a major effort to improve education and public services in the state and assured Negro leaders that Negroes would be included in his appointments to state offices. Shortly before the election, Godwin received the endorsement of two major Negro voters' organizations. For the first time since 1937, the Democratic nominee won the support of the Virginia labor movement.[86] Negro leaders succeeded in delivering a significant majority of the black vote to Godwin, reversing normal preferences for the less race-conscious GOP candidates, and promptly claimed credit for Godwin's narrow victory.[87]

The new Democratic coalition pieced together by Godwin embraced elements ranging from Southside segregationists and conservative businessmen to labor and Negro organizations. Godwin needed to consolidate public support by improving state services while avoiding any issue that could tear the coalition apart. This political situation helps explain the passive attitude of the Virginia congressional delegation and the quiet participation of the Governor's office in the 1965 Federal effort to bring the state's school divisions into compliance with the first guidelines. Opposition would not only have denied Virginia schools needed funds but would also have threatened the urban and Negro support Godwin needed to be elected.

Black political power also limited the force of opposition to the far

[86] *Washington Post*, October 15, 1965, and October 27, 1965; *The Reporter*, Vol. XXXV, October 21, 1965.
[87] *Washington Post*, November 5, 1965.

more sweeping provisions of the 1966 guidelines. Even as implementation of the new regulations began, the state was caught up in an extremely important struggle between the two Democratic factions for both of Virginia's Senate seats. Since the poll tax had been outlawed in elections for Federal office by a 1964 constitutional amendment, the Negro vote could obviously be decisive. For this reason even committed segregationists, like newly appointed Senator Harry Byrd, Jr., attempted to keep the race issue out of their campaigns.

Negro political influence was further increased by a Supreme Court decision in March 1966 (the same month the new guidelines were issued), which declared that the poll tax for state and local elections was an unconstitutional disenfranchisement of those who could not afford to pay.[88] Since the Voting Rights Act denied Virginia politicians the authority to devise new ways of limiting black voting, candidates at all levels confronted a much larger Negro electorate. Within three months Negro voting reached record levels in a number of municipal elections.[89] Thus, while candidates of the Conservative splinter party thundered about HEW dictatorship, all serious candidates for the Senate did their best to avoid the issue.

This decisive primary produced a dramatic confirmation of the new forces in Virginia Democratic politics. Black voters helped defeat Senator Robertson and joined with white moderates in the stunning upset of Representative Howard Smith, the chairman of the House Rules Committee. Even Senator Byrd, Jr. had an embarrassingly narrow victory. Public opinion analyst Louis Harris saw in the returns evidence of a new reform coalition of white suburbanites and Negroes. Pointing to precincts in Richmond and Norfolk, Harris emphasized the "sharp candidate selectivity" of black Democrats, who produced a virtually unanimous vote for President Johnson in 1964 and then delivered similarly overwhelming margins against Senator Byrd, Jr.[90] Negro voters had indeed heeded the call of the *Richmond Afro-American* to turn against the "Byrd Machine ultra-conservatives who have fanatically opposed the progress of the colored man throughout their political lives." [91]

While the political incentives for segregationism were greatly diminished, commitments to furthering integration were still avoided. The Democratic coalition contained not only Negroes and liberals but also crucial support from the old Southside political machines. Godwin had lost important strength in the Southside to the Conservative party in

[88] *Washington Post,* March 25, 1965.
[89] *Richmond Times-Dispatch,* June 9, 1966, June 10, 1966, and June 16, 1966; *Richmond News Leader,* June 15, 1966.
[90] *Newsweek,* July 25, 1966.   [91] *Richmond Times-Dispatch,* July 8, 1966.

1965, and any identification with the HEW guidelines would have invited political disaster. The 1966 guidelines moved the two congressmen representing the deep Southside counties into open opposition and eventually provoked public attacks on the enforcement effort by the Governor. Outside the Southside most politicians, particularly those running for election, were eager to avoid the race issue completely. This fact prevented a concerted attack on the new HEW requirements.

Enforcing the 1966 Guidelines

Virginia schoolmen, operating within a rapidly changing political and educational context, were confronted with the new guidelines late in the 1965–66 school year. Three weeks later 60 educators were called to a session with state and Federal officials. David Barus, the acting deputy director of the Office of Education compliance program, laid the facts on the line. The new rules, he said, meant that the "dual system must go." Free choice had failed in many areas, and school systems must now either find some way to make it work far more effectively or move toward a completely nonracial student assignment policy. School systems that failed to move far more rapidly toward total desegregation or did not make "significant" progress toward an equal distribution of white and black teachers in every school were warned that they faced not only loss of Federal aid but also a Justice Department lawsuit.[92]

In addition to the new standards applicable across the South, Barus explained that 20 Virginia divisions had been notified to suspend their freedom-of-choice plans. The Office of Education had decided to push these districts with relatively few Negro students toward immediate and complete desegregation. This was an important departure from normal policy. Although the new guidelines gave the Commissioner of Education broad authority to reject desegregation plans, it was generally understood that free-choice plans would be accepted if they produced a sufficient rate of change.

The special treatment of the 20 districts resulted from an argument within the Office of Education. The tacit understanding that any district with one-fifth of its black pupils in integrated schools would be in full compliance, David Barus asserted, meant that virtually no additional step would be required in many districts in border states and in northern Virginia and Shenandoah Valley areas having few Negroes. Recognizing the need to maintain the momentum of change, Commissioner Howe gave Barus permission to try a new strategy in three border states, 20 Virginia school divisions, and a few districts in North Carolina.

[92] *Washington Post,* March 30, 1966.

Each district selected received a letter telling the local superintendents that HEW had determined that free choice was no longer appropriate in their situation. Howe's idea was that the letter would provide leverage for negotiations, but he warned the staff to be prepared to back down if the demand was adamantly resisted at the local level. The Commissioner was willing to bluff, but he was not prepared to take the political risk involved in actually denying Federal money to a district where free choice had brought some integration.[93]

On the basis of this understanding, the Office of Education informed all Virginia school divisions with fewer than 10 per cent black students, plus a few other selected districts, that they would "probably" be ineligible for Federal aid unless the local school board adopted either a neighborhood school system or another arrangement to end separate schools. The hope in Washington was to shatter the illusion that free choice fully satisfied the Civil Rights Act, setting a precedent for eventual total desegregation across Virginia.[94]

The negotiating skill of the Federal staff and the fact that some superintendents were privately happy to have the Federal authorities take the heat for closing their small and highly inefficient Negro schools produced important gains. Separate schools were most costly and made least educational sense where a sparse black population forced school administrators to run small, inefficient buildings, to offer inadequate curricula or tolerate half-filled classrooms, and to pay high transportation costs. By midsummer, six such divisions had agreed to complete desegregation. The total reached 12 by summer's end.

The effort to "accelerate" the racial transition won real victories. In some regions of Virginia, segregated schools became only a memory. Needless duplication was ended, and the savings were often used to enrich the curriculum and to improve facilities for children of both races. Neglected problems in black schools became matters for urgent action once the buildings were integrated. School administrators and school boards were able to turn their attention from the divisive race question to the issue of building a better educational system. Those sections of the state with few Negroes and a relatively good tradition of race relations were now largely freed of the caste system in their schools. In some adjacent areas, schoolmen began to seriously plan for what they now viewed as an inevitable transition.

The acceleration attempt, however, had a serious flaw. Since Commissioner Howe was unwilling to back up the bluff, adamant local resistance could destroy the credibility of the threat. When the Office of Education

[93] Barus Interview, May 9, 1967.   [94] Ibid.

included among the 20 chosen districts two large school divisions near the Southside, it was gambling for high stakes. If these divisions integrated, hopes for resistance would be weakened. Balancing this possible gain was the likelihood that public opposition would encourage local officials to call the Federal bluff. This is indeed what happened in Henrico County, the most important district involved. The outcome was a protracted conflict in which everyone lost, a conflict that revealed the political limits of Title VI enforcement power.

The Henrico Controversy

In many ways Henrico was a logical target for acceleration. The rapidly growing suburban school system in metropolitan Richmond had only 6 per cent black students, and one-fifth of them had chosen white schools in the first year of guidelines enforcement. During the first year the superintendent had considered moving beyond free choice. From the outside there seemed to be few obstacles to total integration of one of the state's largest systems.[95]

Although Henrico was basically a moderate area, the county had a reservoir of segregationist sentiment reflected in a series of Ku Klux Klan rallies in 1966. The prospect of forcing some white children to attend predominantly Negro schools produced protests, the political importance of which was magnified by the serious over-representation of the county's rural areas on the malapportioned county board of supervisors. The school board responded to the Federal letter by asking for two more years of free choice, claiming that a building program would make the transition less difficult.[96] Henrico educators felt that they "had gone as far and much further than other divisions," and that they should be given more time.[97]

Frustrated by what they saw as Federal intransigence, county officials prevailed on the local congressman to arrange a meeting for them with Commissioner Howe. The session in Washington was a fiasco. The congressman, perhaps concerned about the alienation of the large black vote in Richmond, skipped the meeting. When Representative David Satterfield failed to arrive, Howe also decided to pass up the meeting. The county delegation was angry and refused to budge in discussions with subordinate officials. Back home, one county supervisor said it was "an insult . . . to have an appointment with one of these bureaucrats and not have him show up." The school board chairman stated his preference for

[95] *Richmond News Leader*, April 21, 1966, and December 30, 1966; Harris interview; Johnson interview.
[96] *Richmond News Leader*, April 26, 1966.
[97] Elmore interview; *Richmond News Leader*, April 4, 1966, and April 8, 1966.

a lawsuit. "I don't believe," he said, "there's a court in the land that would work any greater hardship than these people are trying to do." [98] Henrico opposition became rigid as the superintendent defiantly announced that he would follow Federal free-choice procedures to the letter and let the Office of Education decide what to do about it. The school board chairman's home was flooded with favorable phone calls.[99]

Resistance now developed a momentum of its own. Meeting secretly at a local steak house, the board of education broke off all negotiations. Realizing by now that Federal officials were not eager to cut off funds, the board openly challenged Seeley's office to begin hearing proceedings.[100] Henrico's stubbornness was hailed by that fiery champion of the old order, the *Richmond News Leader*, which denounced the "tinpot despotism of Czar Harold Howe and his army of contemptible commissars":

> Nothing suggests that the U.S. Commissioner of Integration is a reasonable man. Through subordinates, he has sent word that this pace is not fast enough to suit him. More! Faster! And his threat is to cut off Federal funds for Henrico unless the county knuckles under. . . .
>
> But Henrico ought not to be compelled to give up tax funds to which the county is plainly entitled. . . . If Czar Howe can convince a Federal court of the lawfulness and equity of his edicts, we will be vastly amazed.[101]

The school system proceeded on a free-choice basis, and Representative Satterfield asked Howe to consider modifying the Office's "harsh and unyielding position." [102] Now the Office of Education began to temporize. The congressman was told that statistics provided by the county were being studied. Although the Federal deadline was past, a spokesman said that a fund cutoff would "be a long way off" and that negotiations would continue.[103]

The bluff had been called. Federal staff members followed the only remaining course that would prevent a very damaging public defeat—bureaucratic delay.

The upshot was that the schools remained largely segregated and needed Federal programs were lost. Henrico had planned a $121,000 Federally financed program of preschool training and in-school remedial work. More than 70 additional staff members were to be hired.[104] The summer remedial effort was to benefit the children at several Negro grade schools. Although the county would certainly have been reimbursed, the

---

[98] *Ibid.*, May 2, 6, and 7, 1966.   [99] *Ibid.*, May 9, 1966.
[100] *Ibid.*, May 17, 1966.   [101] *Ibid.*
[102] *Ibid.*, May 20, 1966; *Richmond Times-Dispatch*, May 24, 1966.
[103] *Ibid.*, May 24, 1966.   [104] *Richmond News Leader*, April 30, 1966.

program was killed by county board members who feared that they would be stuck with the bill. Only weeks before it was to begin, a project to help almost 500 children from very poor families and to provide extra income for a large number of Henrico teachers was destroyed. Even a Federal announcement that there was no immediate danger of fund cutoff failed to revive the effort.[105]

Cancellation was blamed on Washington. One newspaper accused enforcement officials of "robbing Negro children . . . of educational opportunities." [106] Governor Godwin insisted that the proper Federal objective was "not racial balance or imbalance but to maintain the best possible public school system . . . with the least possible disruption." [107]

The impasse continued for month after month. In spite of periodic speculation about a Federal decision, the entire school year passed without any formal Office of Education action to either accept or reject the local plan.[108] Henrico remained adamant. In spite of a chronic need for more school funds and a public demand for preschool programs, Henrico was unwilling to negotiate the closing of the district's three remaining all-black schools.[109] The county continued to pay the cost of bussing Negro high school students past white schools to an inefficient and inadequate separate school. Positions were frozen and, for a second summer, the county's poor children were denied a needed remedial program.

The chief value of the Henrico story lies in what it reveals about the practical limits on Title VI enforcement. The effort to impose standards permitted but not demanded by the guidelines disrupted valued program relationships with local officials. The Office came under attack both by local politicians and editors. The incident made clear that even a large sum of Federal money could not overbalance aroused local feeling, particularly when the money was going to poor, and therefore largely black, students. The double-edged character of the cutoff weapon, which damaged the agency almost as much as the recipient, was recognized by Henrico officials challenging the Office of Education to accept the onus for destruction of an attempt to help black students.

The Henrico conflict showed flaws in some of the assumptions underlying the guidelines standards. Two years after the Civil Rights Act became

[105] *Richmond Times-Dispatch*, June 4, and June 7, 1966.
[106] *Ibid.*, June 23, 1966.
[107] *Ibid.*
[108] *Ibid.*, July 13, 1966, August 21, 1966, and November 16, 1966; *Richmond News Leader*, July 18, 1966; interview with Robert P. Hilldrup, February 3, 1967.
[109] *Richmond News Leader*, February 15, 1966, January 30, 1967, February 16, 1967, March 1, 1967, and May 23, 1967.

law, the policies were still basically directed toward the problem of getting integration in motion where resistance was strongest. Since Federal court decisions had dealt most explicitly with this stage of the process and HEW had tied its administrative regulations to judicial standards, Federal energy was focused on Deep South recalcitrance. In the absence of a strong commitment from Commissioner Howe and the President to resolve ambiguous court findings through the use of administrative discretion to clearly require prompt total desegregation, Federal power was strictly limited in the border states and in relatively progressive southern communities. The Administration was not prepared to pay the political costs involved in denial of funds to districts with substantial desegregation which refused to take the final step. Once the Federal bluff became evident, it was also clear that either stronger court decisions or a good deal more Federal power would be necessary to finally abolish separate schools in large areas of Virginia.

The Henrico clash illustrated the seriousness of HEW's initial mistake in accepting free-choice plans. Initial acceptance of 1965 freedom-of-choice procedures without any stipulation that they must actually desegregate schools had encouraged southern schoolmen to believe, as they wanted to believe, that a Negro student's rights were fully protected when he was offered a chance to transfer to a white school. Now the Office of Education seemed to be attacking a fair and democratic system. The very words "freedom of choice" had a rhetorical force wholly outweighing the pallid bureaucratic pronouncements about the "dual school system." If there was something wrong with free choice, why had it been accepted as perfectly adequate only a year earlier?

From the local perspective it was easy to characterize the new demands as the product of arrogant bureaucrats committed to "racial balancing" or "forced integration." Operating within a political system in which power is essentially local, in a society profoundly suspicious of Washington bureaucrats, the Office of Education had the disadvantage of advocating a poorly understood position opposed to a system widely seen as completely fair and all that the law required.

The stalemate was to drag on two more years until mid-1968. Henrico sacrificed $290,000 in Federal aid for poor children, while the Office of Education stalled about cutting off hundreds of thousands of dollars still going to the county for other programs. Not until January 1968 was the case reopened and a serious threat made to terminate Federal aid. This threat came only after there had been important court decisions against free choice and a reformulation of the guidelines to state clearly the necessity to abolish separate schools. Even then, in spite of flagrant inadequacies in the existing free-choice plan, another half year went by before

Henrico was cited for a hearing to cut off funds.[110] When there was a strong local resistance on a politically controversial issue, Federal power proved to be much less than awesome.

The Effort to Make Freedom of Choice Work

While the effort to completely desegregate 20 school systems was important for the future of Virginia education, the major goal under the 1966 guidelines was to obtain local commitments to transform freedom of choice from an end in itself to an effective mechanism producing substantial integration. The central issues in this struggle were raised by the new requirements specifying minimum annual rates of progress and demanding faculty integration.

In the more conservative parts of the state, the new requirements generated a wave of concern from local schoolmen convinced that their communities were completely unprepared to accept these changes. School officials who had negotiated what they believed to be long-range agreements with the Office of Education only the year before were angered by what they saw as a repudiation of Washington commitments. This misunderstanding resulted both from an initial Federal failure to make clear that standards would continue to evolve as the case law developed and administrative experience accumulated and from the wishful thinking of schoolmen personally committed to freedom of choice.

When Commissioner Howe invited the Virginia school superintendent to Washington for a session on the new guidelines, Superintendent Woodrow Wilkerson coolly declined. Certain Federal programs, he indicated, had been developed without adequate local consultation. "The genius of American education," he said, "resides in the fact that it has been kept close to the people." [111]

Although the state's top educator refused to cross the Potomac, the trip was soon made by the top political official. Governor Godwin, a Southside Virginia politician, knew the bitter resistance the new guidelines would produce. As his office received reports from local leaders indicating the possibility of widespread cutoffs, his concern deepened. Almost two-thirds of the state's districts failed to submit plans by the original HEW deadline. Although the deadline was extended, Godwin was worried.

The Governor carried his concern to HEW Secretary Gardner. The first southern governor to carry his protest to the capital, Godwin dismissed the new rate-of-progress requirement as an illlegal demand for

---

110 *Richmond News Leader*, January 25, 1968; *Richmond Times-Dispatch*, July 15, 1968. Henrico officials finally announced a desegregation plan in late 1968.
111 *Richmond News Leader*, April 11, 1966.

"racial balance." The Governor believed that Congress had explicitly prohibited directives ordering certain percentages of integration during consideration of the Civil Rights Act. On the equally vexing issue of faculty integration, Godwin argued that even HEW officials had earlier conceded that they lacked authority over employment discrimination. He appealed for caution:

> It must be recognized that full desegregation of an historic dual public school system based on traditional social patterns or mores of a people cannot be achieved by Federal edicts in a relatively short span of time without serious disruptions in the efficient operation of that school system. . . .
>
> During this year much progress has been made. . . . Every county, city, and town . . . is in compliance. In light of the varying problems and complexities faced by Virginia localities . . . the importance of maintaining reasonable flexibility in the administration of the revised guidelines is critical.
>
> We are on the eve of taking some of the greatest steps in the history of our public school system. . . . We ask your understanding and cooperation that we may get on with the job of improving the quality of instruction for all boys and girls without regard to race, color, or national origin.[112]

The meeting was cordial but produced no policy changes. Godwin was told that the controversial percentages had been de-emphasized and that the regulations "carry a certain amount of flexibility with them." [113] In these comments Secretary Gardner was merely amplifying a conciliatory letter he had sent to southern political leaders earlier in the month in response to their bitter criticisms. The suggestion that the guidelines might not really mean what they said further increased the difficulties facing enforcement officials, even as the Governor's well-publicized belief that the rules were illegal magnified the political problems for local superintendents struggling with the decision on the compliance pledge. Once again the pressures of fundamental social change were to focus on subordinate Office of Education bureaucrats and local superintendents, confronted with a decision that could well cost them their position, their local support, or the resources they had to have to do their job properly. In May, when the second deadline arrived, 22 school boards were still holding out.[114]

Although political calculations kept most Virginia politicians out of the school fray, the Governor was to become increasingly involved. Secure for four years in an office for which re-election is forbidden, he decided that the new guidelines were illegal, threatened to stir up dormant racial feelings, and might endanger educational progress. His trip to Washington was only the first in a series of steps he took to increase pressure for Federal policy changes. Godwin was a formidable opponent.

112 *Ibid.*, April 22, 1966; House Judiciary Committee, *Guidelines*, pp. 77–78.
113 *Washington Post*, April 22, 1966.   114 *Ibid.*, May 7, 1966.

Free Choice and the Enforcement Bureaucracy

As the wave of political controversy splashed over the Title VI staff and the Governor committed the authority of his office to the battle, the routine bureaucratic procedures giving substance to the new guidelines went quietly forward.

As usual, the compliance program was chronically understaffed. During the early months of 1966, one woman handled Virginia enforcement— Miss Caroline Davis, a 33-year-old black attorney who was to be a target of one of Governor Godwin's attacks. For Miss Davis these months of growing turbulence in Virginia were largely consumed by endless desk work, processing statistics on free choice sent in by local superintendents.

The new enforcement strategy was based on the provision of the 1966 guidelines that free choice would be accepted only where it worked. To determine whether it was working, the Office needed rapid analysis of the existing situation revealed by the local enrollment projections for the coming fall. There was to be a "second go-round," allowing Federal staff members to propose additional steps to school divisions moving too slowly. The elaborate data-processing system for handling the local statistics broke down, however, and Miss Davis spent her days preparing charts showing the number of black students in a given district, the per cent integrated, the proportion of total enrollment that was Negro, and the teacher integration in each system. Because these four figures were the most important indicators of what was happening in a division, much professional time was invested in the mundane work of assembling statistics.

Contact with confused and angry local superintendents was handled by telephone. The staff shortage ordained by congressional budget-cutters meant that the jobs of answering local questions and trying to persuade local officials to sign compliance forms had to be handled by long-distance calls.

Local problems were many-sided, and negotiations proceeded slowly. Superintendents objected to the replacement of the previous year's individual plans for each locality by a "blank check" form promising to observe the numerous detailed directives of the new guidelines. At first it was expected that many Southside counties would follow the example of similar Deep South areas and simply refuse to sign the pledge. Miss Davis maintained contact with reluctant school officials, telling them they were in a small minority and informing them when systems with similar problems made the decision to sign. A considerate approach to local superintendents, coupled with threats to terminate funds, helped reduce the 22 counties resisting in May to five holdouts as school began.

While negotiation of compliance promises had been the primary concern in 1965, it was only the first step of the process the second year. The basic administrative focus during summer 1966 was on checking out performance.

A serious weakness of the Title VI effort had been the inability of the Washington staff to personally review what was actually happening at the local level and to develop sources of information independent of the local superintendent. It was obviously impossible for one overburdened bureaucrat to visit school divisions all over Virginia. To meet this need and to short-circuit staff ceilings, HEW hired a large group of law students as temporary summer aides. Seven were assigned to assist in the review of Virginia school divisions.

After training, each student was given specific instructions about gathering data and conducting telephone negotiations with certain school divisions. The law students established regular contact with the superintendents, calling them to discuss compliance pledges, to request progress reports, and to encourage action on the difficult faculty integration requirements.

Midsummer field investigations brought the first independent assessment of how desegregation was really working on the local level. Investigating teams were sent to different regions, and one or two students visited each of the five divisions covered during a typical one or two day trip. Thus, in most cases, the first Federal visit to the school division was not by a senior official but by law students in their early twenties.

The investigator's role was a sensitive one. He had to deal successfully with local educators, even though his very presence implicitly questioned the accuracy of their reports. He was instructed to talk not only to local white officials, but also to Negro parents and students who might report violations. If free choice was not working well, he would meet with school officials and discuss possible ways to increase the level of integration.

In some ways the visits to 28 Virginia school divisions strengthened the Title VI effort. In six counties local leaders took Federal warnings seriously, and performance quickly improved. Even more significant was the collection of a bank of data on local conditions. Previously most communities were known in Washington only as names and statistics; now individual school systems could be described in detail. It became far easier to suggest the particular changes needed in a given division and to effectively plan future enforcement activities. Formal reports prepared on 15 counties seriously violating the law specified charges to be made if a fund-cutoff hearing became necessary.[115]

115 Interview with Caroline Davis, March 24, 1967.

The risks involved in sending inexperienced law students into the field, however, had been justified only by the hope for real breakthroughs in the "second go-round." In most cases these gains did not materialize. The visits began too late, and administrative confusion and caution delayed Washington approval of letters to school divisions demanding further progress. Although the Commissioner's authority to require additional local action was very clear, the overburdened administrative structure was unable to digest the data gathered and make the necessary policy decisions. Formal notifications to school administrators were often not mailed until summer was over. When school opened in Virginia, letters to eight divisions in serious danger of losing Federal funds and 27 other systems making inadequate progress were still in desk drawers in Washington.[116] When they were finally sent they reached superintendents right in the midst of the hectic first weeks of a new school year. Officials who might possibly have considered further steps in July were outraged by demands reaching them after all arrangements for the school year had been worked out.

Sensing the reaction, Governor Godwin promptly took the issue to Secretary Gardner. In a September 1 meeting he told the Secretary of numerous complaints from local schoolmen both about the "immaturity" and inexperience of the law student review teams and the ill-timed requests for further changes.

> The major complaint arises from the unreasonable demands . . . when all assignments have been made of instructional personnel, and the school system has been organized for opening. To comply . . . would require delay in opening dates and repeating many detailed operations essential for the orderly administration of a school system.[117]

The Governor was reacting to a double violation of the norms of American Federal-state relations. In the first place, the dispatch of investigators indicated that the standard practice of accepting local promises was being replaced and the good faith of local white officials was being called into question. Rather than quietly accepting the word of the white leadership that blacks were being offered every fair chance to transfer from their inferior schools, Federal officials were prying into local affairs and encouraging black discontent. Second, the Office of Education had violated the strong tradition that Federal-state interaction should be between professionals, in this case between educators at both levels. School officials were insulted when they were asked to deal as equals on the most sensitive local issue with young men lacking both experience and professional

[116] *Richmond Times-Dispatch*, September 1, 1966.
[117] Letter from Governor Godwin to Secretary Gardner, September 1, 1966, reprinted in House Judiciary Committee, *Guidelines*, p. 79.

training. HEW was aware of this dilemma but could not escape from the limitations imposed by an inadequate budget and the unwillingness of southern school administrators to accept jobs with the controversial compliance program.

Governor Godwin asked Secretary Gardner to re-examine the recommendations of the review teams. He pleaded for special consideration of the difficulties faced by backward Southside counties with large black majorities. Speeding up integration there, he argued, would simply expand the private school system.[118] After consideration, HEW refused to jeopardize recommendations across the South by publicly questioning the judgment of the department officials who had approved the letters. HEW defended its staff's work, but ordered yet another attempt to negotiate local problems.[119]

The policy impact of Godwin's four-hour session at HEW was mixed. The department stood firm on terminating funds to seven of the eight divisions most blatantly violating the guidelines.[120] On the other hand little pressure was exerted on behalf of suggestions made to 27 other divisions falling short of guidelines standards. The Office of Education failed to effectively use its authority to insist on further desegregation steps. The idea that the law required only freedom of choice remained very much alive in Virginia. The credibility of Federal enforcement threats began to seriously erode.

Progress in 1966

As the second summer of enforcement ended, a reporter asked a high HEW official for an assessment of the state's record. Virginia, he was told, continued to stand ahead of most of the South. Because of the early start arising from NAACP litigation, much of the state seemed "typical of a border state," but "some of its communities are as hard to crack as Alabama or Mississippi." The fact that some areas had agreed to abandon free choice and end separate schools was especially encouraging. From Washington, the most serious problem seemed to be in the field of faculty integration. Few school divisions had met even the modest Federal standard of one teacher moving across race lines for each school in the system. In concentrating on the more central issue of student transfers, HEW had relaxed this requirement.[121]

The returns in the fall of 1966 showed that the new guidelines had maintained the momentum of change. Another 14 per cent of the Negro

118 *Richmond Times-Dispatch,* September 2, 1966, and *Washington Post,* September 2, 1966.
119 *Ibid.,* September 3, 1966.   120 *Richmond News Leader,* January 31, 1967.
121 *Washington Post,* August 29, 1966.

students entered integrated classrooms, and now one black child in four was being educated outside the traditional Negro school system. In one year, almost as many black students had crossed the racial barrier in the Old Dominion as had entered all the white schools of the South in the first 10 years after the 1954 Supreme Court decision. Even though one-fifth of these children were still in schools more than 95 per cent Negro, the achievement was substantial. Moreover, the first small steps had been taken toward faculty integration in dozens of communities where the idea would have been dismissed as a fantasy two years earlier.

Where local attitudes or the commitment of local officials permitted free choice to work, gains had been made. Behind the promising facade, however, there were ominous signs. Many school divisions had done far less than the guidelines demanded and encountered no difficulty in retaining Federal money. The general enforcement failure noted by the Civil Rights Commission was obvious in Virginia:

> Something far short of these standards was required in practice. No attempt was made to require school districts to live up to each of the two independent standards for student transfers and professional staff desegregation which the guidelines established. Instead, the approach was to enforce Title VI only against those districts where progress was minimal in both categories. Initial efforts to enforce the guidelines as written were abandoned.[122]

In nine Virginia school districts where no action was taken, more than 95 per cent of the black children remained in the old separate schools. Fourteen divisions that had failed to integrate a single teacher continued to receive subsidies.[123] HEW lacked the political and administrative muscle to give substance to its rhetoric, and this fact was becoming increasingly apparent.

The first two years of guidelines enforcement had exhausted most of the relatively easy gains. Most communities prepared for a final solution of the race question had now been committed to total integration. Few remained that would eliminate segregation without unambiguous Federal determination to cut off aid funds. The Henrico case and a number of other instances clearly revealed that this determination was lacking. Most Virginia divisions made some further progress within the free-choice system in 1966, postponing the showdown on the free-choice issue for a year. The easiest part of teacher integration had been accomplished with the placement of some of the best black teachers in white schools and some of the most unprejudiced white teachers in Negro schools. The next steps were crucial, and there were signs of powerful resistance.

122 Civil Rights Commission, *Southern School Desegregation*, p. 38.
123 See Gary Orfield, "How to Beat Integration," *New Republic*, February 3, 1968, p. 17.

Cutoff: The Ultimate Weapon

For almost two years the enforcement program operated in Virginia without withdrawing Federal aid from a single district. The tactics of threat, bluff, and persuasion had normally been enough to produce some vestige of forward movement. Now that HEW was making demands seen as absolutely intolerable in some rural communities, however, the old approach began to break down. Office of Education officials feared that continuance of a permissive attitude toward divisions refusing to make the slightest effort to comply could quickly unravel the whole compliance program. If local leaders saw open defiance go unpunished, they would feel free to stand still or even to permit regression. In a state where 21 districts had less than 50 black students in white schools after two years of guidelines enforcement, it was plain that decisive action was needed if there was ever to be more than token integration in some parts of the state. Well-publicized assertions that the guidelines were illegal encouraged educators to insist that free choice fully satisfied the law.

Finally in September 1966 the Office of Education moved to shore up the credibility of its desegregation effort by deferring new funds for the seven Virginia districts with the worst records. The divisions were concentrated in the black belt. Although all of the divisions had a heavy Negro enrollment, they had an average of only 40 black students in integrated schools in the entire local system. They were small, poor districts, eligible for substantial Federal aid because of their high numbers of students from poor families. Three had no faculty desegregation whatever, and the other four had only a handful of teachers working in schools of the other race. The divisions were in the most rigidly segregationist parts of the state and the areas most in need of educational improvement.[124]

No one wanted to deny money where the need was so obvious. Time after time Washington suggested ways to comply. The most common proposal was to reopen registration in the hope that more Negroes might transfer. Even this, however, seemed unnecessary and disruptive to the local farmers and businessmen on the school boards. Another free-choice period would mean an additional burden for a superintendent who often had only a secretary or two to help with all the details of getting the school year underway. A new choice period meant days of mimeographing and addressing letters, checking returns, reassigning students, and shuffling teachers, classrooms, and even bus arrangements if large num-

[124] *Statistical Summary*, p. 37; Virginia State Department of Education, *Facing Up, Statistical Data on Virginia's Public Schools* (Richmond: State Department of Education, 1966), pp. 3–9, 46–52.

bers transferred. Money would have to be found in the tight school budget for mailing the choice forms. Some school boards simply refused to budge. Where local white resistance was intense, a test of Federal determination became inevitable.

Terminating Sussex County

The first school division in Virginia to feel the full weight of Federal power was the black-belt county of Sussex. A rural area of pine forests and farms that grows rich Virginia peanuts, Sussex has been the home for about 12,000 people ever since the Civil War. Near the site of the Nat Turner slave rebellion, the county today is part of the political fiefdom of the powerful segregationist State Senator, Garland Gray, a leading figure in the state Democratic Organization. The county's four small towns now show only the first faint beginnings of the industrialization transforming much of the state. Although the public-school population is about three-fourths black, only 40 Negro students had entered white schools 12 years after the Supreme Court decision. There had been no integration of full-time classroom teachers. Although Federal subsidies equaled one-fourth of the local school budget, the county refused to obey the 1966 guidelines.

Sussex was one of many hundreds of southern counties where not the slightest step toward recognizing the constitutional rights of black students had been taken between 1954 and the issuance of the 1965 guidelines. In 1965 the Office of Education had approved a free-choice plan opening only four grades the first year. Only 20 black students escaped segregation in the fall of 1965, the very kind of local failure that had prompted the drafting of more explicit Federal requirements.

The county shared in the private-school boom. Tidewater Academy, a poorly financed segregationist school, was formed in 1964 and had drawn 133 students from the county's public schools by 1966. Tuition grants for this and other private schools had produced a loss of more than one-sixth of the county's white pupils. In an adjoining county the public schools had been all black since 1964. Resistance was also reflected in the flowering of the KKK. The local klavern had drawn as many as 200 people to its cross burnings. While token integration had been accepted quietly, local whites found further change unacceptable.

In an area where plantation-style economic dependence was still commonplace, the large local NAACP chapter was not an activist organization. Although Negro schools were crowded and offered inferior training, and although transferring students had not been seriously harassed, black parents remained wary. Like many Deep South communities, Sussex had constructed new Negro schools in the late 1950's in an attempt to ward off pressure for desegregation. Although the buildings were designed to be overcrowded, some families preferred them to the older white schools. In a traditionalistic community, many people simply held back because of an inbred apathy or an undefinable fear of the social or financial consequences of taking an overt step against the caste system.

When the law student review team reached Sussex in August 1966, they negotiated with a superintendent who had grown up in the county and had spent his entire teaching career there. Superintendent Mayes felt that the Federal representatives "didn't come down here with any sense of reason about them." When the school board was told that more desegregation was essential, Mayes decided that the team didn't understand school administration problems and that undoing all the school plans in late August would be a "breach of faith with the people." [125]

After fruitless telephone negotiations, cutoff procedures were begun. Since almost one-third of $1 million would be lost, the school board decided to reopen discussions. The HEW Virginia specialist came down for a futile meeting. County officials said they might be willing to gradually desegregated teachers, but they were intransigent on the student question. In fact, in explicit violation of their guidelines promise, the board had approved the return of 10 black children to Negro schools. Federal toleration of such action would encourage those who were harassing students who dared to cross racial lines and would possibly result in complete resegregation.

The next step in the contest was forced by Congress. An amendment to the Elementary and Secondary Education Act limited to 90 days the time funds could be deferred without a hearing for a final cutoff. By late December 1966 complex discussions between HEW and the Justice Department produced a decision to maintain the credibility of the enforcement program by citing for hearings the 90 worst school districts in the South. One of these was Sussex County.

The HEW statement accompanying the hearing notice asserted that more than 19 in 20 black students remained in separate schools. Even free choice had been denied to high school students. The local caste system was reinforced by segregated bus routes with segregated drivers and a policy against interracial athletic competition. The school board refused to consider transferring any teacher unless the teacher requested it.[126]

Convinced that the guidelines were illegal, the Sussex school board

[125] Interview with Superintendent Mayes, March 9, 1967; interview with Luis Andrews, March 9, 1967.
[126] Docket CR 395 HEW, County School Board of Sussex County, State Board of Education of Virginia. December 3, 1966, "Notice of Opportunity for Hearing," "Requests for Admission of Fact."

retained a Richmond lawyer who specialized in fighting school desegregation. On February 2, 1967, in the courtlike atmosphere of a Washington hearing room, the formal authority of the law was invoked. Across a long table sat the Federal bureaucrats and the defenders of the local status quo. A young HEW lawyer and a young woman from the review team sat next to Caroline Davis, facing the Sussex attorney, nervous local schoolmen, and a quietly confident Virginia assistant attorney general. The hearing examiner took a tall chair at the front of the room. In an hour and a half, it was all over.

Testimony confirmed the essential elements of the Office of Education case. The school board's lawyer based his argument on the claim that HEW had no authority to force Sussex to put 8 or 9 per cent of its black students in white schools. Defiantly, he warned that a cutoff would only hurt Negro education:

> . . . the threat of loss of Federal funds will not make them force school children to go to schools they do not wish to attend. Likewise, the respondent school boards will not make involuntary transfers or assignments of teachers. . . .[127]

Since the legal authority of HEW had been decisively upheld in the courts and the facts of the case were clear, the hearing examiner had little difficulty in recommending final termination of funds.[128] After notification to Congress and another attempt to negotiate, the cutoff order was signed in June by Secretary Gardner.

Sussex was the first Virginia school division to have funds terminated. Things continued much as before, however, and the immediate impact was not great. The county's normal school program was largely undisturbed. What was lacking were the new programs taking hold in other Virginia localities. Special summer remedial programs were cancelled. Local school boards notorious for their frugality faced the alternative of finding more tax revenue or cutting back Federally funded vocational and science programs. The long-term prospects for the county were not bright. Compared with similar systems with one-fourth more money to spend, the school program was certain to become increasingly inadequate.

A year after funds were terminated the school board remained adamant. The Virginia Southern Christian Leadership Conference chose a Sussex community as their focus for the Poor People's Campaign and found school conditions as bad as ever. A reporter found a family with 21 children, all illiterate; few of them had ever attended school because of local unwillingness to enforce compulsory attendance. These black chil-

[127] Henry T. Wickham, attorney, "Brief on Behalf of Respondent School Boards," April 17, 1967.
[128] Docket CR 395 HEW, "Initial Decision of Abraham Gold, Hearing Examiner," April 12, 1967.

dren and others like them lived in a shantytown largely owned by State Senator Gray and not yet served by the local school bus.[129] The existence of such conditions in a relatively progressive southern state in the late 1960's suggests the kind of local resistance Federal officials had to confront. The fact that funds were cut off from only the very worst districts in the South meant that the Federal sanction was being used, not where Federal leverage could most easily be decisive, but against the South's most determined segregationists.

The Civil Rights Act provided a two-pronged attack on school segregation. Not only was HEW directed to end subsidies to communities defying the Constitution, but the Attorney General was also granted power to initiate lawsuits on behalf of black children. One of the most powerful arguments in convincing Southside school divisions to comply with the first guidelines had been that they really had no option, since they would be sued by the Justice Department if they defied HEW. The fact that Sussex chose to ignore the guidelines, as did a number of other Virginia divisions, arose from the failure of the Justice Department to make good on its threat. This failure resulted in part from the department's striking concentration of its limited legal staff on the more blatant resistance encountered in the Deep South and in part from the failure of local black leadership to submit the necessary complaints to Washington. The absence of an effective Justice Department presence made possible at least a temporary escape from the law, encouraging local segregationists to waste irreplaceable funds.

The major immediate impact of cutting off funds was to change attitudes in surrounding areas. The fact that money was finally denied, after two and a half years of talk, made the threat real. In school divisions with very poor performance, such palpable evidence of disastrous loss forced schoolmen to think seriously about ways to accomplish things that had always been unthinkable in their communities.

Political Reaction

The cutoff decision in the first Virginia cases mobilized the entire state congressional delegation. Days after the hearing examiner's judgment, all Virginia congressmen signed a letter asking the powerful House subcommittee handling the HEW budget to strangle the enforcement effort financially because of coercive methods used in Virginia. The letter claimed, once again, that the Civil Rights Act required only free choice. The Office of Education was accused of "exercising direction, supervision

[129] *Washington Post*, September 12, 1968.

and control of school personnel, including faculty assignments, in violation of laws governing Federal educational assistance." [130] Governor
Godwin strongly endorsed the protest.

Hearing decisions against five more districts in May 1967 set off a fresh
fusillade. Byrd Organization leader Representative Wat Abbitt, whose
home county of Appomattox stood to lose $110,000, attacked. He de-
nounced the "Gestapo" tactics of "trying to browbeat, coerce, and black-
jack local school officials," and called on Secretary Gardner to "take a
realistic view of our problem and get on with the goal of helping educate
our children." [131] The Governor again joined the fray with an open
letter quoting the bitter comment of a local schoolman who had told him
that Federal officials were "after percentages . . . they deal with human
being the way you deal with a bag of beans." Federal requirements,
Godwin repeated, were seriously interfering with educational improvement. Godwin again raised the issue when he accompanied other Democratic governors to a meeting at the President's ranch.

In terms of the immediate objective of gaining release of Federal funds,
the Virginia political assault failed. Proceedings were eventually completed, and the flow of funds stopped. Less immediately visible but of far
greater ultimate importance, however, were the lengthy delays and the
future caution in using the enforcement tool in Virginia. When a political
figure as powerful as a governor or a congressional committee chairman
attacked the program, the administrators quickly found themselves on the
defensive. Commissioner Howe explained that the kind of policy and
personnel criticisms made by Virginia leaders do not bring dramatic
policy changes, but do *bring* a variety of more subtle alterations. Once
such a charge was made, "You've got to stop and talk about it . . . and
hold things up while you are doing it." [132] President Johnson continually
demanded, as did Secretary Gardner, that the highest Office of Education
officials be ready to meet with state authorities and answer their charges.
Thus sharp criticism tended to increase normal bureaucratic caution,
building on the normal desire to avoid controversy.

If the state's separate schooling was to be ended, the Office of Education had to be ready to deny funds not only to divisions that adamantly
refused to make any effort, but also where free choice simply produced
insufficient progress toward the abolition of all-black schools. Across the
state were school systems ready to do what was absolutely necessary to
retain Federal money, but nothing more. While action against the very
worst divisions was essential to sustain any Federal program, determina-

[130] *Richmond News Leader*, April 18, 1967.   [131] *Ibid.*, May 12, 1967.
[132] Interview with Harold Howe, II, September 20, 1968.

tion to threaten cutoffs in more typical districts would be required for ultimate success. During the third year of the program the level of political opposition was to make such action very timid indeed.

Loss of Momentum in 1967

In January 1967 the Office of Education announced that there would be no change in the guidelines for the third year of enforcement. Thus school districts would have to continue faculty desegregation at the same annual rate and make substantial progress in student integration. Within HEW adequate progress was defined as rapid total integration in school divisions with less than 20 per cent black students and at least a doubling of the level of integration in systems that had achieved little in 1966.[133] In spite of these formal requirements, however, many districts fell far below and no enforcement action was taken.

During 1967 the standards actually enforced in Virginia demanded so little that NAACP attorneys wondered whether desegregation was actually hampered by implicit Federal approval given many divisions doing less than the minimum demanded by the Constitution, as interpreted in recent court decisions. At first civil rights leaders had hoped that Title VI enforcement would break new ground, closing gaps in existing court-order desegregation standards. Reluctantly they reconciled themselves to the idea that the HEW requirements would merely reflect current constitutional doctrine, and the NAACP Legal Defense Fund returned to the courts in an effort to obtain more explicit rulings on such central issues as faculty desegregation and free choice. The battle was won in the courts, but now HEW was unwilling to incorporate the tougher rulings into its operating standards.

The problem was strikingly apparent in faculty desegregation. A Virginia Federal judge had ordered full integration of one division's faculty in a single year. In a suit against the major Southside city of Petersburg the NAACP had won an agreement for complete integration by the fall of 1967.[134] The Office of Education, however, asked only that one teacher be integrated each year for each school in a system, and it settled for a great deal less than it asked. During 1967, no action was taken against more than 20 school divisions violating even the minimal requirements of the guidelines.[135]

The gap was even more serious on the fundamental question of student

---

[133] Office for Civil Rights, "Procedures for Review of Elementary and Secondary School Desegregation Plans," July 1967, pp. ii–1–ii–2.

[134] *Washington Post*, January 7, 1966; *Richmond Times-Dispatch*, July 1, 1966; *Richmond News Leader*, July 8, 1966.

[135] Office for Civil Rights, compliance status charts, December 1967.

integration. In the courts the loopholes in the case law were rapidly being closed. A historic decision of the Fifth Circuit Court of Appeals undermined the basic assumptions of the free-choice system. In Virginia in March 1967 the NAACP gained a settlement from the Norfolk school board providing for geographic zoning of the city's schools. In August a Virginia Federal judge ordered Loudoun county to abandon free choice and move rapidly toward a unified school system.[136] HEW fell far behind judicial standards.

If the formal Federal standards stated in the guidelines were inadequate, the standards actually enforced were very low indeed. Policy judgments within HEW resulted in virtual suspension of guidelines enforcement in all southern school districts with a majority of black students and in all districts with more than one-fourth of the Negro students in integrated schools. Even in the remaining districts, Federal determination seemed to sag.

During the first two years of enforcement, local confusion and uncertainty about Federal firmness left room for a great deal of bluffing in Washington. Now, as the stakes were mounting, it was becoming increasingly evident that HEW was afraid to deny funds to many districts. Federal caution during the 1967 negotiating session was reflected in the replacement of the investigating teams that had swarmed over the state the summer of 1966 by a small ineffective effort at summer's end. Although a major campaign had been launched to completely desegregate 20 districts in 1966, no such sustained effort appeared in 1967.

Much of the state was balancing between a reluctant decision to move toward total integration and a further consolidation of the existing commitment to freedom of choice. HEW staff members spent much time and energy in urging school divisions to comply with the law. Sanctions were threatened, and, in some cases, the Virginia compliance officer recommended denial of funds only to be reversed by superiors.[137] Although approximately 20 school divisions either went backward or made extremely little progress under free choice, only three districts were cited for cutoff hearings.[138] While a few divisions did make significant progress, the increasingly obvious fact that districts defying the law had little to fear took most of the steam out of the movement for change.

In its simplest terms, the central question was whether HEW would use force to uphold its timid desegregation guidelines. The answer was

[136] *Washington Post*, March 19, 1967, and September 16, 1967.
[137] U.S. Commission on Civil Rights, Virginia State Advisory Committee, *The Federal Role in School Desegregation in Selected Virginia Districts* (September 1968), p. 30.
[138] Office for Civil Rights, compliance status charts.

no. In many areas the continued flow of Federal aid was taken as implicit approval of existing racial practices. In two Southside counties studied by the Virginia State Advisory Committee to the U.S. Civil Rights Commission, this argument was repeatedly raised. Although 95 per cent of the black students in these schools remained segregated and no visible progress was being made, one county board member told the committee "that as long as the school system was receiving Federal funds, the board thought it was in compliance with Federal requirements." [139] When Isle of Wight County black spokesmen complained to their school board, they were told that the board was "meeting the Guidelines and that HEW was satisfied, why weren't we?" The board "repeated that over and over." [140] Thus regulations intended to aid Negro children to obtain their rights were now so seriously diluted that in some cases local segregationists could use them as a shield against black demands.

Under intense political pressure, a program created to make litigation unnecessary allowed school divisions violating the Constitution to continue receiving Federal subsidies. With the national civil rights coalition in death throes as ghettos broke into riots and militants moved toward black separatism, and with HEW facing strong and continuing southern attacks, the Administration moved to placate local leadership by weakening desegregation requirements.

Social Revolution and Local Power in American Federalism

In the mid-1960's Virginia witnessed the local impact of a great national movement, which had won the support of the American people, for a vast expansion of Federal authority to regulate local racial discrimination. In Virginia, as across the entire 17-state region touched by the school guidelines, the first two years of enforcement rapidly accelerated desegregation. In two years' time, 10 times as many black students entered desegregated classrooms as had made the transition in the preceding decade of intensive struggle in the courts.

This vast and rapid social change was the direct result of the sweeping alteration of Federal-state relationships demanded by Title VI of the Civil Rights Act. What had been an issue decided by local white and black leaders and sometimes a Federal judge now became a confrontation between the U.S. Government and the local school board. A passive source of needed funds suddenly claimed the dominant role in determining how the most sensitive local political question would be resolved.

As the confrontation began Virginians, like most Americans, overestimated the extent and permanence of the change. Feeling defeated by the

[139] Virginia State Advisory Committee, pp. 13, 21.   [140] *Ibid.*, p. 23.

overwhelming public demand reflected in the large congressional majorities that had finally cut down southern resistance, resistance seemed futile. Schoolmen and political leaders eventually accepted the requirements of the first guidelines, which seemed to ask only token integration. In a single year the large areas of total segregation were broken as every school division began integration. A few districts actually began to move toward a unified nonracial school system. Growing Negro political power and a strong new drive for educational advancement limited political attacks on the program.

Initial progress, however, did not indicate widespread willingness to end school segregation. In most parts of the state, local officials accepted only a transition from total segregation to token integration, justified under the rubric of freedom of choice. Virginia communities were proud of themselves for successfully doing all that they felt the law demanded.

To a great many Virginians the 1966 guidelines went beyond the limits of easily tolerable change. Local officials who believed that they had made every reasonable accommodation now found themselves confronted by a whole new catalogue of changes that would have seemed hopelessly radical only a year earlier. When it became perfectly evident that Federal authorities were really determined to fundamentally rearrange race relations in all Virginia public schools, a test of Federal power became inevitable. The outcome suggested that the national commitment to alteration of American federalism was relatively ephemeral and that Old Dominion politicians were still able to effectively use the formidable powers of state and local governments to make their protests felt in Washington.

Within the complex institutional structures of American federalism, it is often difficult for officials at one level to know accurately the boundaries of political and administrative power of agencies at other levels. Normally the creation of a new Federal program sets in motion a lengthy process of gradual mutual adjustment among Federal, state, and local authorities. Because of a general public preference for state and local dominance and because political power in the United States is built at the local or state level, the final balance generally favors state and local concerns. For a time in the mid-1960's, civil rights seemed to be the great exception for two reasons. In the first place, most Americans believed that the southern race issue was a special case and were prepared to over-ride normal patterns to protect Negro rights. In the second place, the emergence of this new majority seemed to promise a permanent alteration of the federal system within this sphere. By 1966, however, the southern problem had become a national problem and the southern political reaction a national backlash. With the civil rights coalition disorganized and ineffectual, the Office of Education found itself in a very exposed position as the normal pattern of Federal-state relations began to reassert itself.

Most of the early change had happened without any need for HEW to face the ultimate question of using the powerful but mutually damaging sanction. Negotiations were endlessly prolonged to try to avoid this very issue when districts became recalcitrant. "Whenever we had to take money from somebody," says Commissioner Howe, "we suffered a defeat." [141] Growing local resistance, encouraged by denunciations from the statehouse and the congressional delegation, forced the issue.

Adamant defiance of the law in the Southside forced HEW to terminate funds in 1967 in a handful of districts. This action was the cost of maintaining an enforcement effort with any meaning, but it provoked new political attacks and damaged education in divisions desperately needing help. With this action, much of the political capital of the compliance program had been spent. Under incessant fire and receiving little support, HEW administrators moved toward an accommodation with their political environment, an environment dominated by local and state power.

The early Federal impetus made historic changes in Virginia education. Complete racial separation became a thing of the past everywhere. Almost one-third of Virginia's school divisions moved toward reorganization of their schools on the northern model. By 1967, however, HEW had consumed much of the energy generated by the tidal wave of civil rights reform in 1964. The guidelines had been critically damaged by Federal caution and local resistance.

Success now required some aid from outside the HEW bureaucracy. Within the compliance program, forces were regrouped, and a new enforcement strategy was devised to replace the discredited guidelines. In Virginia, belated investigations of some poorly performing divisions gave a spark of life to the effort in early 1968. To close the gap between the ideal of total integration and the reality of powerful local resistance, however, the program needed the momentum that could be provided only by public anger, a strong new presidential commitment, or a sweeping restatement of the law by the Supreme Court.

Once again the focus of the crusade that began in the marble courtroom on Capitol Hill in 1954 turned toward the courts. The definitive legal answer to the maintenance of separate schools was set out in a May 1968 Supreme Court ruling on a case involving the New Kent County, Virginia, schools. The Court held that freedom of choice rarely provided sufficient protection of the constitutional rights of black students and that all local school boards must rapidly create a single nonracial school system.

[141] Howe interview.

Once again the work of black attorneys and the response of the judiciary was creating a shield behind which the administrative techniques of HEW could be effectively employed. In the wake of the Supreme Court decision against free choice, the NAACP Legal Defense Fund and the Justice Department began to close a legal pincers on the remaining segregated divisions. Districts operating under court-order desegregation plans were now forced to submit plans for final abolition of their separate school systems. With the New Kent precedent on the books and complaints coming in from black parents, the Justice Department belatedly began filing suits, including one in Sussex county. Local lawyers now told school boards that further defiance would only bring a costly and hopeless battle in court. As the 1968 election approached, the only real hope for Virginia segregationists was that a new President would order a change in HEW and Justice Department policies. Virginia's Southside was a hotbed of Wallace support and Richard Nixon's apparent endorsement of freedom of choice was prominently mentioned in the state's newspapers.

Four years of enforcement of the 1964 Civil Rights Act had brought Virginia within sight of the objective of the 1954 Supreme Court decision. Given firmness in Washington and in the Federal district courts, the state was within a year of eliminating the major vestiges of separate schools. The principal legal barriers to equal education were already gone in many school divisions and others were making plans to meet the September, 1969, HEW deadline. Barring a reversal of national policy, Virginia educators would soon complete the first long step toward resolving racial inequality in the schools. Already, however, problems of resegregation and racial separation within nominally unified schools were testing the will of local leadership to build on this historic beginning.

Given the local nature of power within the American political and educational systems, the future of Virginia's black children could never be sure until the people and the leaders of the Old Dominion accepted the idea of equal opportunity for all Virginians. The Civil Rights Act forced Virginia to choose between segregation and progress. The state chose progress. Many areas of the state, however, had yet to make a commitment to equality.

6

Reaction in Congress

The problem of the Negro, the central and persisting dilemma of American life, has always been reflected in that great repository of middle-class American values, the American Congress. In a democratic society professing egalitarian values but maintaining a caste system, sanctioned by law in one region and generally upheld by social pressure in the others, the questions of relations between the castes and between the lower caste and a government based on the assumption of equal rights are always fundamental issues. Because the system is an elemental part of the society, any attempt to bring to bear the power of the government to alter caste relations generates a different kind of politics than any other issue.

The question of Negro rights, unlike most political issues, cannot be quietly resolved by a compromise giving something to each of the interested constituencies. Any right extended to the black as a black is a direct attack on the caste exclusiveness of the white. While most issues are of concern only to small groups directly affected, virtually the entire constituencies of most congressmen feel strongly about basic changes in race relations. Because of the great visibility of the issue, the congressman must be far more a delegate of his constituency and far less an autonomous bargainer than is true on other issues.[1] Thus waves of public sentiment on civil rights issues are quickly reflected in Congress and powerfully condition its activities.

The American system of government, with its lack of centralized party leadership to deliver a dependable majority in Congress, forces Federal administrators to create and maintain effective congressional alliances to see their programs safely through the annual congressional ordeal. At a minimum, agencies must maintain tolerable relationships with the legislators who, by virtue of seniority, hold decisive power over their pro-

---

[1] Gunnar Myrdal, *An American Dilemma* (New York: Harper and Brothers, 1955); Warren E. Miller and Donald E. Stokes, "Constituency Influence in Congress," *American Political Science Review*, Vol. LVII (March 1963), 45–56.

grams and budgets. On a broader scale, each agency must attempt to give prompt and careful attention to administrative questions raised by any member of Congress. This necessity resulted in the creation of congressional relations staffs in all major agencies dedicated to the processing of complaints from congressional offices. The complexity of the total relationship and the multiplicity of points within Congress from which effective pressure can be exerted mean that there are always a vast array of channels open between Capitol Hill and executive agencies, channels that sensitively reflect changes in congressional attitudes. Thus when public opinion changes on civil rights, the resulting change in Congress is felt very rapidly in the enforcement programs of various Federal agencies.

In the Civil Rights Act of 1964 and the Voting Rights Act of 1965 Congress ratified a national demand for a revolutionary change in the exercise of Federal power. The new laws represented a fundamental defeat for the southern strategy of preserving local control over race relations by skillfully exercising decisive leverage from points of power within Congress.

The unique feature and the unique power of the movement that won passage of the civil rights bill was its generality. In the broadest sense, it was the millions of people outraged by the television pictures of the police dogs in Birmingham and by the beating of the peaceful marchers at the Selma bridge. Stirred by the dignity and eloquence of the black protest, people concluded that the South was different and that something had to be done to change plainly intolerable conditions. This consensus, expressing itself in Washington through a powerful but ephemeral coalition of religious leaders, labor spokesmen, and the leaders of a united civil rights movement, and through huge majorities in opinion polls, proved irresistible.

With two sweeping new laws on the books, the movement had run out of clear legislative objectives. Legal barriers to equality in the South, it seemed, had been demolished. Surely the strong public commitment to civil rights reform would continue into the future, insuring the implementation of the legislation. Few could guess that within a few months of President Johnson's historic address to Congress on the Voting Rights bill, in which he made the slogan of the civil rights movement his own, that the tide of public sympathy would begin to recede. By the end of the 1966 session of Congress, the forward impetus was gone, and only the strategic skill of key liberals had prevented serious congressional weakening of the school desegregation program.

In retrospect 1965 had been a year of mixed omens for civil rights. The victory rally in Montgomery at the end of the Selma March was one enduring image. The most vivid event of the year, however, was the shattering destruction of a large segment of the country's third largest city. Day after day, television reported on the killing, burning, and looting in Watts, conveying the strange mixture of hate and carnival that the whites of the nation were unable to comprehend. Antiwhite violence by a relatively successful black community in a prosperous and relatively progressive state gave rise to fear, resentment, and anger.

Reaction Begins: Congress and the Defeat of the 1966 Civil Rights Bill

In January 1966 the 89th Congress assembled in Washington for its second session. Elected in 1964, when the Goldwater fiasco permitted liberal Democrats to win in normally Republican districts, it was the most liberal Congress since the New Deal. In its first session the 89th Congress had indicated its temper by enacting the first general program of Federal aid to education, the Voting Rights Act, and an array of other new social programs. When President Johnson decided to press for another civil rights bill, however, the drift of national opinion was clearly reflected on Capitol Hill.

In late April the President asked Congress for legislation including the expansion of Justice Department authority to bring lawsuits, protection for civil rights workers, jury selection reform, and, most important, nationwide fair housing. "The day has long since passed when problems of race in America could be identified with only one section of the country," the President said.[2] Congress was now asked to move beyond the national consensus to interject Federal authority, if only in a symbolic way, into a problem that closely divided the public. The battering the bill received during its journey across the floors of Congress suggests the political atmosphere within which the Title VI enforcement program had to exist.

From the outset Congress was hesitant about acting on such a controversial proposal in an election year. The housing provision frightened big-city Democrats from the North and was promptly denounced by Senator Dirksen as "absolutely unconstitutional."[3] The Republican leader who in 1964 and 1965 had produced the necessary votes to break the southern filibuster was to stand firm this time.

Southerners who had been limited to adamant and ineffective opposition to earlier bills could now seriously work to add anti-civil rights amendments to the bill. Often these amendments focused on the school

[2] *Congressional Record*, 89th Cong., 2d Sess., April 28, 1966, CXII, 8957. Unless otherwise noted, all citations of the *Congressional Record* in this chapter refer to the second session of the 89th Congress (1966), and all are taken from the daily edition.
[3] *Chicago Daily News*, April 29, 1966; *Washington Post*, April 30, 1966, and May 3, 1966.

desegregation guidelines, which had emerged as the cutting edge of the 1964 act in the South. Senator Sam Ervin of North Carolina promptly called for an amendment to "clarify the ambiguities of Title VI." He proposed language that would permit school districts violating the guidelines to continue receiving aid for new projects until the lengthy hearing process had been completed and federal authorities had proved that the local school board had taken affirmative action to discriminate.[4] The amendment would cripple the enforcement program and write into the law the southern belief that free choice constituted full compliance. Under such a proviso a free-choice plan leaving schools totally segregated would be acceptable indefinitely. This was but the first of a series of similar amendments that were to appear.

As the southern attack began in Washington, the earlier unity of the civil rights movement was coming unravelled. Militant elements were turning away from the cause of integration toward the new slogan of "black power." In late spring young activists in the organization threw out the pro-integration leadership of SNCC and installed Stokeley Carmichael as chairman, de-emphasizing the role of whites in the organization.[5] No more would SNCC be investing its energy in monitoring enforcement of the school guidelines.

Carmichael, soon to emerge as a major national figure, announced that "integration is irrelevant." SNCC decided to boycott the White House Conference on Civil Rights, which the President had called with hopes of giving new impetus and direction to the movement. SNCC was later to oppose the enactment of the new civil rights bill. At the White House conference the delegation from CORE did its best to disrupt the proceedings.[6] The unified voice of the black community that had been so powerful in Congress was reduced to a babel of discord.

The civil rights bill got nowhere until the shooting of James Meredith drew national attention to the need to protect civil rights workers. As Martin Luther King came to claim leadership of Meredith's march through Mississippi, it seemed as if the classic pattern might be repeated. "We are going to put President Johnson on the spot," King said. "We are demanding immediate action by the Federal government." [7]

In Congress, the lagging hearings took on new life. President Johnson predicted rapid passage of the bill. Feeling the pressure of public concern, a group of House Republicans asked that the section of the bill protecting civil rights workers be passed immediately. The Adminstration rejected the move, hoping to win the entire bill.[8]

[4] *Congressional Record*, May 9, 1966, p. 9579.   [5] *Washington Post*, May 17, 1966.
[6] *Ibid.*, June 3, 1966.   [7] *Ibid.*, June 8, 1966.
[8] *Chicago Daily News*, June 8, 1966; *Richmond Times-Dispatch*, June 9, 1966.

Hopes for a new law, however, were in shreds by the end of June, destroyed by Negro divisions and rising white anger. The Mississippi march produced no great new symbol the white community could understand and respond to. Instead it turned into a forum for Stokeley Carmichael. The scene etched on the television screens was that of crowds of Mississippi Negroes shouting "black power" under the leadership of the strident young radical.

Clear evidence of an important shift in white opinion came in California with the overwhelming primary victory of Ronald Reagan. Even as opinion polls appeared attributing his support to public concern with Negro rioting, Reagan appeared in Washington to announce his belief that there were already too many civil rights laws.[9] Within days the outbreak of violence in the Cleveland ghetto gave warning that Watts had not been an isolated occurrence.[10]

As whites turned against the cause of Negro rights, the black power slogan had a growing appeal for civil rights activists. The national CORE convention endorsed the new philosophy of racial separatism. Something of the new militancy was evident in Martin Luther King's campaign in Chicago.[11] The new approach, observed the *Chicago Defender*, the city's black newspaper, "has just begun to blossom and already it has taken the play away from the old conservative racial organizations." Eventually black power "will either consume the old passive institutions or crush them."[12]

The worst of the summer violence was yet to come and with it a further widening of the chasm between whites and blacks. The minor incidents of early summer gave way to sustained and serious eruptions. Amid the killings and uncontrolled fires, police officials charged that the riots had been systematically organized by agitators.[13] In a single month there were riots in eight important cities, with hundreds of arrests and unmeasured destruction; and it was becoming clear that all communities were vulnerable. Violence raced crazily from neighborhood to neighborhood, igniting unpredictably across the nation. Rioters on Chicago's West Side and in other towns were reported to be shouting "Black Power."[14]

What had seemed a wild aberration when it happened in Watts was now rapidly becoming commonplace. White reaction to Negro "ingratitude" was expressed by the President. "If we are not to lose a great many of the gains that we have made in recent years," he warned coldly, "we must recognize that while there is a Negro minority of 10 per cent in this

[9] *Washington Post*, June 13, 1966, and June 17, 1966.
[10] *Chicago Sun-Times*, June 26, 1966.   [11] *Chicago Daily News*, July 11, 1966.
[12] *Chicago Defender*, July 9–15, 1966.   [13] *Chicago's American*, July 22, 1966.
[14] *Chicago Sun-Times*, July 24, 1966; *Chicago Daily News*, July 23, 1966.

country there is a majority of 90 per cent who are not Negroes." [15] A congressman noted approvingly the *Wall Street Journal's* ominous warning: "The point for the leaders to understand is that the Negro needs the white man far more than the other way around." [16]

Urban riots and the shrill calls for a black revolution rapidly influenced public opinion. While 60 per cent of the people had approved President Johnson's leadership in civil rights in the fall of 1965, the figure declined to 49 per cent by July 1966. By September approval had dropped further, to 43 per cent.[17] Civil rights enforcement hopes had been based on what seemed to be a permanent national commitment. Now that commitment was gone.

The same late September day that segregationist Lester Maddox won the Democratic nomination for governor of Georgia, the Gallup Poll reported that resistance to civil rights legislation had reached the highest level since the early 1960's. For the first time a majority was convinced that the Administration was "pushing integration too fast." People in every section of the country reported that race relations was the dominant domestic issue and expressed their concern over the new black racism and the violence in the ghettos.[18]

The changing public temper was faithfully mirrored in Congress. It became clear by the end of June that the Administration bill could not pass, and the housing provision was compromised to exclude individual home owners from coverage. This move failed to placate Senator Dirksen. Confident of public support, the Republican leader denounced the compromise bill as "a majestic piece of opportunism." [19]

During the House debates the sacrifices necessary to obtain a majority were so extensive that much of the Negro leadership turned against the bill. The new mood produced rapidly growing interest in an antiriot amendment. For the first time in years it became possible to write into a civil rights bill language that might well threaten the work of some of the Negro organizations. A New York congressman summarized a growing feeling when he said that "the commonsense approach is impossible to even discuss when these communities erupt into the kind of violence we have witnessed in the past week in Chicago, New York, and Cleveland." He approvingly cited a newspaper editoral that concluded:

> We fear that the hatred and violence are also alienating the generally passive support of the majority, most of whom . . . would like to see the Negro get every

---

[15] *Washington Post,* July 21, 1966.   [16] *Newsweek,* August 8, 1966.
[17] *Chicago Daily News,* July 18, 1966; *Washington Post,* September 12, 1966.
[18] *Richmond Times-Dispatch,* October 25, 1966; *Washington Post,* September 29, 1966.
[19] *Chicago Sun-Times,* June 30, 1966.

break a citizen deserves. But who needs this—year after year of disorder, preach-
ment of contempt of the law, taking to the streets in orgies of pillage and
shooting? [20]

The leading moderate Republican spokesman on civil rights in the House
spoke of the "increasing concern and alarm by law abiding citizens" over
urban violence.[21]

Finding themselves on the defensive and worried that they would be
attacked for passing a bill under pressure from rioters, northern congressmen moved toward support of an amendment directed at riot participants. The NAACP's Roy Wilkins vainly criticized the tendency: "Such
a proposal would be idiotic. It would be ridiculous, an insult to Negroes.
It would set the civil rights clock back 150 years." [22]

The antiriot amendment proved irresistible. In their eagerness to record
their opposition to rioters, members of the House were even willing to
support a very broad provision of highly dubious constitutionality. Debate on this proposal to give state legal authorities the power to obtain
court orders to restrain any person acting on a racial or civil rights
ground from engaging in or preparing to engage in any act that would
deprive others of constitutional privileges or legal rights illustrated the
congressional temper. "A vote against this amendment," said one angry
representative, "in effect is a vote for the riots. . . ." [23] Action, said
Chicago's Representative Pucinski, was essential to prevent "Moboc-
racy." [24] The amendment carried on a standing vote, and only a roll call
vote in which the leadership brought pressure to bear defeated this very
reactionary provision.[25]

The House was not satisfied, however, until a penalty against "outside
agitators" was written into the bill. The device adopted was the provision
of stiff penalties for the use of interstate commerce to incite riots. The
amendment was clearly aimed at the out-of-state civil rights workers who
had been so often blamed for local protests. The target was "the professionals who are making a business out of rioting, and capitalizing on the
recent preaching of civil disobedience." [26] One congressman expressed
the theory behind the amendment:

I . . . am sick and tired of reading and hearing such a wonderful flood of double-
talk from theologians and sociologists trying to explain how it all happens, why it
happens. . . .

It is becoming increasingly clear, that . . . sinister forces are at work within these
movements and behind lawlessness, either before or after it breaks out. These
forces of evil in this land . . . must be found, exposed, convicted, and punished.[27]

[20] *Congressional Record*, July 20, 1966, pp. A3843–844.
[21] *Ibid.*, July 26, 1966, p. 16316.　　　[22] *Chicago Daily News*, July 27, 1966.
[23] *Congressional Record*, August 2, 1966, p. 17055.　　　[24] *Ibid.*, p. 17057.
[25] *Ibid.*, p. 17058.　　　[26] *Ibid.*, August 8, 1966, p. 17657.　　　[27] *Ibid.*, p. 17668.

An aroused House speedily rejected an effort to substitute a more moderate amendment drafted by the Justice Department. By a heavy margin, the antiriot provision was written into the civil rights bill.[28] The tide of civil rights progress had begun to recede.

A Congress that was turning against civil rights was receptive to southern attacks on the Office of Education. Before the end of the session, the southerners were able to launch a brutal attack on the enforcement of the school guidelines and Commissioner Howe. Virtually without challenge, they were able to define the terms in which the enforcement effort was discussed. Before the House was through with the 1966 civil rights bill, it contained an amendment threatening the school guidelines.

Very early in the debate on the Administration bill, the standard southern charges against the guidelines were made. The Office of Education, it was asserted, had blatantly ignored the clear intent of Congress. The central thrust of the regulations, argued a North Carolina congressman, is "racial balance in pupil and teacher assignment according to percentages." Such requirements, he assured the House, were wholly incompatible with the legislative history of Title VI and "fly blindly in the teeth of every Federal judicial decision concerning equal protection of the laws handed down in the last twenty years. . . ."[29] "Congress," said one senator, "has meekly surrendered the control of the Federal purse strings to the 'equal opportunity officer' of each agency which he may use to effectuate his own notions of sociological progress."[30]

Local school superintendents had quickly made their problems under the new guidelines known to their congressmen, and much of the discussion concerned the impact of the new standards in particular school districts. Representative William Jennings Bryan Dorn of South Carolina told of one locality:

> We have freedom of choice in Greenwood. No child is turned away from any school. . . . We have complied with the law, but, Mr. Chairman, when someone in Washington, D.C., far removed from the scene of real education at the local level, issues rules and regulations like the one issued the other day which demands of the board of education the reason a school is built in a certain locality . . . I say this type of conduct on the part of those who are supposed to advance the course of education in America, is destructive of good education at the local level.[31]

Federal administrators were attacked for inconsistency and arbitrariness, and the law student investigating teams were harshly criticized. A Florida congressman denounced one of the teams:

> They are the judge, jury, and prosecuting attorney on school matters in every county into which they go, and they have left nothing but confusion behind them.

[28] *Ibid.*, p. 17670.   [29] *Ibid.*, August 9, 1966, p. 17881.
[30] *Ibid.*, May 9, 1966, p. 9580.   [31] *Ibid.*, August 9, 1966, p. 17883.

They know nothing about education. They care nothing about education. Their only purpose appears to be racemixing.[32]

Virtually nothing was said to defend the Office of Education, and the House soon found itself considering two amendments designed to curtail enforcement powers. The first and more sweeping proposal would have made impossible any enforcement effort by requiring proof of local intent to discriminate. The amendment specified that freedom-of-choice plans must be accepted regardless of performance and forbade deferral of funds for new programs until after the completion of the lengthy hearing process. This striking attempt to turn the most important section of the 1964 Civil Rights Act into nothing more than a wistful memory was narrowly defeated, 127 to 136.[33]

Later in the same day a less comprehensive but very important amendment was adopted. Congressman "Bo" Callaway of Georgia proposed that Federal authorities be prohibited from requiring "assignment of students to public schools in order to overcome racial imbalance." Although the amendment was an obvious attack on the performance requirements for free-choice plans in the 1966 guidelines, it was skillfully drawn to bring together both northern city and southern support. Members of Congress tied the issue with the Office of Education action in Chicago. Clark MacGregor, a moderate Minnesota Republican, expressed his belief that the Office of Education had exceeded its authority in Chicago:

> Without so much as a courtesy call to the Commissioner of Public Instruction of the State of Illinois, and on the basis of an unsubstantiated claim or claims, the U.S. Office of Education decided to withhold Federal money. . . . This step was taken in flagrant violation of existing law, and it contributed nothing toward the goal of nondiscrimination in educational opportunity.

With broad support, the Callaway amendment was adopted by a voice vote.[34]

There was little enthusiasm in the House even for a much weakened civil rights bill. Moves to delete even the weak housing provision and to completely kill the bill came very near success, while the final vote on the antiriot measure produced a huge 389 to 25 majority.[35] The House grudgingly sent to the Senate a bill that Martin Luther King concluded was "not worth passing." [36]

The bill that had consumed so much effort in the House was quickly and painlessly put to death in the Senate. In the best of circumstances, the

[32] *Ibid.*, p. 17888.   [33] *Ibid.*, p. 17894.   [34] *Ibid.*, p. 17897.
[35] *Chicago Daily News*, July 26, 1966; *Washington Post*, August 6, 1966; *Congressional Record*, August 9, 1966, p. 17914.
[36] *Washington Post*, August 6, 1966.

battle to overcome a Senate filibuster would have been arduous. Now it was plainly an impossibility.

As Senate consideration began, Martin Luther King's Chicago Freedom Movement started its open-housing marches into working-class white neighborhoods. The violent white reaction failed to produce a new symbol to rally public support for the bill. Instead, the hostility merely confirmed the disposition to kill the legislation. King, who had always used local resistance to dramatize a need to a sympathetic national majority now found himself aggravating a spreading pattern of national resistance. The Chicago violence, President Johnson speculated, would produce an anti-civil rights backlash in the fall's congressional elections.[37]

Omens of reaction were plentiful. In Arkansas, the moderate candidate supported by Governor Faubus was defeated in the Democratic gubernatorial primary by a bitter-end segregationist. In this climate, Senate Majority Leader Mike Mansfield expressed his belief that the bill could not pass even with Dirksen's support.[38] The *Washington Post* analyzed the change:

> . . . the rioting alienated and frightened much of the white community that had been impelled by conscience to support Negro demands. "We shall overcome" is a pledge that can be endorsed by a reasonable man, even by a President; "burn, baby, burn" has a much more limited appeal. . . .
>
> No doubt some persons, in and out of Congress, who have jumped off the civil rights bandwagon were eager for an excuse to do so; and it is true that open housing awakened prejudices which lay dormant. . . . Nevertheless, many conscientious progressives were alienated by the recklessness of the new adolescent Negro leadership. . . .[39]

The malaise of the civil rights movement permeated the Senate debate. The small corps of southern senators filibustering the earlier bills had now become an unbeatable organization of 30 senators prepared to talk the measure into the ground. The civil rights coalition that had functioned with brilliant effectiveness in 1964 now repeatedly failed to produce the quorum needed to keep pressure on the filibuster. The Senate, said the Majority Leader, was not prepared to pass any bill, even if the open-housing section were removed. The bill died quickly, amid an atmosphere of apathy and defeat.[40] This was the congressional environment for the agency attempting to revolutionize race relations in southern education.

---

[37] *Chicago Sun-Times*, August 25, 1966.   [38] *Washington Post*, September 9, 1966.
[39] *Ibid.*, September 11, 1966.
[40] *Richmond Times-Dispatch*, September 7, 1966, and September 8, 1966; *Washington Post*, September 11, 1966; *Congressional Record*, September 14, 1966, p. 21694.

Congress and the Guidelines

As it became clear that Congress would not authorize new ventures in civil rights, it seemed possible that a congressional majority could now be obtained for proposals to destroy existing enforcement powers. Votes on the amendments to the civil rights bill demonstrated a willingness to limit the powers of the Office of Education and, after the bill was killed, southerners continued to press for limitations, either through Administration action or through an amendment to school legislation or appropriations bills.

When it became clear that the Office of Education actually intended to force through reorganization of southern schools rather than merely approve token integration under the banner of freedom of choice, relatively silent southerners in Congress were transformed into implacable enemies of the agency. Congressmen and senators who earlier had quietly helped to bring school districts into compliance regarded the March 1966 revised guidelines as legally questionable and politically disruptive. A long season of attacks was underway. The early comments of Georgia's Senator Talmadge were typical:

> They are arbitrary and capricious. They are dictatorial. In many respects, they are impossible. In every instance, they are unwarranted and unreasonable. The penalty for noncompliance is to be literally starved out of the Federal Treasury.[41]

Talmadge's initial assault was warmly supported. Senator Russell described the new guidelines as "fanaticism at its very zenith." [42] Even token integration, Senator John Stennis argued, was "an almost complete reversal of education and social systems developed for generations. . . ." [43]

Senate opposition crystallized in a letter to the President. The letter, signed by 18 southern senators, was a formal and stately appeal for help to an old Senate crony. Describing themselves as "friends and former colleagues," the men who had played a major role in making Lyndon Johnson majority leader asked the President to recognize their "solemn petition for a redress of the grave injustice threatened our people." The senators professed their willingness to abide by the Civil Rights Act but claimed that the guidelines were in "direct conflict" with the legislative history of the act and totally ungrounded in court decisions. "We earnestly beseech your personal intervention to right this wrong and have this order revoked." [44]

The letter confronted the President with the basic issues troubling the

[41] *Ibid.*, March 29, 1966, p. 6563.   [42] *Ibid.*, p. 6566.   [43] *Ibid.*
[44] Mimeographed text of letter from southern senators to President Johnson, May 2, 1966.

white South. He was told that the guidelines destroyed "the cherished freedom of choice of pupils and their parents to select the school that such pupil shall attend." Compliance, they warned, was "certain to endanger the local support and interest—financial and otherwise—without which our weaker and most needy schools cannot succeed." "You well know," they told the former southern schoolteacher in the White House, "that a school cannot operate in a small or rural community without the cooperation and local support of the citizens. . . ." After all, even the first guidelines had required a social revolution in many communities, and it was going "far beyond fairness and good conscience" to change the rules so drastically and so soon. "It would be little short of criminal after matters have moved so far as they have until now to nullify the hours of work and explanation by local school authorities to secure acceptance of the original Guidelines that they thought would last at least three years."

> Throughout your Presidency, you have consistently emphasized the importance of an education and particularly in assisting the under-privileged, but I am sure that you will agree that the withdrawal of school funds from communities that are less favored financially will victimize children who are most in need of a chance for an education.[45]

President Johnson delayed his response for several weeks and directed HEW officials to discuss and promptly examine complaints submitted by members of Congress. Finally he wrote to Senator Russell endorsing the guidelines. While telling the senator that the Administration had no intention of demanding racial balancing or bussing of children, he defended the controversial percentages for progress under free choice. The figures, he explained, were not quotas, but only administrative rules of thumb to determine when it was necessary to examine in detail the effectiveness of a given plan.[46]

After this initial failure, there was little discussion of the issue until local school officials began to feel heavy pressure in August. During the early summer much of the congressional concern had focused on the forceful effort to desegregate hospitals thoroughly before they could be certified for participation in the new Medicare program. In spite of bitter criticism over what seemed in much of the South to be a wholly irrational and even unhealthy policy of forcing hospital administrators to assign patients to rooms without regard for race, the President made his commitment absolutely clear and most of the opposition collapsed.[47] By late summer attention was again focused on the school guidelines as the school year approached and review teams roamed the South.

[45] *Ibid.*   [46] *Chicago Daily News,* June 1, 1966.
[47] *Congressional Record,* June 29, 1966, pp. 14018–19.

Members of Congress presented a catalogue of objections to the enforcement procedures. One senator categorized the new compliance form as a "blank check" permitting "an extensive amount of manipulation," and accused the Office of Education of regularly violating its promises to local officials.[48] A Florida congressman denounced the review teams as "totally, and completely unqualified." [49]

Congressional Offices and the Title VI Enforcement Staff

One of the most routine processes in Washington is the referral of a local complaint from an office on Capitol Hill to the appropriate administrative agency for an explanation or for corrective action. Because the political future of a congressman or senator is often related to his effectiveness in processing these local requests, most congressional offices follow up on almost any reasonable request. At a minimum, they expect from the agency involved a polite and prompt reply, and most agencies have adopted special procedures to insure that such requests receive top-priority handling. Depending on the importance of the case and the nature of the congressman's convictions, his office may settle for a letter of explanation or may pursue the case further through additional demands, meetings, pressure at higher levels in the Administration, or, finally, through denunciation of the agency or official involved on the floor of Congress.

When members took to the floor to blast the Office of Education, it was often evident that they were not so disturbed about abstract principles as about crises in particular counties, disruptive local situations that they wanted to end somehow. Criticism became far more bitter in the House than in the Senate not because senators differed with the general opinion that the guidelines were illegal, but because far more school superintendents and school board members called on their congressmen to resolve what were seen as terrible local problems. Following normal procedures, these complaints were referred to the Office of Education. There the real trouble began.

Many southern congressional offices were continually involved in the administrative process, either as intermediaries between local and Federal officials or as advocates for local school authorities. This relationship was obviously of importance both in the shaping of Federal policy and in the development of what became a very serious attack on the Office of Education. In an effort to understand congressional relations with the enforcement staff, interviews were conducted with the staff aides handling civil rights complaints in most southern senators' offices. In addition, a

48 *Ibid.*, August 31, 1966, p. 20634.   49 *Ibid.*, August 23, 1966, p. 19493.

questionnaire was sent to all southern congressmen at the height of the attack on the Office of Education. Although only a third of the congressmen completed the questionnaire, the general consistency of the data with that obtained from Senate interviews and from a careful study of statements on the floor suggests that a reasonably representative sample was obtained.[50]

The basic factor determining congressional attitudes toward the Office of Education was the fact that most southerners simply refused to accept the legitimacy of the basic rules of the game by which the Title VI operation was run. Approximately four out of five southern members both in the House and in the Senate simply believed that the 1966 guidelines exceeded the authority granted under the Civil Rights Act. In spite of the changing pattern of court decisions, the belief persisted that the Supreme Court had ruled against denying a Negro child an opportunity to enter a white school but not in favor of an end to legally separate schools. The initial Federal acceptance of free-choice plans had reinforced this belief.

Given this fundamental difference, there was little room for successful negotiation. The kind of complaints that came to the enforcement program from Congress were very different from the normal sort of Congress "casework" in administrative agencies. Southern members of Congress were often asking, not for speeding up a determination or re-examining the technical details of a particular case, but for concessions that would undermine the entire enforcement effort. Officials faced incessant demands that they approve honestly run free-choice plans that had failed to produce a significant level of integration. Enforcement staff members saw these demands as threats to the entire desegregation effort. When they stubbornly refused to approve a school district where the congressman was convinced that local officials were doing their best to make free choice work, the congressman concluded that the Federal officials were "unreasonable" and arbitrary.

The intensity of feeling varied tremendously both between states and

[50] The questionnaires, simple "checklists," were sent to all southern members of the House in early October 1966, as the session neared its end and the attack on Commissioner Howe peaked. There is, of course, no way of knowing whether the members filled them out personally or whether they tended to overstate their difficulties in the midst of this controversy. The interviews were conducted in September and October with staff assistants in the offices of 20 of the 22 southern senators. Each office generally had one person to whom complaints about the guidelines were referred and who handled most of the office's contacts with HEW. In a few offices there were specialists who spent a large amount of their time pressing individual cases in detail. These interviews varied greatly in quality, but tended to be highly consistent for a given state or region.

within a given state. While one Texas congressman proudly reported on the early desegregation of the city in his district, another saw the Office of Education staff as unreasonable and the guidelines as illegal. "Everyone," he reported, "agrees that the regulations are screwball."

In those states where integration was well underway and where there was a relatively low Negro population and moderate state leadership, few members of Congress became involved in the war on the Office of Education. In effect, there was little political mileage in the issue in the six border states or in most of Tennessee and Texas, as well as certain areas in the Middle South. Resistance was most bitter among those representing states or districts with many Negroes, with segregationist state leadership, and with very little integration before passage of the Civil Rights Act.

Most southern congressmen reported receiving at least 20 letters relating to the school guidelines during the 1966 session, and some offices had been flooded with as many as several hundred complaints. One Florida congressman received letters from every school district in his constituency. Senate offices were much less likely to become involved in the problems of individual school districts, and the extent of their correspondence varied greatly. The issue stimulated about 400 letters of protest to Georgia's Senator Russell, about the same volume he received on the bitterly contested right-to-work question. Russell's office became extensively involved in negotiations affecting about 15 districts with serious problems. On the other hand, Virginia's Senators received few letters and had little involvement.[51]

The complaints that arrived in Washington demanded careful attention. Most of the mail came not from the public at large, but from local school superintendents and boards of education. In some cases county and state officials appealed for the congressman's help. Thus the letters were from important men in the congressional district, officials whose requests could be ignored only at the congressman's peril.

There is no "typical" complaint, but to understand the intensity of the congressional attack it may be useful to consider, from the congressman's perspective, one of hundreds of local problems. In 1966 Franklin County, North Carolina, a county of some 28,000 people in the black belt of the eastern part of the state, applied to the Office of Education for Elementary and Secondary Education Act money to finance a summer program employing six teachers to help Negro students. Although the county's freedom-of-choice plan had produced far less integration than the guidelines demanded, the state department of education had assured the local superintendent that the money would be available. On the strength of this

[51] Interview with Mr. Charles Campbell, Office of Senator Russell, October 11, 1966.

commitment, all the arrangements had been made. The local superintendent did not realize that there was imminent danger of losing the money until a notice arrived from Washington a week before the program was to begin. Suddenly school officials learned that unless drastic changes were made, possibly by interchanging two grades of students between the black and white schools, funds would be cut off at once. Although from the perspective of HEW enforcement officials the action was overdue, the manner in which it was handled enraged the community. The local congressman became deeply concerned by what he saw as uncontrolled and arbitrary action. Eventually his anxiety led him to introduce an amendment to eliminate the Commisioner of Education's power to defer funds before a formal hearing had been completed.

Congressmen's views about the illegality of the Federal requirements were continually reinforced by complaints from their constituents. In fact, no other subject was mentioned so frequently in letters from local officials as their conviction that the Federal standards were invalid. The second most frequent criticism was that the administrative decisions taken under the guidelines were arbitrary. Given these fundamental differences, there was often very little to negotiate.

Most southern congressmen forwarded some complaints to HEW or the Office of Education, but few felt that the problems had been satisfactorily resolved. The typical office sent four complaints over, generally either through a telephone call to the enforcement staff or a letter to Commissioner Howe. In some cases congressmen arranged negotiating sessions, but only about one-third believed the enforcement staff to be "willing to reasonably negotiate." Less than one-fifth of the congressmen responding reported successful resolution of all complaints, while more than two-thirds felt the effort was a total failure.

The intensity of the congressional attack on the Office of Education in the fall of 1966 was related, in part, to the election campaigns then in progress. In more than half of the congressional districts covered by the survey, the members reported that newspaper opinion had been highly critical of the guidelines. In many districts the guidelines were seen as a major political issue, and in a number of others the issue had not emerged only because all candidates agreed that the Federal rules were illegal.

Senators were less involved in the battle, particularly in states where militant segregationism had little statewide political value. Only where the possibility of gaining additional white support clearly outweighed the risk of alienating an increasingly important Negro vote did senators actively join the attack. Alabama's Senator John Sparkman, running for reelection against a leading Goldwater Republican, was an early recruit to Governor Wallace's war against the guidelines. Senator Eastland advised

Mississippi school officials to refuse to sign guidelines pledges, arguing that the Office of Education would give in if all the school officials held firm. In Georgia, where racial reaction was to sweep Lester Maddox into the Governor's mansion, both senators attacked Commissioner Howe. In Senator Russell's office an able young aide coordinated a continuing attack, and the Senator took questions personally to Secretary Gardner and President Johnson. The entire Georgia congressional delegation was assembled for a meeting with Commissioner Howe. The Georgians believed that their efforts explained the removal of a leading official in the HEW regional office in Atlanta and the lowering of demands for faculty integration in the state.

A chronic problem in congressional relations arose from the inadequate staffing of the Office of Education compliance program. When they sent a complaint to the Office, members of Congress naturally expected the same kind of prompt reply that a congressional inquiry generally receives from other Federal agencies.

The Title VI staff, however, was seriously overburdened and had no skilled congressional relations experts to shepherd inquiries from desk to desk. The HEW legislative liaison operation, wishing to keep its handling of program relationships separate from the disruptive civil rights question, had abdicated responsibility for handling desegregation complaints. The letters went directly to the Equal Educational Opportunities Program. When the inquiry finally reached the desk of the terribly overburdened staff member responsible for the district, he would often put it aside while he tried to deal with the urgent questions and demands coming in from school officials making basic decisions about the future of their districts. Often it was weeks and occasionally even months before the case could be reviewed and the policy questions considered.

The program was gravely weakened by the lack of anyone who understood the inner workings of Capitol Hill. Throughout this period efforts to explain and justify the program to potential supporters were minimal and disorganized. Peter Libassi, Special Assistant for Civil Rights to Secretary Gardner, characterized the staff as "grossly inexperienced in Congressional relations" and unable to distinguish between "form and substance." [52]

> There's a ritual to Congressional relations, and if one follows the ritual . . . you can deal on a different level about the substantive issues. Very simply, congressmen like to have their telephone calls answered. It doesn't matter if you call them and say, 'We're going to cut that money off,' but they don't appreciate not getting an answer when they call.[53]

[52] Libassi Interview, July 25, 1968.   [53] *Ibid.*

With smouldering congressmen waiting for something to tell very angry and worried local officials, the situation became serious. The representative or senator involved would try to force a response by writing or talking to Commissioner Howe, Secretary Gardner, or even the President. Some discovered that a letter to the White House was the only way to get a prompt reply. The President was disturbed by complaints that reached him and insisted that each be answered promptly.

The result was a vicious cycle. The staff was unequipped to handle even a typical number of congressional inquiries, but it was flooded by a large volume of complex and difficult questions. Inability to answer these questions deepened bitterness on Capitol Hill, and powerful legislators, who could easily damage HEW or Administration programs in Congress, made increasingly insistent demands. The enforcement staff eventually found itself under pressure not only from congressional offices but also from the Commissioner's office, the Secretary's office, and even the White House to answer particularly important letters. Finally, it became necessary for some staff members to simply suspend work until an answer could be worked out and cleared within the department. Even then, the member of Congress was rarely satisfied with the reply he received.

The intense external pressure generated a kind of seige mentality within the Equal Educational Opportunities Program. Pressing demands for answers added to the normal confusion and heat inherent in the effort. Later, when congressional hearings were called in the fall, the demands on the staff were magnified. With both the Commissioner of Education and the program seriously threatened, many officials spent much of the fall preparing "backup" materials for the hearings, assembling data to permit rebuttal of expected charges.

The work of the compliance staff was perhaps even more profoundly affected by an indirect result of the congressional buffeting. The well-publicized attacks in Washington stiffened local resistance. It became very difficult for local school officials to go along with Federal requirements that their political leaders continually denounced as illegal. Thus Federal-local relationships became increasingly tense, and the enforcement program found itself on the defensive both in the halls of Congress and in the county school offices of the South.

Although disgruntled southern members of Congress often felt that their protests were being ignored, the static from the Capitol doubtless influenced the vigor with which Federal officials were willing to enforce the guidelines requirements. By April 1966 Secretary Gardner was circulating a conciliatory letter to southern congressmen and governors. Drafted largely by top Justice Department officials, the letter stated a determination to administer the numerical standards of progress in the new guidelines "flexibility." Although these standards had been very severely compromised during the drafting process, southern leaders were now put on notice that even these minimums were negotiable. Most importantly, the Gardner letter gave a great deal of ground by attempting to defend the percentage rates of progress figures not as an essential element in eliminating unconstitutional separate school systems but merely as a possible way of checking how "free" a freedom-of-choice plan really was. In other words, the Secretary was conceding the basic validity of the free-choice approach:

> It is our responsibility to review such plans to insure that the choice is, in fact, free and to indicate to the school districts what procedures should be used to assure true freedom of choice.

> If substantial numbers of Negro children choose to go to previously all-white schools, the choice system is clearly operating freely. If few or none choose to do so in a community where there has been a pattern of segregation, then it is appropriate that the free choice plan be reviewed and other factors considered to determine whether the system is operating freely.[54]

In apparently accepting the southern argument that truly free-choice procedures were an end in themselves rather than merely a device justified only when it moved school districts rapidly toward a unified nonracial system, Gardner immensely complicated the administrative part of the enforcement task. The relatively routine job of checking progress statistics was transformed into the highly complex task of attempting to prove that freedom of choice in a given district was not really free.

Neither the Secretary's reassuring comments about free choice nor his down-peddling of the faculty desegregation requirements satisfied angry southerners. Demands continued to mount for nothing less than a total withdrawal of these "illegal" standards. By late summer the southern campaign was to become bitter and vehement and was to come to a focus in a brutal series of attacks on the Commissioner of Education.

Assault on Commissioner Howe

If the Federal government was violating the Civil Rights Act in issuing the new guidelines, some Federal official would have to be responsible. There was relatively little value in attacking the President, since he had avoided any public responsibility for the details of the standards. An attack on Secretary Gardner, a highly respected figure known to enjoy

[54] Secretary Gardner statement, April 9, 1966. The Secretary did not intend the letter as a policy retreat, but its language did accept the Justice Department view that free choice was still an open question and that failure to meet the rate-of-progress figures would only be the beginning point for a detailed investigation of local conditions.

President Johnson's strong support, promised little political profit. Commissioner of Education Harold Howe, II, however, was a far less prominent figure, and the Commissioner's actions during 1966 on the race issue made him a perfect target for southern demagogues.

During the summer of 1966, as the nation began to turn against the cause of Negro rights, Commissioner Howe made the mistake of publicly discussing the possibility of Federal involvement in solving the racial problems of the urban ghetto schools. In a Chicago address, Howe called for sweeping changes in urban education. "The education link in this chain of social slavery," he said, "is the segregated, inferior ghetto school." In a speech movingly describing the problems of the inner-city school, the Commissioner urged localities to allocate their financial and teacher resources to those areas where the need was most urgent. Going beyond these standard prescriptions, however, Howe urged local officials to consider "more drastic measures" including mergers of city and suburban school districts and construction of new schools at locations designed to break up racial and economic segregation. The Office of Education, he said, was prepared to encourage such efforts with Federal grants. The Office had already awarded some planning grants for new school buildings, Howe said, and "if I have my way the Office will provide construction funds before long." He endorsed proposals to build experimental educational parks, school complexes bringing thousands of children from many neighborhoods by bus to a large central campus.

> . . . we are particularly interested in finding one or two great American cities that are adventurous enough to join us in planning the educational park of the future. These entities will house 20,000 or more pupils, and will cut across all geographic, economic, and political boundaries to draw students.[55]

The Commissioner's speeches were widely reported, but he was not attacked in Congress. After a summer of riots, the speeches were to be exhumed and used against Howe. Meanwhile Howe continued to press his effort to draw the attention of schoolmen to what he saw as the central issue facing American education. At a national conference of school administrators, he called on educators to "form a third front for racial equality in the United States." [56] "Unless," he said, "all of us are willing to put our jobs and integrity on the line, we should admit that American educators are no longer prepared to be the prime movers in American education."

> While we have gone on urging moderation, sweet reason, and bigger and better panel discussions, the schools throughout the nation remain almost as segregated

[55] *Congressional Record,* June 8, 1966, p. 12053.
[56] *Chicago Tribune,* June 19, 1966.

today as they were in 1954 when the Supreme Court decided that racially segregated education was illegal.[57]

The black revolution in the cities put it squarely up to the schools "to determine whether the energy of that revolution can be converted into a new and vigorous source of American progress, or whether their explosion will rip this nation into two societies." [58]

As Howe was leading a new rhetorical charge against the bastions of segregation, the array of those sympathetic to his call was dissolving behind him. By summer's end there was no political mileage left in the integration issue. The civil rights movement was in confused retreat, and the public consciousness was filled with vivid images of rioting Negroes chanting "black power." The great wave of energy and commitment to racial justice had crested, and as it receded Howe's immensely quotable phrases remained, to be evaluated in an atmosphere wholly different from that of early summer.

The national reaction on the race question, which immediately permeated an election-year House of Representatives, coincided with the showdown over freedom of choice taking place across the South. As Office of Education investigating teams began to actually check local progress in the field for the first time, and began to demand that hundreds of districts where free choice had failed either run another registration or move at once toward a nonracial student-assignment policy, it became evident that Federal authorities would actually try to enforce the hated guidelines provisions. Facing local turmoil just months before election day and noting the national mood, southern congressmen began to mobilize for a frontal assault on the Office of Education. As the attack proceeded it became increasingly bitter and personal. Demands for Commissioner Howe's resignation mounted.

Few congressmen had time or inclination to probe the subtleties of the Civil Rights Act, but many became indignant as reports of "unreasonable" actions came in from their districts and as David Lawrence and James Kilpatrick began to feature polemics against Howe in their nationally syndicated columns. Howe, claimed one conservative journalist, "had no sooner assumed . . . office earlier this year when he disclosed a strong personal antipathy to the concept of neighborhood schools." Howe's calls for experimentation with education parks now became "fanciful visions of panaceas, among them systems of vast 'educational parks' " . . . "designed to create racial and economic 'balance.' " [59] These columns were cited as proof that Harold Howe was a dangerous social

[57] *Chicago Sun-Times,* June 19, 1966.
[58] *Richmond Times-Dispatch,* June 19, 1966.
[59] *Congressional Record,* August 31, 1966, p. 20638.

planner, determined to misuse his authority to accomplish his personal objectives.

The readiness to see Howe as a devil figure is strikingly illustrated by the history of a remark he never made. In early August James J. Kilpatrick, perhaps the South's most influential journalist, attacked Howe. Describing Howe's attitude, he inserted the following sentence: " 'If I have my way,' schools will be built for the primary purpose of social and economic integration." The only part of the sentence that was a quote was taken out of context from a speech Howe had made in Chicago, while the rest was simply Kilpatrick's opinion. A week later, however, the entire sentence was inserted in the *Congressional Record* as a quote. Soon the "quote" was broadcast by radio and television stations in North Carolina; newspapers reprinted the broadcasts and denounced Howe. In early September the statement was again cited in congressional debate as proof of the Commissioner's arrogant attitude.[60] The statement would not die and was heard again and again on the floor of Congress.

By early September the southern offensive had taken on a strident quality. Accusing Howe of the "most contemptible plot ever hatched by a Federal agency on the American people," Representative Watson described the Office of Education as "a totalitarian regime within the executive branch, bent upon the destruction of local control of education." He called for Howe's resignation in order to preserve the nation's educational system.[61]

Few Federal officials ever experience a siege as heavy as that now beginning in earnest for Commissioner Howe. Belatedly recognizing the seriousness of the storm clouds above the Capitol, the Commissioner took some steps to trim his sails. Howe called in reporters to announce that there would be a new "grass-roots approach" to the enforcement effort. Rather than working out of Washington, he said, staff members would be located in HEW regional offices in the South. Locating the controversial responsibility in southern offices staffed largely by southerners could be expected to moderate the temper of the program. (Indeed, Assistant Secretary Quigley's strenuous efforts to use the regional offices for enforcement had very largely failed.) Howe also announced that a much-denounced official, Stanley Kruger of the Atlanta HEW office, responsible for the program in several Deep South states, had been removed and assigned to another position.[62] At the same time further enforcement action was quietly deferred until after the election in a number of congressional districts. Still the tide of abuse continued to rise.

[60] *Richmond Times-Dispatch*, September 12, 1966. This "quote" was later used repeatedly by Richard Nixon in his 1968 campaign.
[61] *Ibid.*, September 9, 1966.   [62] *Ibid.*

The Northern School Flap

In mid-September, the army of Howe's southern critics was joined by a band from the North. Led by Representative Paul Fino of New York, they loudly insisted that Howe had a sinister plan to reconstruct northern urban school systems in the near future. The Commissioner dismissed the charge that he was planning a massive Federally financed school bussing program as "ridiculous and untrue." [63] The following day Rep. Fino released a draft bill, leaked to him from inside the Office, providing for $6 billion in Federal aid to stimulate new solutions to the school crisis in the cities.

Fino, playing to the backlash in the Bronx, described the draft proposal as the "most radical legislation ever drawn up in these United States." The money, he said, could be used to encourage local authorities to redraw school district lines, to exchange pupils between slum and suburban schools, and to finance school bussing.[64]

Secretary Gardner immediately denied any intention of proposing such legislation, dismissing the document as an "unofficial discussion paper." He pledged that HEW would respect "the historic American principle of local supervision and control of public education." The department would not submit any bill compelling either rezoning or bussing.[65]

Opponents rejoined by revealing that the draft had been prepared by a high-ranking task force within the Office of Education and had been formally submitted to the Secretary. Congressman Fino called Howe "a political liar engaged in tricking the Congress." He demanded that the President repudiate the draft bill by firing Howe. When the Office of Education delayed issuance of a pamphlet containing Howe's controversial speeches, Fino analyzed the action as an effort "to muzzle Harold Howe until after the election." [66] Fino persuaded his fellow Republicans on the House Republican Policy Committee to denounce the draft bill as "a Federally sponsored attack on the concept of neighborhood schools." [67] Howe was being attacked on both flanks in a Congress nervously watching the signs of reaction in primary after primary.

Trouble in the Senate

With an election near, the skittishness of the House on the race question was not surprising. The depth of the reaction in the Senate, however, also became apparent. In September powerful southern senators began to exercise their control of crucial committees to make successful raids on HEW. A number of senators who had supported the 1964 Civil Rights

[63] *Congressional Record*, September 15, 1966, p. 21832.   [64] *Ibid.*, p. 21834.
[65] *Ibid.*   [66] *Ibid.*, p. 21832; *ibid.*, September 28, 1966, p. A4994–95.
[67] *Ibid.*, p. 23200.

Act now quietly acquiesced to southern efforts to set limits on the enforcement program.

Throughout American history until the mid-1960's, with the brief exception of the Reconstruction era, southern strength in the Senate had been sufficient to prevent significant use of Federal power to protect the rights of southern Negroes. The 17 southern and border states with totally segregated schools when the Supreme Court handed down the 1954 decision controlled more than one-third of the votes in the Senate. Only a social revolution that divided the border states and united the North and West in an extremely strong bipartisan coalition, willing to suspend all other legislative business indefinitely to enact civil rights legislation, breached the tenacious southern resistance in 1964 and 1965. By the end of 1966 this coalition was only a memory, and southern power began to reassert itself.

In spite of defeat many southern assets were intact. Only in Tennessee and Texas were there Senators who had broken with the legion of resistance. The South still possessed the resources of seniority that accrued to the representatives of one-party states. From dominant positions on key committees, southern leaders could very powerfully affect the flow of authority and money to executive agencies. An intangible but very real resource of the South was an accumulation of knowledge and skill in manipulating the complex parliamentary procedures through which the business of the Senate was accomplished.

The southern attack came in the form of language buried in the middle of a seemingly routine report from the Appropriations subcommittee accompanying the annual HEW money bill. The subcommittee, chaired by Alabama's Senator Lister Hill, criticized both the school and hospital desegregation procedures of HEW.

The device employed in the attack was well chosen. Comments from the subcommittees that control a department's lifeblood are taken with great seriousness by administrators well aware that they must face the same men the next time they request funds for their programs. The nature of a committee report makes it an ideal vehicle for a minority to influence policy through a powerful committee position without any risk of reversal by a majority. Although the document is taken by the courts and many officials as an expression of the will of the committee, the committee need take no formal action on the report. The document is commonly prepared by a staff member appointed by the chairman. Before the report is circulated in the Senate, it must be sent to committee members, but this can be an unreal protection. A lengthy and seemingly noncontroversial document that reaches members only shortly before it is scheduled to go to the Senate floor may not be carefully scanned.

Another advantage of the report is that it is not voted upon by the entire Senate. Although it is an important part of the legislative record of a bill, it is not part of the bill itself and can neither be rejected nor amended by the entire Senate. Thus manipulation of a procedural device connected with a financial bill can be used to strike forcefully at authority granted to an executive agency by a majority of Congress.

In addition to Senator Hill, the subcommittee included Russell of Georgia and Stennis of Mississippi, two of the most persistent and effective foes of the guidelines. In the subcommittee's executive sessions, HEW civil rights enforcement standards were attacked, and even some of the group's liberal members expressed their willingness to go along with limitations on hospital desegregation.[68] When the report became public, however, it contained strictures against both the hospital and the school policies.

Liberal members of the committee were taken by surprise by the harshly worded denunciation of the Office of Education inserted deep inside the report. "The committee believes," the document stated, "that the revised guidelines contravene and violate the legislative intent of the . . . Civil Rights Act of 1964." The report "strongly" urged reconsideration of compliance standards. The damage was compounded by a slashing attack on the hospital desegregation effort, accusing officials of "harassing people who have shown every indication of abiding by the letter and intent of the Civil Rights Act. . . ." [69] When questioned by reporters, aides to the liberal members said that these senators simply had not been aware of what was in the report.[70]

Knowing that the report would create serious problems for HEW, some strong civil rights advocates attempted to put the Senate on record in support of the program. Senator Javits proposed an amendment to the bill to restore the full HEW request for enforcement staff. A favorable Senate vote, he reasoned, would indicate the Senate's disapproval of the committee's accusation that the guidelines were "onerous or illegal." [71]

Javits encountered unexpectedly heavy sailing in the floor debate. One of the leading Democratic liberals, Senator Pastore of Rhode Island, who had been floor manager for Title VI in 1964, now joined southern critics of the hospital desegregation effort. The Senate learned that a move within the subcommittee to restore half the enforcement positions had failed 10 to 2 partly because of economy and partly, said one member, because "some . . . never had any heart for Title VI of the Civil Rights Act." [72]

[68] *Richmond Times-Dispatch*, September 27, 1966.
[69] *Washington Post*, September 27, 1966.
[70] *Richmond Times-Dispatch*, September 27, 1966.
[71] *Congressional Record*, September 27, 1966, pp. 22955, 22960.
[72] *Ibid.*, pp. 22955, 22963–64.

The economy argument prevailed on the floor. On a roll call vote, the pro-enforcement forces were smashed. The Javits amendment lost 25 to 40. Even such northern liberals as Stephen Young of Ohio, E. L. (Bob) Bartlett of Alaska, Mike Mansfield of Montana, and Daniel Inouye of Hawaii joined most Republican and all southern senators in opposition to the amendment.[73]

Following this triumph, Senator Stennis of Mississippi quickly proposed another amendment giving local medical authorities the right to prescribe segregated facilities when they felt it was necessary for a patient's "physical or mental well-being." This amendment was supported by both Pastore and Saltonstall of Massachusetts.[74] An attempt to make hospitals accountable for the misuse of medical excuses for segregation was overwhelmingly defeated, and the Stennis amendment passed 55 to 11.[75] Nothing was left of the commitment and unity that had made the Civil Rights Act law.

The morning after the votes, reporters crowded around Senate Majority Leader Mansfield. In off-the-cuff comments on his way to the floor, the Administration's leading spokesman in the Senate underlined the change in sentiment. He agreed with the Appropriations report. In a statement that was trumpeted across the South, the Majority Leader agreed with the southern claim that Title VI forbade segregation but did not demand "an affirmative policy of integration." [76] Although he had not read the report or studied the issue, Mansfield stated that desegregation was going too fast. Describing the "mood of the Senate," he said, "In a realm of great delicacy like this, the thing to do is to take it slowly and surely. I think they have gone too fast." [77] In a statement coming the same day as the upset victory of a segregationist in the Georgia Democratic primary, it was hard to give credence to Mansfield's claim that the white backlash had made no impact on his thinking. The next morning the Majority Leader was shocked by the newspaper coverage of his careless off-the-cuff remarks. He set out to repair the damage. Claiming that he had misunderstood the questions, he now said that school desegregation progress was actually too slow.[78] Although he had actually been uninformed when first questioned, it was widely believed that he had initially expressed his true feelings and was reversing himself under pressure.[79] At the very least, the incident demonstrated the southern success in defining the terms with which the issue was discussed.

---

[73] *Ibid.*, p. 22966.   [74] *Ibid.*, p. 22975.   [75] *Ibid.*, p. 22985.
[76] *Washington Post*, September 29, 1966.   [77] *Ibid.*
[78] *Richmond Times-Dispatch*, September 30, 1966.
[79] Interview with Charles Ferris, Senate Democratic Policy Committee, September 30, 1966.

The mood of Senate liberals who cared about civil rights was one of defeat and disillusionment. The votes, said Javits, were an "alarming portent." He wondered aloud "whether resentment against riots and 'black power' sloganeering will now extend to relaxation of enforcement of laws now on the books." "It will be a long time," another senator commented, "before we have another civil rights bill. After what happened Tuesday, we have started to move backward." [80]

The enforcement program was obviously in serious trouble in both houses of Congress. Finally the White House made a gesture toward defending the embattled Administration officials. President Johnson's press secretary announced that the President "believes Secretary Gardner is doing his best to carry out the law the way he sees it." [81] It was hardly a staunch defense, but even this statement took courage at a time when political support for civil rights programs seemed to have evaporated.

House Rules Committee Investigation

With the Administration on the defensive, some congressmen demanded an investigation. Both of the committees that could logically conduct such a probe in the House, however, happened to be controlled by congressmen elected from one-party districts in New York City. There was no likelihood that either Adam Clayton Powell's Education and Labor Committee or Emanuel Celler's Judiciary Committee would permit an attack on civil rights enforcement. Confronted by this rare concentration of liberal seniority, southerners began to call for appointment of a special investigating committee. Congressmen from Georgia and South Carolina introduced similar resolutions, claiming that the Judiciary Committee was blocking legitimate requests for information.[82]

The time was propitious for a frontal assault on the Office of Education. Majorities in both houses were now on record in opposition to the enforcement program. Most northern and western congressmen paid little attention to the issue. The general congressional antagonism toward bureaucratic interference in local affairs and the obvious drift of national opinion encouraged most members to passively watch the southern attack.

At this juncture, Judge Howard Smith, Chairman of the Rules Committee and the South's leading strategist, decided to call Commissioner Howe on the carpet. The resolutions calling for the appointment of a special investigating committee had been sent to the Rules Committee, and now Smith decided to use the committee's discussion of these

80 *Washington Post*, September 29, 1966.
81 *Richmond Times-Dispatch*, September 30, 1966.
82 *Congressional Record*, September 8, 1966, pp. 21105, 21139.

resolutions as a pretext for a public confrontation between Howe and the conservative-dominated committee. The unusual public hearings were designed to provide a national forum for the southern effort to remove Howe and reverse enforcement policy. The Rules Committee staff contacted state officials across the South requesting information on problems with the enforcement program.

As the hearings began in a small hearing room in the Capitol, reporters crowded in to witness a major confrontation. At the head of the green felt-covered committee table sat octogenarian Howard Smith, a frail and crusty Virginian determined to cut one last bureaucrat down to size before his retirement at the end of the session.

The hearings began with statements by several concerned congressmen. Representative Cooley, Chairman of the powerful Agriculture Committee, found the situation "deplorable and intolerable." Cooley was in very serious political trouble in his district, where a young Republican was capitalizing, in part, on resentment caused by guidelines enforcement.

To the North Carolina Congressman, the situation was clear. All that was needed was for someone to convince the President to bring HEW into line. Cooley was indignant that Johnson had ignored a protest telegram from governors of 15 of the 17 states involved. He promised to make a strong personal appeal to the President. "One telephone call from the White House, in my opinion, would put an end to it and we would go back to freedom of choice." [83] Cooley's complaints were echoed by congressmen from several other states. That afternoon, for 45 minutes, Cooley discussed the guidelines with the President, coming away with the feeling that something would be done, but with no specific assurances.[84]

The heat was on the Office of Education. With the entire program in danger, great amounts of time and energy were invested in preparing the Commissioner's statement and assembling back-up materials to respond to particular questions. In the Justice Department, a strong legal memorandum was prepared in support of the much-criticized faculty integration requirement.

The day before the confrontation between Howe and Smith, the Administration seemed to be mounting an orchestrated campaign to strengthen the Office of Education position. Both the President and Secretary Gardner identified themselves with the enforcement program, Senator Mansfield retracted his earlier criticism, and Howe attempted to moderate his public image through a temperate speech in Virginia.

During the day the White House issued two statements, the first sup-

[83] U.S., House, Committee on Rules, *Hearings, Policies and Guidelines for School Desegregation*, 89th Cong., 2d Sess., 1966, p. 3.
[84] *Washington Post*, September 30, 1966.

ported Gardner and the second cautiously endorsed the guidelines. Secretary Gardner insisted that he did not "underestimate in any way the difficulty of this social change" and argued that the rate of progress had been slow.[85] Majority Leader Mansfield told reporters:

> It is twelve years after the decision in the Brown case. Scarcely 10 per cent of the formerly segregated schools of the nation have been desegregated, even on a token basis. That is not "too fast." If anything, it is too slow.[86]

Earlier the Administration had seemed content to let Howe absorb the political flak from Congress. Now some of the power of the executive branch was being brought to bear in his defense.

On September 30 1966 Commissioner Howe walked quietly into the hearing room. Puffing his pipe and calmly defending the program against pointed questions, Howe quickly dispelled his image as a power-mad social planner. The Commissioner and his aides were well prepared to deal with southern assertions that the guidelines were illegal, bringing with them carefully prepared analyses of the decisions of the Supreme Court and the high Federal courts of the South that provided the basis for the guidelines' standards.

Howe came to the committee with disarming answers to a variety of questions. To those who complained about cutoff of funds, he responded that there were only 37 districts in the entire South that had lost all Federal money. To those who objected to specific incidents or procedures, he conceded that some mistakes might have been made. Finally, Howe caught his critics completely by surprise when he stated that he favored decentralization of the enforcement program to the states. Five state departments of education, he told the committee, had already received grants for state programs to assist districts with their desegregation problems.[87]

The issue of action in the North arose, and Howe was confronted with the controversial draft "Equal Educational Opportunity Act which Representative Fino had attacked." Howe conceded that the Office was interested in northern segregation, but said that "certainly we have no authority to enter into it now under existing legislation. . . ."[88] He firmly denied commitment to any specific plan for revamping the urban schools and insisted that his only goal was to persuade local officials to seriously consider possible answers to urgent problems. "I think," he said, "these have got to be worked out locally."[89] Decisions on possible actions were wholly up to local officials. Howe's quiet reasonableness and excellent

[85] *Baltimore Sun*, September 30, 1966.   [86] *Ibid.*

[87] House Rules Committee, *Policies and Guidelines* . . . , pp. 33–35.

[88] *Ibid.*, p. 42.   [89] *Ibid.*, p. 50.

preparation weakened the attack of his critics. During a second session with the committee, Howe explained that his speeches had been misunderstood:

> I am inclined to make strong statements in speeches because you have limited time and it is a way to catch attention. I certainly did not intend to give them the impression that civil rights enforcement activity or Title VI itself was involved in that discussion.[90]

Howe came out of the dreaded hearings without suffering further damage. The lack of an effective and well-prepared inquisitor meant that the committee was no match for a completely calm official effectively drawing on the resources of his bureaucracy, enjoying a great advantage of information, and prepared to take a much more "reasonable" policy line than the southerners had believed possible.

The effective performance of the Commissioner was buttressed by liberal arguments that the Rules Committee was violating the very rules and precedents of the House upon which conservative power had so long rested in the House. Judge Smith was confronted by his fellow Democrat, Emanuel Celler of Brooklyn. Celler, who had come to the Congress eight years earlier than Smith, argued that under the House rules his committee had jurisdiction over enforcement of civil rights laws originating in the committee. The ranking Republican member of Celler's committee also appeared in defense of the prerogatives of the Judiciary Committee.

The Rules Committee was confronted by a committee chairman with very great seniority who was invoking valid precedents. Celler promised that a full investigation would be conducted after the election and that the South would be represented on the investigating subcommittee. Between sessions of the Rules Committee hearings, Representative Celler took the initiative by requesting funds for an investigation and announcing that a South Carolina congressman would be included on the panel to conduct the probe.[91]

This resistance based on venerated traditions of committee independence made it impossible for the Rules Committee to report to the House the resolution to establish a select committee. Committee prerogatives are the central source of power in Congress, and any attempt to diminish the authority of one of the most prestigeful committees in the House would be resisted by many as an attack on the entire system. Ironically, a full-scale hostile investigation of the Office of Education was made impossible by the very devices so cherished by congressional conservatives.

The central fact that made some defense of the Office of Education

---

[90] *Ibid.*, p. 65.　　[91] *Ibid.*, pp. 11, 18, 56.

possible was that the Civil Rights Act was now part of the status quo. For many years before passage of the Act, attempts to pass civil rights legislation had been frustrated by the multiple minority vetoes built into the structure of Congress. In 1966 liberals occupying a few points of power were able to use congressional procedures, designed to protect the status quo, to limit the ability of a hostile majority to damage the enforcement program.

The Attack Continues

Although a destructive public inquisition had been headed off, the intensity of the rhetorical fire rained on Commissioner Howe continued to grow as October wore on and election day drew near. As September ended the national mood of reaction, which had so powerfully affected Congress, was reflected in a Gallup Poll indicating that 58 per cent of white Americans felt that the Administration was moving too fast on civil rights issues. The mood in the House was illustrated by the submission of 60 antiriot bills. In early October the Senate approved a vague and sweeping antiriot amendment to the poverty bill, over-riding Senator Javits' warning that it was an "administrative monstrosity, requiring no judicial finding before a person could be denied all benefits of the poverty program." [92]

Amid this atmosphere of reaction, Representative L. Mendel Rivers of South Carolina, Chairman of the Armed Services Committee, made a brutal attack on Howe. He described the Commissioner as a "misfit" who was not only destroying the American educational system but was also dismantling the Democratic party in the South. Howe was a "foul blot on the escutcheon of decency" and deserved to be fired immediately. "This man," said Rivers, "talks like a Communist. That is why those of us who know him call him the commissar of education." [93]

The same day that the House was listening to Rivers' villification of Howe, the Senate Labor and Public Welfare Committee quietly removed Senator Edward Kennedy's amendment providing aid to northern cities with voluntary desegregation plans from the pending Elementary and Secondary Education bill. Early in the session, prospects for this program had seemed good. Now Congress was not prepared to help cities desegregate, even if they wanted to.[94]

In southern politics, Commissioner Howe was claiming Bobby Kennedy's old position as the most hated Federal official. During October the Commissioner was subjected to at least 15 verbal assaults on the floor of

[92] *Washington Post*, September 30, 1966; U.S., *Congressional Record*, October 4, 1966, pp. 24154–62.
[93] *Washington Star*, September 30, 1966.   [94] *Ibid*.

Congress. At home, candidates were attempting to use the issue. The Democratic administration in South Carolina attempted to head off a Republican challenge by filing a lawsuit claiming that the guidelines were illegal. In Alabama, Governor Wallace threatened to arrest HEW officials for interference with the operation of local school systems. In at least four states, the guidelines became a major issue in contests for governor.[95]

Congressional broadsides became increasingly extravagant. "Harold Howe," declaimed an angry Alabamian, "has pressed down upon the brow of the South a crown of thorns as cruel and as torturous as that pressed upon the head of the Prince of Peace when they crucified Him on the cross." [96] "He has set out," thundered Representative Joe D. Waggonner, Jr., of Louisiana, "on a course of imperial threatening in the name of the Federal Government and the lash he is laying on the backs of school authorities is backed by $2 billion a year of the people's own money." [97]

It was not surprising that congressmen from the Deep South were fighting bitterly against the implementation of a social revolution in southern schools. What was striking was the almost complete lack of interest in defending the Office of Education on the part of the liberals who had fought for the civil rights bill two years earlier. Southern members carried on the attacks for weeks without any forceful rebuttal and were largely successful in defining the terms of the discussion. Once the southern vocabulary and legal arguments were accepted, the conclusion that the guidelines were illegal necessarily followed.

The national mood discouraged close examination of the southern claims and made it easy for northern and western congressmen to sympathize with what seemed to be legitimate local grievances. In a legislative body composed of members elected by local constituencies and deriving their political strength from a local organization rather than a national party structure, there is an automatic receptivity to local complaints that Federal bureaucrats have exceeded their authority. In the area of civil rights, actions of the local officials in Birmingham and Selma had temporarily overcome this inclination. Now the normal pattern was reasserting itself.

The problem was deepened by the Administration's failure to make a significant effort to activate potential supporters in the House. The Office of Education's side of the story simply was not explained to liberals.

[95] *Richmond Times-Dispatch*, October 8, 1966, and October 20, 1966; *Richmond News Leader*, October 15, 1966.
[96] *Congressional Record*, October 6, 1966, p. 24589.
[97] *Ibid.*, October 10, 1966, p. 24922.

Neither the Office of Education nor HEW had sufficient civil rights manpower to put someone to work full-time to develop contacts on Capitol Hill and feed information to sympathetic members. There was a regular congressional relations operation in HEW, under an assistant secretary, but this office saw its function as drafting legislation and handling congressional questions about the grant programs. The congressional relations staff clearly perceived the difference between the cooperative relationships involved in the grant programs and the regulatory responsibility implied by Title VI, and they decided to stand clear of the controversial program that might threaten their legislative effectiveness.

There was very little effort to repair the damage in the House. A Connecticut congressman finally accused the House of "bad taste, bad manners, and uncalled-for behavior" in the vicious personal attacks on Howe.[98]

Near the end of the session, somewhat more success was achieved in the Senate. Senator Joseph Clark, provided with information from HEW, accused southern politicians attacking Howe of "real old-fashioned demagoguery." "He has," said the Pennsylvania liberal, "brought intellectual honesty, deep respect for our local traditions, and enormous energy to bear on the great opportunity of our generation: excellence of education for all our people." [99] Senator Mansfield added his judgment that Howe "fills this position with abundant fitness and great dedication."

> Neither he nor his office has designs upon the responsibilities of State departments of education or local school boards. His only purpose is to prevent circumvention of the law over which Congress has made him responsible.[100]

While a handful of members of Congress thus came forth to defend the integrity of Commissioner Howe, there were no major attempts to explain and defend the substance of the enforcement policy.

The Legislative Impact

While some of the fiery southern speeches were obviously intended to influence local politics rather than national policy, there was a very serious effort to write into law restrictions on Title VI enforcement authority. By early October several votes had indicated that a clear majority in each house had lost its taste for forceful implementation of the civil rights law. Before the President's open-housing bill finally passed the House it had been amended to provide that the guidelines could not demand more than a freedom-of-choice desegregation plan. The House had been quite ready to accept a change that meant that most southern districts would

98 Ibid., October 19, 1966, p. A5431.   99 Ibid., October 18, 1966, pp. 20306–7.
100 Ibid., October 22, 1966, p. 27639.

never move beyond token integration. In the Senate the votes on the HEW appropriations bill reflected the same mood.

The school desegregation controversy tended to infect other pieces of legislation as Congress rushed toward adjournment. The Administration's high-priority Model Cities bill, designed to help communities plan for more effective coordination of the confusing variety of Federal aid programs, was attacked as a disguised effort to bribe school districts into bussing children across boundary lines. "If you are tired of social planners," said Congressman Fino, "tired of Howe and Weaver with their talk of racial balance here, racial balance there, racial balance everywhere, then vote against this bill. Vote against this bill if you believe in the neighborhood school." [101] Before the bill passed, the House wrote in an amendment forbidding that desegregation be required as a precondition for receipt of the funds.[102]

The session's most important skirmish on the guidelines came in the last days, during final consideration of the 1966 Elementary and Secondary Education Act amendments. When the House had passed this extremely important bill extending the 1965 aid-to-education measure, it had adopted an amendment proposed by North Carolina's Representative L. H. Fountain. The effect of the amendment was to cripple the enforcement program by denying the Commissioner of Education authority to defer action on new grants to districts he was convinced were defying Title VI requirements. Only after completion of lengthy hearing procedures, a process with enormous potential for delay, would it be possible to end the flow of new funds to districts plainly violating the Constitution and the guidelines. Since the Office lacked the legal staff to rapidly prepare and conduct hearings for all the districts involved, Commissioner Howe would be forced to release millions of dollars to local officials who had no intention of complying with Federal requirements. Districts would be encouraged to resist, knowing that Federal subsidies would continue to flow as long as they could drag out the procedures.

The Senate bill, however, included no such amendment. Thus the dispute was consigned to a conference committee. This committee, composed of members named by the relevant committee chairman in each house, had power under congressional procedure to settle all issues in dispute between the House and Senate versions of the bill and to return the compromise to both houses. Neither house possesses the authority to amend the bill reported by the conference committee; it can only be accepted or rejected as a whole.

In the normal course of events, the conference committee is a strongly

101 *Ibid.*, October 13, 1966, pp. 22544, 22554–55.
102 *Ibid.*, October 14, 1966, pp. 25858–63.

conservative force. Since the chairmen generally appoint senior members of their committees, the more progressive two-party states tend to be under-represented because of their failure to accumulate seniority. Although conferees for each house are expected to represent the position of their chamber, particularly if there has been a roll-call vote, the members have a good deal of discretion in reaching their decisions.[103]

Once again, however, a circumstantial concentration of liberal seniority served to protect the Office of Education. Until the mid-1960's there had been few significant Federal education programs, and few congressmen had sought seats on the Education and Labor Committee. Adam Clayton Powell had chosen to stay with the committee rather than transfer to a more important committee. In 1961 his seniority made him chairman. Thus the Harlem Democrat had power to select the House conferees who would carry the responsibility of defending the anti-civil rights amendment against Senate objections. In the Senate the committee chairman followed the common practice of making the subcommittee chairman the head of the conference delegation. Thus Wayne Morse, head of the Education subcommittee, led the Senate conferees. Thus circumstances put two of the strongest civil rights supporters in Congress into decisive positions.

The conference committee was strongly liberal. The House delegation did not include a single strong conservative, and the Senate conferees were predominantly liberal.[104] Although the House had adopted the Fountain amendment 2 to 1, the great majority of the House conferees were opposed to the provision. With both delegations predisposed to kill the Fountain proviso, the task was to find an acceptable formula that could be defended on the floor of the House. Powell proposed a compromise limiting Howe's authority to defer funds to a period of 90 days. If the hearing procedure began within that period, the Commissioner could then defer new grants until the hearing examiner made a final decision.[105] The proposal was Powell's last significant contribution to civil rights policy before he was thrown out of Congress at the beginning of the next session.

The education bill was one of the last issues of the session, and the conferees worked far into the night to find suitable language. A more complicated version of the Powell suggestion, drafted by Senator Javits, was adopted.[106]

---

[103] Malcolm E. Jewell and Samuel C. Patterson, *The Legislative Process in the United States* (New York: Random House, 1966), pp. 474–79.
[104] *Congressional Record*, October 19, 1966, p. 26547.
[105] *Chicago Daily News*, October 18, 1966.
[106] *Congressional Record*, October 18, 1966, p. 26475.

The effect of the new language was to transform an amendment that had been intended to outlaw a procedure for which the Commissioner's power was not absolutely clear into an explicit legislative authorization for the deferral procedure, subject only to certain time limits. In fact, the conference language had been checked with and found acceptable by both HEW and the Leadership Conference on Civil Rights before it was reported out.

The possibility remained that the House would choose to reject the entire conference report. To circumvent this threat, House liberals resorted to a bit of parliamentary sleight of hand, executing a maneuver that would have made a southern strategist proud. Because the House had passed the bill first and the Senate subsequently adopted a different version and requested a conference, the conference report would normally be submitted for action first to the House. The House, however, could be expected to promptly send the bill back to conference, demanding inclusion of the original Fountain amendment. Thus the tactical problem facing the liberals was to find some way to deny the House this opportunity.

A rare procedure was invoked. As the conference ended, the papers containing the report were handed to Senator Morse rather than Congressman Powell. The next day, after telling reporters that the new language actually strengthened the legal position of the Office of Education, Morse promptly called up the report for Senate approval.[107] In a brief discussion, the Oregon senator read an analysis stating that the amendment prevented abuse of the deferral power by insuring a prompt opportunity for a formal hearing. He recommended that the Senate consider the provision of additional funds to HEW to meet the new deadlines. In essence, he said, the report was a "very sound compromise." [108] In the last-minute rush, the conference report was adopted by the Senate by unanimous consent, without a record vote.[109]

Once Senate action was completed and one house had adopted the conference report, the conference committee was discharged. The House no longer had the option of returning the bill to conference, since the conference no longer existed. At this late date, there was no possibility of convening a new conference committee. The only choice left to the House was either to accept the entire bill or to kill the highly popular education bill, denying expected funds in every congressional district in the country.

Furious House proponents of the Fountain amendment felt that they had been doubly wronged. Not only had the House conferees failed to represent the position overwhelmingly supported by the House, but they

[107] *Washington Post*, October 19, 1966.
[108] *Congressional Record*, October 19, 1966, pp. 26538, 26554.　　　　[109] *Ibid.*, p. 26556.

had also acquiesced in a parliamentary trick to deny the House majority a chance to demand reconsideration. The southerners were beaten, and the only thing they could do now was to try to influence the legislative history of the new provision through floor debate.

House Education subcommittee chairman Carl Perkins reported that the new provision would prohibit abuse of the deferral power. The Senate conferees, he said, had taken a "very adamant" position in favor of this language, and it had been supported by both Democratic and Republican senators. The amendment, he said, gave the Commissioner no authority he did not have previously, but merely placed limits on the exercise of whatever authority he might have. At any rate, discussion was somewhat academic since there was now "no conference to whom to rerefer the matter. . . ." [110]

Southern congressmen continued to argue that the House majority decision had been totally subverted. Representative Albert Quie, who was to lead a Republican-southern assault on the entire Federal aid-to-education program early in the next session, denounced the parliamentary tactics of the liberals on the conference committee. Representative Celler happily pronounced the new provision a "satisfactory procedure." [111]

In the end, of course, the conference report was adopted, 185 to 76. Civil rights supporters on the conference committee, representing perhaps no more than one-third of the House members, succeeded in frustrating a majority willing to cut back the enforcement program. The same kind of tactics that had so long delayed a social revolution now worked to prolong it. Shortly after completing action on the bill the 89th Congress adjourned, leaving the civil rights enforcement machinery in far better repair than would have seemed possible a few weeks earlier.

The Judiciary Hearings: A Belated Counterattack

The promised House Judiciary Committee investigation provided a final footnote to the congressional furor of 1966. Within days of the election, a liberal-dominated subcommittee with some southern representation assembled in Washington to probe guidelines policies. Just as the Rules Committee hearings had been designed to provide a platform for a southern attack, so the subcommittee proceedings were used to provide a forum for an Office of Education defense. The sessions also gave informed liberal congressmen an opportunity to publicize some of the strong civil rights group criticism of the compromises that had been made within the Office of Education.

The political atmosphere had improved. Election-time passions had

110 *Ibid.*, pp. 27059–64.   111 *Ibid.*

diminished, and the white backlash had assumed less importance than expected. For the first time the program's potential supporters were well prepared. Congressman Byron Rogers, the subcommittee chairman, had arrived in Washington the previous weekend and had been briefed by staff members of the NAACP Legal Defense Fund. An enormous amount of staff work within the enforcement program had been devoted to the preparation of voluminous answers to all of the major southern charges.

Well-designed questions gave Commissioner Howe an opportunity to explain in detail the derivation of the guidelines standards from Federal court decisions. Moreover, Howe had a chance to take the offensive against the free-choice desegregation plan. "The free choice system," he said, "places the burden for school desegregation on the individual Negro pupil or his family. And there seems to me a very real question about how long we should continue to operate our school desegregation progress on the basis of free choice plans. . . ." [112] Assistant Commissioner Seeley gave dramatic testimony on the extent of intimidation, both subtle and violent, that confronted children attempting to exercise their "free choice." Homes had been bombed, he said, people had been directly threatened, the Ku Klux Klan had distributed messages calculated to instill fear, and there had been repeated shootings. In some areas of the South, he argued, the people were virtually as terrorized as the populace of a totalitarian society.[113] In such an atmosphere to talk of freedom of choice was to deceive oneself.

The attitude of most subcommittee members was distinctly sympathetic. A liberal California congressman was highly disturbed that 88 per cent of southern Negro students remained in segregated schools.

> I know of no other precedent in the law where we tolerate a percentage of compliance. I am sure the Internal Revenue Service would not tolerate my paying income tax on 9 or 12, or 98 percent of my taxable income. . . . I think that the most disastrous thing that we can do is to lead the people of this Nation to believe that there is going to continue to be a dual system and a free choice.[114]

A Minnesota Republican accused Federal authorities of transforming what Congress had intended as a simple regulatory function into a negotiating operation permitting widespread segregation to continue.[115]

The hearings were a step toward restoring balance to the civil rights enforcement debate. The testimony helped to move the Office of Education toward the more comfortable public position of taking a moderate middle course between the demands of southern whites and the necessities as seen by the civil rights group. This process was also aided by two

[112] House Judiciary Committee, *School Desegregation Guidelines*, p. 125.
[113] *Ibid.*, pp. 58, 134.   [114] *Ibid.*, p. 149.   [115] *Ibid.*, p. 245.

developments in December: the issuance of a report on the compliance program by the Southern Regional Council and the decision of the Fifth Circuit Court of Appeals in an extremely important case that tested the validity of the guidelines.

The Atlanta-based Southern Regional Council bitterly criticized Federal authorities for continuing to accept freedom-of-choice plans in the Deep South. In the five Deep South states, the group concluded, performance was "far below any reasonable standard for achieving the law's demand that discrimination based on race cease." The council denounced as political cowardice the decision to remove a compliance officer who came under fire in the process of negotiating effective desegregation plans in the Atlanta metropolitan area.[116]

The southern argument that the guidelines were illegal was laid to rest in the historic *Jefferson County* decision, handed down December 29, 1966, by the Fifth Circuit Court of Appeals. This tribunal, with jurisdiction over all school litigation in the Deep South, made an authoritative interpretation of the constitutional requirement for affirmative action to end school segregation:

> The United States Constitution . . . requires public school systems to integrate students, faculties, facilities, and activities. . . . A state with a dual attendance system, one for whites and one for Negroes, must "effectuate a transition to a [single] racially nondiscriminatory system." The two *Brown* decisions . . . compelled seventeen states, which by law had segregated public schools to take affirmative action to reorganize their schools into a unitary, nonracial system.
>
> *The only school desegregation plan that meets constitutional standards is one that works.*[117]

This decision made it extremely difficult to make a plausible legal argument against the moderate requirements of the school guidelines.

Summary

As 1966 ended the most serious congressional assaults had been thrown back, at least for a time. The attempt to remove Commissioner Howe had failed, and the guidelines had not been changed. The Office of Education had been given an opportunity to defend its policies, and some liberal congressional support had been activated.

The threat remained serious, however. The national mood had turned sharply against civil rights. Because the question of national policy to-

---

[116] Southern Regional Council, "School Desegregation 1966: The Slow Undoing," reprinted in House Judiciary Committee, *School Desegregation Guidelines*, pp. 267–69.

[117] *U.S. v. Jefferson County Board of Education*, No. 23345, 5th Circuit Court of Appeals, December 29, 1966, slip opinion, pp. 5–7.

ward the Negro was the central visible question of domestic politics, this mood very rapidly pervaded a Congress that had been hailed as the most liberal in decades. A majority were now quite willing to retrench existing enforcement efforts. This basic problem was deepened in November when the Republicans made significant gains in the congressional elections, returning control of the House to the old conservative coalition.

Very few members of Congress understood the subtleties of the enforcement debate. To do their job, congressmen must deal with the great bulk of the issues that confront them in terms of their general orientations toward broad questions of public policy. In the field of race relations, these orientations vary almost directly with public opinion.[118] So long as the public remained convinced that civil rights progress was too fast, the strongest court decisions or the most eloquent defenses of the Office of Education could have only limited success.

While the power of the Commissioner of Education had been preserved, it had been accomplished through defensive tactics frustrating a majority bent on reaction. In the long run it is extremely difficult for any executive agency to carry on a major program without the active support of Congress. This fact was recognized within HEW as officials discussed the desegregation standards for the coming year. Although there was no question of legal authority, there was serious discussion within the department about dropping the rate-of-progress provision from the standards, thus eliminating the section that forced school districts to move beyond token integration. Unlike the previous year, there was no attempt to strengthen the guidelines by incorporating new developments in constitutional law. It was considered a sign of determination when the same guidelines were reissued. The program was alive, but much of its forward momentum had been lost.

No one has ever claimed that the American Congress was created as an effective instrument for the implementation of vast and rapid social change. Only in rare moments are the web of ties between the decentralized centers of congressional power and the forces of the status quo broken. Only in those moments is the creaking legislative machinery transformed into an agency for the accomplishment of change that is long overdue. These moments are short and they are followed by a reinstatement of the normal pattern. That is the nature of the system.

Only twice in American history has Congress been able to act forcefully to protect the rights of Negro citizens: in the decade following the Civil War and, for a moment, in the mid-1960's. The first was made possible by the subjugation of the South and the creation of an extraordi-

[118] Miller and Stokes, "Constituency Influence in Congress," pp. 47, 51.

nary political situation. The second arose from the irresistible force of a great tide of public anger. The first ended when the public grew weary of contention and turned against the black man and when the political power of southern whites became crucial once again in national politics. The great reforms disappeared, leaving few traces for generations. In late 1966 it became obvious that the strength was gone, at least for a time, from the second wave of reform. Leading black moderates pointed to the ominous parallel:

> Ninety years ago this Nation permitted the democratic promise of emancipation to wither and die before a rampant reaction which condemned the Negro to segregation, disenfranchisement, peonage and death. Then as now the voices of temporary liberalism sounded discouragement and disillusionment with the capacity of the freedman for full citizenship.[119]

As the extraordinary public commitment to racial change rapidly dissolved, opponents in Congress began to use their sources of power to harass the enforcement effort and to try to curtail its power. As normalcy returned to Congress, the majority of members were prepared to accept apparently reasonable southern proposals without close scrutiny. Only the strategic skill of liberals, placed by circumstance in some positions of influence, saved the Federal power to protect the right of Negro children to a desegregated education.

The skill of a handful of defenders prevented sudden dismantling of the effort that had become the cutting edge of civil rights enforcement. Even as southern minorities had so often used their leverage within the structure of Congress to frustrate a majority committed to racial progress, so now a liberal minority was able to buy time for the desegregation program. In the long run, however, the survival and success of the attempt to remake race relations in southern schools could be insured only by a general public commitment to racial justice. As Congress went home in 1966, this commitment seemed alive only in memory.

[119] Advertisement in *New York Times*, reported in *Washington Post*, October 14, 1966.

7

Federalism and the Reconstruction

of Southern Education

We come then to the question presented: Does segregation of children in the public schools solely on the basis of race, even though the physical facilities and other "tangible" factors may be equal, deprive the children of the minority group of equal education opportunities? We believe that it does. . . .

To separate them from others of similar age and qualifications solely because of their race generates a feeling of inferiority as to their status in the community that may affect their hearts and minds in a way unlikely ever to be undone.

Brown versus Board of Education

It all began in the solemn, classic building across from the Capitol. The words read by a gray-haired man in judicial robes called for the most basic peacetime transformation in the nature of American federalism. To make the rights recognized by the Supreme Court a reality, the authority of the national government would have to be brought to bear on the most sensitive issue in thousands of localities. It is not easy for any democracy to restructure fundamental facts of social existence, and it is particularly difficult within a governmental structure consciously designed to protect local and regional interests. The Supreme Court's decision set in motion a social revolution arising from the core problem of American life, a revolution that was to threaten some of the most cherished and most abused of our traditions of government.

First through the Court and much later through action by Congress, the national government became involved in a crusade to eradicate any official manifestation of one of the most basic social and cultural patterns of a vast region of the country. Segregation is much more than a mere unexamined set of beliefs that pass when reason and power are brought to bear. "Segregation," wrote a sensitive student of the struggle, "is a 'way of life,' a social phenomenon shared, intensely shared, by whole towns and states." [1] Rarely does any nation self-consciously set out to use long-established and stable institutions of government to remake the society that government serves. This history, the traditions, and the very structure of American federalism had been compatible with local racial tyrannies. Federalism magnified the difficulties of implementing change.

Change within Federalism

The American system of government provides multiple opportunities for an intensely concerned minority to delay or simply veto government action. For the South, the question of eliminating racially separate schools was an issue of such sovereign importance that political leaders were impelled to use every possible means of opposition. In spite of the Supreme Court decision, the accurate southern perception that integrated schools would destroy the rigid stereotypes basic to maintenance of the caste system stimulated resistance of very great intensity. The Federal judicial machinery proved unable to bring more than symbolic recognition of the rights proclaimed by the Supreme Court. Within the legislative machinery, even symbolic commitment to the cause of Negro rights had been prevented for decades.

In Congress, legislation can be killed at any of a large number of critical steps except in the rare situation when a large majority is intensely committed and ready to override normal legislative practices. A hostile subcommittee or committee chairman, a concentration of opponents on a critical subcommittee or committee or on the Rules Committee that controls the business of the House, the existence of a sizeable minority willing to filibuster in the Senate, or the skillful use or misuse of parliamentary procedure can doom a piece of legislation. For decades the South built and consolidated its power within Congress, protecting its ability to segregate. Only in 1964 did the civil rights coalition assemble a majority sufficiently large and sufficiently committed to overcome the internal barriers in Congress. Even then the commitment remained largely symbolic and its implementation uncertain. The South still retained much of its power for resistance in Congress.

Reform almost always comes slow in America, and none have been slower than civil rights reforms. Power is not only fractionated within Congress, but also between national and state and local officials, among the myriad executive agencies with their various constituencies and bases

[1] Robert Coles, *Children of Crisis* (Boston: Atlantic-Little Brown, 1967), p. 31.

of political support, and even within a judicial system in which most appointments are very heavily influenced by locally oriented politicians. Reform often begins at the local or state level and only gradually becomes a national issue. Reform leaders must come to understand the workings of the Congress and put together sufficient support to produce a majority at all of the veto points built into the congressional process. In the case of major regulatory legislation, one expert observes, this stage of the struggle may take more than two decades. Even when legislation finally passes, it is often compromised or even outmoded.[2]

Within the American system, waves of reform sentiment generally culminate in the enactment of a piece of legislation. The battle typically focuses on the problem of producing a congressional majority, and the history books record the names of the great legislative accomplishments and their principal congressional sponsors.

Few members of the concerned public understand that passage of a law means very little until the resources of the executive bureaucracies are committed to its implementation and until the validity of the law and the administrative regulations issued under the law have been tested in the courts. Thus, after a reform is written into law the forces that have given impetus to the legislative battle often dissolve. The task of turning the broad generalities of legislation into the minute day-to-day realities of administrative requirements takes place in a setting understood by few, a setting in which most of the advantages lie with the custodians of existing relationships and with those organized interests that have learned through experience to effectively influence administrative decision-making. Often those representing the status quo also enjoy similar advantages of legal expertise in the judicial battles over the definition of new legislation.

It is thus a common experience that legislation already compromised in Congress is further emasculated within the executive agencies and in the courts. These problems are further heightened by the fact that minorities in Congress can frequently manipulate the decisive committees in the appropriations process to sap the power of agencies that seriously attempt to implement reforms. Therefore an administrator attempting to accomplish basic change operates in an extremely difficult situation, a situation that generally forces an agency either to come to terms with its existing constituency or to try to create a new constituency able to generate broadly based support in Congress.

The difficulties hampering implementation of reform are all present in accentuated form in the field of civil rights. Significant civil rights reform took not a generation but almost a century. It became a normal and

---

[2] Marver H. Bernstein, *Regulating Business by Independent Commission* (Princeton: Princeton University Press, 1955), pp. 74–76.

expected part of the American political process that the South could use any parliamentary device and indeed threaten a complete shutdown of the legislative business of the nation to resist even symbolic commitment of the nation to the cause of Negro rights. The best talent produced by southern politics was invested in this defensive effort, and the effort enjoyed great success.

After passage of civil rights legislation, the administrative obstacles to enforcement were of unequaled dimensions. This was the most sensitive local issue across the South and the one question that often threatened total disruption of program relationships. Thus administrators with very large investments in existing programs had to weigh against these valued relationships a responsibility for which few had enthusiasm. Moreover the intense resistance to the entire Office of Education, which could be expected in Congress, was of enormous importance within a legislative system in which program administrators were regularly dependent upon committees and subcommittees led by southerners. The transient quality of the civil rights coalition and the slight interest of northern congressmen in the details of civil rights enforcement were in sharp contrast to the continuing strength of southern congressmen and the passionate interest taken by many of them in what they saw as illegitimate actions in their districts. In the important field of school desegregation, these problems were further magnified by the tradition of local control of the schools.

The nature of the American system of government puts civil rights reform at an enormous disadvantage. In fact significant administrative action is possible only in special conditions. Real change is possible only when the public is overwhelmingly committed, when a presidential election creates a powerful incentive to appeal for black votes, or when a President is willing to draw on his political capital to meet the inevitable and heavy political attack. It was a combination of these factors which made important progress possible between 1964 and 1966. Typically, however, these conditions exist for only brief periods. A good deal of time is consumed in working through the complexities of the governmental apparatus before actual change can begin. Within a system of genuine decentralization of power, a system deeply committed to the belief in localism, a single legislative pronouncement can never resolve a great issue. Irreconcilable opponents of change will inevitably continue to take advantage of the multiple opportunities always available to launch direct or hidden attacks through various instruments of government.

Ultimately legislation protecting Negro rights can only be sustained by success in so changing the society that there will no longer be an overwhelming political incentive to attack such legislation. Across the South the central element in this social change is the successful integration of the schools. Once local schools are fully integrated, local officials committed to peaceful operation under the new order, and local stereotypes broken, the issue becomes of distinctly secondary importance. Thus the crucial question is one of time, time to defy the normal political gravity of the American political system toward localism while Federal power is used to transform the local conditions. This time can be bought only by the expenditure of political power, either the raw political power of highly activated public opinion or the institutionalized political power of key members of Congress or of a President with a good deal of political strength. The waves of national emotion arising from Birmingham, the assassination of President Kennedy, and the 1965 Selma March together with the enormius political power of a President elected by an immense majority in 1964 allowed the process of transformation to begin. By 1966, however, public support for change had faded and the power of President Johnson had sharply declined. Those attempting to lead the revolution found themselves on the defensive.

Equality vs. Localism: Federal Intervention in Education and Civil Rights

A dominant theme of American political thought is the preference for localism, for the concentration of important governmental functions at the grass-roots level. This commitment is reflected both in the locally centered character of American politics and in the highly decentralized character of the administration of nominally "Federal" programs. In no field of activity has this popularly supported tradition of localism been more highly valued than in public education.

Although the national government began granting public lands to support local schools even before the Constitution was adopted, the financing of education is still the most important local responsibility. The great leaders of the movement to create public school systems had been local and state rather than national figures. As the common school movement gained success, educational leadership came to be concentrated in the large city school systems and in the state departments of education. This arrangement was nicely consonant with the prevailing constitutional theory of the day, with its emphasis on states' rights and limited Federal authority. By the late 1800's, the idea of state control of the school curriculum was the American way. Any suggestion of change aroused the abiding public suspicion of strong central government.

The decades of struggle to create universal public education implanted in the public understanding a set of deeply held beliefs about the nature of education. Public schools came to be seen both as the essential precondition for the maintenance of democracy and as the chief pathway to opportunity. The great leaders of the common school movement burned into the public consciousness the perception of the local school district as "a bulwark of the Republic and repository of popular hopes and aspirations." [3]

American democracy, it was held, depended on the strength of the schools. Schoolmen echoed the words of Thomas Jefferson: "If a nation expects to be ignorant and free, in a state of civilization, it expects what never was and never will be." [4] The schools could only be strong if they drew upon the fundamental source of democratic energy, the local community. Local leaders would make certain that education reflected local values and met the needs of the community.

Americans came to believe not only that political freedom rested with the schools, but also that the social ideal of the society, the ideal of equal opportunity, could only be realized through the schools. Public education, Horace Mann proclaimed, is the "great equalizer." [5] This persisting belief has often meant that American movements for social reform are transformed into movements for educational change.

The American faith in education as the road to opportunity and the solution to social problems has been almost unbounded. Recently the conviction that fundamental economic and social disorders can be remedied in the schools has been particularly striking in the War on Poverty. The enthusiasm with which the country greeted Operation Headstart, an expensive, untried, and short nursery-school program was matched only by lack of interest in alternative approaches. Although education programs rapidly gain acceptance, proposals for public creation of jobs or for direct income supplements to the poor produce deep ideological divisions. The schools occupy a central place in the public mind, and this very fact magnifies the importance of change in the schools.

There has been a grievous flaw in the vision of the American school. After the Civil War it became evident in the South that, given local determination to segregate, the two great principles—local control of the schools and equal opportunity through education—were mutually incompatible. Concern over the southern failure to provide schools for Negroes helped spur the northern drive for Federal aid in the decades after the war. Fear that the local status quo would be threatened led the South to an increasingly rigid defense of states' rights and local control of the schools. Appeals to the strong American tradition of localism in education helped defeat Federal programs and thus limit the ability of the nation to

---

[3] Cremin, *The Transformation of the School*, p. 9.
[4] Cremin, *The Genius of American Education* (New York: Vintage, 1965), p. 5.
[5] Cremin, *The Transformation of the School*, p. 9.

threaten the caste system by making economic, cultural, and political mobility possible for the Negro.

The goal of equal opportunity had been largely forgotten by the turn of the century. As the first education grant programs took shape, they set a pattern eminently acceptable in the South. Theoretically the ruling principle was "separate but equal," but in practice the determination of "equality" was left to state and local officials. With few exceptions, this was the dominant pattern until the 1960's. It was within an administrative tradition of rampant localism that the Title VI enforcement program was forged.

Only the 1954 Supreme Court decision forced Americans to confront the fundamental contradiction in the ideas of American education. The court sensitively analyzed both the central importance of the schools in local government and the hope for equal opportunity. The decision described education as "perhaps the most important function of state and local governments."

> It is required in the performance of our most basic public responsibilities. . . . Today it is a principal instrument in awakening the child to cultural values, in preparing him for later professional training, and in helping him to adjust normally to his environment. In these days, it is doubtful that any child may reasonably be expected to succeed in life if he is denied the opportunity of an education. Such an opportunity, where the state has undertaken to provide it, is a right which must be made available to all on equal terms.[6]

In fact, the court concluded, for both psychological and educational reasons equal education was impossible within the context of legally separate segregated schools. On this issue, local control would have to yield to what the court saw as basic constitutionally protected rights.

The 1954 decision and a decade of litigation following it forced recognition both of this basic clash of values and of the impossibility of effectively guaranteeing equal opportunity within the normal processes of American federalism. Finally, after Birmingham made the extent of local abuses vivid to the nation, a powerful movement developed to vastly expand Federal power to limit local discrimination. The 1964 Civil Rights Act made the central government responsible for active protection of certain Negro rights, even while the generally passive relationship with local authority in other fields was to continue. In no field of Federal activity was the tension between the existing administrative relationships and the requirements of the new law to be more acute than in education.

[6] *Brown v. Board of Education*, 347 U.S. 483 (1954), reprinted in Daniel M. Berman, *It is So Ordered* (New York: W. W. Norton and Co., 1966), pp. 139–40.

At every stage, the tradition of educational localism was to be invoked against those who attempted to enforce the Federal right.

The Administration Setting

The Office of Education was caught in the conflict between equality and localism in 1964. While most Americans clearly believed that southern schools should be integrated, most also remained firmly attached to the ideal of local control of the schools. The Office of Education was expected to force local officials to recognize the rights of Negro children, but do nothing else to threaten the tradition of local dominance. It rapidly became apparent, however, that the two kinds of responsibilities could not be easily separated. Experience soon revealed that, without tightly drawn requirements, nothing would change at the local level. Effective standards, however, demanded Federal regulation of such processes as student assignment, school districting, and racial distribution of teachers. From the local perspective, it was obvious to school officials that their traditional sphere of authority had been drastically limited. Naturally they protested in the name of local control. Their protests endangered the carefully developed image of the Office of Education as a cautious respecter of state and local primacy.

Historically, the Office of Education had responded to the decentralized structure of American politics and to the strength of local control sentiment by fervently and genuinely denying any intention to supplant local authority. Administrators operating within the context of American government must seek political support for their programs. Because Congress and the President have independent bases of power, the survival and prosperity of any program demands not only executive support but continuing approval in Congress, a body composed of men chosen and reelected by separate political organizations built in and responsive to localities. Federal education officials had responded to this practical necessity by protecting local power. Now, suddenly, without any basic change in either the decentralized character of the political system or the commitment to localism in education, a unique historical development placed the Office of Education in an extremely difficult position.

Reaction against school desegregation requirements soon threatened to jeopardize the entire array of Federal aid programs. Commissioner Howe described the problem the Office was encountering in the South:

> To meet its legal obligations the Office of Education has had to set standards for school desegregation. . . . There are considerable differences between Office of Education responsibilities in the realm of civil rights and our administration of financial aid programs, but the distinctions have been blurred by the strong feelings which pervade the issue of civil rights. The result of this blurring is additional

difficulty in the federal-state-local relationship in education; feelings engendered by the controversy . . . frequently are transferred to programs sponsored by the Office for totally unrelated purposes.[7]

Congressmen from the affected states now found their offices constantly receiving complaints that the Office of Education was grossly violating local prerogatives.

The significance of the controversy was magnified by the rapidly growing Federal role in American education. The Office of Education had normally been of very slight importance in the total national effort. Between 1964 and 1966, however, the number of Federal education authorizations more than doubled, and a vast new program for elementary and secondary schools went into operation.[8] Although delighted by the tide of new money, state and local schoolmen were uneasy about the implications of the change for the traditional pattern of educational decision-making. In this sensitive period, the Office of Education could ill afford an image of vigorous intervention in local affairs.

Congressional worries about the new role of the Office of Education were reflected in the hearings of a special House subcommittee in late 1966. As it crossed the country seeking to assess new Federal programs, the group heard complaints both about civil rights enforcement and about the administration of the Elementary and Secondary Education Act. Predictably, the attack of the local schoolmen on Federal authority was most bitter in the South.

A broad attack was launched against the Office of Education at the subcommittee's Atlanta hearing. Georgia school officials urged that aid to the schools be separated from extraneous concerns about social reform. The Federal government should do nothing more than provide general unrestricted funds for state authorities to divide according to normal state procedures. The Georgia department of education complained of the need to travel repeatedly to Washington and of incessant Federal demands for information that Georgia officials considered irrelevant.[9]

The southern protest was not isolated; it was part of a national reaction against the expansion of Federal influence in education. At the same time they were forcing local racial change, Federal officials were also administering the new Elementary and Secondary Education Act, a set of pro-

[7] Harold Howe, II, "The U.S. Office of Education: Growth and Growing Pains," *Saturday Review*, Vol. XLIX (December 17, 1966), p. 69.
[8] U.S., Office of the Vice President, *Vice President's Handbook for Local Officials* (Washington: Government Printing Office, 1967), p. 4.
[9] U.S., Congress, House, Committee on Education and Labor, Special Subcommittee on Education, Hearings, *U.S. Office of Education*, 89th Cong., 2d Sess., 1966, pp. 649–52.

grams designed to reorder the priorities of local schools. The Act, in the words of Commissioner Keppel, was intended to "put funds in such quantity at particular points so that it is possible to get a leverage to raise the quality. . . ." The money was a "crowbar" which was "put in at the point where we can get some leverage." [10] By demanding that the bulk of the new funds be used to improve schools for children from poor areas, the Office of Education was directly attacking local practice. The subcommittee heard a good many hostile comments on this practice, including these from leading schoolmen in Maine:

> It is felt that the State and State officials should know the needs of the State better than someone at a more remote point. What is innovation or change in Scarsdale, N.Y., may not be in Meddybemps, Maine. . . .[11]

> I have strong conviction that the State department and the people of Maine could spend this money more wisely, more prudently and with greater impact on the local education scene. . . .[12]

Local criticism troubled those congressmen for whom the commitment to local control of the schools was a more basic article of political faith than Federal aid to education. Even Commissioner Howe conceded the existence of widespread "concern about the possibility of shifts in power. . . ." School people, he said, "are concerned lest future Federal policy grow more specific in pinpointing activities for the use of Federal funds." [13]

Congresswoman Edith Green, chairman of the House subcommittee, reflected perfectly the conflict between civil rights and localism. A liberal with a perfect voting record on civil rights, her earlier career as an employee of the Oregon Education Association had given her a fervent belief in locally controlled schools. When she heard the head of the Georgia School Boards Association testify that civil rights enforcement had "very gravely affected the administration of all of the other programs of education," she became deeply worried about the maintenance of local control. The Georgia spokesman testified that Federal officials refused to accept the word of local educators but readily believed the claims of Negro parents. Local superintendents, the subcommittee was told, were considered "guilty . . . until they prove themselves innocent." [14] Mrs. Green decided that the actions of the Federal enforcement staff had been improper. She said angrily:

[10] U.S., Congress, Senate, Committee on Labor and Public Welfare, Subcommittee on Education, *Hearings, Elementary and Secondary Education Act of 1965*, 89th Cong., 1st Sess., 1965, p. 887.
[11] House Special Subcommittee on Education, p. 419.   [12] *Ibid.*, p. 438.
[13] Howe, "The U.S. Office of Education," pp. 68–69.
[14] House Special Subcommittee on Education, pp. 663–65.

I would like to read . . . a section that is in almost every education bill passed by Congress. . . .

Nothing contained in this title shall be construed so as to authorize any officer, employee, or agent of the United States to exercise any supervision or control over the curriculum, the program of instruction or the personnel of any educational institution or school system. . . .

. . . If I were in your position, and I received requests which I felt perhaps were contrary to this law, I would fire back a similar telegram and quote it.

I say this as a person long interested in civil rights, but one . . . deeply committed to the local and State control of education, and one who insists that the Federal Government be the junior partner.[15]

During the 1967 session of Congress, Mrs. Green was to become the leader in an effort to restrict Office of Education powers both under the Civil Rights Act and under the Elementary and Secondary Education Act.

During 1964 and 1965, as the Johnson Administration won passage of historic school and civil rights legislation, it seemed as if a century of heated debate over the propriety of Federal intervention in these sensitive local matters had been conclusively resolved. The Office of Education had been given two powerful tools to equalize educational opportunity for those discriminated against on racial or economic grounds. It very soon became evident that these two instruments worked powerfully together, each deepening the impact of the other. Across the South, the tide of new Federal money provided an extremely strong incentive to desegregate and made it possible for schools undergoing integration to simultaneously improve their educational programs. An important alteration of the federal system was underway. By 1966 it was becoming evident that Federal officials truly possessed the power to transform some central features of American education.

The dilemma faced by the Office of Education in 1966 arose from the fact that the agency now possessed more power than the public believed it should exercise. As support for civil rights faded, it became a basic political necessity for the Office to reach some kind of tolerable relationship with state and local educators. Eventually Congress, reflecting local concerns, was to force the Office of Education to choose between continuance of its civil rights responsibility and the preservation of its authority under the Elementary and Secondary Education Act.

The Context in Congress: Resurgence of Localism

When the 1966 congressional election produced significant Republican gains, ending a brief interval of liberal control of the House, a serious

[15] *Ibid.*, p. 653.

debate about the condition of American federalism became inevitable. Dozens of new Johnson programs posed potential threats to the status quo in localities, state bureaucracies, or professional groups where Federal power had previously been either nonexistent or wholly passive. All over Washington agencies were going through the confusing processes involved in transforming the enormous legislative output of the last Congress into routine administrative operations.

From the local perspective it seemed that program after program held out the lure of needed dollars but only entrapped local officials in an endless and seemingly pointless paper blizzard. Inadequately staffed state agencies found themselves completely overloaded. A natural result was resentment against "red tape" and a growing demand that local officials be allowed to use their own judgment in spending Federal aid funds.

The sudden and many-sided expansion of Federal power had been the product of a historic anomaly. The disastrous Goldwater defeat in 1964 happened to coincide with the cresting of the civil rights movement; Goldwater's defeat was so massive that he carried down with him Republican congressmen from a number of normally Republican districts, thus breaking the congressional power of the conservative coalition.

The Republican comeback in the 1966 election restored the old balance. The conservative GOP newcomers in the 1967 Congress insured a reexamination of these changes, including the revolution implied by vigorous enforcement of the 1964 Civil Rights Act.

As the 1967 session began many congressmen were reacting against the new grant programs, including the education act, and asking whether it wouldn't simply be easier to turn over a part of Federal tax receipts to the states to use as they saw fit. Since new Federal undertakings were often justified by reference to the fact that Federal income tax revenues automatically expanded as the economy grew while state and local tax systems were tied to relatively static income sources, the answer might be "revenue sharing."

The revenue sharing idea, originally popularized by economist Walter Heller in 1964, became a basic objective of the Republican party in the 90th Congress. The idea, of course, posed a direct threat to the agencies administering the new Great Society programs. Given the level of expenditures now demanded by the Vietnam War, it was clear that funds transferred to the states would have to be taken from existing agencies in Washington.

The assumptions behind the Heller Plan appealed to the localistic orientation of many members of Congress. Heller saw the need to strengthen state and local bureaucracies so that they could "meet the Federal bureaucracy on reasonably even terms." Otherwise, he feared arid centralism.

The tendency for Federal grant programs, Heller argued, was to aid specialized objectives, thus creating a "web of particularism, complexity, and Federal direction." [16] Many members of the House were sympathetic to Heller's proposal to combine existing categorical programs into broader grants, leaving more discretion to state and local authorities.[17] This idea was used by House Republicans in a major attempt to end Federal influence in the new education programs.

Even liberals were dissatisfied with the older grant programs. Congressmen were disturbed by the spectacle of confused and angry local officials loaded down with large catalogs of complicated and overlapping programs, each operating out of a different regional office. HEW Secretary Gardner summarized the problem:

> In almost every domestic program we are encountering crises of organization. Coordination among Federal agencies leaves much to be desired. Communication between the various levels of government—Federal, state and local—is casual and ineffective.[18]

At well-publicized hearings on the urban crisis, city leaders repeatedly attacked the cumbersome Federal machinery.

As the 90th Congress assembled, many members brought with them bills designed to alter the grant system. The proposed attack on Federal power had broad public support. A Gallup Poll found that seven of every 10 Americans were in favor of simply transferring 3 per cent of income tax revenue to the states where, they felt, it would be spent better. Across the nation the fear of "big government" remained a very serious public concern.[19] GOP leaders promptly called for enactment of a revenue sharing program. They proposed that the attempt to exert Federal leverage at certain crucial points in the educational system be transformed into a program of unrestricted educational grants to the states. Republican leaders promised that these steps would "restore vital State and local initiative and reinvigorate our federal system." [20] The Administration found itself on the defensive, attacked even by Democratic governors who felt that their offices were being ignored. A number of governors were particularly disturbed about the school desegregation guidelines, an issue that was to recur constantly as congressional action proceeded.

[16] Walter W. Heller, *New Dimensions of Political Economy* (New York: W.W. Norton and Co., 1967), pp. 123–24, 142.

[17] *Ibid.*, pp. 142–44.   [18] *Washington Post*, January 18, 1967.

[19] House Republican Policy Committee, "Strengthening the Federal System—The Case for Revenue Sharing," January 15, 1967.

[20] *Congressional Record*, 90th Cong., 1st Sess., 1967, CXIII (January 30, 1967), H774. All future references to the *Congressional Record* in this chapter refer to Vol. CXIII, covering the first session of the 90th Congress, except when noted. All refer to the daily edition.

President Johnson's 1967 State of the Union address revealed his reading of the congressional climate. The speech devoted a good deal of attention to problems of Federal-state cooperation and buried a passing reference to civil rights deep in the text.[21] The new Congress, which began with House expulsion of the most powerful Negro congressman, Adam Clayton Powell, found the Administration forces abandoning the role of innovator and concentrating energy on the attempt to preserve Federal authority built into programs adopted by the last Congress. High Administration officials were assigned to the task of improving relationships with state and local executives, and meetings were organized across the country to encourage the exchange of ideas.[22] Already the hard-won Federal leverage over backward local institutions was seriously endangered.

Attack on the Elementary and Secondary Education Act

The congressional struggle over Federal programs rapidly came to a focus in the area where the ideology of localism was strongest and the break with tradition the most recent—in the field of education. The historic 1965 Elementary and Secondary Education Act was up for renewal, and the program had been received with distinct reservations from many powers within the education profession. Groups including the National Education Association and the PTA called for weakening Federal controls, while an advisory commission criticized the "piecemeal" and "fragmented" character of many of the programs funded.[23] Rushed into operation, the new program had little of substance to show for its first year's operation. Even before its administrative arrangements were sorted out, however, the very existence of the program was to be imperiled.

President Johnson attempted to disarm critics in his education message. He described the program as "a new alliance with America's States and local communities" in which the Office of Education remained the "junior partner." [24] The message contained a number of minor changes designed to lessen state and local opposition.

Rhetoric was not enough. A study for the GOP leadership concluded that the federal system and the Constitution itself were endangered by the specter of "an omnipotent national government." The array of Federal programs with "minute conditions and close supervision" was destroying local authority.[25] The solution proposed was to combine all

---

[21] *Chicago Sun-Times*, January 11, 1967.   [22] *Washington Post*, January 18, 1967.
[23] *Ibid.*, January 19, 1967; *ibid.*, January 17, 1967.
[24] *Congressional Record*, February 28, 1967, p. S2678.
[25] *Ibid.*, April 10, 1967, p. H3835.

education programs into a single "block grant" to be used as state and local school officials decided.

The Republicans seized the initiative in an area where the public, political leaders, and the professionals all agreed that local authority should prevail. The party's remedy was Representative Quie's amendment to the pending education bill, which provided for block grants and for an end to the National Teachers Corps. Extensive Republican and southern support very rapidly crystallized for the amendment. Although Quie insisted that the change would have absolutely no impact on civil rights enforcement, the measure appeared to southerners as both a state's rights issue and a way to retaliate against the Office of Education. The conservative coalition was reappearing in the House, and, as the battle began, it was clear that a majority would support the dismantling of the education program. The Democratic leadership delayed the vote.[26]

Facing this dilemma, leaders of Administration forces adopted a two-pronged strategy of neutralizing as far as possible the race issue and activating resistance to change on the part of those with a vested interest in the formula embodied in the existing program. Civil rights complaints were deflected by an administrative reshuffle ending the authority of the controversial Commissioner of Education, Harold Howe, over civil rights enforcement. At the same time tacit approval was given to the less damaging of the proposed House amendments limiting civil rights enforcement. Even as the opposition was being divided, the Administration worked hard to change the focus of debate from the issue of local control to the practical question of which groups in the population would be hurt and who would gain if the Republican alternative were substituted for the 1965 law. In this effort Democrats were able to draw on the advantages of those defending a known status quo against fundamental change.

Administration spokesmen warned the big cities and the South that they would lose money if funds were no longer distributed on the basis of the number of poor children within a given district. The fear that parochial schools would not receive existing benefits if state authorities controlled the funds activated a powerful Catholic lobby. Commissioner Howe played on the worry of urban schoolmen that traditionalistic state superintendents would not respond to city school problems.[27] The GOP proposal, said a Democratic congressman, "is based on an old Republican operational philosophy: the people be damned, especially those in need. . . ."[28] President Johnson entered the battle directly, warning

[26] *Washington Post*, April 23, 1967.
[27] *Congressional Record*, April 24, 1967, p. H4675; *Washington Post*, April 25, 1967.
[28] *Congressional Record*, April 26, 1967, pp. H4675, 4712.

against reactivating the "feuds" that had prevented enactment of a broad aid-to-education bill for almost two decades.

> They have stirred up the suspicions of the poor states toward the wealthy states. They are reviving ancient and bitter feuds between church and public school leaders.
> They have aroused the fears of the big city school superintendents. . . .[29]

While this tactic did produce a series of statements attacking the GOP proposal and did change the minds of some congressmen, it was not enough. The passage of the amendment sponsored by Representative Quie had become a major party issue for the Republicans. The votes of southern Democrats would decide the issue. Something had to be done to make it politically possible for southerners to vote down an amendment that not only punished the Office of Education for its interfering ways but also promised "states' rights."

The Tranfer of Civil Rights Enforcement

Part of the price for southern votes to renew the Elementary and Secondary Education Act was paid when Secretary Gardner took civil rights enforcement authority away from the Office of Education. Embattled Commissioner Howe had been in an increasingly untenable position. He was far better known for what he had said about civil rights than for his leadership in education. It was almost impossible for him to effectively argue that the Office of Education respected the preeminence of local authority while leading a showdown battle with local politicians over desegregation. Southern moderates opposed granting discretionary authority to the hated Commissioner as long as he was enforcing the guidelines. Federal education officials, said one southern congressman, had taken to issuing "their orders to local school officials and boards much like the reading or posting of a proclamation in the days before a democratic government with checks and balances was even envisioned." [30]

Obviously the hope for the bill would improve dramatically if the race issue could be defused. Given the President's commitment to hold firm on policy, the opportunities for compromises were limited. Fortunately, much of the southern criticism had focused not on issues but on the personal beliefs and administrative leadership of Commissioner Howe. While the Commissioner could not be fired without destroying the morale of the enforcement program, it was possible to shift responsibility for civil rights compliance within HEW.

After consultation with the White House, Secretary Gardner called

---

[29] *Ibid.*, April 27, 1967, p. A2073.   [30] *Congressional Record*, April 3, 1967, p. S4441.

together a few selected reporters to announce a major reorganization of civil rights activities. A new centralized staff in the Secretary's office was to take over the compliance responsibility from HEW's constituent agencies. Shortly before the announcement, Assistant Commissioner Seeley resigned.[31] The two Office of Education men most identified with civil rights were removed from the chain of command.

Although the reorganization was officially described as nothing more than routine compliance with a long-ignored directive of a House Appropriations subcommittee, its impact on the fate of the pending bill was obvious. Gardner told the press that the powerful chairman of the subcommittee controlling the HEW budget had demanded rapid action.[32]

On the surface, the change seemed to be by mutual consent. Things would return to normal and the Commissioner of Education would spend his time on more traditional school problems. His Office would resume the role of respectful junior partner in the national educational enterprise. In fact, however, the reorganization was a basic alteration in HEW enforcement strategy and one that Commissioner Howe believed wrong. Howe would have preferred to have delayed the change until after the beginning of the next school year, permitting him to supervise another critical summer period of negotiations.[33] Secretary Gardner had earlier refused to centralize enforcement activities in spite of congressional pressure because of a conviction that the program was strengthened by the influence of the professionals in the operating agencies. Some HEW leaders had also subscribed to the theory that the civil rights effort was less vulnerable scattered about the agency than would be a centralized effort easily abolished by a "single bullet" from an angry Congress. Only three weeks before the reorganization was announced, the department had testified against such a change in House appropriations hearings.[34] The transfer was far more important than Secretary Gardner suggested. Congressional pressure had forced the federal education agency to relinquish its responsibility for equal opportunity in southern schools.

The reorganization, together with several other moves, won on needed southern votes to defeat the GOP attack on the school program. After Secretary Gardner met with Lester Maddox, Georgia's segregationist governor, reports began to come out of Atlanta that Gardner had prom-

31 *Washington Post*, May 1, 1967.
32 Secretary Gardner Statement, May 12, 1967 (Mimeographed.)
33 Interview with Harold Howe, II, September 20, 1968.
34 U.S., House, Committee on Appropriations, Subcommittee on Departments of Labor and Health, Education, and Welfare and Related Agencies, *Hearings, Departments of Labor and Health, Education and Welfare Appropriations for 1968*, 90th Cong., 1st Sess., 1967, pp. 1283–88.

ised changes.[35] House Democratic leaders now revealed that they were ready to accept the Fountain amendment limiting the time HEW could defer Federal funds without a formal hearing.[36] These concessions produced a majority for the education bill. After reorganization was announced, action was quickly scheduled on the long-postponed bill.

Reorganization, in the words of Gardner's top civil rights advisor, "gave the southern congressmen a victory—Howe was removed—and that took all the southern congressmen off the political hooks." The Secretary's asssistant, Peter Libassi, had earlier convinced Gardner to oppose the reorganization as "a concession which would only be interpreted as the Administration backing down." Finally, however, it had become "very clear that there was a convergence of political problems on the Hill which, in effect, forced the department to consolidate . . . because the pressure was too great."[37]

As the floor debate on the school bill began, the race question put both parties in uncomfortable positions. While all leaders proclaimed that the bill had nothing to do with civil rights, each side clearly wanted support from southern members concerned with little else. For a time, GOP members on the HEW appropriations subcommittee were tempted to outbid the Democratic concessions by joining southern members in writing into the department's money bill a provision forbidding HEW to require anything more than freedom of choice. GOP House leaders finally decided, however, that such an action might damage the party's major effort to develop an image of constructive action to help win a majority in the next Congress.[38] At the same time, rumors of further Administration concessions were swirling around Washington. Vice-President Humphrey found it necessary to tell a group of educators that it was "absolutely clear that the Administration is not minimizing its commitment to complete and equal education for all."[39] The very day Humphrey made his pledge, a Louisiana Congressman told a meeting of southern Democrats that the House Democratic leadership had accepted nine out of 10 southern-supported changes in guidelines enforcement.[40]

The lengthy floor debate on civil rights was a study in confusion. Controversy revolved around a series of amendments proposed by Congresswoman Edith Green of Oregon. As debate began, the conservative coalition was solidly behind her proposals that all HEW guidelines be

[35] *Washington Star*, May 11, 1967; *Baltimore Sun*, May 12, 1967; *Washington Post*, May 14, 1967.
[36] *New York Times*, May 12, 1967.   [37] Libassi Interview, July 25, 1968.
[38] *New York Times*, May 14, 1967, and May 22, 1967; Congressional Record, May 11, 1967, p. H5345; May 18, 1967, p. H5779.
[39] *Washington Post*, May 17, 1967.   [40] *Ibid.*

specifically based on statutory language and that they be applied equally to all 50 states. The amendments were believed to severely limit administrative discretion under the Civil Rights Act and to force HEW to end demands for positive local action against segregation in the South unless it was prepared to make the same kind of demand in the infinitely less favorable conditions of the North. The unpredictable Oregon Congresswoman, however, confounded everyone by readily accepting a change in the language of one provision to permit HEW to cite court decisions to justify administrative requirements; then she told the House that the "50 state" amendment was not intended to hamstring enforcement in the South but to provide a clear congressional mandate for accelerating northern desegregation. Citing the HEW backdown in Chicago, Mrs. Green promised "progress in eliminating discrimination now occurring in States where the Office of Education says the guidelines do not apply." [41] In the end, even the leading black spokesman, Representative John Conyers, Jr., of Detroit, supported the change. It would, he said, "enable us to go forward throughout all the States, North and South, to end segregation in education in whatever invidious form it may be encountered." [42] It was one of those rare occasions where votes were really changed in hastily called caucuses on the floor of the House. "I do not know," said a tired and troubled Republican leader, "who installed the turntable on the floor of the House, but it has certainly been spinning around here today." [43]

The civil rights program was the beneficiary of parliamentary confusion and of the erratic performance of the gentlewoman from Oregon. The debate was a classic demonstration of the difficulty of settling a complicated, emotional, and little understood issue on the House floor. The Green amendments were adopted with very few objections. Southerners hoped that the "illegal" provisions of the guidelines would now be outlawed. Some liberals believed that the new language actually enlarged Federal responsibility. Many members must simply have been uncertain. At any rate, the South could claim a victory and the education bill was saved. Later HEW could find ample latitude in the language written into the law.

When the vote on the Republican proposal to restructure the education program finally came, the change was easily defeated by a 29-vote margin.[44] With the race question settled, at least for the moment, the Democratic factions closed ranks. Although later amendments did move toward decentralization of some portions of the program, the Administration emerged from the House with a stronger school bill and less real

[41] *Congressional Record*, May 23, 1967, p. H5939; *ibid.*, p. H5941.
[42] *Ibid.*, p. H5951.   [43] *Ibid.*, p. H5953.   [44] *Ibid.*, May 24, 1967, p. H6069.

damage to civil rights authority than would have seemed possible a few weeks earlier.

The brief surge of reform sparked by the civil rights movement and fed by the Goldwater fiasco was now ebbing. The traditional issues of local control of the schools and Federal nonintervention in local race relations were again assuming their normal importance in the struggle to put together a congressional majority. Although the education bill survived, it bore the imprint of the new majority. Changes augmented the authority of state departments of education while cutting back the influence of the Office of Education over some types of grants. During the congressional maneuvers, the Office was stripped of responsibility for school desegregation and lost control of the largest program of educational experimentation. Congress clearly desired to return to the kind of Federal-state relationship prevailing before the Office of Education encounter with the civil rights movement and the 89th Congress. Localism was again central.

The survival of both the school aid program and the guidelines can perhaps be best credited to the basic bias of the congressional forum in favor of the status quo. Confronting the GOP challenge, many congressmen supported a staus quo they understood in preference to a sudden major change that might damage vital local concerns. Members had to balance predictable constituency attacks against a philosophical preference. The basic question of local control was obscured by a series of crosscutting alliances reflecting the desire of various interests to preserve the status quo expressed in the delicate compromises built into the program. The existing distribution formula favored the big cities and the poor southern states while offering some important indirect aid to parochial schools. Once the race issue was disposed of, the question of constituency interest became primary. The southern attitude was symbolized by a Mississippi newspaper attack on the GOP effort to trade a little states' rights for a formula cutting the Mississippi allocation 50 per cent. The Georgia state superintendent supported a compromise, keeping most of the urgently needed funds flowing but making some gains on the states' rights question.[45] Those with a vested interest in the existing program were convinced that marginal changes were preferable to a basic rethinking of the entire program.

The managers of the bill were able to play on fears that the whole education program might come unraveled. The civil rights amendments were scheduled first to neutralize the race issue. An amendment was adopted raising further the amount of money going to the South. The

[45] *Ibid.*, May 22, 1967, p. H5892.

sequence of the votes allowed a succession of alliances of minorities to frustrate the abstract philosophic preference of the majority. The Office of Education was saved in spite of itself.

Civil Rights in the Senate

As the Senate had traditionally turned back waves of sentiment for civil rights legislation, so it held firm against the public reaction. While many liberals elected to the House in 1964 had lost their seats in 1966, the Senate beneficiaries of the Johnson landslide didn't have to face reelection campaigns for three more years. While the 1966 Republican gains in the House were overwhelmingly conservative, five of the six new GOP senators were from the party's more progressive side, several elected with significant black support. Senate liberals were strongly represented on the education subcommittee, where a battle over the House amendments was inevitable.

Originally the hope had been to pass the education bill early in the year to permit improved local planning to use the funds. Within the Senate committee, however, the struggle over civil rights and localism dragged on until well after the beginning of the school year. Subcommittee Chairman Wayne Morse was determined to eliminate the major House civil rights amendment. The southern caucus, however, was determined to write further limitations into the bill. The stage for confrontation was set on October 10, when the subcommittee reached a tentative decision to delete from the bill the "Fountain amendment" ending Federal authority to deny funds pending the completion of the hearing process.[46] The subcommittee was responding to testimony from Secretary Gardner and civil rights spokesmen that the House amendment would seriously weaken enforcement.

The South began to threaten use of its ultimate weapon against civil rights legislation, the filibuster. The school bill had been singled out for attack at a southern caucus. Under the leadership of Senator Russell, southern members were determined to exact some limit on the fund-deferral process as their price for allowing passage of the bill. Senator Morse, however, insisted that the House amendment be eliminated.[47]

Senate maneuvers took place against a national backdrop of rising conservatism. For the first time in a decade, the November 1967 Gallup Poll revealed, most Americans were convinced that the Republican party was best able to deal with urgent problems, including civil rights.[48] A major survey by Roper Research Associates showed that 55 per cent of the

[46] Letter from Senator Wayne Morse to author, October 23, 1967.
[47] *Washington Post*, November 11, 1967.   [48] *Ibid.*, November 12, 1967.

white population felt that the Federal government was pushing integration too rapidly.[49]

When the bill reached the Senate floor on December 1, the issue had still not been resolved. As debate began Senator Morse revealed that negotiations between HEW officials, committee members, and southern spokesmen were still underway. The bill reported to the floor accepted the Green amendments but still rejected limitation of the deferral power. Morse explained that the compromise on civil rights and the extent of local control had been worked out in close consultation with the White House, including personal discussion with the President.[50] Morse told the Senate that many senators had asked him to accept further civil rights changes, but that he was adamant. In response to the southern threat to filibuster, Morse threatened to try to gain the two-thirds majority necessary to cut off debate.

> As far as I am concerned . . . I would rather go home at Christmas time without an education bill than walk out on what I think is the clear responsibility of the Senate of the United States to sustain the Civil Rights Act of 1964.[51]

Stennis of Mississippi openly threatened a filibuster:

> Let us not try to push this thing. . . . I have plenty of time. I am not in a hurry about this matter. . . . We have been in every other forum except the Senate, trying to obtain some relief, and we are not going to rush now.[52]

The managers of the bill did not have only a southern attack to cope with. Minority Leader Dirksen, always one of the last aboard the civil rights bandwagon, sensed that the tide of public opinion was moving in the other direction. He submitted an amendment prohibiting use of the Federal aid funds for programs designed by local officials to remedy racial imbalance in the schools. "Bussing pupils, students, and teachers from one school to another or from one school district to another to achieve a chromatic balance," he argued, "is not an educational function. . . ."[53]

Dirksen, however, had miscalculated the changing temper of his own party's Senate delegation. Opponents turned the ideology of localism against the Illinois Senator. Congress had no business, they argued, making decisions about local educational programs. Most significantly, the Republican leader was directly challenged by a freshman member from his own party. Michigan's Senator Griffin, narrowly elected in a normally Democratic state with a large black population, proposed to cripple the Dirksen amendment by adding:

---

[49] *Congressional Record,* November 28, 1967, p. S17271.
[50] *Ibid.,* December 4, 1967, p. S17781.   [51] *Ibid.,* p. S17782.
[52] *Ibid.,* p. S17791.   [53] *Ibid.,* p. S17827.

. . . unless such use is in accordance with a policy formally and freely made by the affected State or . . . local educational agency without the exercise of direction, supervision, or control with respect thereto by any Department, agency or officer of the United States.[54]

The vote on the Griffin proposal ended in a tie. Eventually, Minority Leader Dirksen decided to withdraw his amendment.

The lengthy Senate debate ended in a compromise. Senator Morse produced a letter from Secretary Gardner promising further restraints on the use of the deferral power. He promised that HEW would continue Federal aid payments to a defiant school district throughout the school year unless the local officials were notified at least six months before school began. Except for certain districts with particularly flagrant violations, all southern school systems would be guaranteed by each March 1 that they would continue to receive aid during the next year and a half.[55] This concession satisfied the southern caucus and saved the bill.

The policy change further diminished the administrative flexibility available to HEW. The war of nerves throughout the summer negotiating seasons that had produced important breakthroughs in the past was no longer possible, except in the case of districts warned in March. Few tactical changes were possible in a system where the department was forced to formally threaten use of its ultimate weapon a half year in advance. This was to become particularly apparent in 1968, when the new circumstances created by the President's decision not to run again and an extremely important Supreme Court decision against freedom of choice found HEW locked into an enforcement strategy developed for far less favorable conditions.

Once the compromise was settled upon, the Senate quickly approved the bill. The bill still had to go to a conference committee, but liberal seniority in both Houses on committees controlling education legislation assured a favorable hearing. The conference committee quickly met and accepted the Senate position on the race issue. Once again the House was confronted with an urgent bill lacking the desired strictures on civil rights enforcement. In the rush of the final day of the session, the conference report was easily approved. Once again skillful defensive efforts had forestalled fundamental damage to civil rights enforcement powers.

The ordeal of the 1967 education bill reflected both the resurgence of localism in American politics and the continuing political crisis created by the enforced revolution in the southern schools. Growing conservative sentiment in the country meant that urgent concern with the use of Federal power to realize the goal of equal opportunity was being replaced

[54] *Ibid.*, p. S17838.   [55] *New York Times*, December 12, 1967.

by a concern with protecting the tradition of highly decentralized power. There was little enthusiasm for the unfinished work of the second reconstruction.

The Office for Civil Rights: Reorganization and Decentralization

When civil rights enforcement responsibilities were transferred from the Office of Education at a crucial moment during maneuvers on the education bill, southern members of Congress obviously felt that the change would make a difference. The timing of the announcement and the fact that the Administration's most articulate civil rights supporter was now removed from responsibility suggested compromise. In fact, as the bill languished in Congress, desegregation progress had already slackened significantly. The administrative practices most irritating to southern schoolmen had been modified, and Federal pressure for progress beyond inadequate freedom-of-choice plans was not sufficient to maintain the rate of change established in earlier years. Finally, the willingness of HEW to accept another limitation on administrative powers to extract the education bill from the Senate suggested a continuing willingness to compromise. Obviously the new enforcement program was going to have to face a series of basic questions during its early months.

When Secretary Gardner announced the transfer, no one knew just what shape the new office would take or which staff members would remain with the program. It was clear, however, that the new organization would be expected to carry out the department's commitment to decentralization of operating authority to regional HEW offices. Thus some way would have to be found to maintain control of widely separated programs with personnel in Atlanta, Dallas, Charlottesville, Virginia, and various northern cities. It was also clear that chronic personnel shortages would continue. The earlier expedient of hiring law students in the summer to help meet the urgent need for field investigations was now ruled out. The new office was also under a congressional directive to do something about discrimination in northern cities. The new Office for Civil Rights faced the necessity of coming to terms with these problems in the months when HEW leadership was still concerned with the ultimate fate of the education program, in months when another season of urban riots was again sapping the reservoir of potential support for basic social change.

One matter of central importance about the new office was soon apparent; it would be headed by Peter Libassi, the man who had served as Gardner's Special Assistant for Civil Rights for more than a year. The job of restructuring the program and trying to find a way to implement change without stirring up a mortal political attack was handed to the 37-

year-old attorney. Libassi had spent virtually his entire career as a civil rights specialist in New York and with the Civil Rights Commission. He came to HEW recommended by the Leadership Conference on Civil Rights and with a personal pledge of complete support from Secretary Gardner. One of Libassi's functions had been to give the Secretary control over decisions such as that leading to the politically disastrous confrontation with Mayor Daley in Chicago. Libassi soon gained a reputation both as a skilled civil rights technician and a politically astute administrator. Before reorganization, he had been more closely identified with a rapid and highly successful hospital desegregation drive than with the Office of Education school effort.

The dramatic contrast in style of leadership between Seeley and Libassi would obviously affect the new organization. Seeley's deep interest in education and his immersion in the process of persuasion had been both assets and weaknesses. Confronting overwhelming initial reluctance to take any step, Seeley's staff had accomplished a great deal through manipulation of undefined threats and through endless negotiations. The psychological barriers to the first steps had been overcome, and the painful transition was underway. By 1967, however, Seeley's strategy was confronting the extraordinarily difficult problem of abolishing free choice, with nothing more to rely upon than another set of threats similar to those that had already been proven empty. Lacking Administration support for a broad program of actual fund cutoffs, the future usefulness of the Seeley approach was dubious.

Libassi was not an educator, and he was to work within the context of a distinctive civil rights office concerned with enforcement across the vast spectrum of HEW programs. Libassi had little regard for Seeley's approach and was determined to develop a controlled, orderly, and more legalistic mechanism for handling the compliance job. Libassi brought to his assignment a good relationship with the Justice and HEW legal staffs. He replaced the political clumsiness of the Office of Education with a highly developed political sensitivity and a set of excellent relationships with the White House.

Seeley's style had been one of obvious commitment. He spoke with a frankness so uncommon in higher bureaucratic echelons that it was sometimes mistaken for naiveté. While Libassi had spent more than a decade in civil rights enforcement positions and fully shared Seeley's profound commitment, he tended to carefully qualify his public statements and to remain close to the case law. One reporter concluded that Libassi believed Seeley had been "too abrasive," while Seeley "thought Libassi was too busy soothing politicians." [56]

[56] *Southern Education Report*, Vol. III (September–October, 1967), p. 4.

Libassi felt that perhaps the most serious difficulty of the enforcement program was a very poor record of congressional relations. He had learned about the inner workings of Capitol Hill in the course of representing HEW during the 1966 assault on the Office of Education and was determined to set up a congressional relations staff to ease needless misunderstandings. The enforcement staff, in Libassi's words, was "grossly inexperienced" and failed to recognize the distinction between "form and substance."

The new centralized operation was to put a far greater premium on political sensitivity. Libassi insisted on respect, courtesy, and promptness in dealings with Congress and tended to weigh much more consciously than before the political implications of given enforcement actions. Both because of his legal training and because of his political judgment, Libassi spurned the dual role of national policy spokesman and adjudicator of cases that had been filled by Commissioner Howe. This confusion of roles, he felt, had merely "added fuel to the political fire" by mixing up perceptions of policy recommendations with statements of enforcement policy. "I made very few controversial speeches, if any," he recalls, "and the style of the program changed to one of speak little and cut off the money." [57]

The change in style alienated some staff members. The more militant officials had long felt that the program had been administered with an excess of caution. The new approach seemed to be another step in the wrong direction. From Libassi's perspective, the staff "misinterpreted courteousness with congressional sellout, and anyone who could be courteous to a congressman was immediately suspect by some of the enthusiastic staff members. . . . I'm sure most of the staff considered me the . . . architect for the great HEW sellout." [58] It was an essentially defensive stance, designed to preserve a program operating in a hostile environment with little public support.

Political skill was urgently needed because the new structure would inevitably focus greatly increased pressure on the Secretary's office. Commissioner Howe no longer provided a lightning rod drawing off the thunderbolts from Capitol Hill. No longer would Seeley's confusing administrative procedures and endless negotiations leave opponents unclear about what existing policy was and where the responsibility lay.

The New Organization: Conception and Reality

During the summer of 1967 Libassi gave much thought to the design of the centralized enforcement effort. As an old regional office worker in

[57] Libassi interview, July 25, 1968.   [58] *Ibid.*

state government, he was firmly committed to decentralizing most of the staff to regional offices. This change, he was convinced, would increase staff impact on local problems, make travel less costly, and decrease the resentment against the "Washington bureaucracy." A school superintendent, he reasoned, would be far less likely to call his congressman when visiting an office in Dallas or Atlanta than on a trip to Washington.

Decentralization, however, posed clear dangers to the program. An experiment in placing one enforcement staff member in the Charlottesville regional office had produced an intolerable conflict between the regional assistant commissioner of education and the Title VI official, who insisted that his first loyalty was to the Washington program rather than the regional office. Some southerners hoped that the transfer of critical decisions to the southern field offices would dilute Federal pressure for change. HEW had to find a way to regionalize without compromising national desegregation standards.

The change eventually approved by the Secretary called for the transfer of most staff members under an arrangement attempting to protect the policy-making authority of the Office for Civil Rights. The regional directors agreed to merely provide physical facilities and administrative support services for the civil rights staff, which would be supervised from Washington. The regional Office for Civil Rights leadership was given all powers except the final decision on fund cutoffs. The regional HEW leadership was to be protected from political flak in the same manner Commissioner Howe was now protected—by denying them any authority for civil rights decisions. Since the most politically sensitive decisions could be made only in Washington and the regional offices were insulated from the process, Libassi hoped to avoid some of the dangers of decentralization.

Basic problems remained, however. Regional offices, staffed largely by southerners and located in southern towns, hardly promised a congenial environment for militant staff members, black or white. The basic justification for the existence of regional offices was the facilitation of program relationships between Washington and state and local officials, and forceful civil rights enforcement impaired these relations. While an HEW Secretary strongly committed to the Title VI effort could protect the special status of the civil rights staff, there was little long-run likelihood that regional office leaders would allow themselves to be frozen out of decisions affecting the whole climate of Federal-state cooperation in their regions.

When time for implementation came, the organizational reality proved to be far less adequate than the design, in part because of inadequate staffing. Of the new positions authorized by the House, Libassi lost 10 in a general congressional budget cut and more than 20 others as a result of a government-wide staffing ceiling imposed as an economy measure by the President. Difficulties in finding competent people who would take jobs in the regional offices led to a large number of vacancies, reducing actual staff strength below the level authorized the previous year.[59] Although the responsibilities of the program (including the mandate for a northern program) and the difficulties of administration had been greatly increased, the organization was forced to operate with a staff that had been highly inadequate even for the more limited assignment of monitoring southern school desegregation from a single central office.

The Evolution of a New Enforcement Strategy

Even before the structure of the Office for Civil Rights had coalesced, it was perfectly evident that a new enforcement strategy was urgently needed. Experience clearly revealed to many southern educators that there was very little risk in falling behind the performance standards of the guidelines. The standards had been watered down by the Justice Department, with HEW acquiescence, to the point where the violation had to be flagrant. Even then, enforcement personnel and HEW lawyers had to invest a tremendous amount of time in working up each individual case finally approved for cutoff. The need to demonstrate the credibility of Federal enforcement threats was paramount.

The immediate problem of the new office was to restore respect for Federal demands. Libassi's basic answer was to categorize all districts not desegregated, isolate certain manageable targets, and then make threats stick. His solution was to abandon any psychological threats and to "mean what you say and say exactly what you mean." Since threats no one was prepared to carry out were producing rapidly diminishing returns, the new director decided to limit cutoff threats to only those districts falling below Justice Department standards and to no more districts than his administrative machinery could actually process. This meant that fewer districts were under direct pressure. Libassi hoped that this decrease would be more than compensated for by a spreading awareness that HEW pronouncements actually meant what they said.[60]

Until 1967 virtually no use had been made of the power to terminate funds. The tendency had been to indefinitely delay Federal funds for new projects or programs where local resistance seemed completely unmoveable. Only after the 1966 Congress limited the length of time new programs could be deferred did HEW seriously face the absolute necessity of a final break with some school districts.

[59] Libassi interview, April 5, 1968.
[60] Libassi interviews, April 5, 1968, and July 25, 1968.

Fund Termination and Justice Department Influence

Libassi first came to HEW before the process of actually citing significant numbers of districts for cutoff hearings began. He told Secretary Gardner that the law would be meaningless unless the sanction was finally invoked and obtained the Secretary's full support for this action as a precondition for coming to the department. "We still," Libassi recalls, "had not conducted a single investigation of a school desegregation case." The only cases that the department had even considered involved the districts that refused to make even the pretense of submitting a desegregation plan. "The job that we had was to get the field staffs out and start getting the cases through the system." [61]

The basic question raised by this decision, of course, was which districts to begin action against. The Justice Department was to play a decisive role in answering this question. While HEW had full power to bluff as much as it wished, its use of the ultimate enforcement weapon was very carefully supervised by the Justice Department authorities. After the Chicago fiasco, President Johnson had issued an executive order vesting responsibility in the Attorney General's office. This action insured both a centralized judgment on the risks to the President involved in specific enforcement actions and policy control by an agency more inclined toward a cautious interpretation of the case law than toward independent use of administrative power. Under the executive order, the Attorney General had issued guidelines making it extremely difficult to defer funds from any northern school system and giving the Justice Department power of review over every cutoff action in any agency.

The Justice Department's Civil Rights Division, to which HEW enforcement actions had to be submitted, was charged with the responsibility of processing complaints and litigating violations of a variety of civil rights laws. Under Attorney General Kennedy, the division had given voting discrimination cases top priority, and this continued until the enactment of the 1965 Voting Rights Act. The theory was that these actions would provide a basis of black political power essential to insure protection of other rights. Only in 1965 did attention really turn toward the school question.

When the Civil Rights Act passed, the major impact on school desegregation was expected to come not under Title VI, but under the Title IV grant of power to the Attorney General to initiate lawsuits when he received complaints from black parents. Complaints came in very slowly, however, and only six suits were begun by mid-1965. In late summer of

[61] Libassi interview, July 25, 1968.

that year, the Division finally received enough manpower to begin the effort that got more than 100 cases into the courts by early 1967.[62] As the Division developed a very substantial commitment in this field, both bureaucratic self-interest and the professional preferences of the attorneys involved created an attitude that favored settlement of issues through the courts and was skeptical of the value of fund withholding.

The Division's director, Assistant Attorney General John Doar, was deeply troubled by the idea of Title VI. A man with superb civil rights credentials, earned through participation in the great Federal-state showdowns of the early 1960's, Doar's fundamental orientation was toward case-by-case litigation. He believed that any administrative enforcement actions must be based on very conservative interpretations of the case law. Yet he was in a position to exercise a veto at the decisive stage of the HEW enforcement process.

The Assistant Attorney General was deeply admired and respected by Libassi, and he used his authority to provide coordination and consistency between HEW actions and Justice's school litigation, which he saw as the primary tool in the fight against discrimination. From his perspective litigation and the guidelines were the two blades of a scissors, a scissors that was operated by the head of the Civil Rights Division. In an early use of his authority, Doar had delayed any cutoff actions until he received an overall analysis of the number of cases that would be necessary.[63]

Doar developed an effective working relationship with Libassi, and the two attorneys came to agree on an enforcement strategy. HEW accepted the Justice argument that "the first cases that come through you have to win, you have to win clean, you have to win big." [64] Given this fundamental assumption, the safest approach was to begin with the very worst cases and to make a determined effort to avoid any issues that were not already settled in the case law. This meant that, in effect, HEW could not cut off money simply because a school district failed to meet the minimum rates of progress specified in the guidelines. The strategy demanded every possible effort to avoid the "pure issue" of whether a fairly run free-choice plan was all that the Constitution demanded. Thus for every case in which HEW staff members wished to deny funds because free choice was not working, they would have to prove not merely that the black students were still overwhelmingly segregated but also that there was something wrong with the local free-choice plan. Either they would have to find evidence that the school administrators had neglected some of the prescribed steps or they would have to show that a pattern of local harassment or intimidation made any real freedom of choice impos-

[62] Interview with St. John Barrett, April 11, 1967.
[63] Doar interview, August 10, 1967.   [64] Libassi interview, July 25, 1968.

sible. Before Justice would approve a hearing citation, HEW was required to prepare a detailed summary of the total racial pattern of the school system involved.

This approach was reasonable enough until the guidelines had been tested in the courts and until there was some definite evidence that an unsuccessful free-choice plan would be considered unconstitutional. Even after HEW standards were sweepingly upheld in the courts, however, this time-consuming approach continued. Even after the important decision of the Fifth Circuit Court of Appeals against free-choice plans that failed to produce integration, HEW was not permitted to deny funds on that ground in itself. When confronted by the objection that he was forcing a return to the very case-by-case proceedings Title VI was designed to replace, Mr. Doar replied simply: "Due process requires no less." [65]

Doar's lawyerly concern for due process was shared by Libassi. He felt that the early staff work within HEW had not been adequate to justify cutoff actions:

> When you are adjudicating the rights of individual school districts with respect to their qualifications for Federal funds there really isn't any blanket way. . . . You have to adjudicate everything on a case-by-case basis. . . . I'd be very worried about any government agency that didn't have to measure up to the standards which our program ultimately began to measure up to, because I worry just as much about totalitarian government for so-called good causes as for bad causes.[66]

Thus neither of the men charged with the basic decisions in administering the law really believed that it was proper to deny Federal funds merely because a district violated the guidelines. Failure to meet the minimum standards of the HEW regulations was nothing more than an indication that further investigation of local conditions was in order.

The Justice Department demands reflected several important facts. In the first place the Administration was feeling no public pressure to speed civil rights progress. With no external imperative for action like that generated by the Selma crisis in 1965, the normal caution of Justice administrators tended to be decisive. The excellent civil rights attorneys on the Civil Rights Division staff tended to judge the adequacy of HEW preparation by the exacting legal standards they applied to their own work in the courts. All other things being equal, Justice didn't want to take the least risk of losing a case. Thus the strategy was to begin with the very worst cases and gradually work up the list.

The resulting strategy was better designed to protect the courtroom records of Federal attorneys than to maximize school integration. Cases

[65] Doar interview, August 10, 1967.   [66] Libassi interview, July 25, 1968.

were concentrated in the Deep South, where the legal issues were most clearly drawn but the prospects for enforcing local change least favorable. The districts that had made significant progress and needed a push to move toward total desegregation were ignored. The practical result was that it soon became obvious to many southern schoolmen that they were safe if they ignored the guidelines and simply stayed a few jumps ahead of the worst districts still receiving funds. Thus the caution and professional standards of Justice's Civil Rights Division magnified the difficulties confronted by the Office for Civil Rights.

Crystallization of Priorities

The limitations of staff and policy under which the Office for Civil Rights labored forced Libassi to make a series of hard decisions about how to use his limited resources. Both in 1967 and 1968 Libassi calculated the administrative capacity of his existing staff to carry out field reviews and to do the necessary background work to meet Justice Department standards for a hearing citation. Then he worked out with Doar the total number of enforcement actions planned. Given his determination not to make idle threats, Libassi then faced the problem of deciding how to use the 350 reviews his office was capable of conducting in 1967 to make maximum impact on more than 1000 districts still desegregating under the guidelines.

A series of basic priorities began to emerge in written directives by the midsummer of 1967. By this time it was finally becoming apparent that little was gained by concentrating all energies on the very worst violators. A first decision was to simply end enforcement efforts in the black-belt districts with a majority of Negro students. Terminations in many such districts led to a judgment that the slim chance that the localities would integrate without law suits was not worth the certainty that black students in very weak school systems would be further damaged.[67]

Of the remaining districts, priority was to be given to those that had completely defied the faculty integration requirements or in which less than one black student in 20 was in an integrated school. Thus, while passing up the most hopeless cases, emphasis was still placed on the cases where the legal situation was clearest and judicial defense most easily formulated. Beyond this point, attention was to be turned to closing up small Negro schools in districts with few black students and to moving large school systems with fewer than 30 per cent black students up to 10 per cent integration.[68] Thus both the worst centers of unreconstructed

[67] Libassi interview, April 5, 1968; Office for Civil Rights, "Procedures for Review of Elementary and Secondary School Desegregation Plans," July, 1967, p. ii–3.
[68] *Ibid.*, pp. iii–3–iii–4.

racism and all the districts where freedom of choice had worked reasonable well were automatically excluded from further pressure in 1967.

The 1967 guidelines had demanded much more, in theory, than the new Office for Civil Rights standards, but the Office of Education had actually enforced much less. A study revealed that most of the districts being cited by the Office of Education in the spring of 1967 had less than 1 per cent integration and that very few districts with more than 3 per cent were called to hearings.[69] Thus Libassi proposed to triple the real minimum. The fact remained, however, that by in effect creating a maximum demand for 10 per cent integration and eliminating bluffs, Libassi was eliminating much of the incentive for further progress in school systems that already had made a good beginning. In many parts of the Middle South these standards were simply irrelevant, and a chance was lost to build momentum toward complete desegregation.

The limitations on the categories selected for review were related to continuing legal doubts in the Justice Department. In spite of a historic decision in favor of unified nonracial school systems by the Fifth Circuit Court of Appeals in early 1967, John Doar still felt that freedom of choice might be all the Constitution demanded. Doar was perfectly willing to bring lawsuits to explore the free-choice question further in the courts, but he felt that it was improper for HEW administrative standards to directly attack this plan. In a case in which a fairly operated free-choice plan had brought as many as one-tenth of the black children into white schools, Doar's personal judgment was that fund withholding was no longer appropriate.

One important element limiting administrative discretion was the ambiguous standing of the guidelines under the Civil Rights Act. Title VI had specified that the nondiscrimination requirement be implemented by presidentially approved regulations. Although the initial HEW regulation met this standard and the President had privately approved the guidelines, the fact that he had not formally issued them as regulations opened the way for a possible legal attack. The courts, Doar felt, would be far less willing to sustain administrative discretion moving beyond the case law in departmental guidelines than if the President had drawn on his authority under the law. Doar had not presented this issue to the White House, however, because he believed that leading the courts was not the proper function of administrative rule-making in the HEW compliance program.

The carefully designed new strategy failed to break the back of southern resistance. In fact large numbers of districts adamantly refused to move a single step beyond free choice although the system was obviously

[69] Commission on Civil Rights, *Southern School Desegregation, 1966–67* (Washington: Government Printing Office, 1967), p. 45.

failing to produce further progress. In a disturbing number of cases, especially in majority Negro districts, school systems actually began to regress toward total segregation. While Libassi did accomplish the difficult feat of beginning cutoff proceedings against a large number of districts with some integration, the effort was insufficient to sustain the momentum of change in the face of stronger southern resistance. The geometric increases in integration of the past two years gave way to a much slower rate of change. While southern school integration had tripled the first year and doubled the second, the fall of 1967 saw a far slower rate of change. More than 80 per cent of southern black students remained in segregated schools. It seemed as if the steam was going out of the enforcement program.

Creation of a Deadline: The 1968 Guidelines

Reports in the fall of 1967 documented the disappointing rate of progress. It was clear that a new approach was essential if local fixation on freedom of choice was to be broken. The rate of progress percentage figures in the guidelines had provided some leverage for further change, particularly in 1966. In effect, the requirement had created a vested interest on the part of local schoolmen in making free choice work. School officials in some areas found ways to let the community know that transferring students would be welcome in the white schools. In most areas, however, the percentage requirements had not been sufficient to induce large numbers of districts to move toward a unified school system. A further problem was related to the fact that the guidelines figures ended at a 20 per cent level of integration. If a school district had one-fifth of its black students in integrated schools, nothing more was required.

A major new departure in enforcement policy was announced in a speech by Office for Civil Rights Director Libassi to the Education Writers Association on October 10, 1967. While attempting to paint a favorable picture of the accomplishments of the past year, he clearly indicated that HEW was moving away from concern with numerical rates of progress toward abolition of separate schools. In most areas, he said, free choice had outlived its usefulness.

Where free choice had failed, Libassi said, school districts would now have to submit "comprehensive plans for the elimination of the dual system," plans to be fully implemented by September 1969. In justifying this new requirement, he quoted from the historic March decision of the Fifth Circuit Court of Appeals: "Boards and officials adminstering public schools in this circuit have the affirmative duty under the Fourteenth amendment to bring about an integrated, unitary school system in which there are no Negro schools and no white schools—just schools." Just the day before the Libassi speech the Supreme Court had let the decision stand by refusing to consider an appeal.[70] Pressure was to be especially focused on the largest school districts enrolling most of the black students.

After announcing this departure, Libassi went on to reveal a tentative beginning in the effort demanded by Congress to extend HEW surveillance to school districts across the nation. While disclaiming any intention to act against de facto segregation, Libassi said that HEW would collect racial distribution statistics from all northern districts with more than 3000 students and examine them for patterns suggesting gerrymandering, faculty segregation, or inequalities between black and white schools.[71] In the months to come a carefully managed HEW effort was to collect data and conduct a number of preliminary field investigations and a handful of serious studies. Learning from the Chicago fiasco, the Office for Civil Rights concentrated on smaller, less powerful communities. Although strong warning letters were sent to Wichita, Kansas, and to a small town in Pennsylvania, there was no plan to cut off funds anywhere, at least before the presidential election.[72] HEW was creating the outlines of an enforcement program that might have a substantial impact on northern school segregation, but this possibility would be realized only if the program received the support of the new President.

The Libassi statement was reflected in the new guidelines issued in March 1968. The document clearly demanded local action:

> A school system which has maintained a system of separate school facilities for students based on their race . . . has the affirmative duty under law to take prompt and effective action to eliminate such a dual school structure and bring about an integrated unitary school system. Compliance with the law requires integration of faculties, facilities and activities, as well as students, so that there are no Negro . . . schools and no white schools—just schools.[73]

The document directed school officials to submit plans to complete desegregation by the fall of 1969. The words of the guidelines were unambiguous, and the new policy perspective turned the enforcement program away from a political dead end. The task of transforming the new standards into real local changes, however, still remained.

[70] Peter Libassi, "Outline of Developments in School Desegregation," a speech delivered to the Education Writers Association, October 10, 1967, pp. 3–4.
[71] *Ibid.*, p. 7.   [72] Interview with Mrs. Ruby Martin, September 23, 1968.
[73] Office for Civil Rights, "Policies on Elementary and Secondary School Compliance with Title VI of the Civil Rights Act of 1964," March, 1968, Subpart B, section 11.

Aid from the Courts

The policy shift announced by the Office for Civil Rights was possible only because of a series of helpful court decisions, and it was to be powerfully underwritten by an important Supreme Court pronouncement in May 1968. Both because of the political vulnerability of the enforcement program and because of the official interpretation of the intent of Congress in drafting Title VI, enforcement standards had always been very largely derived from current constitutional doctrine in the circuit courts and the Supreme Court. Since the HEW program had very little public or political strength, it was less able than ever to implement a policy asking for anything more than the courts were demanding as the minimum consonant with the Constitution. Thus the very reliance on case law that had slowed down the enforcement battle in the early period when public support still existed now provided a way to inject some new momentum into the lagging effort.

The great progress made possible by enforcement of the Civil Rights Act had pushed a new range of constitutional questions to the top of the judicial agenda, and now the courts were handing down their decisions. Earlier, Federal courts had accepted free choice as a satisfactory desegregation plan. Now, however, both the day-to-day, district-by-district effort to begin integration and much of the intense political pressure against change had been removed from the judicial system as a result of HEW action, and the courts were freed to rethink the basic legal issues. This reassessment was aided by the vast and organized body of administrative experience accumulated by the Title VI program. Freedom of choice was no longer a philosophic approach to fulfilling constitutional demands; it was a plan that had been tried in many hundreds of school districts under exacting conditions and had not succeeded. Now, political vulnerability, public disinterest, and executive caution prevented HEW initiatives; the slower but more insulated processes of the courts began to produce the needed policy redefinitions.

The legal development that received its first powerful expression in the March 1967 decision of the Fifth Circuit Court of Appeals reached a climax in the decision of the Supreme Court in the case of *Green v. County School Board of New Kent County*. In the late fall of 1967, the Supreme Court had accepted cases challenging the freedom-of-choice system from Arkansas, Virginia, and Tennessee; the following May it handed down its decision on this issue, which had now become central to the desegregation struggle. Considering the case of a Southside Virginia school district with a majority of black students, which had achieved token integration under a freedom-of-choice plan, the Court held that the pattern of separate white and black schools was "precisely the pattern of segregation" that the 1954 decision held unconstitutional.[74]

Thirteen years after the Supreme Court decision implementing the 1954 order, an "initial break" in a pattern of separate schools no longer met minimum standards of compliance with the Constitution. The "first step" had been "obtaining for those Negro children courageous enough to break with tradition a place in the 'white' schools," but the Court had always envisaged the final goal of "a system of public education freed of racial discrimination." The Constitution, the Court held, requires local authorities "to take whatever steps might be necessary to convert to a unitary system in which racial discrimination would be eliminated root and branch." While not asserting that free choice was unconstitutional in all possible cases, the Court dealt a fatal blow to the legal justification for the approach, holding that if other approaches promise "speedier and more effective conversion to a unitary, nonracial school system, 'freedom of choice' must be held unacceptable." [75]

At a time when the momentum of school desegregation was fading and the tide of public opinion was turning against racial reconciliation, the Supreme Court decision strengthened the enforcement program. Inevitably, serious efforts to make the 1968 guidelines stick would generate local claims that HEW was exceeding its congressional mandate. The Supreme Court decision made clear the fact that the Office for Civil Rights was asking nothing more than the minimum demanded by the constitutional guarantee of "equal protection of the laws." The decision did not, of course, end the policy debate, but it did close off most local hopes for relief from HEW demands through the courts. The decision helped keep alive the possibility that the 1954 Supreme Court decision would indeed be the law of the land in the vast majority of southern school districts in September 1969.

The Conservative Tide: Congress and the Presidency

In a democracy the ultimate fate of a movement for fundamental social change rests with the people and their representatives. In a political system where a great deal of discretion and political power is focused at the local level, the condition of forcing unwanted local change is the existence of powerful national support. In a society that cherishes local self-government, the condition of extending national power is a continuing public perception that the issue involved is so unique or so central that a departure from tradition is justified. These conditions existed in 1964. By

---

[74] *Green v. County School Board of New Kent County* (1968), slip opinion, p. 3.
[75] *Ibid.*, pp. 5, 7, 10–11.

1968, as congressional and presidential elections approached, they seemed to be crumbling.

In 1964 the great majority of Americans believed that there was a need for racial progress and supported the use of national authority in the fight against discrimination. This sentiment faded by late 1966, and with it, much of the civil rights support in the House of Representatives. The effort to enforce the laws still enjoyed the strong support of the President and the courts. The President, however, had decided to leave office at the end of the year, and the courts, particularly the Supreme Court, were at a low point in national esteem.

By early 1968 it was evident that President Johnson had spent much of his political capital in Vietnam and that he was trying to lead a nation in which the primary racial question was not equal rights but "law and order," a phrase that crystallized the white fears of ghetto riots and expressed a widespread desire for more repressive police tactics. The racist candidacy of Alabama's George Wallace, constantly hammering on the need to end HEW control of local schools, already suggested the possibility of a segregationist upheaval in southern politics.

Although the fate of the civil rights program now rested far more on the choice of the electorate than on actions within the bureaucracies, HEW quietly proceeded in its effort to collect pledges to totally desegregate local school systems by the fall of 1969. Obviously, promises enforceable only a year after the presidential election would be meaningless should the election put in office a President who would repudiate the HEW standards.

The influence the Office for Civil Rights could exercise was further limited. Well before the election year began, Libassi had circulated through the Administration a memo estimating that only 300 districts would be cited for noncompliance and that about 150 would lose funds during this politically sensitive year. This commitment was made on the basis of an assumption that the President would run again. Libassi saw the enforcement program continuing under a Democratic administration and largely completing its southern assignment by 1972.[76] Following this strategy, Libassi rejected his staff's recommendation that 450 districts be warned that they were risking a fund cutoff.[77] Since the HEW agreement with the southern caucus of the Senate limited any effective enforcement activity for the following school year to those districts receiving warning letters by March 1, the program was locked into a narrow and inflexible position by the time of President Johnson's announcement in which he withdrew his name from the presidential contest. There was

[76] Libassi interviews, April 5, 1968, and July 25, 1968.
[77] Libassi interview, April 5, 1968.

no way to capitalize on the President's new insulation from politics, on the surge of public concern following the assassination of Martin Luther King, Jr., or on the Supreme Court decision against freedom-of-choice desegregation plans. Three-fourths of the districts operating under the guidelines had been guaranteed immunity from any enforcement until after the election. The hard issues had been postponed. The final outcome would be determined by a new President and a new Congress, elected by a new coalition and responding to whatever racial climate existed as he assumed power. In this area, at least, President Johnson's proud record in civil rights was to end in a bureaucratic whimper.

As the campaign unfolded, prospects for completion of the desegregation of southern schools became increasingly bleak. From the outset of his highly visible campaign, third-party candidate George Wallace made HEW enforcement of the school guidelines an absolutely central issue, continually raising it in the standard speech he gave to audiences in all parts of the country. As the campaign warmed up and the Republicans became increasingly concerned by Wallace inroads on the middle South and border states that the GOP ticket hoped to carry, Richard Nixon endorsed the freedom-of-choice desegregation plan as all that the law demanded and indicated his general skepticism about the fund-with-holding approach.

The public drift toward blatant racism was symbolized by the emergence of Wallace as a presidential candidate with sufficient political strength to accomplish the remarkable feat of qualifying his third-party ticket on state ballots across the country. This was the man who had first attracted national notice with the peroration of his Alabama inaugural address: "I say segregation now, segregation tomorrow, segregation forever!" [78] In 1963 Governor Wallace symbolized the resistance of the old South when he stood in the door to bar the entrance of black students at the University of Alabama and attempted to use the state's national guard to prevent integration of primary and high schools.[79] After the passage of the 1964 Civil Rights Act, Wallace again led the resistance. Both Wallace and his state school superintendent pressured local school systems to retract pledges of compliance they made to HEW, threatening to deny state aid and offering special state assistance to continue segregation.[80] The state legislature accepted Wallace programs designed to encourage the creation of private schools, guaranteeing free choice, and requiring "all students, acting through their parent or guardian . . . to exercise a choice . . . of the race of the teacher desired." [81] After a Federal court order directing prompt integration of all Alabama school districts the

[78] Lewis, pp. 166–67.   [79] Ibid., pp. 170–71.
[80] *Washington Post*, December 1, 1966.   [81] *Ibid.*, April 4, 1967.

Wallace administration asked the legislature for complete control of all Alabama schools and for an increase in state troopers.

> I am serving notice that whatever power I possess under the Constitution of Alabama as Governor of Alabama shall be used to prevent the destruction of our public school system, and they better understand what the people of Alabama mean.[82]

As a presidential candidate, George Wallace carried the issue of Federal nondiscrimination guidelines into all corners of the country. "We are not going to better race relations," he said, "so long as these theoreticians and bureaucrats—these pseudo-intellectuals—attempt to tell the people of every State from New York to Alabama about bussing their children to school; who can teach their children and who can't; and what books they can read." [83] He promised to eliminate the HEW employees "hired to oversee everything in the country involving schools and so forth" and to throw the briefcases of the Federal guideline writers into the Potomac.[84] Thus the issue of the revolution in southern education was being exploited with great skill. Federal enforcement activities were distorted beyond recognition by a politician described by one careful observer as "the complete democratic demagogue," a man who could say:

> Let 'em call me a racist. It don't make any difference. Whole heap of folks in this country feel the same way I do. Race is what's gonna win this thing for me.[85]

While many politicians initially discounted support for Wallace in public opinion polls as a gesture of protest that would fade as the election approached, the Alabama segregationist continued to gain strength. In the South the growth of Wallace support was particularly striking. In April, 1968, the Gallup Poll showed him receiving 26 per cent of the southern vote; by June this figure had climbed to 29 per cent and he was far ahead of the major party candidates in five Deep South states. In late summer, polls appeared that showed him leading the GOP and Democratic candidates across the entire southern region. Of his major issues, the one with most support from the general public was his commitment to "leave race relations to the states." Only four years after passage of the 1964 Civil Rights Act, almost half of the public was ready to support this long step backward.[86] Clearly the Alabamian was speaking for a large fol-

82 *Ibid.*, March 13, 1967.

83 John J. Synon, ed., *George Wallace, Profile of a Presidential Candidate* (Kilmarnock, Virginia: Manuscripts, Inc., 1968), p. 83.

84 *U.S. News & World Report*, September 30, 1968; *Chicago Daily News*, October 2, 1968.

85 Marshall Frady, *Wallace* (New York: World Publishing, 1968), pp. viii, 7.

86 *Richmond Times-Dispatch*, June 19, 1968; *Washington Post*, July 15, 1968, and September 23, 1968.

lowing, a following activated, in part, by Federal civil rights enforcement.

This enormous shift in partisan alignments in the presidential campaign soon began to influence the calculations and the positions of major party candidates. Both parties had to seriously consider the real possibility that neither the Democratic or Republican ticket would carry the required electoral vote majority and that Wallace might hold the balance of power. Wallace had made clear his terms for delivering what could have been the decisive votes:

> Enter into a solemn covenant with the people of our country, face-to-face with them: That, for our votes, they will provide a change in domestic policy; will allow representation upon the Supreme Court of the United States by people with experience in the judicial field—supporters of sound doctrine—instead of putting political hacks on the bench; hacks or college professors who have always been theorists and have never been in any actual practice or actual contact; will allow the people of the various States to control their own domestic institutions.[87]

Of even greater importance was the fact that Wallace had raised issues the Republicans had to answer if they were to compete effectively for the votes of the southern conservatives. Richard Nixon's successful pursuit of the GOP nomination depended on southern support as did his victory. In order to hold the support of southern politicians worried about the Wallace threat, Nixon found it necessary to take a position favoring a cutback in civil rights enforcement. During the Republican convention, Nixon not only agreed to pick a running mate acceptable to the South, but also told a caucus of southern delegates that "I don't believe you should use the South as a whipping boy." [88] He told the caucus that he would name "strict constitutionalists" to the Supreme Court and that he believed that open housing was properly a local responsibility. No judge, in any court, he said "is qualified to be a local school district and to make the decision as your local school board." [89] What remained of the bipartisan coalition for civil rights enforcement seemed to be rapidly dissolving.

In his first southern television program of the campaign, Nixon attacked the school guidelines and endorsed free choice, thus identifying himself with the leading slogan of southern resistance and denying himself the most important enforcement tool. While proclaiming his support for the theory of the 1954 Supreme Court decision, he added:

> But, on the other hand, while that decision dealt with segregation and said that we would not have segregation, when you go beyond that and say that it is the responsibility of the Federal Government and the Federal courts to, in effect,

[87] Synon, p. 88.   [88] Newsweek, August 19, 1968.
[89] Washington Post, August 9, 1968.

act as local school districts in determining how we carry that out, and then to use the power of the Federal Treasury to withhold funds or give funds in order to carry it out, then I think we are going too far.

In my view, that kind of activity should be very scrupulously examined and in many cases I think should be rescinded.[90]

The GOP nominee endorsed the idea of "true freedom of choice" for black students.[91] The Republican nominee said he opposed the "dangerous" idea of using fund withholding "to force a local community to carry out what a Federal administrator or bureaucrat may think is best for that local community." [92]

After being criticized by civil rights supporters within his own party, Mr. Nixon began to qualify his remarks. When free choice was a "subterfuge for segregation" Federal aid should be denied, but the Office of Education must not go "beyond the mandate of Congress" or use the withholding threat "for the purpose of integration in a positive way." He denounced any enforcement effort involving bussing of children.[93] Nixon accused HEW of having a policy that "we should build schools primarily for integration." [94] Taking another phrase from the rhetoric of the southern resistance, he said that he would not withhold funds to achieve what Federal bureaucrats decided was "racial balance." [95] On his next sojourn into the South, Nixon told a Virginia audience that he supported fairly operated free-choice plans.[96]

Ironically, the clear Nixon identification with the cause of southern resistance helped civil rights supporters in their efforts to assemble a congressional coalition large enough to turn back the annual southern flanker attack on the enforcement program. When the annual HEW appropriations bill had been passed by the House in June, a southern show of strength in a midnight vote with almost 200 congressmen not present succeeded in writing into the bill an amendment providing that HEW would no longer be permitted to withhold money to enforce any desegregation plan that would involve bussing or "the abolishment of any school or the attendance of students at a particular school. . . ." [97] The Senate added to this provision language that would nullify the damage to the compliance program. When the bill went to a conference committee, however, the distribution of seniority within the Appropriations commit-

[90] New York Times, September 13, 1968.
[91] Washington Post, September 13, 1968.
[92] New York Times, September 13, 1968.
[93] Washington Post, September 18, 1968.
[94] Richmond Times-Dispatch, October 2, 1968.
[95] New York Times, October 2, 1968.
[96] Charlottesville Daily Progress, October 3, 1968.
[97] Richmond Times-Dispatch, September 14, 1968.

tees produced a committee dominated by influential southern senators and other conservatives.

The conference committee reported back a bill incorporating the House amendment, facing HEW with a probable choice between mortal damage to the civil rights program or a wrangle during the closing days of a Congress eager to adjourn, which could leave the department without an approved appropriation. The conference report, however, was rejected in the House after an intensive lobbying effort and a switch of position by a group of GOP conservatives apparently concerned that the Nixon campaign not be further hampered by another anti-civil rights move.[98] Thus HEW was once again spared the wrath of an unsympathetic Congress. The law remained intact, and the final choice belonged to the electorate.

As the campaign unfolded it was clear that the great crusade of 1964 had settled down to desultory trench warfare. Many of the powerful allies of the civil rights cause had left the ranks, and a few had even deserted to the opposition. What had seemed a tattered and permanently defeated remnant of segregationist politicians in 1964 had found new strength. Indeed the most unreconstructed of the southern leaders was successfully raiding the North in 1968, drawing crowds to equal those of the major-party candidates and cutting deeply enough into popular support to frighten both Republicans and Democrats. The nation seemed to be rapidly polarizing on the race issue, turning away from concern with Negro rights and toward the normal pattern of local control.

The final great battle in the war on racism in southern education still lay ahead, as did any serious engagement between the power of the Federal bureaucracy and the segregated school systems of the North. Only the perspective of the future will permit a final evaluation of the strategy chosen by the responsible officials of the Johnson Administration. It was clear, however, that the forces of localism and prejudice were growing and that the energy for domestic change gathered in the great election victory four years earlier had been spent at home and in Southeast Asia. The Administration had chosen to invest political capital and a good deal of administrative energy in an attack on the southern caste system. The civil rights program had been unable to achieve a decisive victory in the first years when the public supported change. After the tide of opinion turned in mid-1966, only skillful leadership and political maneuvers had protected the small enforcement bureaucracy against fierce attacks.

As the 1968 election approached, the banner had been raised for the final engagement, but the troops were exhausted and reinforcements urgently needed. With the resignations of Secretary Gardner and Peter

---

[98] *Washington Post,* October 5, 1968.

Libassi in early 1968, it was evident that the entire command would be new when the next President made decisions that would determine the future of the national effort to protect the rights of the black schoolchildren of the South.

Once again the 1968 presidential campaign found the question of race to be the crucial domestic issue before the nation. To a degree highly unusual in American politics, the three candidates offered three distinctive answers. In a certain broad sense the people's choice among the men representing continued rapid change, a slowing down of the process, and a radical reversal of direction will decide the final outcome of the great effort at social reconstruction begun four years earlier. A clear electoral verdict against racial reconciliation could mean that the episode of the school guidelines may recede into history as an interesting but futile experiment. Once again the schools, the most basic public institution in American culture, would deepen and reinforce the most fundamental flaw of American society.

Revolution is an overused word, but it is the only word appropriate to the profound changes set in motion when separate schools are abolished.

Pg 349

Reconstruction of Southern Edu

8

Racial Change and the Structure
of American Government

The intensity and bitterness of the protracted battle over integration of southern schools reveal much not only about the ultimate importance of this issue to southern society but also about the structure of political institutions within which the struggle had to be waged. To a person not understanding the racial assumptions of our culture or our strong tradition of decentralized government, the dimensions and the significance of the contest would be simply incomprehensible. The simple task of bringing children of a darker shade into classrooms formerly reserved for whites alone has demanded a historic restructuring of national-state relations and has constituted a fundamental element of an unprecedented peacetime social revolution.

SCHOOL DESEGREGATION AND RACIAL CHANGE

Revolution is an overused word, but it is the only word appropriate to the profound changes set in motion when separate schools are abolished. The significance of a highly visible and obviously important breach in a system of rigid caste separation and systematic inequality must be judged against the background of the pervasive corrosive consequences of official segregation, both on the race branded publicly as inferior and on the race that must devise beliefs and practices to support behavior based on the proposition that all people of another color are different and somehow less human.

The fact is that caste separation of the degree common in the South cannot survive long in integrated schools. Once black children in any numbers enter the classrooms neither the stereotypes nor the customs of racial exclusiveness can remain unquestioned. Margaret Anderson, an educator intimately involved in a decade of transition in one southern high school has described the way change comes:

> Integration begins to become a reality through the very fact that the children are mutually involved in attaining an education and are in daily association with each other. . . . The contact provides them an opportunity to measure and sift their experiences with each other. . . .
>
> They see their friends changing their attitudes. A white student . . . discovers that much of what he has heard about the Negro is false. For example, youngsters sometimes have the idea that all Negroes are dirty or small and cannot learn. A class experience contradicts this. . . .
>
> An accumulation of such changes begins to produce some measure of change in the individual.[1]

In the Deep South, where racism becomes most explicit and complete, school integration can produce deep personality changes. Robert Coles, the man who has most carefully studied the impact of the change on individual children, reports striking findings in his book *Children of Crisis*. To suggest both the strength of the caste system and the possibilities for change, Coles analyzed the drawings made by a Negro girl and a white boy in the first grade of the first integrated school in New Orleans.

[1] Margaret Anderson, *The Children of the South* (New York: Delta Books, 1967), pp. 103–4.

In its recent report, *Racial Isolation in the Public Schools*, the U.S. Civil Rights Commission cites a variety of studies demonstrating the impact of school desegregation in changing basic racial attitudes. An integrated school experience, particularly at an early age and particularly where interracial friendships are formed, greatly diminishes racial prejudice. Negro graduates of integrated schools are more confident, more willing to trust whites, more eager to live in integrated neighborhoods, more likely to have white friends, and more determined to send their children to integrated schools. A similar pattern of changed racial attitudes was found among whites who had attended integrated schools. See U.S. Commission on Civil Rights, *Racial Isolation in the Public Schools* (Washington: Government Printing Office, 1967), p. 112.

Supporting evidence is also found in James S. Coleman *et. al., Equality of Educational Opportunity* (Washington: Government Printing Office, 1966), the report on the largest national survey ever made of the impact of segregation on educational opportunity. Teacher attitudes were clearly related to the racial composition of the student body and the fact that Negro schools are commonly regarded as inferior within the teaching profession. Teachers were aware of this difference and are inclined to view their students as having less academic motivation and ability than white students. (Coleman report, pp. 163, 165.) Since the expectations of the teacher play a significant role in stimulating student achievement, the racial identification of the school by the community clearly diminishes the opportunities of the Negro student. "Every pupil," the Civil Rights Commission reports, "knows that, regardless of his personal attainments, the group with which he is identified is viewed as less able, less successful, and less acceptable than the majority of the community." (*Racial Isolation*, p. 104.)

Ruby, the little girl, began school already accepting the role of inferiority forced upon her by the community.

> For a long time . . . Ruby never used brown or black except to indicate soil or ground; even then she always made sure they were covered by a solid covering of green grass. . . . She did, however, distinguish between white and Negro people. She drew white people larger and more lifelike. Negroes were smaller, their bodies less intact. A white girl we both knew to be her own size appeared several times taller. While Ruby's own face . . . lacked an eye in one drawing, an ear in another, the white girl never lacked any features. . . .
>
> The ears of Negroes appeared larger than those of white people. . . . In contrast, quite often a Negro appeared with no mouth—it would be "forgotten." . . .[2]

Only after she had been in school with whites for most of a year could she draw a clear and undistorted picture of a Negro.[3]

Jimmie, the white boy, came to school with the feeling that Negroes were either somehow "related to animals" or were "dirty human beings—and dangerous too." [4] At first he drew Ruby small, without any feet, and with only a trace of a mouth. When he drew the school building, he refused to put her inside with other children.[5] As time passed a change took place:

> In time Jimmie took Ruby into the building he drew, and in time he regularly came to see her as an individual. Amorphous spots and smudges of brown slowly took on form and structure. Ruby began to look human every time, rather than, say, a rodent. . . . Eventually she gained eyes and well-formed ears. It took more time for her to obtain a normal mouth; and only after a year of knowing her would Jimmie credit her with the pretty clothes he often gave to other girls.[6]

Even in Alabama, where the first significant group of black students entered public schools after passage of the Civil Rights Act, some change soon occurred. Although black students often encountered overt hostility from classmates, they soon lost their acceptance of white superiority, an acceptance basic to a stable caste system. Before the students entered white schools, almost two-thirds of them thought that the whites would be more intelligent. After a year in white schools, only one student in five retained this belief.[7]

While school integration, in itself, cannot destroy racial bias, it does inevitably weaken the extreme stereotypes held by both races that provide the basis for the southern social order. Once children can be put into integrated classrooms, the machinery of one of the most powerful social

[2] Coles, p. 47.   [3] *Ibid.*, p. 49.   [4] *Ibid.*, p. 53.   [5] *Ibid.*, p. 54.
[6] *Ibid.*, p. 56.
[7] Mark Chesler and Phyllis Segal, "Southern Negroes' Initial Experiences and Reactions in School Desegregation," *Integrated Education*, Vol. VI (January–February, 1968), p. 27.

and cultural institutions is committed to peacefully and successfully dealing with day-to-day situations in which children must be treated as equal individuals.

Not only does school integration produce far-reaching personal and cultural changes, it also makes possible some approach to the American ideal of equal educational opportunity. In 1954 the Supreme Court decided that the old view of equal opportunity as merely the provision of schools approximately equal in various tangible ways was no longer adequate. In deciding that racially separate school systems were "inherently unequal," the court expanded the definition of equality in the schools. Not until 10 years after the court decision, however, did Congress provide funds for a national survey to clearly analyze the educational impact of segregation. The resulting summary of findings, *Equality of Educational Opportunity*, popularly known as the Coleman Report, immediately became the best available interpretation of this issue.

This survey of some 600,000 students showed that there was relatively little difference between white and black schools in facilities, equipment, and curricula. It also showed, however, that although Negro students were very highly motivated, the longer they stayed in segregated schools the further they fell behind white students. Thus segregation, or, as it turned out, a factor closely related to racial separation, was clearly crucial to school achievement.

The differences in levels of achievement were very wide, particularly in the South. Across the nation less than one Negro student in six scored as well as the typical white at the time of high school graduation. The typical Negro student was a year and a half behind his white counterpart by the sixth grade, and before graduation, fell more than three years behind.[8]

Black students were very highly motivated to learn. Contrary to expectation, the report noted that no major population group was more highly motivated than the black students of the South and Southwest. Negro students did more homework than any group except the tiny oriental minority, and one out of four hoped to become a professional. "Negroes," the report concluded, "are expecially strongly oriented toward the school as a path for mobility." In a subsociety in which the middle class had always been largely limited to men with professional training in law, religion, education, and medicine, this orientation was a natural one.

The central problem was to explain why highly motivated students in apparently equal schools perform so differently. The data of the Coleman Report strongly suggested that the single factor most influential in a given

[8] Coleman report, pp. 219–20, 273.

school was the background of the student body. "Higher achievement
. . . is largely, perhaps wholly, related to effects associated with the student body's education background and aspirations." [9] The formal aspects
of the school counted for less than the opportunity for students to learn
from other students. Students who come from families with poorly educated parents gain sharply when they share classes with students from
middle-class families. It is, obviously, "a simple fact that the teacher can
not teach beyond the level of the most advanced students in the class."

> It is also clear that going to school with other children whose vocabulary is larger
> than one's own demands and creates a larger vocabulary. Sitting next to a child
> who is performing at a high level provides a challenge to better performance.[10]

Since most Negro families are near the bottom of the educational and
economic ladders, the implications of this central finding were obvious.
"In a segregated system," the report concluded, "if one group begins at
an educationally impoverished level, it will tend to remain at that level."

> Ordinarily, one has a conception of schools' effects as consisting of a strong
> stimulus from the outside, independent of the immediate social context of the
> students. . . . It appears that a more appropriate conception may be that of a
> self-reproducing system, in which most of the effects are not independent of the
> social context, but are, rather, internal ones.[11]

Thus the study gave very dramatic support to the belief that integration was of central importance educationally. Negro and other impoverished minority groups gained substantially when placed in white middle-class schools. The white children, less dependent on the schools and learning more at home, lost nothing when almost half the class was made up of
black students. When Negro children entered white working-class
schools, they gained an average of a year in achievement levels. In white
middle-class schools improvement amounted to "more than two grade
levels." [12]

The educational issue is simple. With very few exceptions, the segregated ghetto school serves to perpetuate a pattern of inferior education,
thus making a mockery of the American ideal of equal educational opportunity. While the data of the Coleman Report is far from complete and
its methodology continues to be debated,[13] the best information now
available suggests that an integrated school experience is far more impor-

[9] *Ibid.*, p. 310; James S. Coleman, "Toward Open Schools," *Public Interest*, No. 9
(Fall, 1967), pp. 20–27.
[10] Coleman, "Toward Open Schools," p. 23.   [11] Coleman report, p. 307.
[12] Civil Rights Commission, *Racial Isolation . . .* , p. 91.
[13] "Equal Educational Opportunity," a special issue of the *Harvard Educational
Review*, Vol. XXXVIII (Winter, 1968).

tant educationally than buildings, equipment, curriculum, or even teacher quality.

Black parents clearly recognize the stakes. At the time of the Birmingham crisis, seven out of 10 wished to enroll their children in integrated schools. In mid-1966, amid mounting white hostility and in spite of the black power movement, this belief remained just as strong.[14] The parents recognized the seriousness of this need, a need particularly critical in the South where the school differences are most debilitating.

Since the emergence of the black power movement, of course, some black leaders have given up hope for integration and have begun, particularly in New York City, to advocate control of local schools by the ghetto residents. Such demands have generally arisen after it has become evident that local authorities either cannot or will not integrate the black schools. In the vast unbroken ghettos that enclose hundreds of thousands of people in some of the nation's largest cities, Negro students have very little hope for integration in the near future, barring a dramatic change in the law or in public attitudes. In these communities an argument can be made that the schools are failing so seriously that an experiment in community control is justified. The Coleman Report's measurement of school expenditures were crude and there was, of course, no way to determine whether massive compensatory programs, far larger than present ones, might actually produce important and lasting educational gains.[15] Southern civil rights spokesmen, representing a people with a century of experience with the kind of separate schools the white majority is willing to provide, are understandably skeptical of the separatist rhetoric of the northern urban militants and of their hope that the white community will finance revolutionary changes in separate schools.

Fortunately, the problems of realizing integration in the South have generally been far more simple than those arising from the ghettos of the North and West. Most of the black students affected by the school desegregation guidelines live in rural areas or small towns without any insurmountable logistical barriers to integration. In fact, the rural areas often have very little residential segregation. Southern cities are far smaller and more manageable in terms of planning integration than the handful of northern metropolitan centers that had served as the focal point for black

[14] William Brink and Louis Harris, *Black and White* (New York: Simon and Schuster, 1966), p. 234.
[15] Samuel Bowles and Henry M. Levin, "The Determinants of Scholastic Achievement—an Appraisal of Some Recent Evidence," *Journal of Human Resources*, III (Winter, 1968), 1–24; Robert C. Nichols, "Schools and the Disadvantaged," *Science*, CLIV (December 9, 1966), 1312–14; Henry S. Dyer, "School Factors and Equal Educational Opportunity," *Harvard Educational Review*, XXXVIII (Winter, 1968), 38–56.

migration from the South. HEW enforcement efforts were very largely confined to smaller cities, since most of the major southern cities were desegregating under previous court orders at the time the guidelines took effect. Thus the Federal officials generally had to confront only the most unambiguous desegregation problems, cases in which the ideals of racial justice and equal educational opportunity could generally be realized through a relatively simple unification of the existing separate school systems.

Southern school desegregation had been on dead center for a decade after the 1954 decision not because of any problems of educational administration, but because the southern public was determined not to do more than the minimum necessary. The most important fact about the extension of Federal power under Title VI was the determination, with recurring hesitations, to use the powerful leverage of Federal money in a confrontation with local centers of political power.

Even though the reordering of race relations in southern schools was halting and incomplete, it was, in the context of American federalism, a remarkable achievement. It has been said that no nation has accomplished, without war or revolution, a social transformation as profound and as rapid as that implied by the partial integration of the schools of the South. A generation ago the image of any black and white children studying together, eating together, sharing buses and athletic teams, and sitting together in classes taught by black teachers would have been simply inconceivable in most sections of the South. Now these sights are commonplace. In the Middle South, a basic prop of the society and culture has been very seriously damaged in less than a decade. The Deep South has had half that time to face the first beginnings of a change made even more dramatic by the rigidity of local custom and the bitter defiance of political leaders. A political system that, normally, passively reflects the interests of local elites had actively intervened on behalf of a basic interest of the most despised local minority.

THE INSTITUTIONS OF GOVERNMENT

The revolution begun by the school guidelines took shape within a set of political institutions far better designed to stifle change than to implement a basic reconstruction. The American federal system is an intricate, slowly operating, and highly decentralized set of power relationships far better suited to protect the local status quo and to make excessively powerful central leadership impossible than to force any unpopular local action. The change was accomplished within a political system in which both the structure of the political parties and the nature of popular ideology concentrate great power at the local and state levels. Even when a congressional majority favoring national action against local vested interests has finally been obtained, localities have commonly been able to modify policy through intervention in the administrative process.

Only unique historical circumstances permitted the creation of the school desegregation effort. Although the excesses of southern racial practices had periodically aroused the anger of the nation, local authority had rarely been disturbed. Only during the brief interlude of Reconstruction had national power temporarily overcome the resistance of a politically prostrate region. In normal times, a national legislative system allowing and encouraging minority vetoes gave the unified region, the "solid South," the opportunity to reject any Federal action that might disrupt race relations.

After Reconstruction was liquidated and the northern public acquiesced in the southern view of the race question, the Federal government betrayed the commitment to Negro rights so bravely set out in the Fourteenth and Fifteenth Amendments. As Southern public school systems arose from the ashes of war, education of blacks was systematically neglected. When Federal money began to flow South, locally approved patterns of racial separation were scrupulously observed and even reinforced. The Supreme Court's 1896 "separate but equal" doctrine, when combined with congressional insistence that Federal administrators leave the judgment about equality to local officials, meant that racism was unchallenged.

Only intervention from the Supreme Court, the one element of the American political system most insulated from localism, finally forced the contradiction between equal rights and local control to the center of American politics. Skillful use of the court system by black litigants won a theoretical recognition of a set of basic rights.

The 1954 decision proclaimed an extremely important principle of constitutional law and stripped away a facade of legal justifications for segregation. It generated the hope for change that produced the modern civil rights movement. The eloquence of the decision, however, did not integrate many schools. The decision called for a revolution, but the judicial machinery was able to administer change only at a symbolic level. Limitations inherent both in the case-by-case procedures of the courts and in the fact that appointments to Federal district courts reflect local political preferences strictly limited change. Outside the areas of voluntary compliance in the border states, progress was very slow. The courts could proclaim the overthrow of a deeply rooted custom; they could not administer it.

Fundamental change demanded that the resources of the great Federal bureaucracies be engaged in the battle. The NAACP quickly recognized this fact, and Representative Adam Clayton Powell tried unsuccessfully throughout the late 1950's to make compliance with the Constitution a precondition for participation in Federal programs. This effort was so unrealistic within the context of southern power in Congress that liberal groups denounced the "Powell amendment" as hopeless and destructive of other legislation. Both the Eisenhower and Kennedy administrations rejected proposals to implement this idea by drawing on the general executive authority of the President. President Kennedy expressed the prevailing American political tradition when he dismissed as radical the early 1963 proposal of the Civil Rights Commission for fund withholding.

The second reconstruction could not begin in earnest until there was an overwhelming and intensely aroused national majority prepared to indefinitely suspend all other business in Congress. Only the clarity and anger born on the streets of Birmingham and the national commitment crystallized by the words of John Kennedy and the leadership of Lyndon Johnson made possible a change in the very nature of American federalism.

While all major reform legislation must somehow survive passage through a series of congressional bottlenecks, the difficulties involved in civil rights proposals were unmatched. Southern politicians simply could not afford any appearance of compromise on civil rights. The result was intense and unified pressure brought to bear by skilled and powerful practitioners at every step. The fact that the seniority system had magnified southern strength by rewarding one-party regularity with control of decisive committees increased the odds against change. Finally, any significant expansion of Federal power required the extraordinary Senate majority needed to break the hallowed Senate tradition of unlimited debate, a tradition that had given the South and a handful of conservative allies a conclusive veto over national action. Finally, in late 1963 and early 1964, sufficient strength was gathered to override normal procedures and extend Federal authority.

Passage of the Civil Rights Act convinced the nation that the battle had been won. Before a single school system could be forced to change, however, the congressional directive had to be meshed into the ponderous machinery of day-to-day bureaucratic action. In this process the sweeping injunction for change was to be softened by program officials sensitive to the national ideology of local control of the schools and sensitive to the need to maintain established constituency relationships, relationships essential to the success of the new aid-to-education program.

A serious enforcement effort was made possible both by intervention from outside HEW in drafting the initial administrative regulations and by the initiative of the Commissioner of Education in creating a separate and largely independent staff within the Office of Education. The commitment of the President and his representatives in the Justice Department to enforcement of the law as written overcame the localistic preferences of grant program administrators. The legal technicians gave the broad and sweeping language of Title VI both the specificity and the limitations of the body of school desegregation law evolved by the Federal courts. Commissioner Keppel's creation and support of a compliance office provided the essential machinery for a real attempt to enforce the law.

In the first guidelines, the Administration forged the policy tools needed for the first step in the orderly transformation of race relations in southern schools. It had proved impossible to deal with thousands of southern communities on this vital local issue without issuing specific enforcement standards. Because the crucial decision-makers were lawyers, because the case law provided the only readily available body of detailed desegregation standards, and because principles derived from the courts would be far easier to defend against attack in the courts, judicial standards were readily accepted as administrative standards. Thus, at the outset, much of the discretion conferred by Title VI was sacrificed in favor of a mission built around generalizing and implementing court standards on a massive basis. The Equal Educational Opportunities Program provided the bureaucratic strength needed to implement the revolution the courts had ordained but could not enforce.

The new bureaucracy soon accumulated an unequaled body of knowledge about administering school desegregation on a mass production basis. It became clear that the principles in the first guidelines could not move most districts beyond token integration. The initial guidelines did, however, greatly lighten the administrative and political pressures on the court system and were quickly supported in the courts. Recognizing the national commitment, profiting from a rapidly accumulating body of administrative experience, and freed from much of the onerous case-by-case responsibility, the Federal courts confronted new legal questions in decisions that rapidly strengthened judicial standards for a desegregation plan. Thus the bureaucracy consolidated judicial gains, leaving the judges free to break new ground.

Court decisions, new administrative expertise, and continuing presidential support for civil rights brought a great strengthening of the guidelines in early 1966. Still riding the tide of the movement for Negro rights, the Administration committed itself to the complete restructuring of the legally separate schools of the South. The initial struggle for symbolic concessions now became a war on the entire system of separate schools.

For a time after passage of the 1964 Civil Rights Act, the extent of the public commitment to civil rights made southern attacks on enforcement largely irrelevant. Ironically the first serious political reversal came not at the hands of irate southerners but from Chicago, one of the very bastions of northern Democratic strength that had provided the votes for the 1964 act. When a series of administrative miscalculations put the Office of Education in the middle of the most explosive racial controversy in the city with the most powerful Democratic machine in the nation, a political disaster became inevitable. The Office became involved in Chicago without any policies for handling the complex problems of school discrimination in the North. After funds were deferred without adequate documentation of segregation, the Office of Education found itself exposed to the full weight of aroused localism. The nature and scope of the local power that Chicago could bring to bear and the ease and effectiveness with which Chicago officials could invoke the ideology of local control of the schools crushed any significant Federal attack on northern segregation. The Federal defeat encouraged local resistance in the South.

Fed by a national racial polarization, southern segregationist influence in Congress put the civil rights program in serious political trouble by the fall of 1966. As southern communities realized that the 1966 guidelines would rapidly doom segregation, a massive onslaught on the Office of Education took form. As national concern receded, southern congressmen responded with increasing effectiveness to constituency complaints. Impelled by the conviction that the law demanded only voluntary token integration, southerners accused Commissioner Howe of usurping authority.

As the protest mounted, the unique civil rights coalition that had made possible a temporary reversal of the norms of American federalism was speedily dissolving. Angry white reaction to ghetto riots and the shrill slogans of the black power movement made congressmen increasingly willing to accept southern claims. The Chicago incident had created a lingering suspicion in the minds of some northern representatives that the enforcement weapon might one day be turned against their cities. The strong public support needed to effectively challenge entrenched and aroused local power was gone.

Although Congress acts as a national body at times of great crisis or clear national consensus, it normally accurately reflects the decentralized and local nature of political power in America. Congressmen are acutely sensitive to changes of local opinion on the race issue, an issue of such universal visibility and high intensity that most members want to accurately reflect local feeling. As a wave of racial reaction rolled across the land in 1966, both houses demonstrated an inclination to curb agencies trying to accelerate the rate of racial change. The public thought that things were going too fast. Even in the Congress with the largest liberal representation since the New Deal, few members defended the Federally sponsored revolution in local race relations.

Once again southerners were able to draw both on their accumulated congressional seniority and the general congressional readiness to accept local claims of bureaucratic abuse. Federal civil rights powers were very seriously challenged in the 1966 Congress and again during the 1967 struggle over the renewal of the education program. A further attack was made during consideration of the 1968 HEW appropriation bill.

The preservation of the civil rights program from mortal damage was less a tribute to the extent of congressional support than to the skill of a few liberals in exploiting the tactical advantages accruing to defenders of the status quo within Congress. In both 1966 and 1967, civil rights supporters found themselves in the uncharacteristic position of exercising minority vetoes to limit the damage wrought by a hostile majority. In 1968 only the fact that George Wallace's candidacy had divided the anti-civil rights vote convinced GOP leaders in the House to aid their national ticket by turning against an amendment that would destroy the compliance program of the Office for Civil Rights and lend substance to Democratic charges against their presidential candidate. While the legal authority of the program remained largely intact, continuing congressional attacks brought compromises in the enforcement effort.

The price for crucial southern support on the 1967 education bill was reorganization of the compliance program, returning the Office of Education to its normal passive relationship with state and local authority. The new Office for Civil Rights very carefully avoided the controversial defenses of integration that had generated such antagonism toward Commissioner Howe. The new organization took on a legalistic tone and set out to quietly and cautiously enforce the law.

The initial task of the Office for Civil Rights was to liquidate a set of policies that congressional attacks and Administration timidity had made unenforceable. The staff shifted attention from specific rates of annual progress to winning local acceptance of plans for complete desegregation by the fall of 1969, promises collectable almost a year after the presidential election. At the same time, the staff began to gather data and quietly probe a few northern districts. The ground work was laid for possible fulfillment of the mission of the new organization, but the decision on implementing the new policies would be up to the man assuming the presidency in January 1969.

As administrators marked time, awaiting the change of national leadership, the courts again emerged at the forefront of the battle. Insulated from the vagaries of elections and the pull of localism, the Supreme Court acted in May 1968 to settle the legal issues posed by the free-choice scheme. Strong judicial intervention on behalf of the idea of rapid creation of unified, nonracial school systems across the South once again provided highly important support, support that could no longer be obtained within the political system.

As the 1968 presidential contest unfolded, the three major candidates offered a strikingly clear set of alternatives on the future of the revolution in southern race relations. George Wallace spoke to a large, bitter, alienated segment of the population when he promised to send all the bureaucrats packing and restore full power over local racial affairs to state and local governments. The Republican candidate, Richard Nixon, argued that things had gone too far and that he would use Title VI sparingly. The Democratic candidate, Hubert Humphrey, pledged to fully enforce the law. The election of Nixon created doubts about the future meaning of the Civil Rights Act.

There are very few questions in American life of greater ultimate importance to our society than the deceivingly simple problem of moving a child from a black to an integrated classroom. Destruction of the walls of legal separation in southern schools is an absolutely fundamental part of the national commitment required to destroy the caste system and make equal opportunity a reality rather than a mockery. Yet, years after the solemn proclamation of this basic right by the nation's highest court and by its supreme legislative body, the revolution remains incomplete. The structure of American federalism has eroded the force of the official commitment and seriously delayed its realization. Recalcitrant local power has imposed critical limits on the exercise of administrative authority in the protection of Negro rights.

Only shocked and angry public consciousness of the total incompatibility between the American belief in equality and the continuance of unbridled local abuses permitted the extraordinary extension of Federal power embodied in the Civil Rights Act. In four years, the political energy arising from this consensus has been largely consumed.

The reconstruction of southern education has been well begun, but its completion demands a renewal of national commitment. The traditions of our federal system mean that finishing this work in the South and seriously beginning in the North will be possible only with determined leadership in Congress and from the new Administration. Normal local concerns must again be suspended to guarantee the elemental rights of black children. Almost a century ago, America had one short and bitterly futile experiment with racial reconstruction. It cannot afford another.

Bibliography

Books

Allen, Hollis P. *The Federal Government and Education.* New York: McGraw-Hill, 1950.

Anderson, J. W. *Eisenhower, Brownell, and the Congress.* ("The Inter-University Case Program.") University, Alabama: University of Alabama Press, 1964.

Anderson, Margaret. *The Children of the South.* New York: Delta Books, 1967.

Banfield, Edward C. *Big City Politics.* New York: Random House, 1965.

———. *Political Influence.* New York: Free Press of Glencoe, 1961.

Banfield, Edward C., and Wilson, James Q. *City Politics.* New York: Vintage Books, 1963.

Bauer, Raymond A., Pool, Ithiel de Sola, and Dexter, Lewis. *American Business and Public Policy.* New York: Atherton, 1963.

Bendiner, Robert. *Obstacle Course on Capitol Hill.* New York: McGraw-Hill, 1964.

Bennett, Walter Hartwell, *American Theories of Federalism.* University, Alabama: University of Alabama Press, 1964.

Berman, Daniel M. *It is So Ordered, The Supreme Court Rules on School Segregation.* New York: W. W. Norton and Co., 1966.

Bernstein, Marver H. *Regulating Business by Independent Commission.* Princeton: Princeton University Press, 1955.

Bickel, Alexander M. *Politics and the Warren Court.* New York: Harper and Row, 1965.

Binkley, Wilfred E. *President and Congress.* New York: Vintage Books, 1962.

Brink, William, and Harris, Louis. *Black and White.* New York: Simon and Schuster, 1960.

Brodie, Fawn M. *Thaddeus Stevens.* New York: W. W. Norton and Co., 1959.

Callahan, Raymond E. *Education and the Cult of Efficiency.* Chicago: University of Chicago Press, 1962.

Carter, Hodding, III. *The South Strikes Back.* New York: Doubleday, 1959.

Clayton, Edward T. *The Negro Politician.* Chicago: Johnson Publishing Co., 1964.

Coles, Robert. *Children of Crisis.* Boston: Atlantic-Little Brown, 1967.

Connery, Robert H., and Leach, Richard H. *The Federal Government and Metropolitan Areas.* Cambridge, Mass.: Harvard University Press, 1960.

Council of State Governments. *Federal Grants-In-Aid.* Chicago: Council of State Governments, 1949.

Counts, George S. *School and Society in Chicago.* New York: Harcourt, Brace and Co., 1928.

Cremin, Lawrence A. *The Genius of American Education.* New York: Vintage Books, 1965.

————. *The Transformation of the School.* New York: Vintage Books, 1964.

Curti, Merle. *The Social Ideas of American Educators.* Paterson, N.J.: Pageant Books, 1959.

Dabney, Charles W. *Universal Education in the South.* 2 vols. Chapel Hill: University of North Carolina Press, 1936.

Dentler, Robert, Mackler, Bernard, and Warshauer, Mary, eds. *The Urban R's.* New York: Praeger, 1967.

Dorman, Michael. *We Shall Overcome.* New York: Delacorte Press, 1964.

Educational Policies Commission. *Educational Responsibilities of the Federal Government.* Washington: National Education Association, 1964.

Elazar, Daniel J. *The American Partnership, Intergovernmental Co-operation in the Nineteenth-Century United States.* Chicago: University of Chicago Press, 1962.

Evans, Rowland, and Novak, Robert. *Lyndon B. Johnson: The Exercise of Power.* New York: New American Library, 1966.

Fenton, John M. *In Your Opinion.* Boston: Little, Brown, 1960.

Fosdick, Raymond B. *Adventure in Giving, The Story of the General Education Board.* New York: Harper and Row, 1962.

Franklin, John Hope. *Reconstruction: After the Civil War.* Chicago: University of Chicago Press, 1961.

Frazier, E. Franklin. *The Negro Family in Chicago.* Chicago: University of Chicago Press, 1932.

Friedman, Leonard, Ed. *Southern Justice.* New York: Pantheon Books, 1965.

Galloway, George B. *The Legislative Process in Congress.* New York: Thomas Y. Crowell Co., 1953.

Gates, Robbins L. *The Making of Massive Resistance.* Chapel Hill: University of North Carolina Press, 1964.

Gosnell, Harold F. *Machine Politics, Chicago Model.* Chicago: University of Chicago Press, 1937.

————. *Negro Politicians.* Chicago: University of Chicago Press, 1935.

Graves, W. Brooke. *American Intergovernmental Relations.* New York: Charles Scribner's Sons, 1964.

Hales, Dawson. *Federal Control of Public Education, A Critical Appraisal.* (Teachers College Studies in Education.) New York: Columbia University Press, 1954.

Harris, Seymour E., and Levensohn, Alan, Eds. *Education and Public Policy.* Berkeley, Calif.: McCutchan Publishing, 1965.

Havighurst, Robert J. *The Public Schools of Chicago.* Chicago: Chicago Board of Education, 1964.

Heller, Walter W. *New Dimensions of Political Economy.* New York: W. W. Norton and Co., 1965.

Hickey, Neil, and Edward, Edwin. *Adam Clayton Powell.* New York: Fleet Publishing Corp., 1965.

Humphrey, Hubert H., Ed. *School Desegregation: Documents and Commentaries.* New York: Thomas Y. Crowell Co., 1964.

Jewell, Malcolm E., and Patterson, Samuel C. *The Legislative Process in the United States.* New York: Random House, 1966.

Johnson, Lyndon B. *Public Papers of the Presidents of the United States.* 4 vols. Washington: Government Printing Office, 1966, 1967.

Johnson, Philip A. *Call Me Neighbor, Call Me Friend, A Case Study of the Integra-*

tion of a Neighborhood on Chicago's South Side. Garden City, N.Y.: Doubleday and Co., 1965.

Karlen, Harvey M. *The Governments of Chicago.* Chicago: Courier Publishing Co., 1958.

Kennedy, John F. *The Public Papers of the Presidents of the United States.* Washington: Government Printing Office, 1964.

Keppel, Francis. *The Necessary Revolution in American Education.* New York: Harper and Row, 1966.

Key, V. O., Jr. *The Administration of Federal Grants to States.* Chicago: Public Administration Service, 1937.

Kimbrough, Ralph B. *Political Power and Educational Decision-Making.* Chicago: Rand McNally and Co., 1964.

Kofmehl, Kenneth. *Professional Staffs of Congress.* West Lafayette, Ind.: Purdue University, 1962.

Kursh, Harry. *The United States Office of Education.* Philadelphia: Chilton Books, 1965.

Lee, Gordon Canfield. *The Struggle for Federal Aid, First Phase.* ("Teachers College, Columbia University, Contributions to Education," No. 957.) New York: Teachers College Bureau of Publications, 1949.

Lewis, Anthony, and the *New York Times. Portrait of a Decade.* New York: Bantam Books, 1965.

Link, Arthur S. *Woodrow Wilson and the Progressive Era.* New York: Harper and Row, 1963.

Logan, Rayford W. *The Betrayal of the Negro.* New York: Collier Books, 1965.

McClure, William P. *A Study of the Public Schools of Illinois.* Springfield, Ill.: Research and Development Department, Office of the Superintendent of Public Instruction, 1965.

MacNeil, Neil. *Forge of Democracy.* New York: David McKay Co., 1963.

Marshall, Burke. *Federalism and Civil Rights.* New York: Columbia University Press, 1964.

Masters, Nicholas A., Salisbury, Robert H., and Eliot, Thomas H. *State Politics and the Public Schools.* New York: Alfred A. Knopf, 1964.

Miller, Clem. *Member of the House.* New York: Charles Scribner's Sons, 1962.

Mort, Paul R., Reusser, Walter C., and Polley, John W. *Public School Finance.* New York: McGraw-Hill, 1960.

Munger, Frank J., and Fenno, Richard F., Jr. *National Politics and Federal Aid to Education.* ("The Economics and Politics of Public Education," No. 3.) Syracuse, N.Y.: Syracuse University Press, 1962.

Muse, Benjamin. *Virginia's Massive Resistance.* Bloomington, Ind.: Indiana University Press, 1961.

Myrdahl, Gunnar. *An American Dilemma.* New York: Harper and Brothers, 1962.

National Education Association, National Commission for the Defense of Democracy through Education. *Certain Personnel Practices in the Chicago Public Schools.* Washington: National Education Association, 1945.

Neustadt, Richard E. *Presidential Power.* New York: John Wiley and Sons, 1960.

Page, Walter H. *The Rebuilding of Old Commonwealths.* New York: Doubleday, Page and Co., 1902.

Peabody, Robert L., and Polsby, Nelson W., Eds. *New Perspectives on the House of Representatives.* Chicago: Rand McNally and Co., 1963.

Peltason, Jack W. *Federal Courts in the Political Process.* ("Studies in Political Science.") New York: Random House, 1955.

————. *Fifty-Eight Lonely Men.* New York: Harcourt, Brace and World, 1961.

Pois, Joseph. *The School Board Crisis, A Chicago Case Study.* Chicago: Aldine Publishing Co., 1964.

Reichley, James, Ed. *States in Crisis.* Chapel Hill: University of North Carolina Press, 1964.

Rhode, William E. *Committee Clearance of Administrative Decisions.* East Lansing, Mich.: Bureau of Social and Political Research, Michigan State University, 1959.

Sarratt, Reed. *The Ordeal of Desegregation.* New York: Harper and Row, 1966.

Schlesinger, Arthur M., Jr. *A Thousand Days.* Boston: Houghton Mifflin Co., 1965.

Schroeder, Oliver, Jr., and Smith, David T., Eds. *De Facto Segregation and Civil Rights.* New York: William S. Hein and Co., 1965.

Seidner, F. J. *Federal Support for Education.* Washington: Public Affairs Institute, 1959.

Selznick, Philip. *TVA and the Grass Roots.* Berkeley and Los Angeles: University of California Press, 1953.

Silberman, Charles E. *Crisis in Black and White.* New York: Vintage Books, 1964.

Simon, Herbert A. *Administrative Behavior.* New York: The Free Press, 1965.

Sorensen, Theodore C. *Kennedy.* New York: Harper and Row, 1965.

Southern Education Reporting Service. *Statistical Summary of School Segregation-Desegregation in the Southern and Border States.* Nashville: Southern Education Reporting Service, 1967.

Stampp, Kenneth M. *The Era of Reconstruction 1865–1877.* New York, Alfred A. Knopf, 1965.

Sufrin, Sidney C. *Administering the National Defense Education Act.* ("The Economics and Politics of Public Education," No. 8.) Syracuse, N.Y.: Syracuse University Press, 1963.

————. *Issues in Federal Aid to Education.* ("The Economics and Politics of Public Education," No. 4.) Syracuse, N.Y.: Syracuse University Press, 1962.

Thompson, Robert E., and Myers, Hortense. *Robert F. Kennedy: The Brother Within.* New York: Dell Books, 1962.

Tipton, James H. *Community in Crisis, The Elimination of Segregation from a Public School System.* ("Teachers College Studies in Education.") New York: Columbia University Teachers College Bureau of Publications, 1953.

Vose, Clement E. *Caucasions Only.* Berkeley and Los Angeles: University of California Press, 1959.

Weinberg, Meyer, Ed. *Learning Together.* Chicago: Integrated Education Associates, 1964.

Welter, Rush. *Popular Education and Democratic Thought in America.* New York: Columbia University Press, 1962.

Wesley, Edgar B. *NEA: The First Hundred Years.* New York: Harper and Row, 1957.

Wilson, James Q. *Negro Politics.* Glencoe, Ill.: The Free Press, 1960.

Woodward, C. Van. *Reunion and Reaction.* New York: Doubleday Anchor Books, 1956.

Federal Public Documents

Coleman, James S., *et al. Equality of Educational Opportunity.* Report to the U.S. Office of Education, 1966.

Judd, Charles H. *Research in the United States Office of Education.* Advisory Committee on Education Staff Study Number 19, 1939.

Shiras, Alexander. *The National Bureau of Education.* Prepared under the direction of the Commissioner of Education, 1875.

Seeley, David, and Anderson, Lucille. *Chronological Statement on Civil Rights in the Office of Education.* October, 1965.

U.S., Commission on Civil Rights. *Civil Rights U.S.A., Public Schools in the North and West.* Staff reports, 1962.

———. *Civil Rights U.S.A., Public Schools in Southern States.* Staff reports, 1962.

———. *Public Education.* Staff report, 1964.

———. *Racial Isolation in the Public Schools.* Vol. I, 1967.

———. *Southern School Desegregation 1966–67*, 1967.

———. *Survey of School Desegregation in the Southern and Border States, 1965–1966*, 1966.

———. *Title VI . . . One Year After, A Survey of Desegregation of Health and Welfare Services in the South*, 1966.

———. Massachusetts Advisory Committee. *Report on Racial Imbalance in the Boston Public Schools*, 1965.

———. Virginia State Advisory Committee. *The Federal Role in School Desegregation in Selected Virginia Districts*, 1968.

Weinberg, Meyer. *Race and Place*, 1967.

Wilkerson, Doxey A. *Special Problems of Negro Education.* Advisory Committee on Education, Staff Study Number 12, 1939.

U.S., Congress, House, Committee on Appropriations. *Report, Departments of Labor, and Health, Education and Welfare and Related Agencies Appropriation Bill, 1968.* Committee print. 90th Cong., 1st Sess., 1967.

———. Subcommittee on Departments of Labor and Health, Education and Welfare and Related Agencies. *Hearings, Departments of Labor and Health, Education and Welfare Appropriations for 1968.* 90th Cong., 1st Sess., 1967.

———. Subcommittee on Departments of State, Justice, and Commerce, the Judiciary, and Related Agencies. *Hearings, Departments of State, Justice, and Commerce, the Judiciary, and Related Agencies Appropriations for 1966, Department of Justice.* 89th Cong., 1st Sess., 1965.

U.S., Congress, House, Committee on Education and Labor. *The Federal Government and Education.* House Document No. 159, 88th Cong., 1st Sess., 1963.

———. *Report, Elementary and Secondary Education Amendments of 1966.* Report No. 1814. 89th Cong., 2d Sess., 1966.

———. *Report, Elementary and Secondary Education Amendments of 1967.* Report No. 188. 90th Cong., 1st Sess., 1967.

———. Special Subcommittee. *Hearings, Investigation of De Facto Segregation in Chicago's Public Schools.* 89th Cong., 1st Sess., 1965.

———. Special Subcommittee on Education. *Hearings, U.S. Office of Education.* 89th Cong., 2d Sess., 1966.

———. Subcommittee on Integration in Federally Assisted Public Education Programs. *Integration in Public Education Programs.* 87th Cong., 2d Sess., 1962.

U.S., Congress, House, Committee on the Judiciary. *Report, Civil Rights Act of 1963.* Report No. 914. 88th Cong., 1st Sess., 1963.

———. Subcommittee No. 5. *Hearings, Civil Rights.* 88th Cong., 1st Sess., 1963.

———. Subcommittee No. 5. *Hearings, Civil Rights, 1966.* 89th Cong., 2d Sess., 1966.

———. Special Subcommittee. *Hearings, Guidelines for School Desegregation.* 89th Cong., 2d Sess., 1966.

U.S., Congress, House, Committee on Rules. *Hearings, Policies and Guidelines for School Desegregation.* 89th Cong., 2d Sess., 1966.

U.S., Congress, Senate, Committee on Commerce. *Hearings, Civil Rights—Public Accommodations.* 88th Cong., 1st Sess., 1963.

U.S., Congress, Senate, Committee on Finance. *Hearings, Proposed Cutoff of Welfare Funds to the State of Alabama.* 90th Cong., 1st Sess., 1967.

U.S., Congress, Senate, Committee on Government Operations. Subcommittee on Intergovernmental Relations. *The Federal System as Seen by Federal Aid Officials.* 89th Cong., 1st Sess., 1965.

———. *The Federal System as Seen by State and Local Officials.* 88th Cong., 1st Sess., 1963.

U.S. Senate. Committee on the Judiciary. *Hearings, Civil Rights—The President's Program, 1963.* 88th Cong., 1st Sess., 1963.

U.S., Congress, Senate, Committee on Labor and Public Welfare. *White House Conference on Education.* 89th Cong., 1st Sess., 1965.

———. Subcommittee on Education. *Hearings, Education Legislation, 1967.* 90th Cong., 1st Sess., 1967.

———. Subcommittee on Education. *Hearings, Elementary and Secondary Education Act of 1965.* 89th Cong., 1st Sess., 1965.

———. Subcommittee on Education. *Hearings, Elementary and Secondary Education Act of 1966.* 89th Cong., 2d Sess., 1966.

U.S., Congressional Globe. 39th Cong., 1st Sess.–40th Cong., 2d Sess., 1866–69.

U.S., Congressional Record. 88th Cong., 1st Sess.–90th Cong., 2d Sess., 1963–68.

State and Local Public Documents

City of Chicago. Board of Education. Advisory Panel on Integration of the Public Schools. *Report.* 1964.

———. Proceedings. July 1960–June 1966.

———. Office of the General Superintendent. *Recommendations and Statements Concerning the Chicago Public Schools.* December 23, 1964.

———. Office of the General Superintendent. *Response to Recommendations 4 through 10 of the . . . Advisory Panel on Integration of the Public Schools.* 1964.

Governors' Conference. *Is Education the Business of the Federal Government?* A preliminary study for the Governors' Conference in Cleveland, Ohio, June 8, 1964.

Massachusetts State Board of Education. Advisory Committee on Racial Imbalance and Education. *Because it is Right—Educationally.* 1965.

Sheppard, Victor H. *A Brief History of the Office of Public Instruction.* Springfield, Ill., 1956.

Virginia State Department of Education. *Facing Up, Statistical Data on Virginia's Public Schools,* 1966.

———. Superintendent of Public Instruction. *Annual Report.* 1954–1965.

Articles and Periodicals

Baron, Harold. "History of Chicago School Segregation to 1953," in Meyer Weinberg, Ed., *Learning Together* (Chicago: Integrated Education Associates, 1964), 14 18.

Chicago Daily News, 1963–68.

Chicago Defender, 1966.

Chicago Sun-Times, 1965–67.

Chicago Tribune, 1965–68.

Coleman, James S. "Toward Open Schools," *Public Interest*, No. 9 (Fall 1967), 20–27.

Crain, Robert L. "Urban School Integration: Strategy for Peace," *Saturday Review*, Vol. L (February 18, 1967), 76–77, 97–98.

Dodson, Dan W. "School Administration, Control and Public Policy Concerning Integration," *Journal of Negro Education*, XXXIV (Winter 1965), 249–57.

Goodwin, George, Jr. "Subcommittees: The Miniature Legislatures of Congress," *American Political Science Review*, Vol. LVI (September 1962), 596–604.

Grodzins, Morton. "Centralization and Decentralization in the American Federal System," in Robert A. Goldwin, Ed., *A Nation of States* (Chicago: Rand McNally, 1961), 1–23.

———. "Local Strength in the American Federal System," in Marian D. Irish, Ed., *Continuing Crisis in American Politics* (Englewood Cliffs, N.J.: Prentice-Hall, 1963), 132–52.

Hauser, Philip M. "Dynamic Inaction in Chicago's Schools," *Integrated Education*, Vol. II (October–November 1964), 44–47.

Henry, David D. "Some Observations on Federal Relations to Education," *Illinois Journal of Education*, Vol. LVII (February 1966), 51–55.

Howe, Harold, II. "The U.S. Office of Education: Growth and Growing Pains," *Saturday Review*, Vol. XLIX, No. 51 (December 17, 1966), 68–70, 87.

Huitt, Ralph K. "The Roles of Congressional Committee Members," in John C. Wahlke and Heinz Eulau, Eds., *Legislative Behavior* (Glencoe, Ill.: Free Press, 1959), 317–30.

Integrated Education, 1965–68.

Keppel, Francis. "The Emerging Partnership of Education and Civil Rights," *Journal of Negro Education*, Vol. XXXIV (Summer 1965), 204–8.

———. "Thank God for the Civil Rights Movement," *Integrated Education*, Vol. II (April–May 1964), 9–12.

Leeson, Jim. "The Deliberate Speed of Title VI," *Saturday Review*, Vol. XLIX (December 17, 1966), 74, 87–88.

Miller, Warren E., and Stokes, Donald E. "Constituency Influence in Congress," *American Political Science Review*, Vol. LVII (March 1963), 45–56.

Morsell, John A. "Legislation and Its Implementation," *Journal of Negro Education*, Vol. XXXIV (Summer 1965), 232–38.

New York Times, 1966–68.

Page, Ray. "Editorial," *Illinois Journal of Education*, Vol. LVII (February 1966), 1.

Pasnick, Raymond W. "Chicago's School Crisis," *Integrated Education*, Vol. II (April–May, 1964), 21–24.

Price, Hugh Douglas. "Race, Religion, and the Rules Committee: The Kennedy Aid-to-Education Bills," in Alan F. Westin, Ed., *The Uses of Power* (New York: Harcourt, Brace and World, 1962), 1–71.

Richmond News Leader, 1964–68.

Richmond Times-Dispatch, 1964–68.

Rivera, Ramon J., McWorter, Gerald A., and Lillienstein, Ernest. "Freedom Day II in Chicago," *Integrated Education*, Vol. II (August–September 1964), 34–40.

Smith, Ralph Lee. "New Tools for School Integration," *The Progressive*, Vol. XXX (May 1966), 25–28.

Southern Education Report, 1965–68.

Southern School News, 1964.

Vespa, Marcia Lane. "Chicago's Regional School Plans," in Meyer Weinberg, Ed., *Learning Together*. (Chicago: Integrated Education Associates, 1964), 118–27.

Washington Post, 1963–68.

Unpublished Material

Bailey, Stephen K. "The Office of Education: The Politics of Rapid Growth." Paper read at the 1966 Annual Meeting of the American Political Science Association, New York, N.Y., September, 1966.

Beis, Edward. Transcript of interview with David Seeley, November 23, 1965.

Coordinating Council of Community Organizations. "Complaint of the Coordinating Council of Community Organizations," July 4, 1965. (Mimeographed.)

Coordinating Council of Community Organizations. "Handbook of Chicago School Segregation." Chicago, 1963. (Mimeographed.)

Edley, Lucille. "Strategies and Techniques of Politics, A Study of Ten Selected Precinct Captains from Chicago's Third Ward." Unpublished Master's dissertation, Department of Political Science, University of Chicago, 1955.

Public Administration Service. "A Report on An Administrative Survey of the U.S. Office of Education of the Federal Security Agency." Washington: Office of Education, 1951. (Mimeographed.)

Quigley, James. Tape recording of a meeting with school officials in Memphis, Tennessee, July 1964.

Seeley, David. Tape recording of a meeting with school officials in Biloxi, Mississippi, July 25, 1964.

Snowiss, Leo M. "Chicago and Congress, A Study of Municipal Representation." Unpublished Ph.D. dissertation, Department of Political Science, University of Chicago, 1965.

Student Non-Violent Coordinating Committee. "Special Report." Washington, September 30, 1965. (Mimeographed.)

Index